Appellate Mediation

A GUIDEBOOK FOR ATTORNEYS AND MEDIATORS

Brendon Ishikawa and Dana Curtis

Foreword by Judge Dorothy W. Nelson,
U.S. Court of Appeals (Ninth Circuit)

AMERICAN BAR ASSOCIATION
Section of
Dispute Resolution

Cover design by Jill Tedhams/ABA Design

The materials contained herein represent the opinions of the authors and/or the editors, and should not be construed to be the views or opinions of the law firms or companies with whom such persons are in partnership with, associated with, or employed by, nor of the American Bar Association or the Dispute Resolution Section unless adopted pursuant to the bylaws of the Association.

Nothing contained in this book is to be considered as the rendering of legal advice for specific cases, and readers are responsible for obtaining such advice from their own legal counsel. This book is intended for educational and informational purposes only.

Printed in the United States of America.

20 19 18 17 16   5 4 3 2 1

Library of Congress Cataloging-in-Publication Data

Names: Ishikawa, Brendon, author. | Curtis, Dana L., author.
Title: Appellate mediation : a guidebook for attorneys and mediators / By
    Brendon Ishikawa and Dana Curtis.
Description: Chicago : American Bar Association, 2015. | Includes
    bibliographical references and index.
Identifiers: LCCN 2015047942 | ISBN 9781634253482 (print : alk. paper)
Subjects: LCSH: Appellate procedure—United States—Handbooks, manuals, etc. |
    Mediation—United States—Handbooks, manuals, etc. | Mediators (Persons)—
    United States—Handbooks, manuals, etc.
Classification: LCC KF9050 .I84 2015 | DDC 347.73/9—dc23
LC record available at http://lccn.loc.gov/2015047942

Discounts are available for books ordered in bulk. Special consideration is given to state bars, CLE programs, and other bar-related organizations. Inquire at Book Publishing, ABA Publishing, American Bar Association, 321 N. Clark Street, Chicago, Illinois 60654-7598.

www.ShopABA.org

With love and admiration for my wife, Cathy.
—Brendon

With love and gratitude to Daniel Bowling, my colleague,
editor, friend, and husband, who encouraged and supported
me during the writing of this book. And to my friend
and colleague John Toker, former Mediation Program
Administrator of the California Court of Appeal, First
Appellate District, and my friends and mentors at the Ninth
Circuit, Claudia Bernard and Chris Goeltz, who were there
in the beginning.
—Dana

Contents

Foreword

Although much has been written about mediation before trial, the benefits of mediation after the court or jury has issued its verdict have received much less attention. The authors of this book, Brendon Ishikawa and Dana Curtis—both outstanding, experienced appellate attorneys and neutrals—are filling this void. They have written a superbly organized and comprehensive book on appellate mediation that should serve as a guide for every appellate judge, lawyer, mediator, professor, or student engaged in the practice or study of appellate law.

The authors emphasize that appellate mediation is profoundly different from pretrial mediation. The appellate mediator should expand the parties' understanding of their own and the other parties' perspectives of the dispute, their needs and interests, and the legal risks and opportunities that exist and inform resolution. Therefore, the appellate mediator must understand the basics of appellate procedures, rules, and process. For instance, the only records that an appellate court has on appeal are the trial court records, and effective analysis of the case begins with the standards of review. Importantly, to the greatest extent possible, appellate mediation is much more client-involved; discussions should be problem-solving not argument-generating, should be collaborative and engaging rather than isolating, and should be facilitative rather than coercive or threatening. The parties' relationships, goals, and cultural differences should be considered, and therefore joint sessions are desirable.

This book includes important material on how to evaluate a civil appeal. The section on decision-tree analysis includes helpful worksheets for participants to calculate the value of a case. There are excellent suggestions on pre-mediation preparation including agreements as to confidentiality and logistics (serve food if possible!), explanations as to the role of the mediator and participants, communication guidelines, and an agenda for the mediation. The authors relate how to initiate a mediation, how to conclude a mediation, how to conduct post mediation follow-up, and what to do if the parties do not reach an agreement. Important practice tips and forms are included. Their final advice on how to grow an appellate mediation practice is invaluable.

Appellate mediation practice has become an important part of our justice system. Those who study this book will have all the tools necessary to become successful in this field.

Dorothy W. Nelson
Senior Judge, U.S. Court of Appeals (Ninth Circuit)

About the Authors

Brendon Ishikawa is certified as a specialist in appellate law by the State Bar of California Board of Legal Specialization and has practiced appellate law for the past twenty years. He serves as a lead appellate court attorney at the California Court of Appeal, Third District. In his prior private practice, Mr. Ishikawa served as counsel in more than 100 appeals and writ proceedings. He regularly writes about and teaches appellate law, risk analysis, and other mediation-related skills to attorneys and mediators.

Dana Curtis was among the first attorneys in the country to devote her career exclusively to mediation of civil matters, beginning her full-time practice in 1991. Since serving as a Circuit Mediator with the U.S. Court of Appeals for the Ninth Circuit, Ms. Curtis has maintained a private mediation practice in the Bay Area for which the *Los Angeles Daily Journal* has recognized her as one of the 50 "Best Neutrals" in California. Ms. Curtis taught mediation at Stanford Law School for 10 years and presently co-teaches Mediating Disputes for Harvard Law School's Program on Negotiation. For over 20 years, Ms. Curtis has designed and facilitated appellate mediation training programs throughout the United States.

Introduction

A. The Growing Field of Appellate Mediation

Mediation of cases on appeal has continued to increase in the United States since the Second Circuit started the first appellate mediation program in 1974.[1] Today every federal circuit court (except the Federal Circuit) has an appellate mediation program.[2] And the appellate courts in 33 states and the District of Columbia have court-connected mediation programs. Although some early efforts at court-connected appellate mediation in the 1980s fizzled for lack of financial and judicial support, since 2000 reviewing courts have embraced mediation.[3] Enthusiasm for appellate mediation continues to grow among courts of review and litigants themselves for a compelling reason: it works! Almost six out of ten civil appeals in the federal courts are successfully settled prior to decision by a court of appeals.[4] Even after years of litigation and failed settlement efforts in the trial courts, appellate mediations frequently resolve appeals in a single mediation session.

Because voluntary appellate mediation tends to occur with less frequency than court-ordered mediation, the trend is to make participation in court-connected mediation programs mandatory.[5] Thus, many parties to civil appeals in a majority of states and nearly all federal circuits have no choice but to participate in appellate mediation. In some appellate courts, mandatory mediation is not just possible, it is probable.[6] As a consequence, effective advocacy on appeal now requires lawyers to develop skills in negotiating and representing their clients in mediation in addition to the ability to write briefs and present oral arguments. This book serves as a guide to lawyers serving clients participating in appellate mediation.

---

1. Sandra Schultz Newman & Scott E. Friedman, *Appellate Mediation in Pennsylvania: Looking Back at the History and Forward to the Future*, J. Appellate Practice & Process 5 (2003): 410; *see also* Robert W. Rack Jr., *Thoughts of a Chief Circuit Mediator on Federal Court-Annexed Mediation*, 17 Ohio State J. Dispute Resolution 609 n.3 (2001) (asserting that the Sixth Circuit's program is the longest continuously operating program since its inception in 1981).
2. Rack, *supra* note 1, at 610.
3. Newman & Friedman, *supra* note 1, at 419–21.
4. Theodore Eisenberg & Michael Heise, *Plaintiphobia in State Courts? An Empirical Study of State Court Trials on Appeal*, 38(1) J. Leg. Stud. 133 (2009).
5. Ignazio J. Ruvolo, *Appellate Mediation-Settling the Last Frontier of ADR*, 42 San Diego L. Rev. 185 (2005); Irving R. Kaufman, *Must Every Appeal Run the Gamut—The Civil Appeals Management Plan*, 95 Yale L.J. 755 (1985).
6. Robert J. Niemic, Mediation and Conference Programs in the Federal Courts of Appeals: A Sourcebook for Judges and Lawyers 6 (1997).

The demand is also growing for neutrals adept at mediating cases in the appellate arena, with all of its unique procedures and substantive rules. Appellate mediation is a growing opportunity for professional mediators, and this book provides them with essential information about appellate law and the idiosyncrasies of appellate mediation. It guides them through a process developed over the past 20 years in scores of appellate mediation trainings and programs throughout the United States in both state and federal courts. This book also offers pointers for professional neutrals who are interested in expanding their mediation practices to include appellate mediation.

Despite the prevalence of appellate mediation, the literature on appellate mediation is sparse—usually limited to law review articles, court guides focused on whether and how to implement a mediation program, and short chapters in works otherwise devoted to mediation of disputes in the prelitigation or trial court contexts. Although a number of texts address mediation in general, these have limited utility for appellate cases, given their unique rules and procedures.

Until now, legal advocates and neutrals have lacked a resource to guide them in understanding mediation in the appellate context and to advise them about what works and does not work for mediation of appeals. This book fills that gap: it is a comprehensive guide to appellate mediation for legal advocates and mediators. We offer a time-tested approach that can guide first-time participants in appellate mediation and enhance the practice of those who regularly conduct or attend such mediations.

B.   Terms We Use in This Book

Before we explore what distinguishes appellate mediation from other alternative dispute resolution processes, we need to define a few basic terms to describe the progression of a case through appeal.

1. *Terms Relating to the Appellate Process*

- **Trial court** refers to the court in which the legal action was filed and that makes the findings of fact (either by jury or bench trial).

- **Judgment,** as used in this book, refers to the decision by the trial court challenged by the appellant in the appellate court. Judgment thus encompasses any order, ruling, interlocutory judgment (entered in an intermediate stage between the commencement and termination of a case), or final judgment for which a party seeks reversal or modification on appeal.

- **Party** refers to any person, company, or entity entitled to appear in the appellate court to challenge or defend the judgment or order being appealed. Party does not include amicus curiae, or attorneys providing legal representation. In short, a party stands to gain or lose personally depending on the outcome of the appeal.

- **Appellant** refers to the party who files an appeal in order to reverse the judgment or challenged order.

- **Respondent** refers to the party defending a judgment or order. In the federal circuits and some states, the respondent is called an appellee. In some cases, the respondent may also wish to challenge the same judgment or order on appeal—perhaps because the respondent believes the judgment awarded too much or too little in damages, or perhaps because the judgment did not provide the full extent of legal or equitable relief to which the respondent may lay claim. In such a situation, the respondent may file a cross-appeal.

  In many court documents a respondent who appeals is additionally called a cross-appellant and the appellant, a cross-respondent (or cross-appellee in the federal circuits). For our purposes, we will refer to the parties according to their position vis-à-vis the judgment when the first notice of appeal is filed. If a party is both an appellant and a cross-respondent, it is easiest to analyze that party's position in the reviewing court as two separate appeals. Thus, the analysis for the appellant will apply for the initial appeal, and the analysis for the respondent will apply to that same party with respect to the cross-appeal. Attorneys and mediators should be sure to consult portions of this book addressed to appellants and to respondents for the respective aspects of the case with two or more notices of appeal.

- **Appellate court** refers to any court that has power to affirm, modify, or reverse decisions of a lower court.

- **Appellate mediation** refers to the process in which parties work to resolve a dispute with the assistance of a mediator after a judgment or appealable order has been entered by the trial court. Appellate mediations may be court ordered, may merely be encouraged by a program within a reviewing court, or may be conducted outside the court context by parties who have hired a private mediator. Although the judgment or appealable order addresses the legal issues between the parties on appeal, a mediated agreement may also resolve disputes other than the appeal or include stakeholders who are not party to the appeal. Thus, mediation allows the parties to an appeal to craft agreements that reach beyond the limits of a court's power in order to address the needs, interests, and concerns of the parties.

2. Terms Relating to the Mediation Process

In practice, mediators vary in how they perceive their roles and their interactions with the parties and attorneys. Moreover, mediators vary in their mediation styles, even within a single mediation, depending on what the situation demands. Thus, the following terms are helpful to describe the varying styles and approaches taken during the mediation process.

- **Facilitative.** Facilitative mediators emphasize the creation of a safe, nonjudgmental atmosphere in which the parties and lawyers explain their positions and interests and negotiate for and among themselves. The facilitative mediator's role is to ask questions, demonstrate and ensure understanding, and help explain the other side's perspectives. Facilitative mediation is especially appropriate for disputes in which emotions and personalities are as important as legal or factual issues and the parties' needs to speak and to be heard are critical first steps to discussing a settlement. Some mediators with a facilitative style work with the parties and counsel in joint session throughout the mediation to encourage the cooperation required to produce a mutually developed and acceptable resolution.

- **Evaluative.** Evaluative mediators tend to use their status and subject matter expertise to evaluate the strengths and weaknesses of each side's positions and legal arguments and to communicate those evaluations in an effort to affect the parties' risk analysis. Mediators with an evaluative style often conduct most of the mediation in confidential meetings with each side rather than in joint session. They believe this approach minimizes polarization of the parties' positions and allows room for the face-saving that this approach often provides. An evaluative approach may be most appropriate for disputes in which the parties have developed divergent assessments of the probable outcome of litigation or when the principle the parties have fought for has become more important than a reasoned legal analysis of the case.

- **Directive**. In addition to, and independent of, being evaluative or facilitative, mediators may be more or less directive about both process and substantive issues. Mediators inclined to be directive regarding process will prescribe a fixed mediation structure that is not easily influenced by the participants. Sometimes known as "muscle mediators," mediators who are more directive about substantive issues are more aggressive in asserting their evaluative predictions about litigation outcomes and rely heavily on their powers to persuade to encourage parties to reach agreements that are consistent with mediator predictions.

- **Less-directive** mediators seek process input from participants before and during mediation and are more inclined to focus on understanding and to elicit the parties' evaluations of settlement proposals in reaching decisions about how to approach resolution of the case. They believe process decisions should be based on the parties' expression of their needs and interests as well as their predictions about litigation outcomes, which are informed by what they learn from their attorneys and from the other side.

C. Significant Differences between Appellate Mediation and Mediation Occurring before a Trial Court Judgment

Mediations before and after entry of a judgment differ significantly. The existence of a court judgment or appealable order has critical implications for risk analysis, settlement options, and timing of appellate mediations. Appellate mediations occur after at least one party has prevailed legally and another has lost and therefore focus their risk analysis and case valuations on whether the trial court made a mistake. By contrast, prejudgment settlement conferences and mediations focus on this question: "Who's going to win at trial?"

After what may be years of litigation and substantial financial costs, the positions of the parties have often hardened into inflexibility and an adversarial mindset. Respondents usually feel vindicated—at least to a certain extent—that the jury or judge credited their position. A boost in their confidence exacerbates the entrenchment in their positions. By contrast, appellants are frustrated that the legal process failed to give them justice and may therefore redouble their efforts to seek legal relief by pursing the appeal.

The very existence of the judgment requires that the trial court's decision be addressed if the mediation is to succeed. If there is a money judgment in favor of the respondent, the respondent's attorney is usually entitled to begin efforts to collect from the appellant even while the appeal and appellate mediation are occurring. If the judgment grants injunctive relief, the appellant (and perhaps both parties) may be obligated to comply with the court's order during the appeal. Sometimes parties—especially institutional or business entities—facing a judgment that negatively affects their reputation will seek to erase the judgment completely through a settlement in which the parties agree jointly to request a reversal of the judgment in the appellate court.

Moreover, parties need to account for the appeal itself as they attempt to negotiate a settlement. Questions of timing become critical. Should the parties seek a stay of the appeal in order to mediate without the pressure of appellate briefing deadlines? If the terms of a settlement agreement cannot be immediately fulfilled, when should the appeal be dismissed? Can appellate mediation occur too late, given that appellate courts sometimes refuse to dismiss cases imminently set for oral argument or the release of the court's decisions? Questions of appellate procedure also become important. Does the mediation automatically stay the appeal by rule of the appellate court, or does the appeal proceed on a parallel track to the mediation—without affecting the appellate briefing schedule?

Finally, appellate advocacy is profoundly different from trial practice. Appellate practice, procedure, and substantive law have many differences from the rules that govern trials. Parties must decide whether to bring in an appellate specialist—whether just to help with the mediation or also to handle the appeal. Mediators in appeals must understand at least the basics of appellate procedure and substantive law, too.

The expense and delay inherent in appeals make exploring voluntary settlement negotiations worthwhile even for appeals in appellate courts without formal mediation programs. Many courts that do not maintain a mediation program nevertheless retain policies for conducting settlement conferences in cases in which the parties stipulate to participate in such conferences. Settlement conferences in these courts are often handled by judges appointed for that purpose.

D.   Appellate Mediation Benefits from a Client-Centered, Problem-Solving, and Primarily Facilitative Approach

The art of appellate mediation is in helping parties successfully explore solutions that have previously eluded them because they have not been able to open channels of candid communication, uncover hidden or erroneous assumptions, or engage in constructive negotiations.

In defining a successful mediation, we focus on the *process*, not the *result*. First, in a successful mediation the parties explore as fully as possible—from their own and the other party's perspectives—the *background* of the dispute and its *impact*, their personal and/or business *needs and interests* going forward, and the legal *risks and opportunities* they face absent a negotiated agreement. With this information, the parties develop and then evaluate options for resolution that are immediately available to them that either reflect their informed analysis of the present value of their legal case or otherwise address their needs and interests, or both. Most of the time this process enables parties to reach an agreement that leaves them better off than pursuing an appeal. Sometimes, the best available option is to go forward with the appeal.

By the time a case is on appeal, parties have almost always engaged in direct negotiations and participated in both mediation and settlement conferences, sometimes on multiple occasions. Nevertheless, options that were better for them than continuing the legal battle—and remain available—have eluded them. Settlement conferences are, almost without exception, attorney-centered, evaluative, directive processes, the goal of which is a resolution based on the settlement officer's best guess about what will happen if the parties fail to reach an agreement. In our experience, a majority of pretrial mediations follow this same approach as well.

As Dana began mediating appeals full time as a Circuit Court Mediator for the Ninth Circuit, she was disconcerted to discover that the settlement conference approach to mediation predominated in pretrial mediations and was, in fact, what the lawyers expected in appellate mediation. This model was in contrast to her previous private mediation practice, where she offered the approach we take in this book. In settlement conferences, what motivated the parties to settle was fear of an adverse judgment as predicted by the mediator. Thus, focus in this style of mediation was to instill fear by arguing the legal case, hearing the mediator's adverse predictions of the outcome (which are often different for each party), and struggling back and forth to reach a settlement that usually approximates the mediator's prognostication. The primary function of the mediator was to browbeat the parties into "agreement."

As Dana considered this approach, she began to wonder: *Why would we offer parties in appellate mediation the same approach—one that is attorney-focused, directive, and evaluative—that did not work the first time?* Thus, during her tenure as a Ninth Circuit Mediator, Dana and her colleagues experimented with another approach. For Dana, this meant a focus that was more closely aligned with her belief that mediation should offer parties the opportunity to reach agreements that address their interests, strengthen relationships, and improve upon the option of continuing to litigate. For over 20 years as she mediated appeals and taught appellate mediation she honed this approach, which is based on the following principles:

- **Understanding-based.** We strive toward a process that expands the parties' understanding of their own and the other party's perspectives on the dispute, their underlying needs and interests, the legal risks and opportunities on appeal, and the practical realities that exist and inform resolution.[7]

- **Client-involved.** To the greatest extent possible in both joint and separate sessions, clients participate *actively* in discussion of a broad range of topics of importance to them because the dispute—and any resolution—belongs to them, not to the mediator or the lawyers. They must live with the result of litigation or any settlement—and they must fund it. This approach contrasts with the more common

---

7. For a thorough and thoughtful discussion of client-centered, understanding-based mediation, we recommend Gary J. Friedman & Jack Himmelstein, Challenging Conflict: Mediation Through Understanding (ABA 2008).

attorney-centered approach, in which the mediator works mostly with the attorneys to negotiate a resolution on behalf of their clients. The discussions generally focus on legal arguments and probable litigation outcomes absent a resolution. The clients generally interact very little, or not at all, with the other side and often take a back seat with the mediator, as well.

- **Discussions that are problem-solving, not argument-generating.** Problem solving has two aspects in our approach to mediation. First, it maintains a broad problem definition, encouraging parties to examine the problems underlying the conflict and develop solutions to address their needs and interests that go beyond the relief an appellate court might provide. It also extends beyond the narrow problem definition of the settlement conference model—to predict the likely outcome on appeal and craft a settlement that consists of the limited relief available in court.

  When discussions turn to legal analysis, problem solving means that attorneys work to educate the parties about the law, rather than to argue about it, in contrast to a typical settlement conference model where lawyers argue their case to the mediator in order to defeat the other side and gain a more favorable prediction from the mediator.

- **Collaborative and engaging rather than isolating.** Sadly in our view, in many—if not most—jurisdictions, joint sessions are no longer fashionable among lawyers. Even more distressing is the trend toward rejection of joint meetings altogether, even for the limited purpose of introductions and discussions of procedural matters at the beginning of the mediation. When asked the reason for refusing joint sessions, lawyers express concern that frank and open discussions of opposing points of view may negatively affect settlement. With a skilled mediator to help shape conversations, participants can minimize the downside and maximize the upside of meeting together.

- **Facilitative rather than coercive or threatening.** Mediators *facilitate* discussions about the differing perspectives on what happened and on the law rather than simply presenting their personal opinions about the legal outcomes. We believe much of the trepidation experienced by parties ahead of a mediation session comes from unpleasant experiences in which judges and other settlement conference officers tried to browbeat them into acquiescence. We believe coercion is not a good path toward satisfying resolutions of legal disputes.

Finally, our approach translates into real practice in the form of an appellate mediation process that (1) is carefully structured as understanding-based, client-involved, problem-solving, collaborative, and primarily facilitative; (2) includes all necessary activities for achieving a successful outcome; (3) organizes the process into phases that build on one another and allow participants to anticipate the process and to focus their discussions on the topics at hand; and (4) discourages premature bargaining over money to the exclusion of more creative, interest-based discussions.

E.   The Promise of Appellate Mediation

Even with a sound approach to appellate mediation, you may wonder whether settlement after protracted trial court litigation is a realistic possibility. Is appellate mediation really worth the effort? With hardened positions, winners and losers in the trial court, and litigation that has resisted any prior settlement efforts, it would seem that mediation on appeal would be futile. Far from it. Mediations often prove successful on appeal. In some court-connected mediation programs, a *majority* of appeals reach a negotiated settlement.[8] Interestingly, "there is no evidence that the settlement rate varies among different kinds of cases."[9] Even "significant public policy issues can be successfully mediated."[10] Thus, we believe parties should seriously consider mediation in every civil appeal.

Although the parties will argue about whether the rulings made in the trial court will stand, the existence of a judgment provides some certainty about the outcome of the lawsuit that enables the parties to assess their cases in a clearer and more logical manner. On appeal, parties know exactly which legal issues they must address to challenge or defend the judgment, and they can use the judgment as a springboard to determine how much their case is worth in light of the risk factors inherent in an appeal and possible retrial. Based on the information and the analytic tools available to the parties to value cases on appeal, it usually becomes clear to them that they have settlement options that are more advantageous for *all* parties than the appeal.[11]

---

8. *E.g.*, Brendon Ishikawa & Rene Ackerman, *Appellate Mediation: The Appellate Mediation Program of the California Court of Appeal, Third Appellate District*, SACRAMENTO LAWYER MAG. 16–17 (May/June 2014) (reporting that two-thirds of appeals ordered to mediation in the Third District result in settlement); *Report of the Appellate Mediation Task Force* 1–2 (Tennessee, June 2007 (reporting similar settlement rates of 62–69 percent in Oregon, 56 percent in Nevada, 54 percent in Hawaii, and 50 percent in Alabama). *See* http://www.tsc.state.tn.us/sites/default/files/report_and_recommendation_06-05-2007.pdf.

9. Irving R. Kaufman, *Must Every Appeal Run the Gamut—The Civil Appeals Management Plan*, 95 YALE L.J. 759 (1985).

10. Jerrold J. Ganzfried, *Bringing Business Judgment to Business Litigation: Mediation and Settlement in the Federal Courts of Appeals*, 65 GEORGE WASHINGTON L. REV. 539 (1996).

11. In Chapter 3, we show how to calculate the dollar value of a civil appeal. Using a quantitative evaluation for both parties to an appeal, it becomes clear that there is almost always a settlement range that makes logical sense for all parties due to the costs and fees necessary for appellate litigation.

For experienced mediators who are growing weary of—or worried about—the trend toward a settlement conference-style mediation, where the focus is on evaluation and mediation occurs entirely in separate sessions, appellate mediation may offer a welcome return to mediation that includes a broader problem definition, a greater focus on the parties and their needs, and a renewed opportunity for discussions that lead to a satisfying resolution.[12]

Parties on appeal have a number of reasons to settle a case—even on appeal. These incentives to reach a settlement include (1) poor odds of prevailing on appeal, (2) the appellant's need to avoid further loss or the respondent's need to preserve a favorable judgment, (3) the goal to avoid additional legal fees, (4) the disruptive effect of litigation on personal and business relationships, (5) the potential to structure installment payments on the judgment, (6) avoidance of additional time delays due to further litigation in the appellate courts, (7) litigation fatigue, (8) the opportunity for parties to solve their own problems rather than having a result imposed by a court, (9) possible tax advantages, (10) a party's immediate financial need for money awarded in the judgment, (11) privacy that can be achieved with a confidential settlement agreement, (12) the potential for global settlement that resolves the controversy entirely, including issues that are not part of the single case being appealed or parties that are not involved in the appeal, and (13) peace of mind.[13] We explore these incentives later in this book and discuss how a skilled mediator can use them to encourage settlement.

F.   How to Read This Book

The fact that you are taking the time to read this book probably signals that you are already quite skilled in providing legal representation or mediation services. It also shows a willingness to do your homework. Sometimes, however, highly skilled people have developed such successful habits and analytic approaches that it can be challenging to learn something new.[14] If you have created a successful trial court mediation practice, you may find it uncomfortable to try a very different philosophy and approach for an appellate mediation. And if you are an appellate specialist wondering how the mediation concepts in this book might be relevant to your work, you are in good company. During one of Dana's first appellate mediation training courses, a preeminent appellate specialist piped up, "I just got it! I just figured out why we are having such a hard time with the idea

---

12. *See, e.g.,* Jacqueline Nolan-Haley, *Mediation: The "New Arbitration,"* 17 HARVARD NEGOTIATION LAW REVIEW 61 (2012); John Lande, *Lessons from Mediators' Stories,* 34 CARDOZO LAW REVIEW 2423 (2013); and JEFFREY KRIVIS, THE PREVENTABLE DEATH OF MEDIATION (2012), *available at* http://www.mediate.com/articles/KrivisJbl20121221.cfm.
13. *See generally* Thomas F. Ball, III, *Settling Cases on Appeal: An Option to Consider,* 11 W. VIRGINIA L. REV. 14–15 (1997).
14. Chris Argyris, *Teaching Smart People How to Learn,* 69 HARVARD BUS. REV. 99, 100 (1991).

of facilitative mediation! We never meet our clients!" We ask that you keep an open mind. You, too, may have a eureka moment like this. If you are skeptical about a process that focuses so much on the parties' needs and interests, we urge you to bear with us while we make the case for an approach that respects participants and encourages collaboration, client-empowerment, and creative problem solving. Whether you are a skeptic or a true believer who is already familiar with our approach, we hope you will give it a try. We appreciate appellate mediation enough to have devoted a great deal of thought, care, and effort toward crafting an approach that we believe will set you up for success.

G. What You Will Find in This Book

This comprehensive guide to appellate mediation for both mediators and lawyers representing clients in mediation provides a fundamental understanding of appellate law and procedures that are relevant to mediation, a basic understanding of mediation in the appellate context, and a demonstrably effective process for mediating cases on appeal. And for those readers who are interested in expanding into the area of appellate mediation, we provide information about doing so. To these ends, we have divided this book into the following four sections.

1. Section I: Fundamentals of Appeals

The first section introduces readers to the fundamentals of appellate law. We have ordered our chapters to help you understand the basic appellate rules that will apply to a civil case, evaluate the odds and outcomes for the case on appeal, determine what options each party currently has, and calculate the dollar value of an appeal to each party. Each of these tasks requires different—and sometimes independent—considerations.

Chapter 1 focuses on the *basics* of appellate law and helps answer the question "Do I have good arguments on appeal?" We discuss various appellate issues and the applicable standards of review. We also present a basic analytical framework for appellate issues: (1) whether the trial court erred; (2) if so, whether the errors were prejudicial; (3) whether the prejudicial errors were preserved, forfeited, or waived; and (4) whether the appellate record provides sufficient evidence of the error.

Chapter 2 provides a guide to case *evaluation*. This chapter helps you to assess the likelihood of winning on appeal and compare the likely outcome with all other presently available options such as dismissing the appeal, continuing with only part of the appeal, and engaging in settlement negotiations. This chapter provides you with a solid grounding in case evaluation of the options available to the opposing party as well. Finally, it helps you answer the questions "What are the options?" and "Can I improve upon them?"

Chapter 3 gives you a step-by-step approach to case *valuation* using decision-tree risk analysis. With this quantitative approach, you can calculate the present value in dollars of a civil appeal based on potential outcomes and odds of succeeding. In short, Chapter 3 helps you answer the question "What is my appeal worth?"

2. Section II: The Appellate Mediation Process

Section II is a phase-by-phase description of the appellate mediation process. It describes each phase and offers suggestions to mediators and lawyers about how to make the most of each.

Chapter 4 covers premediation considerations and preparations. Beginning with how to assess the suitability of an appeal for mediation, we explore the differences between trial court mediation and how to initiate an appellate mediation, how appellate mediation differs from trial court settlement efforts, and how to prepare for the mediation session. Preparation can mean the difference between a successful mediation and one doomed from the start for lack of adequate settlement authority, ground rules, or familiarity with the problem and its potential solutions. This chapter answers the following questions: "How do I know if an appeal is suitable for mediation?"; "What do I need to accomplish before the mediation session starts?"; and "How do we enhance the potential for resolution?"

Chapter 5 explores the opening phase of the mediation session (Phase 1). Although this chapter covers the briefest of the five phases of appellate mediation, it focuses on a crucial part of the process. A good opening sets the process on the path to success by instilling confidence in the process and participants. Conversely, a bad start leads to either a failed mediation or inordinate and unnecessary time and energy to bring the process back on the right track. Thus, this chapter answers the question "How do we get off to a good start in this mediation session?"

Chapter 6 explores the phase in which the parties are exchanging information (Phase 2). Because no new evidence is admitted on appeal and the parties have presumably revealed their best strategies in trying to win in the trial court, there is little or no incentive to withhold information during an appellate mediation. Moreover, the strong mediation confidentiality provided in most jurisdictions further facilitates a free and frank exchange of information. Thus, the exchange of information in an appellate mediation looks quite different from the exchange of information in a trial court or pretrial mediation, where the parties are likely more guarded, and this chapter provides guidance in talking about the merits of appeals.

Although parties and mediators might see little point in exchanging information at this point—especially after lengthy litigation—new and important information frequently comes to light in appellate mediation. Also, if previous mediations were of the settlement conference variety, the appellate mediation may be the first opportunity the parties have had to be in the same room to discuss resolution or to address each other directly. Thus, the ability to share with and listen to one another is a hallmark of a successful and productive appellate mediation. For this reason, we offer this chapter to answer the question "What do we need to understand in order resolve this appeal to the benefit of the parties?"

Chapter 7 focuses on defining the problem and organizing the issues (Phase 3). Once parties understand the problem underlying the litigation as well as the legal and procedural posture of the case on appeal, they are ready to identify the issues they need to address during the remainder of the mediation and, then, to create an agenda. This chapter, which offers suggestions about how to facilitate these tasks, addresses the question "What do the parties need to discuss and decide during this mediation session to resolve their dispute— and in what order?"

Chapter 8 concerns the developing and negotiating of solutions (Phase 4). Only with the great amount of groundwork laid in the prior phases are parties ready to figure out how to resolve their dispute. Even then, parties, perhaps with the help of the mediator, should formulate a negotiation plan before conveying the first offer. Thus, this phase poses the question "Are there options we can all agree are better than continuing with the appeal?" Chapter 8 provides guidance on how to use the appellate mediation process to facilitate the analysis of risks, opportunities, and uncertainties facing the parties and how parties can become future-oriented by turning their attention away from strife and toward a constructive resolution.

Chapter 9 offers insight into the concluding phase of appellate mediation (Phase 5). Important—and sometimes extensive—work remains to be completed even after the moment a party says "I accept the settlement offer." The terms of the settlement agreement must be clarified and refined for enforceability. Under the laws of most jurisdictions, settlement agreements must be reduced to writing and signed by the attorneys and/or their clients. And the appeal must be dismissed. Thus, this chapter answers the question "How do we make sure the agreement works and is enforceable?"

3. Section III: Practice Tips for Appellate Attorneys

Section III offers appellate attorneys practice tips to ensure that they provide the best advocacy possible for their clients.

Chapter 10 addresses the following question for attorneys: "How do I get myself and my clients ready for the appellate mediation session?" This chapter includes guidance on preparation of mediation statements, client preparation, and premediation communications. In short, this chapter provides helpful guidance on premediation preparations for counsel.

Chapter 11 focuses on the mediation session and offers advice on how best to use joint sessions and private caucuses. Also, we provide some tips on enlisting the aid of the mediator to facilitate better negotiation. This chapter answers the question "What strategies work best in an appellate mediation session to reach a successful conclusion?"

Chapter 12 concerns concluding the mediation session. This is one of the phases of mediation during which the attorneys can provide the most value because of their familiarity with contract drafting, enforcement of agreements, and understanding of confidentiality rules. Thus, we offer a few insights and tips for successfully concluding the process. This chapter answers the question "How do I make sure my client gets the benefit of a clear and enforceable settlement agreement?"

4. Section IV: Practice Tips for Appellate Mediators

Section IV offers guidance and encouragement to neutrals who wish to develop an expertise in the unique context of appellate mediation. We offer suggestions about how to mediate appeals effectively, how to expand your mediation practice to include appellate mediation, and how to develop personally and professionally as an appellate mediator.

Chapter 13 helps mediators in the earliest phases set the case on a path to success by emphasizing the essential nature of effective preparation of (1) the case on appeal, (2) the lawyers and parties, and (3) the mediator. Beginning with the convening of the case and the premediation communications and ending with the opening face-to-face mediation session, this chapter helps mediators understand the special importance of beginning activities in the appellate context and provides practical, creative ideas for handling them effectively.

Chapter 14 focuses on the phases in which the parties exchange perspectives on the situation that gave rise to litigation and the legal risks and opportunities on appeal as well as what matters to them and must be considered in any interest-based negotiation. It encourages mediators to maximize the time spent in face-to-face discussions, or joint sessions, and provides understandings and tools for working effectively with parties and lawyers in this forum. Finally, it offers suggestions for making the most of separate sessions, or caucuses, during these phases.

Chapter 15 concerns what we call the concluding phase of a mediation session. We offer ideas about how to expand the pie and divide it, including negotiating interest-based solutions and distributive agreements, especially about money. We also address the often-overlooked but crucial responsibility to document and test any agreement the parties reach. Finally, we emphasize the importance of following up after the mediation and offer ideas for doing so when the mediation ends with a settlement and when it does not.

Chapter 16 gives appellate mediators suggestions for professional development in two aspects: (1) developing themselves as appellate mediators and (2) developing an appellate mediation practice.

5. *Section V: Appendix*

In Section V, we provide relevant resources. For mediators, we include a script of a typical premediation telephone conference, examples of an engagement e-mail and a mediation and confidentiality agreement, and a one-page outline of the appellate mediation process. For attorneys, we provide examples of mediation statements for appellants and respondents and a settlement agreement. For attorneys and mediators, we include lists of our favorite books and articles.

H.   We Wish You Success in the Challenging and Rewarding World of Appellate Mediation

After what often turns out to be years of frustrating and costly litigation, appellate mediation can provide parties a satisfactory end to the legal battle. It is empowering, cost-effective, and quick.

For mediators, appellate mediation offers the intellectual and emotional challenge of a demanding and interesting practice area. And it provides a satisfying opportunity for mediators to help parties do more than "make a deal." They can help parties to be thoughtful and thorough in predicting the no-deal alternative of an appellate decision. And they can facilitate a process in which parties can create agreements that best address their interests and needs.

In addition, the role of representing clients in appellate mediation presents new challenges and opportunities for appellate lawyers by requiring them to expand their understanding and skills in entirely new directions. It offers a refreshing departure from the routine of legal analysis, brief writing, and argument. And it demands attention to the human aspects of conflict and an opportunity to examine their own relationship to it. We wish you success and fulfillment in appellate mediation!

Section I: Fundamentals of Appeals
Overview

A. Effective Negotiation Requires Mediators and Lawyers to Understand Appellate Rules and Procedures

Not surprisingly, parties routinely misapprehend how appellate rules and procedures governing civil appeals differ from those of trial court proceedings.[1] What *is* surprising is the extent to which *lawyers* fail to understand both the differences between appellate and trial practice and the implications of these differences for the negotiation and mediation of cases on appeal. Especially given the recent trend toward mediation of civil appeals, it is becoming increasingly important for attorneys, mediators, and parties to be familiar with the unique facets of the appellate process. To be effective advocates, attorneys must know how the rules on appeal affect the prospects of success for both appellants and respondents. And appellate mediators must be sufficiently knowledgeable in the appellate arena to understand the legal contentions and analyses offered by attorneys and parties to bolster their settlement demands.

In a rational world, appellate cases settle when the parties conclude that the available terms of an agreement are better than the prospects of continuing with an appeal. To determine whether a party is better served by an agreement or pursuing an appeal, parties should consider their needs and interests, and should analyze their risks and opportunities on appeal. If, as in many cases, the parties and their attorneys lack a comprehensive understanding of substantive appellate law, they are not equipped to make a realistic comparison between continuing with the appeal and accepting a negotiated settlement. Mediators who understand basic appellate law can offer valuable insight and help participants assess the strengths and weaknesses of their appeal, as well as the costs of pursuing it.

This section offers a simple guide to the rules and procedures of appeals relevant to negotiation and mediation. Chapter 1 distills the essence of appellate court review that applies to determine whether an appellate court will affirm or reverse a judgment. Chapter 2 offers an approach to appellate risk

---

1. With only rare exception, voluntary and court-connected mediations are limited to civil rather than criminal, conservatorship, or juvenile delinquency cases. Robert W. Rack Jr., *Thoughts of a Chief Circuit Mediator on Federal Court-Annexed Mediation*, 17 Ohio State Journal of Dispute Resolution 609, 611 n.9, 617 n.33 (2001); *but see* http://www.ca9 .uscourts.gov/mediation/ (noting that the Ninth Circuit Court of Appeals mediation program has even successfully mediated criminal appeals, including death penalty cases). In this book, we focus on the rules and procedures governing civil appeals.

analysis and explores the key implications of appellate rules on the prospects for success on appeal. Chapter 3 provides a step-by-step method for calculating the economic value of a case pending on appeal.

In this section, we provide information about appellate rules and procedure to enable attorneys, parties, and mediators to participate knowledgeably in an appellate mediation. Although our concise treatment of this broad subject will not make the reader an appellate expert, it will show how to assess the strengths, weaknesses, financial consequences, and pitfalls of a civil appeal, an ability that is particularly important at the early stage of an appeal when many cases successfully settle through mediation.

In addition to understanding the appellate rules and procedures we discuss next, participants in appellate mediation will need to be familiar with the local rules of court and any required court forms governing court-connected mediation programs. Mediation program rules usually cover requirements and deadlines for court forms, mediation statements, and communications with staff that shepherd cases through the mediation process. Even for voluntary mediations (i.e., settlement efforts independent of any formal appellate court program), the local rules are important because they inform whether parties may obtain a stay of proceedings, extensions of time to complete the appellate record or briefing, and the requirements for a stipulated reversal of the judgment. Although we do not cite specific rules of court or forms, the requirements of many appellate courts are sufficiently similar that we touch upon them generally when appropriate.

B.   Appeals Differ Dramatically from Trials

An appeal differs greatly from a trial in substance, procedure, and strategy (see Table 1), even in the same case. Until the trier of fact reaches a verdict or the trial court rules on a dispositive motion, the animating question for the parties is "Whose perspective is going to prevail?" Thus, in the trial court, parties focus on which witnesses appear most credible, which experts have the most impressive credentials, and what manner of presenting evidence leaves the most vivid impression. In negotiations prior to the appellate stage, discussions about the law often come down to dueling views of whether plaintiffs can prove their causes of action, whether defendants can marshal evidence of affirmative defenses, and how a jury may weigh the evidence. As we shall see, some of the most important legal questions for parties to assess during trial court negotiations become irrelevant on appeal.

Most fundamentally, every appeal involves a "winner" and a "loser." By definition, the appealing party feels sufficiently aggrieved to incur the time and expense to challenge the judgment. In some cases, all of the parties are dissatisfied and appeal the judgment.

The appeal also represents certainty about key issues that were undetermined before entry of judgment, most notably which evidence the trial court would admit or exclude, whether the plaintiff or defendant would prevail, the amount of damages and attorney fees, and whether any sanctions would be imposed. Whereas the primary issues before trial are *factual*, the issues to be resolved on appeal are exclusively *legal* in nature.

On appeal, the reviewing court only considers whether the trial court violated any laws—whether substantive or procedural in nature—in arriving at the judgment. In conducting its review, the appellate court cannot reweigh the relative strengths of the evidence or reassess witness credibility. At the appellate stage, the trial court's factual determinations are essentially set in stone.

Parties may fear that entry of the judgment hardens bargaining demands of the prevailing party into stone as well. To the contrary, the appeal marks a new opportunity to negotiate on the basis of concrete information, in the form of a judgment, and a set of well-defined legal challenges the parties intend to raise on appeal. Rather than speculating about every aspect of the case, the parties on appeal can usually confine their guesswork to a few legal arguments. Thus, quantitative risk analysis at this stage is often easier than before trial.

Table 1: Key Differences between Trials and Appeals

Trials	Appeals
No party has won or lost yet.	There is a "loser" who feels aggrieved by at least part of the judgment and a "winner" defending the challenged part of the judgment.
There is uncertainty about what evidence will be admitted at trial.	There is an appellate record of trial court proceedings to which no more evidence can be added.
There are guesses as to how persuasive a witness or piece of evidence will be to the trier of fact.	There is a conclusive presumption of credibility for witnesses who testified in support of the judgment.
It is uncertain whether the defendant is liable for economic or punitive damages.	Damages are certain, often with an explanation of their bases, if resulting from a court trial or a jury trial employing a detailed special verdict form.
It is unknown whether and what amount of damages and attorney fees may be awarded.	Damages, costs, and fees are set forth in the judgment.
Dispositive legal issues are not yet fixed with any certainty.	Key legal issues are known.
The trial court or jury will consider the relative persuasiveness of testimony, documents, and other evidence.	The appellate court will not reweigh the evidence or second guess the persuasiveness of the parties' evidence.

Now that we understand that an analysis of a case's outcome on appeal has little in common with a pre-trial estimation of a case outcome, we can proceed to learn what makes an appeal succeed or fail in the reviewing court.

Chapter 1
Appellate Law in a Nutshell

A. Appellate Law Fundamentally Rests on Two Questions: "Was There Error?" and "If There Was Error, Was It Prejudicial?"

As difficult and abstruse as appellate law may seem to newcomers, the entirety of a reviewing court's analysis of whether to affirm or reverse a judgment can be distilled into two questions about trial: (1) Was there error? and (2) If there was error, was it prejudicial? Reversal depends on whether the appellant can convince the appellate court to answer yes to both questions.

It is helpful to think about these two questions as follows: (1) Was the judge legally wrong in making a decision, evidentiary ruling, or finding of fact? Or, if the judgment rests on a jury verdict, did the jury make a factual finding without any evidentiary support? and (2) Did the error change the outcome? In other words, did the error result in an unfair trial for the appellant? Another way appellate courts formulate this second question is: Could the appellant have expected a more favorable judgment if the error had not occurred?

These two questions of error and prejudice constitute appellate law in a nutshell. Although appellate advocates engage in additional legal research, record review, and analysis, all of their efforts ultimately go toward answering these questions in a light most favorable to their clients. Issues of law and fact—although they might have been important during trial court proceedings—are not relevant on appeal if they do not address the questions of error and prejudice.

Determining whether error and prejudice occurred in the trial court is not an unbounded, free form inquiry. It requires basic familiarity with substantive appellate law to understand (1) how an appellate court measures whether a trial court's ruling exceeded lawful bounds and (2) what threshold error or errors the appellant must surmount to topple a judgment. Appellate courts in our common law system have developed specific tests—standards of review—to determine whether a complained-of action constituted legal error and whether this error (or errors cumulatively) had a result-changing effect on the judgment. Fortunately, the tests used by appellate courts to determine whether error occurred at trial are not difficult to understand. Thus, we proceed to explore these tests for error.

B. Appellate Courts Use Standards of Review to Determine Whether There Was Legal Error at Trial

An appellate court begins its assessment of whether the trial court erred by determining how much deference it will show to the lower court. The reality that appellate courts are better suited to answering questions of "pure law" than challenges to trial court rulings that are factual or discretionary in nature has resulted in standards of review employed by the appellate court.

For factual issues, appellate courts are highly deferential. They acknowledge the lower court's sole ability to determine witness credibility and evidentiary authenticity based on the trial judge's opportunities to observe witness testimony, examine exhibits, and interact directly with attorneys and parties. By contrast, appellate courts learn about the facts of a case only through the "cold" record—trial transcripts, original documents filed in the trial court, and, often, photocopies of exhibits—and thus are extremely reluctant to find trial court error on factual issues.

Appellate courts *are* well suited to determine questions of law and interpret the terms of a contract. They are well equipped to determine the legally permissible range of options available to a trial court in ruling on issues such as the amount of damages or sanctions. But they *are not* well suited to micromanage trial judges on matters subject to trial judges' discretion. Thus, so long as a trial court made a decision falling within the legally permissible limits of its discretion, an appellate court will defer to the trial judge's decision.

C. Effective Analysis of Appeals Begins with Standards of Review

1. What Are Standards of Review?

Standards of review are the lenses through which the appellate court analyzes the record to determine whether it reveals trial court error. They fall into three categories and apply to nearly all of the issues raised in civil appeals.[2] Our discussion summarizes the standards of review in a manner that will apply in both federal circuit or intermediate state court of appeal cases. Although the technical labels for particular standards of review may differ somewhat in various jurisdictions, each of the three fundamental standard of review categories operate in functionally identical ways. The fundamental standards of review are

- Substantial evidence (and the functionally equivalent "clearly errone-ous" standard),

- Abuse of discretion, and

- Independent (sometimes called de novo review).

---

2. Unique standards of review applying to criminal, conservatorship, habeas corpus, and extraordinary writ proceedings lie beyond the scope of this book. An excellent history and overview of standards of review may be found in Amanda J. Peters, *The Meaning, Measure, and Misuse of Standards of Review*, 13 LEWIS & CLARK L. REV. 233 (2009). Interestingly, appellate courts have begun identifying the applicable standards of review only relatively recently—starting around the 1970s and 1980s. *Id.* at 237–38. The varying levels of deference appellate courts show to trial judges' decisions, however, are not a new phenomenon.

If you understand the rationale for the varying levels of deference to particular arguments—whether attacks on the sufficiency of the evidence, the trial judge's procedural ruling, or the proper application of a statute—you will be able to analyze and describe accurately how the appellate court will analyze the appeal. For this reason, the standards of review "give the parties in a lawsuit an idea of their chances of success on appeal."[3] When an appellate court applies the highly deferential standard of review of substantial evidence to evidentiary issues, the odds of a reversal decline precipitously. By contrast, with independent review that applies to questions of law, the odds increase substantially. Although there are nuances and exceptions—as there are in every other area of law—standard of review constitutes the most important factor in a preliminary assessment of prospects for a reversal.

Appellate courts begin with the presumption that all went well in the trial court—that the judgment is correct and is supported by both law and fact. To prevail on appeal, the appellant has the burden of proof and persuasion to show otherwise. To do so, the appellant must support all claims of error by citing to the appellate record and must convince the appellate court that the conduct complained of actually constituted error.

In contrast, once the appellant files an appeal, the respondent may win the appeal and secure an affirmance of the judgment without filing any briefs or making any appearance in the appellate court. There is no such thing as a default judgment in a court of appeal.

Standards of review fundamentally differ from *evidentiary standards of proof* at trial.[4] The evidentiary standard of proof at trial refers to the weight of evidence necessary to prove a cause of action or affirmative defense, while the standard of review refers to how willing the appellate court is to defer to the trier of fact. Regardless of what weight of evidence the plaintiff had the burden to introduce in the trial court—whether a preponderance of the evidence, clear and convincing evidence, or proof beyond a reasonable doubt—the standard of review of evidentiary issues on appeal is always substantial evidence. Consequently, it is equally difficult for an appellant to convince the appellate court of trial court error when the appellant had a low burden of evidentiary proof—such "a reasonable suspicion" or "some evidence"—as it is to persuade the court when the burden was "beyond reasonable doubt."[5] Likewise, the standard of review of issues of pure law is always de novo, regardless of the plaintiff's burden of evidentiary proof in the trial court.

Unlike the level playing field of the trial court, where either party may succeed by a preponderance of the evidence or lose by failing to rebut the opposing party's evidence, appeals are an uphill battle for appellants. Any evidentiary

---

3. *Id.* at 238.
4. SSIH Equip. SA v. U.S. Int'l Trade Comm'n, 718 F.2d 365, 371 n10 (Fed. Cir. 1983).
5. Although these standards of evidentiary proof usually apply to criminal proceedings, they aptly illustrate that even the extreme opposite ends of the burden of proof spectrum are subject to the same standard of review on appeal.

problems the appellant encounters for any reason—including lack of a sufficient appellate record, ambiguity in the proceedings, or an alternate basis justifying the result—necessarily inure to the benefit of the respondent. As we shall see, the rules governing standards of review explain why the vast majority of respondents emerge victorious in appellate proceedings. For now though, let us delve into how exactly the appellate courts apply the three primary standards of review.

2. The Substantial Evidence and the Clearly Erroneous Standards Apply to Review of Challenges to Factual Findings

The substantial evidence and clearly erroneous standards of review are functionally equivalent, and we refer to both as the substantial evidence standard for ease of reference.[6] Both standards of review rest on the idea that appellate courts show great deference to the trier of fact—whether a jury or a judge—on factual findings.

The substantial evidence standard of review applies to challenges to the sufficiency, persuasiveness, and authenticity of the evidence supporting the jury's verdict. Under the substantial evidence standard of review, the appellate court inquires whether the judgment "'is supported by reasonable, substantial, and probative evidence on the record considered as a whole.' Under this standard, reversal requires finding 'that the record not only supports reversal, but compels it.'"[7] This standard of review is extremely strict in the sense that all factual inferences, questions of credibility, and issues concerning the weight of the evidence are drawn in favor of the judgment.[8]

Appellate courts review trial court rulings resting on findings of fact to determine whether they are "clearly erroneous."[9] As one appellate court memorably explained, "To be clearly erroneous, a decision must strike us as more than just maybe or probably wrong; it must . . . strike us as wrong with the force of a five-week-old, unrefrigerated dead fish."[10]

---

6. In searching for the distinction between substantial evidence and clearly erroneous standards of review, the U.S. Supreme Court, in Dickinson v. Zurko, 527 U.S. 150, 162–63, 119 S. Ct. 1816, 144 L. Ed. 2d 143 (1999), stated that it "failed to uncover a single instance in which a reviewing court conceded that use of one standard rather than the other would in fact have produced a different outcome." Nonetheless, the court noted that substantial evidence applies to assess the reliability of findings of fact made by a jury (or an agency), while clearly erroneous applies when the trial court's decision rests on its own fact finding. Id.; In re Zurko, 258 F.3d 1379, 1384 (Fed. Cir. 2001).
7. Zhou Hua Zhu v. U.S. Attorney Gen., 703 F.3d 1303, 1307 (11th Cir. 2013), quoting Imelda v. U.S. Attorney Gen., 611 F.3d 724, 727 (11th Cir. 2010) (citations omitted).
8. In this sense, review is even more constrained than it is under the abuse of discretion test discussed in part C.3. See Aircraft Owners and Pilots Ass'n v. FAA, 600 F.2d 965, 969 n21 (D.C. Cir. 1979).
9. Peters, supra note 1, at 245.
10. Parts and Elec. Motors, Inc. v. Sterling Elec., Inc., 866 F.2d 228, 233 (7th Cir. 1989).

Although evidentiary appeals as bad as stinky fish are almost nonexistent, parties and their attorneys frequently try to make the case for evidentiary error in appellate mediations. Having recently been through trial, or proceedings designed to lead to trial, many parties and attorneys retain their focus on witness credibility, expert witness qualifications, strengths and weaknesses of the parties' competing documents and exhibits, document authenticity, and the relative persuasiveness of their evidentiary cases. These complaints are usually grounded on a belief that the jury's verdict or court's judgment reached a conclusion that cannot be defended based on the evidence introduced in the trial court.

The desire to dwell on evidentiary persuasiveness is understandable: those arguments win at trial! The parties and their attorneys (especially those who have taken a case on a contingency fee arrangement) may have recently spent astronomical sums of money to amass evidence, pay expert witnesses, and litigate the case through judgment in the trial court. Moreover, parties are all too aware of the moment during the testimony at trial when their case may have tilted toward loss. Parties disappointed by jury verdicts and judgments are often upset and may believe the trier of fact ignored what they consider to be the overwhelmingly convincing evidence—or, worse, that the judge was biased against them.

Participants in an appellate mediation, including mediators, can adjust their understanding of the importance of evidentiary issues on appeal by remembering a few key points:

- *Appeals are not retrials.* An appeal is not a *second* opportunity to present a case but an inquiry into whether there was legal error at the *first* proceeding that requires some correction to the judgment or even retrial by the lower court.

- *Courts of appeal do not allow new or additional evidence.* At the moment the appellant files a notice of appeal, the record of proceedings to which parties on appeal may refer is closed. If after the judgment is final parties realize they forgot to introduce some document or testimony or discover more convincing evidence, that's too bad. They are stuck with the evidence as already presented.

- *Appellate courts deem respondents' evidence to be conclusively credible.* Even if the appellate court believes it might have drawn different conclusions from the documents or testimony, it must defer to the trier of fact's findings. As the U.S. Supreme Court has explained, "If the [trial] court's account of the evidence is plausible in light of the record viewed in its entirety, the court of appeals may not reverse it even though convinced that had it been sitting as the trier of fact, it would have weighed the evidence differently."[11]

---

11.   Anderson v. Bessemer City, 470 U.S. 564, 105 S. Ct. 1504, 84 L. Ed. 2d 518, 573–74 (1985).

- *Appellate courts usually disregard the testimony of appellants and appellants' witnesses.* Appellants are often chagrined to discover that the reviewing court will likely ignore their testimony and, instead, credit all testimony and documents supporting the judgment.

- *Reviewing courts presume that vague or ambiguous evidence favors respondents.* Whenever appellate courts can plausibly interpret testimony or documents in more than one way, they will adopt the interpretation that supports the judgment.

- *Courts of appeal will not reweigh the evidence.* Even if the appellant introduced a greater volume of evidence, produced witnesses with greater credentials, or had seemingly more convincing evidence, the appellate court will not reverse on this basis because it does not reassess the relative persuasiveness of the parties' cases. Put another way, testimony by a convicted felon that supports a verdict will not be rejected by an appellate court even if the pope and several cardinals testified to the contrary.

- *The emotional impact, vividness, and intonation of evidence usually does not come though the cold appellate record.* Testimony that evokes gasps in the courtroom often comes across as utterly unremarkable in the reporter's transcript. Thus, the emotional impact of witness testimony is usually lost when an appellate court reviews the transcripts.

- *Many evidentiary issues cannot even be raised on appeal.* As discussed next, most evidentiary rulings of a trial court cannot be challenged in the appellate court unless the appellant's trial attorney made a timely and specific objection when the evidence was admitted or excluded.

- *Gaps in the record favor the respondent.* An incomplete record of the proceedings invariably accrues to favor the party defending the judgment.

- *The testimony of a single witness suffices.* No matter how untrustworthy witnesses for the respondent seemed to the appellant, the testimony of a single witness suffices to buttress the judgment against a claim of insufficient evidence.

- *The burden to prove error is exclusively on the appellant.* The appellant "has the burden to clearly demonstrate error in the court's findings. This is a strong burden where . . . the findings are primarily based upon oral testimony and the trial judge has viewed the demeanor and credibility of witnesses."[12] The respondent does not have the duty to prove that the evidence at trial was enough.

---

12.   Snodgrass v. Nelson, 503 F.2d 94, 96 (8th Cir. 1974).

Given these rules for the substantial evidence standard of review, reversals based on insufficiency of the evidence are exceedingly rare. Reversals based on a showing that the appellant's testimony "really was more truthful or persuasive" than that of the opposing party are essentially nonexistent.

However, it would be a mistake to think that appellants never succeed on insufficiency of the evidence claims. Sufficiency of the evidence challenges can succeed, when (1) they are targeted at the failure of proof for a particular element of a cause of action or (2) if the appellant can demonstrate that a key piece of evidence or category of documents was erroneously excluded by the trial court. Successful challenges to sufficiency of the evidence often have the following hallmarks:

- *There is no evidence to prove a particular element of a cause of action.* Especially for new or revised statutes setting forth specific causes of action, parties may forget to introduce evidence on a new, technical, or obscure element of their claims. As one court explained, "The evidence may be reasonable, credible, and of solid value in light of the whole record, and may clearly establish facts A, B, and C. The judgment must still be reversed if fact D, which is essential, is not established by facts A, B, and C or by other substantial evidence. That is unchanged by whole record review. A reviewing court must merely determine whether any reasonable trier of fact could have inferred fact D from facts A, B and C, or from other substantial evidence."[13] Challenges to the sufficiency of the evidence can and do succeed when the party with the burden of proof has simply overlooked a necessary element. Surprisingly, this actually happens with more regularity than one might anticipate

- *The appellant introduced the wrong type of evidence in an attempt to prove the claim.* When a statute or rule requires particular types of evidence, as in the case of certain types of medical malpractice claims, the evidence may be insufficient.

Finally, we note that if the appellate court determines that evidence challenged on appeal was erroneously admitted in the trial court, the previously prevailing party might be left with insufficient evidence to support the judgment.

Attorneys and mediators who understand the substantial evidence standard are able to help parties adjust their expectations regarding the slim odds of success for factual contentions on appeal. The appellate court tends to be extremely deferential to the trier of fact. For this reason, factual contentions focusing on lack of proof, witness credibility, and reweighing the evidence tend to be very weak issues on appeal.

---

13. Rivard v. Bd. of Pension Comm'rs, 164 Cal. App. 3d 405, 414, 210 Cal. Rptr. 509 (Ct. App. 1985).

3. The Abuse of Discretion Standard of Review Applies When the Trial Court Had the Prerogative to Choose from a Range of Options

The abuse of discretion standard of review applies when, in making its decision, the trial court had discretion to select from more than one option. A trial court abuses its discretion when it exceeds the bounds of *permissible* options. Courts usually word this standard broadly, such as in this example: "A district court abuses its discretion when it misconstrues its proper role, ignores or misunderstands the relevant evidence, and bases its decision upon considerations having little factual support."[14] For example, a trial court might have discretion to grant a continuance for a day, or even a month, but not a year. Or the trial court might have the prerogative to grant only a very short continuance but would deny a party due process by refusing any continuance to secure a key witness. Likewise, a trial court might have statutory authority to award fees and costs for a specific cause of action, but it would abuse its discretion by awarding fees for a separate cause of action for which no contract or statute provides fee shifting.

Because trial courts usually have a range of permissible options at any time to allow for the management of courtroom procedure and to oversee trials, many—if not most—decisions of a trial court can only be challenged under the abuse of discretion standard of review. Thus, this standard of review "span[s] the variegated landscape of the law."[15] Examples of rulings reviewed for abuse of discretion include

- The amount of statutory or contractual attorney fees to be awarded or sanctions for improper litigation conduct,

- The relevance of evidence,

- Whether to bifurcate trial,

- The amount and duration of spousal support orders (within statutory guidelines),

- Visitation orders,

- Continuances of trial, and

- Change of venue.[16]

---

14. Arlook v. S. Lichtenberg & Co., 952 F.2d 367, 374 (11th Cir. 1992).
15. Hurtado v. Statewide Home Loan Co., 167 Cal. App. 3d 1019, 1023, 213 Cal. Rptr. 712 (Ct. App. 1985).
16. Research Automation, Inc. v. Schrader-Bridgeport Int'l, Inc., 626 F.3d 973, 977 (7th Cir. 2010).

Under the abuse of discretion standard, the burden is entirely on the appellant to show that the trial record establishes that the court exceeded the lawful bounds of its power or selected an option outside the permissible range. The following are a few key points to keep in mind for the abuse of discretion standard of review:

- *The trial court's decision must fall entirely outside the range of lawful options.*[17] Or, as some courts put it, "A court abuses its discretion when its ruling 'falls outside the bounds of reason.'"[18]

- *The appellate court will not reverse even if it can think of a "better" decision than the one made by the trial court.* Although appellants invariably believe the judge could have made a better ruling, appellate courts will not reverse simply because they too can imagine a better ruling. Thus, "unless a clear case of abuse is shown . . . a reviewing court will not substitute its opinion and thereby divest the trial court of its discretionary power."[19]

- *The trial court's decision must have been arbitrary, capricious, or irrational.* "A trial court abuses its discretion when it acts arbitrarily, acts without conscientious judgment, or, in view of all of the circumstances, exceeds the bounds of reason and ignores recognized principles of law, resulting in substantial injustice."[20]

- *Abuse of discretion is a very difficult standard for an appellant to overcome.*[21] Some courts go so far as to describe abuse of discretion as "the most deferential of appellate review standards."[22]

Nonetheless, abuse of discretion claims can succeed. Trial courts are under enormous time constraints and often labor under staggeringly large dockets. Given these challenges, trial courts sometimes make decisions that prove indefensible with the benefit of hindsight. Appellants secure reversals by showing that the trial court did one of the following:

- *Misunderstood the boundaries of its discretion.* Especially when called upon to construe a new, complex, or especially lengthy statute, a trial court can err in determining the limits of its discretion. Even if a trial court

---

17. Johnson v. Univ. of Rochester Med. Ctr., 642 F.3d 121, 125 (2d Cir. 2011).
18. People v. Carter, 36 Cal. 4th 1114, 1149, 32 Cal. Rptr. 3d 759, 117 P.3d 476 (Cal. 2005).
19. Denham v. Superior Court, 2 Cal. 3d 557, 566, 86 Cal. Rptr. 65, 468 P.2d 193 (Cal. 1970).
20. *In re* Marriage of Pond, 379 Ill. App. 3d 982, 987–88, 319 Ill. Dec. 182, 885 N.E.2d 453 (Ct. App. 2008).
21. Lorentzen v. Anderson Pest Control, 64 F.3d 327, 331 (7th Cir. 1995).
22. Arneson v. Arneson, 2003 S.D. 125, 670 N.W.2d 904, 910 (S.D. 2003).

does not actually exceed the lawful limits of its discretion, an appellant can demonstrate error by showing the court actually misunderstood the range of options available. "A trial court abuses its discretion when it applies the wrong legal standards applicable to the issue at hand."[23]

- *Did not actually exercise its discretion when asked to do so by a party.* For example, a trial court errs when failing to rule on (rather than simply denying) a motion brought by a party.[24]

- *Used impermissible factors in reaching its decision.* Because parties are entitled to have the trial court make a decision guided only by the legal considerations allowed by the applicable statute or case law, the appellate court will reverse when the record shows the trial judge relied on any other factors to make the decision.[25] For example, a trial court may err by considering any of the following inadmissible evidence: a party's ability to pay when a particular statutory civil penalty may be mandatory; post-injury improvements to a product to prove design defect in a products liability action; settlement offers to prove liability; or any immutable characteristic such as race, gender, or age of the party to establish fault.

Participants in appellate mediations should therefore understand the abuse of discretion standard of review:

- It applies broadly to decisions made by the trial court,

- The scope of review is extremely deferential, and

- Appellants who challenge trial court judgments under this standard rarely succeed.

4. *The Independent (De Novo) Standard of Review Applies to Questions of Law*

An appellate court's disadvantage in reviewing factual issues on a cold record evaporates when it comes to issues requiring the interpretation of writing. Thus, the least deferential standard of review—independent or de novo review— applies to the interpretation of statutes, constitutional provisions, regulations, and private contracts.

---

23. Cook ex rel. Estate of Tessier v. Sheriff of Monroe Cnty., Fla., 402 F.3d 1092, 1104 (11th Cir. 2005).
24. *See, e.g.,* Miles v. Dep't of Army, 881 F.2d 777, 784 (9th Cir. 1989).
25. For example, in People v. Abbaszadeh, 106 Cal. App. 4th 642, 644–50, 130 Cal. Rptr. 2d 873 (Ct. App. 2003), the trial court encouraged prospective jurors who could not put aside racial biases to get off the jury even if jurors had to do so by false pretenses.

For such issues, appellate courts apply their "independent judgment in interpreting the [matter] without giving any deference to the trial court's ruling."[26] Examples of the types of decisions reviewed under this standard are judgments on the pleadings and decisions interpreting the provisions of a contract.[27]

Although independent review offers appellants the best odds, by far, for reversal on appeal, it is these types of appellate issues that cause the parties' eyes to glaze over. It is rare for a party to show up at an appellate mediation and exclaim, "The judge misinterpreted subdivision (b)(7)(G) of Section 47689, and that's why we haven't yet settled this case!" Even so, issues subject to independent review deserve close examination, because the appellate court will declare error if it interprets a statute, rule, or regulation even slightly differently from the trial court; or the appellate court will determine the meaning of private contracts without deference to the trial court's construction of the terms of the agreement.

Given the total lack of deference shown to the trial court under independent review, there is a misconception that appellants have 50/50 odds of winning under this standard. Independent review does not yield reversals as often as affirmances for these reasons:

- The trial court's interpretation must still be *wrong*. Trial judges usually construe writings correctly and their decisions are therefore affirmed.

- Even if an appellant establishes error, reversal is not automatic. The appellate court may deem an error of law to be harmless.

Although independent review does not offer an equal-odds bet for reversal, it is the standard most favorable to appellants and the one under which a respondent's position is most vulnerable. Because appellate courts do not defer to trial court interpretations of statutes or contracts, the outcome of independent review is significantly less certain than it is under the other two standards.

D. Determining Which Standard of Review Applies

There is no simple list that categorizes trial court rulings and jury decisions by standards of review, because the applicable standard is not determined by the particular *decision* being appealed. Rather, it is determined by the *nature of*

---

26. Campbell v. Scripps Bank, 78 Cal. App. 4th 1328, 1336, 93 Cal. Rptr. 2d 635 (Ct. App. 2000).

27. There is also a hybrid standard of review called mixed question of law and fact that applies when the appellate court must determine which law or standard applies before it can even consider which facts are relevant for the applicable legal test. This standard of review usually receives the same deference as independent review. NLRB v. Hearst Publications, Inc., 322 U.S. 111, 130–31, 64 S. Ct. 851, 88 L. Ed. 1170 (1944). Questions under this standard are predominantly legal in nature with the attending lack of deference.

appellant's challenge. An appeal from an order granting statutory attorney fees provides a good illustration. The *substantial evidence* standard of review applies when an appellant argues that an $80,000 statutory attorney fee award was unsupported by declarations of counsel or an itemized statement of hours spent on the litigation. The *abuse of discretion* standard applies when an appellant argues that an $80,000 statutory attorney fee award was excessive because the trial court should have concluded that the legal work was so poor that it was worth only $20,000. *Independent review* applies to an appellant's argument that the statute relied upon by the trial court in granting fees does not actually authorize the award. Thus, an appellant has better prospects for success in arguing that fees should be reduced to zero under the independent standard than in arguing fees should be reduced by even one dollar under an abuse of discretion standard.

Determining the applicable standard of review can be difficult. This task is especially challenging in appeals with multiple grounds for reversal, as each issue requires a separate standard of review analysis. Even so, the challenge of identifying the applicable standard(s) of review for a case is worth the effort because it provides a very good indication of how likely or unlikely the appellate court is to conclude that the trial court erred on issues raised by the appellant.

E.   Appellate Courts Will Not Reverse in the Absence of Prejudicial Error

It is not that hard to establish error. Indeed, most lengthy or complex trials involve some sort of error. As the U.S. Supreme Court has observed, "[a litigant] is entitled to a fair trial but not a perfect one, for there are no perfect trials."[28] Given the prevalence of errors committed at trial, appellate courts apply a second test to determine whether to reverse judgments. They ask this question: Was the effect of the error so grave that the appellant received an unfair trial? In other words, in the absence of error, would the trial court have reached a different result? As essential as the analysis of prejudice is to an appeal, surprisingly, appellants frequently fail even to address it at all in arguing for reversal. Mediation can help parties who might have ignored prejudice in evaluating their appeal to focus on this important analysis.

In establishing prejudice, several principles apply to make it difficult for an appellant to prevail:

- *Prejudice requires error that "almost surely affected the outcome of the case."*[29] Even if the appellate court finds error, this stringent test often compels affirmance of the judgment.

---

28. McDonough Power Equip., Inc. v. Greenwood, 464 U.S. 548, 553, 104 S. Ct. 845, 78 L. Ed. 2d 663 (1984).
29. Champagne v. U.S., 40 F.3d 946, 947 (8th Cir. 1994).

- *Appellants have the burden to demonstrate prejudice.*[30] Just as respondents have no burden to disprove error, neither must they show that errors were harmless.

- *Even multiple errors do not guarantee a reversal.* If redundant bases support the judgment, an appellant must demonstrate prejudicial error *as to each* before the judgment will be overturned. For example, if the trial court entered judgment for the defense based on lack of evidence by the plaintiff as well as on the untimeliness of the claim, the plaintiff/ appellant must demonstrate error as to both grounds in order to secure reversal.

- *Appellate courts will affirm judgments based on any reasonable legal grounds—even if that basis was not relied upon by the trial court in entering judgment.* If the respondent can formulate a new, legally justified reason for affirming the judgment based on the appellate record, the appellate court will deny the appeal, even if that reason had not been first argued in the trial court. And the appellate court can base its decision on legal grounds it formulated on its own.

- *A very few types of errors are inherently prejudicial.* These errors do not require an appellant to demonstrate prejudice. These errors are as rare as they are obviously fatal to a fair trial. Such errors usually involve denial of a party's right to testify at all, denial of the right to cross-examine a witness, entirely preventing a party from introducing admissible evidence, denial of a party's right to legal representation, or refusal to follow statutory imperatives for which no discretion is granted. The limited instances of inherently prejudicial errors indicate how rarely they appear. A demonstration of prejudice is nearly always necessary for an appellant to secure a reversal of the judgment.

One way to understand the inquiry into prejudice is to imagine trials or trial court rulings as ships to the appellant's desired legal outcome. The appellate court will not provide the vehicle of a new trial if the errors at the first trial were just a few splashes overboard or a small leak. Instead, the errors complained of had to sink the ship. For example, appellants can demonstrate prejudice by establishing the following:

- *A trial court's misinterpretation of an applicable statute or term in the parties' contract.* Such errors are likely to affect the outcome.

- *Errors in instructing the jury on key elements of the causes of action.*

- *Errors that are compounded by repetition to the jury.* Trial rulings are vulnerable to the prejudice analysis when errors (usually in

---

30. Waldorf v. Shuta, 3 F.3d 705, 710 (3d Cir. 1993).

misinterpreting the law) are repeatedly reinforced to the jury, by, for example, attorneys who emphasize the error in arguments to the jury or in faulty hypotheticals to witnesses who are told to make assumptions based on misinterpretation of the law.

- *Pretrial rulings that have the effect of wrongly eliminating entire categories of evidence.* A judge's erroneous ruling that effectively excludes all evidence a party needs to prove or defend against a cause of action is prejudicial. Pre-trial rulings that exclude expert testimony, a large set of documents, or an entire category of evidence based on lack of scientific reliability can, if in error, establish prejudice because a party never "got to put on a case."

- *Errors that rendered the process unfair to one side.* For example, evidentiary rulings that allowed one party to introduce a category of evidence—such as an expert witness's statistical analysis of data—but prevented the opposing party from introducing counter evidence of the same type.

Parties routinely underestimate, or even ignore, the importance of the requirement of prejudice. One of the many services mediators provide is to help parties focus on this crucial analysis. As appellate lawyers recognize, if a judgment is supported on redundant bases—through either multiple theories of liability or more than one legal basis—the best appellate attack on one ground can do nothing to disturb the judgment. Similarly, winning an argument about evidentiary error does not help the appellant if the court deems the evidence of the opposing party to have been overwhelming. Any evaluation regarding the strength of an appeal must include the question of *whether the error made a difference.*

The requirement of prejudice explains why appellate courts affirm the overwhelming majority of civil appeals. The U.S. Courts of Appeals affirm approximately 81 percent of all civil appeals.[31] Even though state appellate courts have a lower affirmance rate of approximately 68 percent for civil appeals, appellants lose most of the time.[32]

F.   Appellate Courts Will Not Usually Reverse If the Appellant Did Not Raise the Issue in the Trial Court

In general, a court will not consider arguments on appeal unless the appellant first made the same argument in the trial court. Failure to preserve an issue for

---

31.   Kevin M. Clermont & Theodore Eisenberg, *Appeal from Jury or Judge Trial: Defendants' Advantage,* 3 Am. L. & Econ. Rev. 125, 130 (2001). We examine differing rates of success for appellants and respondents among varying categories of civil cases in Chapter 2.

32.   Theodore Eisenberg & Michael Heise, *Plaintiphobia in State Courts? An Empirical Study of State Court Trials on Appeal,* J. Legal Stud. 38 (2009).

appeal can be difficult to ferret out without the appellate record. Even so, in preparation for negotiations and mediation, lawyers and mediators can be on the lookout for the following most obvious issues related to forfeiture:

- *Did the appellant raise the issue in the trial court?*[33] Except in limited circumstances, as described below, in order to preserve issues for appeal, parties must raise objections in the trial court. Appellants are almost always limited to arguments they made in the trial court, even if further reflection and legal research seem to yield promising new theories to challenge the judgment. Sometimes though, appellate courts will consider novel issues when they are purely legal in nature or the claimed error is so obvious that the failure to consider it would result in a miscarriage of justice.[34]

- *Did the appellant who is complaining about the exclusion of evidence first make an offer of proof in the trial court?* An appellant usually cannot challenge the exclusion of evidence without first (1) expressly objecting to the exclusion of evidence, (2) doing so in a timely manner, and (3) describing the proffered evidence in sufficient detail to allow the trial court to understand the evidence to be admitted.[35]

- *Did the appellant make a timely objection about the admission of evidence before raising the issue on appeal?*[36] Generally, the evidentiary objection in the trial court must have been made on the same grounds as raised on appeal. For example, an objection based on relevance does not preserve an appellate challenge that the evidence constituted inadmissible hearsay.[37]

---

33. "'[I]t is the general rule . . . that a federal appellate court does not consider an issue not passed upon below.' . . . Our precedent generally counsels against entertaining arguments not presented to the district court." Golden Bridge Tech., Inc. v. Nokia, Inc., 527 F.3d 1318, 1322 (Fed. Cir. 2008). Exceptions to this rule are narrow, usually involving new statutes or Supreme Court cases. *Id.* at 1323. Sometimes though, self-represented litigants are not held to the same preclusive rule. *Id.*

34. For example, if the new issue is a purely legal one, it is proper to resolve it on appeal, because doing so would not require the parties to develop new or different facts. Hansen v. Morgan, 582 F.2d 1214, 1218 (9th Cir. 1978); United States v. Patrin, 575 F.2d 708, 712 (9th Cir. 1978). Because the question here is purely "one of statutory construction that is both central to this case and important to the public, we exercise our discretion to decide it." Commodity Futures Trading Comm'n v. Co Petro Mktg. Grp., Inc., 680 F.2d 573, 581 (9th Cir. 1982).

35. Although federal appellate review may still be possible under the plain error standard (Perkins v. Silver Mountain Sports Club & Spa, LLC, 557 F.3d 1141, 1151 (10th Cir. 2009)), some courts deem the evidentiary contention conclusively forfeited in the absence of an offer of proof. Shaw v. County of Santa Cruz, 170 Cal. App. 4th 229, 286–87, 88 Cal. Rptr. 3d 186 (Ct. App. 2008).

36. Christmas v. City of Chicago, 682 F.3d 632, 640 (7th Cir. 2012).

37. Green v. Schutt Sports Mfg. Co., 369 Fed. Appx. 630, 639 (5th Cir. 2010).

- *Does the appellate record contain information about the errors the appellant wishes to assert?* Assertions of trial court error usually cannot succeed without a reporter's transcript to demonstrate the mistake—most likely a reporter's transcript of the entire trial. Similarly, no procedural issue can succeed without a record of the pertinent motions and pleadings from all parties.

- *Did the appellant who is challenging a jury's award of damages as excessive or inadequate first object on the same ground before the trial court?*[38] Appellants cannot assert new theories of damages on appeal.[39] Conversely, respondents cannot assert factual defenses for the first time on appeal.[40]

- *Is the appellant arguing against a position he or she took in trial?* Appellants cannot raise issues of "invited error" by contradicting themselves.[41] This means that a party cannot request a particular ruling, remedy, or jury instruction in the trial court and then argue on appeal that the requested relief was erroneously granted.[42] For example, a parent who initiates a legal proceeding to establish parentage cannot later argue that the trial court did not have jurisdiction to decide the question.[43]

Without a complete record, lawyers and parties cannot fully assess issues of waiver and forfeiture. Nevertheless, effective case evaluation, even in the absence of a complete record, requires parties to inquire into whether the appellant properly preserved issues at the trial level. Mediation offers parties a good opportunity to do so.

G.   Appeals Offer Only a Limited Scope of Relief

Appellate courts have few options for resolving appeals. They are constrained to the following:

- *Affirm.* This result keeps the judgment intact.

- *Reverse.* This ruling vacates the judgment in whole or in part. Reversal almost always results in the case's return to the trial court for further proceedings or a new trial.[44]

---

38. "It is well-established that there can be no appellate review of allegedly excessive or inadequate damages if the trial court was not given the opportunity to exercise its discretion on a motion for a new trial." Bueno v. City of Donna, 714 F.2d 484, 493–94 (5th Cir. 1983).

39. *See* Kantlehner v. Bisceglia, 102 Cal. App. 2d 1, 6, 226 P.2d 636 (Ct. App. 1951).

40. *See* Curcio v. Svanevik, 155 Cal. App. 3d 955, 960, 202 Cal. Rptr. 499 (Ct. App. 1984).

41. Fryman v. Fed. Crop Ins. Corp., 936 F.2d 244, 250 (6th Cir. 1991).

42. Allen v. Zurich Ins. Co., 667 F.2d 1162, 1166 (4th Cir. 1982) ("In certain circumstances a party may properly be precluded as a matter of law from adopting a legal position in conflict with one earlier taken in the same or related litigation.").

43. Kristine H. v. Lisa R., 37 Cal. 4th 156, 166, 117 P.3d 690 (Cal. 2005).

44. *See* Hampton v. Superior Court, 38 Cal. 2d 652, 655, 242 P.2d 1 (Cal. 1952).

- *Modify.* Sometimes an appellate court will change the judgment when it determines that there can be only one lawful result. For example, a court of appeal may modify a punitive damages award if it concludes the award was unconstitutionally excessive as compared to a lawful multiplier of compensatory damages.[45] A court may also modify a judgment to correct portions of the trial court's decision for which the correct amount of damages and viable causes of action can be ascertained as a matter of law.[46] A judgment may also be modified to strike improperly awarded costs and fees or to impose the correct rate of post-judgment interest when the correct amount is legally certain even without the need for further hearing in the trial court.[47]

These constraints have significant implications for parties on appeal. They should bear in the mind that an appellate court *will not* do the following:

- *Substitute a judgment with a "better" or "wiser" solution.* Even if a win-win solution for all parties is obvious to the appellate court, it will not "improve" upon the judgment for the benefit of the parties.

- *Declare the appellant to have had better or more persuasive evidence.* Appellate courts do not weigh the evidence. They simply determine whether the evidence submitted was sufficient to support the judgment and treat the insufficient evidence as a failure of proof. In making this determination, they ignore altogether evidence submitted by the opposing party. If the appellant had a "full and fair opportunity" to present evidence, ordinarily an appellate court will not order a new trial absent an intervening change in the law or newly discovered evidence that could not have been discovered through proper diligence.[48]

- *Award damages or other relief.* Even if a losing plaintiff demonstrates that the trial court erred by, for example, improperly excluding evidence or wrongly instructing the jury, a court of appeal will not change the award in the plaintiff's favor. It will merely remand the case to the trial court for a new trial.

The limited relief available in an appellate court enhances the attractiveness of a negotiated settlement that can offer a better, wiser, more efficient alternative to the trial court's judgment.

---

45. *E.g.,* Arizona v. ASARCO LLC, 733 F.3d 882, 891–92 (9th Cir. 2013); Las Palmas Assoc. v. Las Palmas Center Assoc., 235 Cal. App. 3d 1220, 1254–56, 1 Cal. Rptr. 2d 301 (Ct. App. 1991).
46. *E.g.,* Ronga v. New York City Dep't of Educ., 980 N.Y.S.2d 426, 114 A.D.3d 527 (N.Y. App. Div. 2014) (modifying judgment to strike certain allegations of misconduct for which the appellant did not receive due process).
47. Crossman v. Fontainebleau Hotel Corp., 346 F.2d 152, 153 (5th Cir. 1965); United States v. Thornton, 245 F.2d 230, 231 (9th Cir. 1950).
48. Viner v. Sweet, 117 Cal. App. 4th 1218, 12 Cal. Rptr. 3d 533 (Ct. App. 2004).

H.   "Winning" on Appeal Rarely Ends a Controversy

"Sometimes, winning your case is only half the battle . . . and not even the worst part."[49] To an uninitiated appellant, the promise of an appeal lies in undoing a bad judgment. However, appellants generally do not appreciate that winning an appeal usually means they get *another trial*—along with the attendant attorney fees, court costs, and emotional turmoil.

Even if the court does not order a new trial, in reversing a judgment, reviewing courts almost always remand a case to the trial court for further proceedings. For example, appellate courts seldom rule on the amount of attorney fees to be awarded a prevailing party. And money judgments frequently result in further trial court proceedings aimed at collecting the debt. Thus, reversals almost invariably require extensive additional litigation in the trial court. Indeed, we know of only two situations in which a reversal does *not* result in further trial court proceedings: (1) a holding by the appellate court that the defendant owed plaintiff no duty (either in tort or contract), and (2) a holding that the insured had no coverage under a policy issued by an insurer. Note that in either of these instances, a fee-shifting clause in the statute, contract, or insurance policy at issue would still require further trial court proceedings to determine the amount of fees to be awarded to the prevailing party for the appeal.

Even in cases in which the respondent succeeds in securing a full affirmance of the judgment, the appellate court's decision rarely ends the litigation. Appellants often petition for review or certiorari with the next higher appellate court. And after the appellate proceedings, disputes often return to the trial court on requests for appellate attorney fees based on contracts that shift fees.

Equally important, a decision by the appellate court does nothing to resolve the underlying human problem that gave rise to the legal action. A cogent analysis of error and prejudice by the appellate court does not mend broken relationships or address the emotional or business needs of the parties. Thus, a resolution of the appellate proceedings rarely ends the personal difficulties underlying the case.

I.   Appeals Can Be Very Slow

As a basic rule of thumb, an average civil appeal will require about a year and a half to two years to be decided.[50] Complex, multi-party, or long-record appeals can easily take two or even three years in an intermediate appellate court. And a grant of review by the jurisdiction's highest court can easily add two or three more years of uncertainty and expense.

---

49.   http://www.gotlaw.org/areas-of-practice/civil-litigation/collecting-on-a-judgment/.

50.   In the U.S. Courts of Appeals, the average time to final disposition after filing the notice of appeal is a little more than 11 months for civil appeals. *See* http://www .uscourts.gov/statistics/table/b-4a/judicial-business/2014/09/30 (Table B-4A (Sept. 30, 2014)). In California, the average time from notice of appeal to decision in its intermediate appellate court is just over two years. Court Statistics Report: Statewide Caseload Trends 2003–2004 through 2012–2013 28 (Judicial Council of California 2014).

Chapter 2
Case Evaluation for Civil Appeals

A.   What Is Case Evaluation?

In Chapter 1, we covered the basics of appellate law. In this chapter, we demonstrate how to use this information for case evaluation, the purpose of which is to determine the odds and potential outcomes of pursuing an appeal, to examine alternatives to litigation, and to compare the *presently available* options to the option of pursuing the appeal.

Case evaluation aims to answer the question: "What is my best presently available option?" To this end, this chapter offers guidance on how to (1) assess the risks and opportunities of continuing with an appeal and determine the financial cost of doing so, and (2) explore and evaluate other presently available options. We explore the implications of appellate rules and procedures on case evaluation for both appellants and respondents.

Perhaps one of the most helpful things to understand about case evaluation is what it is not. Case evaluation is *not* an exercise in dreaming up hopes, yearnings, and wants in order to have the other party fulfill them. Parties often pursue civil appeals based on fantasies of emotional vindication, enough money to change their lives or businesses for the better, justice, or relief from humiliation. When parties judge settlement options by the standard of what they *want*, appeals are unlikely to settle. The opposing party almost never offers everything the other party wants. (If it were otherwise, the case would have already settled!)

Case evaluation does not depend upon what *the opposing party* believes or is doing. Moreover, it does not involve forcing the other party to do anything, whether that be making a concession, extending an offer, or accepting a settlement. Instead, case evaluation focuses on a party's own case, his or her own options, and how a party can improve upon them without the cooperation of the other party.

Parents understand this principle intuitively. For example, one evening Brendon was making dinner and asked his then four-year-old daughter whether she preferred rice or quinoa. She exclaimed, "French fries and a burger!" Like many other four-year-olds, she adored French fries and burgers. However, as Brendon explained, there were no French fries in the house, and it was too late to run to the store to buy some. His explanation triggered the insistent response, "I want French fries!" After a temper tantrum failed to resolve the issue, dinner ended up being rice and tuna. For dinner, the four-year-old faced a choice: have rice and tuna or skip dinner. She opted for what she *needed*, a dinner that satisfied her hunger, though it was not what she *wanted*. In the same way, parties do well for themselves when they surrender an exploration of wants to focus on their interests—what is important to them—and on the options available to address their interests.

Importantly, case evaluation is not the bottom-line analysis that usually precedes negotiations. Parties often determine their bottom line or "walk-away number" because they fear that they may accept a settlement offer they will eventually bitterly regret. However, as Fisher and Ury note, "While adopting a bottom line may protect you from accepting a very bad agreement, it may keep you both from inventing and agreeing to a solution that would be wise to accept. An arbitrarily selected figure is no measure of what you should accept."[1] Rather than an arbitrary bottom-line, or other sort of line in the sand metric that serves as a way to judge settlement proposals, case evaluation is an analytical process based on the specific realities of the dispute. Case evaluation enables parties to closely examine the option of pursuing the appeal and explore other presently available options and compare them to determine the best available option. This exercise allows parties to enter negotiation with information they need to make sound settlement decisions.

B.   How Does Case Evaluation Differ from Legal Assessment of the Appeal, Decision Tree Risk Analysis, and Negotiation?

In addition to understanding that case evaluation involves the comparison of presently available options, it is important also to remember where case evaluation fits within the larger process of appellate mediation. The tasks of *legal assessment*, case evaluation, *calculation* of the present economic value of the appeal, and, finally, the actual *negotiation* of a resolution are distinct activities that should be accomplished in order.

Legal assessment answers the question "How strong are the arguments on appeal?" As you identify the appellate issues, the standards of review that apply, whether any errors were prejudicial, and whether the arguments were preserved or forfeited, the strength and weakness of the appeal become apparent. A thorough legal assessment of the appellate issues results in a clear understanding of the strengths and weaknesses of the arguments and allows you to engage in case evaluation. Case evaluation involves the following tasks: (1) an estimate of the likelihood of winning on appeal (What are the odds on appeal?); (2) the exploration of other presently available alternatives to the appeal, such as dismissing the appeal, continuing with only part of the appeal, and engaging in settlement negotiations (What are the other options?); and (3) the comparison between continuing with the appeal and pursuing other available options.

Case evaluation generates the information necessary to complete the next task: calculation, in dollars, of the present economic value of the appeal (What is my appeal worth?). (Chapter 3 addresses this topic.)

---

1.   ROGER FISHER, WILLIAM L. URY & BRUCE PATTON, GETTING TO YES: NEGOTIATING AGREEMENT WITHOUT GIVING IN 99 (Penguin, 2nd ed. 2011).

Case evaluation is the bridge between the legal analysis of your case and the eventual negotiation that seeks an agreeable option that is preferable to the appeal. Only after completing these tasks, should the final task of negotiation begin. Negotiation constitutes an effort to improve on presently available options by creating a new and better option, namely a settlement agreement whose terms are more advantageous than all others, especially loss on appeal, but perhaps even better than winning the appeal. This is the search for an answer to the question "Are there options we can agree on together that are better than continuing with the appeal—or other options that are available to us by acting alone?". (Section II describes the appellate mediation process in which negotiations can occur.)

C.   Why Do Case Evaluation *before* Negotiating?

Parties and their attorneys regularly arrive at an appellate mediation without having thought about what they will gain or lose if they continue with the appeal. They also may not have devoted any serious effort to determining the costs of appellate litigation. Most importantly, they may not yet appreciate the implications of what it means to "win" an appeal. Negotiating with only hazy concepts of what it means to continue with the appeal invites regrettable results—whether in rejecting a disappointing offer that is nonetheless better than continuing to appeal or in accepting a settlement that unintentionally discounts a very strong position on appeal. Once the parties understand the implications of continuing with an appeal, they become able to negotiate with a clear understanding of their options and how a settlement needs to improve on those options to be acceptable as a negotiated agreement. As Fisher and Ury admonish, "[i]f you have not thought carefully about what you will do if you fail to reach an agreement, you are negotiating with your eyes closed."[2]

There is an important though obvious caveat: Although case evaluation is best begun before negotiations commence, it is in fact an ongoing process. During mediation and negotiation, parties often learn additional information and explore previously unidentified risks and gains. Moreover, parties sometimes signal unexpected willingness to make certain concessions or extend unanticipated offers. This means that the options available usually change in the process of negotiating. Thus, case evaluation should recommence whenever new information comes to light that materially changes the options that a party has available. Thus, the steps for case evaluation that we set forth below are applicable at any stage of the mediation.

D.   How to Do Case Evaluation for Civil Appeals

Our step-by-step approach walks you through the process of case evaluation for any civil appeal. Here it is.

---

2.   *Id.* at 100.

1. Step 1: Identify the Best Case Outcome

One major difference between trial and appellate litigation is what it means to win. Parties generally come to trial mediation having analyzed their expected outcomes regarding damages or injunctive relief. Surprisingly often, participants come to appellate mediation with no concrete idea of what winning an appeal means. For this reason, one of the most useful questions for appellate mediation is "What exactly do you win if you win on appeal?"

The answer to this question can be startling for parties and attorneys stuck on fantastical settlement positions based on what they want or their perceived strengths of their legal arguments. Appeals have serious drawbacks, and appellate courts offer at best only limited relief, yet even represented parties attend an appellate mediation without a clear understanding of what winning means in the appellate court.

Because winning on appeal differs substantially for appellants and respondents, we address these perspectives separately.

a. What Winning Means for an Appellant

Winning on appeal almost always means getting the opportunity to continue litigating in the trial court. In most appeals, appellants ask for a reversal of the judgment. If they succeed, the appellate court sends the case back to the trial court for a new trial or further proceedings. Like a pie-eating contest where the prize is more pie, a prevailing appellant wins the opportunity to spend more time, money, effort, and emotional energy to win in the trial court—and in some cases, in the appellate court for a second time.[3] Most parties did not enjoy the trial court process the first time. To the contrary, they found it to be among the most stressful experiences in their lives. Yet a request for reversal seeks to repeat this constellation of unpleasant experiences.

If the appellant lost on a procedural point *before* trial—such as by motion to dismiss, demurrer, or summary judgment—then winning an appeal usually confers the opportunity to proceed to trial for the first time. Thus, the appellant has secured the right to be cross-examined, spend money on trial, and live with uncertainty for months or years to come.

The cost implications of winning can be sobering for an appellant. Conclusive legal success arrives only after paying for

- The trial court proceedings being appealed,
- The appeal,
- Further trial court proceedings, and
- Quite likely, a new trial—and perhaps another appeal.

Thus, appellants who win appeals are often shocked at how little they gain.

---

3. Dana's appellate mediation record for the length of time a mediation case was in litigation is 17 years. The dispute was before the appellate court four times, and it was tried three times. Unfortunately, it did not settle.

Winning on appeal can ultimately lead to loss. Sometimes the prospect of losing during a remanded trial court proceeding can make a successful appeal the cure that is worse than the disease. This was the consequence for the appellant in *Hasson v. Ford Motor Company*, where the defendant successfully appealed a $1.1 million jury verdict for the plaintiff. The appellate court granted the defendant a new trial, which culminated with the second jury's awarding the plaintiffs more than $11.5 million. Although the trial court reduced damages to $9.2 million, the defendant appealed a second time. The second appeal, however, resulted in an affirmance by the California Supreme Court more than 12 years after the accident giving rise to the claim. The defendant would have been much better off simply abandoning the litigation before taking the first appeal.[4]

b. *What Winning Means for a Respondent*

Winning preserves the judgment. Winning for the respondent means preservation of the judgment by the appellate court. As we discussed in Chapter 1, an appellate court will not improve on the judgment for a respondent even if the court can think of a better, wiser solution. Thus, winning essentially means not getting worse. Zero gain in the judgment is a pretty faint win. Even though the *judgment* may not get worse, it is possible for the circumstances to worsen for respondents during the appellate process. Here's how:

A judgment is not a check. Respondents basking in the glow of a judgment for monetary damages are often dismayed to find that entry of judgment does not mean money put into their pockets. The appellate process often delays payment by years.

For plaintiff/respondents, winning on appeal marks the stage at which the judgment is final and collectable (if, for example, the defendant/appellant has received a stay or posted an appeal bond). These respondents do experience a tangible gain when they win on appeal. However, viewed in another way, they are simply getting the money to which they were entitled during the entire appeal. In short, it is ending the litigation—more than winning on appeal—that marks the event when circumstances finally start improving for respondents.

A word on cross-appeals by respondents. Respondents sometimes do file cross-appeals to "improve" upon disappointing judgments. However, cross-appeals involve the same considerations as for the initial appellants. Thus, a successful cross-appeal most likely will require a remand for retrial or further proceedings in the trial court. Thus, the same costly drawbacks and risks apply as for the initial appeal.

---

4. Hasson v. Ford Motor Co., 32 Cal. 3d 388, 396–98, 650 P. 2d 1171 (Cal. 1982).

c. Implications for Any Party's Win on Appeal

Winning can be expensive. Appeals often carry a high price tag for attorney fees and costs. Almost always, appellants pay substantially more to litigate in the appellate courts than do respondents. Practitioners report that a typical civil appeal costs the appellant $20,000 to $50,000 in attorney fees in an intermediate court of appeal.[5] Although attorney fees are generally lower for respondents, the cost can be substantial—$15,000 to $25,000.[6] If a higher court subsequently grants review, to secure a final outcome appellate legal fees will easily double.

In addition to attorney fees, appellate costs are often substantial. A successful appeal usually requires a complete reporter's transcript of trial or other court proceedings as well as the motions and pleadings filed by the parties. A reporter's transcript of trial court proceedings often costs between $500 to $1,000 for each day of trial. A clerk's transcript contains the written documents, exhibits, and court orders found in the trial court's file. These usually cost approximately a dollar per page. To make a rough estimate of the cost to produce the appellate record, multiply the number of full days of hearing and trial by $1,000. Almost invariably the appellant bears the cost of producing the record. Moreover, the appellant usually has to pay the entirety of the record production costs shortly after the notice of appeal has been filed. Although costs may ultimately be recovered from the respondent if the appellant wins on appeal, the unfavorable odds that appellants face mean that appellants should not count on reimbursement.

Although many courts allow respondents to reduce their court costs by borrowing the appellant's copy of the appellate record, respondents still face filing fees and the cost of producing additional appellate records not submitted by appellants. Even if these costs are ultimately collectable, the lengthy nature of the appellate process means that these costs may not be recovered for years.

What about fee-shifting agreements and statutes? Historically, the "American rule" has required litigants to pay their own attorney fees.[7] Thus, the usual rule on appeal is that winners must pay their own attorney fees, with the result that the win becomes less valuable after deducting the cost of attorney

---

5. http://www.anappealtoreason.com/faq/; http://www.myronmoskovitz.com/frequently -asked-questions/.

6. http://www.californiaappeals.com/flat-fees-for-appeals.html; http://www.anappealtoreason .com/faq/.

7. As the U.S. Supreme Court has noted, "In the United States, the prevailing litigant is ordinarily not entitled to collect a reasonable attorneys' fee from the loser." Alyeska Pipeline Service Co. v. Wilderness Society, 421 U.S. 240, 247, 95 S. Ct. 1612, 44 L. Ed. 2d 141 (1975). This practice is nearly unique to the United States, as most other legal systems normally shift attorney fees to the prevailing party. Id.; Thomas D. Rowe, *Predicting the Effects of Attorney Fee Shifting*, LAW AND CONTEMPORARY PROBLEMS 139, 139 (1984).

fees. This is true even if costs are shifted by rule of court. Costs to produce the appellate record and photocopy briefs tend to be dwarfed by the attorney fees required for an appeal. In the absence of any fee-shifting provision, an appellate win may be an expensive victory.

However, in the past three or four decades, there has been a strong trend toward attorney-fee-shifting contractual provisions and statutes.[8] Thus, many contracts and statutes provide for shifting of attorney fees from the winner to the loser. In such a case, the winner on appeal may be reimbursed—in full or in part—if the court discounts the bill in its fee award. Reimbursement, however, is not a gain. It is simply mitigation of an earlier loss, namely the outlay of attorney fees to engage in the appellate process.

Emotional cost. Parties on appeal have varying experiences. Some people find litigation extremely stressful—even if they are only employees or members of the companies or institutions that are the actual parties on appeal. Moreover, the stress of litigation tends to be prolonged given the lengthy nature of the appellate process. Juries regularly award noneconomic damages for mental anguish and stress arising out of wrongful conduct—in other words, stress *is* costly. There is no compensation for the stress of an appeal. If the mental anguish and depression connected with an appeal are unbearable, a favorable disposition by the appellate court may not feel like a win at all.

Opportunity costs of appeal. In addition to the emotional toll and direct financial costs, the large investment of time, money, and emotional energy required to pursue an appeal also has indirect financial consequences. Parties may be foreclosed from pursing business and personal opportunities. Individuals might be stuck in financial limbo while awaiting determinations of custody, support, and visitation. Businesses may have too much capital tied up in a judgment bond to seize a promising prospect for expansion. Continuing litigation might interfere with merger and acquisition opportunities. Lives and businesses are put on hold until the certainty of an appellate decision allows people to pursue again the opportunities that seemed unavailable under the cloud of litigation.

Winning on appeal probably does not end the legal war. If the appellant wins, the result will almost certainly be further proceedings (and perhaps a full new trial) in the trial court. However, even if the respondent wins, the probable result is further trial court proceedings—if only to claim attorney fees and/or costs. Respondents who are judgment creditors may have to engage in the process of collecting on the judgment. If the judgment awarded injunctive or other non-monetary relief, further litigation over compliance issues may be necessary. In short, winning on appeal almost certainly will not end the litigation.

---

8. Note, *State Attorney Fee Shifting Statutes: Are We Quietly Repealing the American Rule?*, Law and Contemporary Problems 321, 322 (1984) (counting approximately 2,000 fee-shifting statutes in the United States). Of these statutes, only a fifth were enacted before 1950. *Id.* at 341.

2. Step 2: Identify the Worst Case Outcome

a. What Losing Means for an Appellant

Losing means getting stuck with a bad judgment (or worse). An appellant who loses on appeal is subject to all of the terms in the unfavorable judgment. For appellants who are appealing from money damages, the judgment has likely become worse due to postjudgment interest. For example, a $1 million judgment becomes a judgment for $1.2 million in a jurisdiction in which a civil appeal takes two years and a 10 percent postjudgment interest rate applies. On a $1 million judgment, the appellant pays about $274 in postjudgment interest *every day* during the appeal.

Appellants who challenge defense verdicts or pretrial rulings dismissing their cases are left with nothing but bills—for attorney fees and/or costs. For them, litigation has been all loss and no gain. Not only have they not won in a judgment, but they have also not had the opportunity to testify during trial because they lost on a pretrial motion.

b. What Losing Means for a Respondent

Losing as a respondent means more litigation. By definition, respondents have the most to lose on appeal. So when respondents lose, they often lose big. Rather than having a favorable judgment, respondents who lose on appeal face much more litigation after reversal by the appellate court. To win, respondents probably need to go through another trial. If the discovery process reopens, the consequence is even more escalating costs and fees.

Moreover, a losing respondent is likely in a worse position than before entry of the original judgment because the appellate court may have eviscerated the respondent's best legal arguments or rendered inadmissible the respondent's best evidence. Consequently, retrial may be a more difficult contest than the first time around.

c. Implications of Losing an Appeal for Any Party

Damage to reputation. The very rules of appellate procedure practically guarantee an unflattering portrait of the losing party on appeal. When the appellate court affirms a trial court decision, the opinion begins with a recitation of the facts. This summary first states the facts in support of the judgment. In other words, it draws from the record of facts least flattering to the appellant and sets them forth with the official imprimatur of a court of law.

Respondents are also vulnerable to an unflattering portrait. If the appellate court reverses, it will marshal the facts against the respondent to support its decision. In some cases, the court may paint *all* parties in a negative light. For example, in analyzing prejudice, the appellate court may compare the unflattering evidence adduced by each party to determine whether the error(s) affected the outcome.

Thus, in addition to the risk of loss, the modern risk of an adverse written decision can have a long-standing unfavorable effect on reputations. Large institutions and companies will inevitably face litigation over regrettable— and perhaps sensationally ugly—conduct by someone in the organization.[9] Individuals too can suffer long-lived consequences from the recounting of short lapses in judgment or freak occurrences.

Just about every appellate court in the United States engages in selective publication—the inclusion of only some cases in the official bound volumes of the appellate reports. Approximately 20 percent of federal appellate court decisions are published in the sense that they are bound in a paper book with page and volume citation.[10] In California, approximately 9 percent of intermediate appellate court and 100 percent of supreme court decisions are published.[11]

Unlike appeals, trial court decisions are rarely published in the official court reports. And although some trial court proceedings make the newspapers, most fly under the radar even if the records are open to the public. Published decisions of intermediate appellate and supreme courts, on the other hand, last forever in the official reports. Published decisions often make headlines as well. In addition, countless blogs and other Internet sites digest and comment on newly reported appellate court decisions. And traditional newspapers frequently report on published decisions, especially when cases involve salacious facts or public figures. Even unpublished decisions have a way of generating news now that search engines make Internet searching free, fast, and easy. Moreover, online legal research providers such as Westlaw and Lexis have searchable databases of unreported appellate decisions.[12]

Attorney fees may be doubled (or more). In a very real sense, fee shifting constitutes financial roulette. To the drafters of a contract or a statute, it must be tempting to think that the blameless party will emerge victorious in the justice system. However, the vicissitudes of litigation often turn attorney fee-shifting provisions into a game of chance. A losing party on appeal must pay not only

---

9. As Warren Buffett, chief executive officer of Berkshire Hathaway, once observed: "We have 180,000 employees, so it's guaranteed that something will go wrong." http://www.thebuffett.com/quotes/Berkshire.html#.UnQl3_nrwTY.

10. Aaron S. Bayer, *Unpublished Appellate Opinions Are Still Commonplace*, Nat'l L.J. (Aug. 24, 2009).

11. Court Statistics Report: Statewide Caseload Trends 2003–2004 through 2012–2013 Preface (Judicial Council of California, 2014).

12. Even judges cannot keep unpublished cases from being widely disseminated. *See* Debra C. Weiss, *A Judge's Unusual Request: Don't Print This in Westlaw or Lexis*, ABA J. (Mar. 11, 2010) (noting that one federal judge's addition of language that "[t]his order is not intended for publication or for inclusion in the databases of Westlaw or Lexis" has been entirely ignored by the electronic databases).

its own attorney but also for the opposing party's. In some cases, the loser must pay *four* attorneys: (1) the loser's own trial attorney, (2) the loser's appellate attorney, (3) the prevailing party's trial attorney, *and* (4) the prevailing party's appellate attorney.

For the respondent, this can be a sudden and massive loss. One minute, under the trial court order, the opposing party is to pay the respondent's trial counsel's fees. The next, under the appellate court decision, the respondent is to pay its own trial and appellate attorney's fees *and* the opposing party's trial and appellate attorney fees. This threat of attorney fees to respondents in cases with fee shifting can easily equal or exceed the amount of the judgment against appellants.

Unfavorable factors and case weaknesses will likely persist. Even if a party secures a reversal on appeal, many (if not most) of the unfavorable factors of the case will continue to plague that litigant. Adverse judgments frequently signal problems with the losing party's case. A losing party may have trouble proving a claim or defense. It may have an unsympathetic (even if technically legally defensible) position or suffer from inadequate preparation or insufficient litigation resources. In addition, the long, difficult process of litigation may leave parties road weary and harboring hard feelings. These problems will not be solved even by success on appeal, but will persist even after reversal and remand. In short, these difficulties will likely reassert themselves on retrial or in any further trial court proceedings.

3. Step 3: Estimate the Odds of Various Case Outcomes

Every appeal has a unique set of facts, procedural history, and set of legal issues. For this reason, estimating the odds of reversal for an appeal can be the hardest part of the case evaluation process to do accurately. Studies of attorneys' abilities to forecast the outcomes of litigation have shown that "[o]verall, lawyers were overconfident in their predictions, and calibration did not increase with years of legal experience."[13] Overconfidence increases as the task becomes more difficult, and civil appeals are intellectually and emotionally difficult.[14] Additionally, overconfidence also grows over time "to justify commitment to a goal."[15] Yet accuracy is critical because an attorney's estimate regarding the odds of success is often the most heavily weighted factor informing the decision whether to settle a case or continue litigating.[16] In other words, a wild guess about the odds of success can lead to unjustified perseverance in continuing

---

13. Jane Goodman-Delahunty, Pär Anders Granhag, Maria Hartwig & Elizabeth F. Loftus, *Insightful or Wishful: Lawyers' Ability to Predict Case Outcomes*, 16 PSYCHOLOGY, PUB. POL'Y & L. 133 (2010).
14. *Id.* at 135.
15. *Id.* at 136.
16. *Id.* at 134.

with the appeal or, conversely, an acquiescence to a settlement offer that may not reflect the true, more favorable odds of success.

So, how do you make good estimates of the odds of succeeding in a civil appeal? We suggest three tools to help you. First, we explore the reversal rates in state and federal courts, with consideration of a few factors tending to increase or decrease prospects for favorable outcomes. Second, we help guard against the natural inclination to overestimate your own chances of success with a method called "consider the opposite." Third, we suggest consulting with an appellate law specialist to evaluate the case with a fresh and expert perspective.

a. Reversal Rate Variability

Reversal rates range widely among appellate courts in the United States— from a low of 12.5 percent in one state to a high of 56.3 percent in another.[17] So too, reversal rates differ greatly among the various types of cases, from 7.98 percent for plaintiffs appealing adverse judgments in civil rights cases in federal appellate courts to the 75 percent for some state court defendants in medical malpractice appeals.[18] Keep this variation in mind when we offer a "rule of thumb" that approximately 25 to 30 percent of appeals yield at least a partial success for the appellant.[19] (See Part 3.b.)

There is an important corollary to reversal rate variability: individual case factors do make a big difference in forecasting the likelihood of success. The biggest factors that determine success are those we described in Chapter 1, namely standards of review and analysis of prejudice. Thus, de novo issues on appeal succeed more often than do claims of abuse of discretion.[20] Notably, one study of Illinois appellate court decisions found that de novo issues resulted in nearly twice the reversal rate of abuse of discretion issues.[21]

Individual case factors also significantly affect the outcome when appellate courts consider whether errors resulted in prejudice. Because appellate judges do not simply count the number of errors or use predefined categories for various types of errors, analysis of prejudice tends to be one of

---

17. Theodore Eisenberg & Michael Heise, *Plaintiphobia in State Courts? An Empirical Study of State Court Trials on Appeal*, 38 J. LEGAL STUD. 121, 140 (2009).
18. *Id.* at 134 (Table 2).
19. By "rule of thumb," we refer to a term "thought to originate with carpenters who used the width of their thumbs (i.e., inches) rather than rulers for measuring things, cementing its modern use as an imprecise yet reliable and convenient standard." http://en.wikipedia.org/wiki/Rule_of_thumb#cite_note-Sommers1994-2. This useful term with an uncertain origin seems particularly appropriate to describe the useful-ness of making estimates of odds on appeal even when we are not entirely certain how we came to the precise number upon which we settle.
20. Timothy J. Storm, *Standard of Review Does Matter: Evidence of Judicial Self-Restraint in the Illinois Appellate Court*, 34 S. ILL. U. L.J. 98 (2009).
21. *Id.*

the most subjective aspects of appellate judging.[22] For these reasons, harmless error analysis uniquely defies quantitative study because it rests upon the appellate jurist's guess as to what would have resulted if the claimed error had not occurred. As an example of the many ways prejudice may be shown—and thus affect reversal rates—consider California Chief Justice Roger Traynor's observations:

- the record "recurringly" reflects the effect of the errors on trial,

- there was evidence (in addition to that erroneously admitted) that supports the judgment,

- there was evidence actually admitted into evidence that was redundant to the erroneously excluded evidence,

- the error was emphasized by the trial judge or attorneys in their opening or closing arguments,

- the jury requested read-backs of erroneously admitted evidence or inaccurate jury instructions in a way showing reliance on the error, and/or

- the trial judge admonished the jury or gave instructions that cured the error.[23]

Reversal rate variability is the most important determinant of success or loss on appeal. Nonetheless, it is helpful to know how civil cases fare generally in the appellate courts.

b. Odds That an Appellant Should Consider

If you do not know anything about a particular civil appeal, the best rule of thumb might be to guess that appellant has about a 30-percent chance of getting *any* relief from the appellate court. The overwhelming majority of civil appeals result in full affirmance—a resounding defeat for appellants. Thus,

---

22. William Henry Beatty, Chief Justice of California from 1884 to 1914, memorably stated, "When we find that a substantial injustice has been done, we look through the [appellate] record for errors, and we damn well find them." Quoted in ROBERT H. FROST, THE MOONEY CASE 243 (Stanford University Press 1969). "Only judges, and their law clerks, who have participated in the appellate process, know what agony it can be to decide when error is really harmless enough to be harmless." Murray Gurfein, quoted in Daniel J. Kornstein, *A Bayesian Model of Harmless Error*, J. LEGAL STUD. 121 (1976).
23. ROGER J. TRAYNOR, THE RIDDLE OF HARMLESS ERROR 75–76 (Ohio State University Press, 1970).

the best estimate might be about a 25-percent chance of reversal, a 5-percent chance of modification, and a 70-percent chance of full affirmance.[24]

State appellate courts. On average, appellants in state court succeed in 32.1 percent of civil appeals.[25] Defendants do much better than do plaintiffs as appellants. The one easy generalization about reversal odds is that defendants win on appeal far more often than do plaintiffs. Another generalization— although the spread is not as significant—is that jury trials are reversed more frequently (33.7 percent) than bench trials (27.5 percent).[26]

Federal appellate courts. In the U.S. Courts of Appeals, appellants succeed in only 18.4 percent of civil appeals.[27] Thus, even an appeal considered to be "twice as strong" as the average federal civil appeal has less than even odds of reversal. In federal appellate courts, defendant/appellants secure reversals after trial in 33 percent of civil cases while plaintiff/appellants win only 12 percent of the time.[28] Some appellants face dismal odds. For example, in federal appellate courts, plaintiffs win only 7.98 percent of civil rights cases and 11.48 percent of personal injury actions.[29]

Many civil appeals never make it to decision on their merits. A hidden peril for appellants is that many never make it to decision on the merits of their appeals. For example, in the federal appellate courts, voluntary withdrawal and involuntary dismissals amounted to almost 40 percent of civil appeals.[30]

Anything that goes wrong in an appeal is usually bad for the appellant. Problems arising during appeals are myriad: a late or defective notice of appeal, an inadequate reporter's transcript, missing documents that the trial court clerk cannot find for inclusion in the appellate record, lack of timely objection

---

24. For example, of civil appeals filed in the California intermediate appellate courts, 79 percent resulted in full affirmance and 18 percent in reversal, and 3 percent were involuntarily dismissed. COURT STATISTICS REPORT, *supra* note 11, at 26. Of the affirmances, about 10 percent are modified. *Id.* at 69.
25. Eisenberg & Heise, *supra* note 17, at 137.
26. *Id.* at 121.
27. *Id.* at 137. The reason state reversal rates are so much higher than in federal civil appeals remains a mystery and "is not a consequence of a different mix of case types because only one category of federal cases, fraud, achieves the overall state reversal rate of about 32 percent. No other federal case category has a reversal rate as high as 30 percent." *Id.* at 137–38, n. 10. Remarkably, the federal appellate courts themselves report that only 12.3 percent of private civil appeals are reversed. Table available at http://www.uscourts.gov/statistics/table/b-5/statistical-tables-federal-judiciary/2014/12/31. This figure, however, is deceptively low because it does not include modifications favorable to appellants and includes as a reversal only dispositions requiring a full retrial. Thus, it significantly understates instances in which appellants secure limited but meaningful appellate relief.
28. Kevin M. Clermont & Theodore Eisenberg, *Plaintiphobia in the Appellate Courts: Civil Rights Really Do Differ from Negotiable Instruments?*, U. ILL. L. REV. 947 (2002).
29. *Id.* at 954.
30. THOMAS H. COHEN & DONALD J. FAROLE JR., APPEALS OF CIVIL TRIALS CONCLUDED IN 2005 at 1 (Bureau of Justice Statistics, U.S. Dep't of Justice, Office of Justice Programs, 2011).

sufficient to preserve an argument for appeal, exhibits returned to the parties and no longer available for forwarding to the appellate court, and many more. What do these problems all have in common? They all disadvantage appellants rather than respondents. Our experience with appeals—as advocates and attorneys within the appellate courts—suggests that one reason the odds of prevailing are so low for appellants is that anything that can go wrong for an appellant generally will. Unanticipated problems arising during an appeal almost invariably prove harmful to appellants rather than respondents. In short, appellants uniquely bear the risks of unanticipated developments on appeal.

c. Odds That the Respondent Should Consider

If you do not know anything about a specific civil appeal, it is reasonable to assume that the respondent has a 70-percent chance of winning. However, in several categories of cases the odds are worse for the respondent than for the appellant. Even with all of the rules and presumptions that favor respondents on appeal, here are a few of the types of cases in which respondents can *expect* to lose:

- Nearly 60 percent of cases are reversed in which the U.S. government is the appellant.[31]

- In state appellate courts, defendants who are appellants win 75 percent of professional malpractice, 73.3 percent of slander and libel, and 61.5 percent of employment contract cases.[32]

Respondents also do poorly in the following types of cases:

- State and local governments win 41.2 percent of appeals in federal court.

- In state courts, defendants as appellants win 46.3 percent of contract, 36 percent of tort, and 33.3 percent of medical malpractice cases.[33]

- Also in state courts, plaintiffs as appellants win 37.5 percent of dangerous premises and 38.5 percent of employment contract cases.[34]

---

31. Donald R. Songer & Reginald S. Sheehan, *Who Wins on Appeal? Upperdogs and Underdogs in the United States Courts of Appeals*, Am. J. Pol. Sci. 235, 241 (1992). However, this astonishing percentage must be taken with a grain of salt. "Frivolous appeals by individuals inflate the winning percentages of governments and businesses. In contrast, repeat players with substantial resources are less likely to bring appeals to any court if they have little realistic chance of winning." *Id.* at 256. *See also generally* Stanton Wheeler, Bliss Cartwright, Robert A. Kagan & Lawrence M. Friedman, *Do the Haves Come out Ahead—Winning and Losing in State Supreme Courts, 1870–1970*, 21 Law and Society Review 403 (1987).
32. Eisenberg & Heise, *supra* note 17, at 134.
33. *Id.*
34. *Id.*

And, plaintiff/respondents should be wary of the 41.5-percent overall reversal rate when defendants appeal. "Indeed, from the perspective of a plaintiff victorious at trial, the appeals process offer[s] a chance to retain victory not far from what a coin flip would predict."[35]

d. How to Increase the Accuracy of Your Estimates of the Odds on Appeal

Attorneys generally believe they help clients by calculating how to win, not by imagining how to lose. When formulating a litigation plan, attorneys usually focus only on what they believe to be the strongest set of arguments or the best litigation strategy. Then they stop. In other words, attorneys usually expend no more effort than required to formulate the single best explanation for how to win.

Imagining how you *can* win does not logically answer how *likely* it is that you *will* win. However, if you only imagine how you can win, you will overestimate how probable it is that victory will result. This is because people overweigh what they imagine and ignore risks they do not imagine. This process of envisioning only a desired end gives rise to an erroneous estimation of the likely outcome. This error in estimation has been described by scholars as single-explanation bias. Single-explanation bias is the norm for estimates about uncertain events because people almost always end their analysis as soon as they figure out how to achieve their desired result.[36] For example, 93 percent of us consider ourselves to be better-than-average drivers![37] This is because we usually think only about our strengths, not the weaknesses in our skills.

Single-explanation bias leads to overconfidence in prediction and is immune to correction by just "trying harder" to be more accurate and objective.[38] Yet unwarranted overconfidence by attorneys is a problem in that it distorts the parties' attempts to make sound decisions about whether to pursue further litigation. An attorney's estimate of the odds of success is usually the primary factor that determines whether a party continues to litigate or decides to settle or abandon the litigation.

Unfortunately, single-explanation bias continues to exert its effect long after the initial case analysis is undertaken.[39] Thus, even though appellate counsel may spend considerable time researching the law, writing briefs, and presenting oral argument, *all* of these tasks are in service to a *single* explanation in support of the client. In other words, additional work and effort usually do

---

35. *Id.* at 138.
36. Edward R. Hirt & Keith D. Markman, *Multiple Explanation: A Consider-an-Alternative Strategy for Debiasing Judgments*, 69 J. PERSONALITY & SOC. PSYCHOLOGY 1069, 1084 (1995).
37. Ola Svenson, *Are We All Less Risky and More Skillful Than Our Fellow Drivers?*, 47 ACTA PSYCHOLOGICA 143–48 (1981).
38. Charles G. Lord, Mark R. Lepper & Elizabeth Preston, *Considering the Opposite: A Corrective Strategy for Social Judgment*, 47 J. PERSONALITY & SOC. PSYCHOLOGY 1231 (1984).
39. Hirt & Markman, *supra* note 36, at 1069.

not help debias an attorney's estimates of odds. To the contrary, additional work on the "best" argument for the client usually makes the attorney even more overconfident due to confirmation bias.[40]

For single-explanation bias and overconfidence, we present a remedy: multiple explanations. Multiple explanations provide an effective way to reduce the analytic traps that make us more certain that we are right than is objectively warranted; such mental traps include single-explanation bias, overconfidence, hindsight bias, and confirmation bias.[41] The multiple-explanations approach has proven more effective than increased efforts to be objective or even financial rewards for making less biased estimates.[42] Rather than working harder, it's better to work smarter.

The multiple-explanations approach, as you might surmise, involves coming up with additional *and different* explanations for how an outcome will be achieved. This approach does not require you to acquiesce to loss. It merely requires you to identify *different plausible outcomes* and the reasons for each.

To demonstrate this approach, assume you believe appellant will win by showing, under a de novo standard of review, that the trial court misconstrued the governing statute. A multiple-explanations approach requires you to come up with alternate, *plausible* bases for the appellate court's decision. For example, the appellant might lose on the de novo review issue but win by arguing that the judge abused his or her discretion in excluding a particular piece of evidence. Or the appellant might suffer a narrow loss in which the appellate court reluctantly affirms. Even though the court disagrees with the wisdom of the trial court's decision, it must affirm nonetheless under the abuse of discretion standard of review. Or the appellant might lose in a blowout decision if the appellate court concludes none of the issues have been preserved for appeal. Anyone who participates in or observes appellate courts is regularly surprised at both the results in cases and the reasoning employed to reach those surprising results. Indeed, appellate commentators have developed an entire industry devoted to surprising voting blocs, unexpected rationales, and surprising results in appellate cases.

The multiple-explanations approach requires you to come up with at least one explanation for all of the following: (1) a *plausible but different* rationale the appellate court can use to get to the result for which you already have figured out a rationale or approach, (2) a *plausible* approach that the appellate court can take to reach the opposite result reluctantly or based on reasoning

---

40. *See* Lord et al., *supra* note 38, at 1232, 1237.
41. Hirt & Markman, *supra* note 36, at 1070.
42. Lord et al., *supra* note 38, at 1240; Adam D. Galinsky & Thomas Mussweiler, *First Offers as Anchors: The Role of Perspective-Taking and Negotiator Focus*, 81 J. PERSONALITY & SOC. PSYCHOLOGY 659 (2001).

reserved for the closest cases, and (3) a *plausible* approach that the appellate court may take that will reach the opposite result in a blow-out decision (that will probably not even be decided on the merits of the parties' arguments). It is important to write out these different rationales for the same and different outcomes, even if you do so only briefly and informally.

The most important requirement of this exercise is that each additional rationale must be *plausible*, meaning that there is a very real possibility that it could occur. In other words, you must find each additional explanation to be believable. If you do not believe the result to be possible, discarding possibilities that seem impossible will not help you.[43] With the exception of appeals dismissed for lack of jurisdiction for a late-filed notice of appeal, the authors have rarely, if ever, worked on a case in which another legitimate rationale could not have been used to reach the same outcome. Perhaps the alternatives would not have been as strong or as convincing, but they would have been valid. For the multiple-explanations approach to work, additional explanations need not all be equally convincing—they only need to be *plausible*. Nonetheless, the more plausible the considered alternatives, the better they are at providing overall clarity.[44] To help you achieve clarity, please refer to the worksheets that appear on pages 40–43. They provide a few samples of rationales by which parties lose in close cases when appellate courts are sympathetic to positions or arguments that they must rule against.

The worksheets also give you a few examples of blowout losses that frequently take parties by surprise in the appellate courts. Every case that involves parties who are extremely confident will yield a result that will be considered a very surprising loss to at least one of the parties. Thus, we include some rationales that regularly stun parties.

Important: for the debiasing exercise to work, you must complete all four worksheets with plausible rationales. The order in which you complete the sheets does not matter.[45]

Although considering multiple explanations may not be a pleasant, ego-stroking exercise, it is nonetheless the exercise most likely to help parties and attorneys adjust their sole analysis of a desired outcome to arrive at a more objective and accurate estimation of the odds of success. As we shall see in Chapter 3, an accurate estimate of the odds of success is crucial to accurate calculation of the dollar value for a civil appeal. Moreover, accurate estimation of a case outcome will benefit parties throughout the litigation and negotiations by ensuring they act on a more accurate and objective case evaluation.

---

43. Hirt & Markman, *supra* note 36, at 1080.
44. *Id.* at 1084.
45. *Id.* at 1074.

Debiasing Worksheet for _____ *(name)* **Page 1 of 4**

Case title _____ Worksheet prepared by _____
Notice: This worksheet may be protected by mediation confidentiality and/or attorney-client privilege.

Examples of explanations for any party's narrow loss

The question of whether the trial court abused its discretion is a close one in this case, but we ultimately conclude that...	The present argument sufficiently differs from that in the trial court to disallow the changes in position on appeal...	Although not discussed by the parties, we determine the dispositive consideration on the question of whether to affirm or reverse to be...	We are constrained to apply the newly issued high court guidance, which requires us to...	Despite the obvious appeal of the argument, it has become moot in light of...

Examples of explanations for appellant's narrow loss

Though we would not have made the same decision, we cannot say the trial court abused its discretion by reasoning that...

Although no evidence proved the point at trial, the evidence admitted suffices to support the judgment based on the inference...

Although appellant presents a reasonable statutory (or contract) interpretation, we believe the better reading is...

We agree that the trial court committed several errors but disagree that the errors—even cumulatively—changed the outcome because...

Although appellant has demonstrated error, we affirm because the judgment is separately supported by...

Plausible rationales for **appellant's** narrow loss *in this case*...

Important: complete *all* four worksheet pages with *plausible* explanations for each outcome.

Debiasing Worksheet for _____ *(name)* Page 2 of 4

Case title _____ Worksheet prepared by _____
Notice: This worksheet may be protected by mediation confidentiality and/or attorney-client privilege.

Examples of explanations for any party's narrow loss

The question of whether the trial court abused its discretion is a close one in this case, but we ultimately conclude that...	The present argument sufficiently differs from that in the trial court to disallow the changes in position on appeal...	Although not discussed by the parties, we determine the dispositive consideration on the question of whether to affirm or reverse to be...	We are constrained to apply the newly issued high court guidance, which requires us to...	Despite the obvious appeal of the argument, it has become moot in light of...

Examples of explanations for respondent's narrow loss

Perhaps the trial court would have reached the same decision under the correct test, but we reverse to allow the court to consider...

Although respondent's evidence was strong, it failed to address the following element of the cause of action (or affirmative defense)...

On questions of law, we conclude the trial court errs when misconstruing the laws even slightly, such as here where...

We reluctantly reverse because we cannot declare that the error had no effect on the outcome at trial given that...

Respondent correctly sets forth the rule. The unique facts of this case, however, require an exception on grounds that...

Plausible rationales for **respondent's** narrow loss *in this case...*

Important: complete *all* four worksheet pages with *plausible* explanations for each outcome.

Debiasing Worksheet for _____ (name) Page 3 of 4

Case title _____ Worksheet prepared by _____

Notice: This worksheet may be protected by mediation confidentiality and/or attorney-client privilege.

Examples of explanations for any party's blow-out loss

We do not consider the argument for failure to properly present it in this court because we require that...	We consider the argument to have no merit because prior decisions clearly indicate that...	We publish this opinion in hopes of discouraging the sort of conduct in this case where...	We need not consider the argument regarding error because prejudice in this case...	The contention was forfeited in the trial court due to waiver/invited error/forfeiture...

Examples of explanations for appellant's blow-out loss

Appellant's argument fails to comprehend the deferential nature of the review we will apply in this instance where...

Appellant's objection at trial was insufficient to allow us to reach the issue on appeal...

We need not reach the merits of the claim of error because appellant cannot demonstrate prejudice where...

Appellant invited the complained of error when arguing in the trial court that...

A defective notice of appeal being fatal, the appeal is dismissed...

Plausible rationales for **appellant's** blow-out loss *in this case...*

Important: complete *all* four worksheet pages with *plausible* explanations for each outcome.

Debiasing Worksheet for _____ *(name)* **Page 4 of 4**

Case title _____ Worksheet prepared by _____

Notice: This worksheet may be protected by mediation confidentiality and/or attorney-client privilege.

Examples of explanations for any party's blow-out loss

We do not consider the argument for failure to properly present it in this court because we require that...	We consider the argument to have no merit because prior decisions clearly indicate that...	We publish this opinion in hopes of discouraging the sort of conduct in this case where...	We need not consider the argument regarding error because prejudice in this case...	The contention was forfeited in the trial court due to waiver/-invited error/forfeiture...

Examples of explanations for respondent's blow-out loss

Plausible rationales for **respondent's** blow-out loss *in this case...*

The trial court adopted respondent's argument, which we reject as unfounded and therefore refuse to consider on remand for new trial...

Respondent's argument distorts the record and reaches the wrong result by drawing inference that...

On retrial, the trial court shall exclude the following evidence erroneously admitted during the first trial...

We reverse with instructions for the trial court to vacate its prior decision and to apply the test set forth in this decision where...

The error necessarily requires reversal because it directly affected the outcome by...

Important: complete *all* four worksheet pages with *plausible* explanations for each outcome.

e. Enlist Help from an Appellate Law Expert

The vast majority of appellate mediations do not involve an appellate law expert or specialist. For a variety of reasons, trial attorneys continue their representation during appellate mediations. Of course, there is nothing wrong with this. Having a dedicated attorney who has personal knowledge of the history of the case in the trial court is helpful. Even so, trial attorneys may become so entrenched and so imbued with the emotion of the contest that they lack the perspective that someone new can offer.

Studies show that "specialized lawyers were better calibrated than general practitioners" at estimating litigation outcomes in their areas of expertise.[46] Thus, a part of case evaluation worth considering is enlisting the help of an attorney who focuses on appellate practice in the court in which the case is pending. Appellate specialists are well suited to lend a fresh, objective, and well-informed perspective of the case. They can also ferret out the implications of appellate rules and procedure for a particular case or party on appeal. Issues of forfeiture, waiver, issue preservation, standards of review, and analysis of prejudice are the appellate attorney's stock in trade. An appellate specialist need not take over the case but can offer substantial help simply by consulting on the appeal. Research shows that the mere expectation that your analysis will be subject to later review by a specialist makes for a more accurate initial evaluation.[47] Thus, a case evaluation by an appellate specialist is an option that should be considered.

4. Step 4: Compare All Presently Available Options

As single-explanation bias theory reveals, for most lawyers the analysis of the outcome on appeal ends once they convince themselves of a way to litigate to a successful result. Having demonstrated the value of expanding this analysis to include multiple alternatives available to appellate judges in deciding an appeal, we now explore the important fourth step: considering all options available to a party. Some of these paths are obvious, some less so. Some seemingly obvious but unattractive paths may actually turn out to be quite desirable upon careful examination. Consider the following options:

a. Continue with the Appeal

The most obvious option for the appellant is to continue with the appeal. Continuing with the appeal is necessary to secure any relief from the appellate court and necessarily means expenditures of substantial sums. Meanwhile, the judgment being appealed is probably already effective. An appeal does not vacate or even stay a trial court judgment. Only a decision by the appellate court

---

46. Goodman-Delahunty et al., *supra* note 13, at 137.
47. Hirt & Markman, *supra* note 36, at 1084.

can do that. Thus, the mere filing of an appeal does not enable an appellant to escape the consequences of a judgment. In fact, judgments for injunctive relief requiring an appellant to take or refrain from certain actions may require an appellant to comply long before the court decides the appeal.

Likewise, unless the trial court has expressly issued a stay, a money judgment is fully collectable while the appeal is pending.[48] To avoid collection proceedings or the risk that the judgment will be uncollectable after a successful appeal, an appellant must post a judgment bond, usually in an amount that exceeds the judgment and sometimes at 150 percent of the damages awarded.[49]

Judgment bond companies usually require appellants to pledge or actually transfer assets in an amount equal to the judgment,[50] which may include not only money damages but also attorney fees and court costs, if awarded. In addition, bonding companies charge a small premium for the service. Thus, an appellant will tie up assets for a long time simply to avoid paying the judgment during the appeal.[51]

For respondents, continuing with an appeal may seem like the only option because the respondent cannot dismiss the appellant's appeal. Although respondents increase their odds of affirmance by filing an appellate brief and presenting oral argument, they are generally not required to take any action in the appellate court. Thus, a respondent should only continue with appellate efforts if the time and effort increase the odds of affirmance enough to justify the further expenditure of resources.

b. *Continue with Only Part of the Appeal*

With rare exception, an appellant does not have more than one or two strong arguments that stand a chance on appeal.[52] Nevertheless, appellants usually

---

48. For example, a judgment in federal court is automatically stayed for only ten days after entry. FED. R. CIV. P. 62(a). The filing of an appeal does not extend the stay. Newball v. Offshore Logistics Intern., 803 F.2d 821, 827 (5th Cir. 1986).

49. In federal and some state courts, an appeal bond must cover the amount of the judgment, interest, and costs. FED. R. CIV. P. 62(a), (d); ILL. RULE OF COURT 305(a). Other states may require substantially more. For example, in California, an appeal bond must be 1.5 times the judgment. CAL. CODE CIV. PROC., sec. 917.1(a). Florida requires an appeal bond in the amount of the judgment plus two years of statutory interest. FLA. R. APP. P. 9.310(b)(1).

50. *See* http://jurisco.com/?page_id=192.

51. In *Pennzoil Co. v. Texaco Inc.*, 481 U.S. 1, 5, 107 S. Ct. 1519, 95 L. Ed. 2d 1 (1987), the court required Texaco to post an appeal bond of more than $13 billion to stay enforcement of a state court judgment during the appeal.

52. In Brendon's experience, as both an advocate and an appellate court attorney, even meritorious appeals usually have a single source of error giving rise to a winning argument. When there are multiple winning arguments, they usually relate in different ways to the same prejudicial error committed in the trial court. Cases with separate *and independent* sources of reversible error are extremely rare—usually being the product of a breakdown in the trial process.

file briefs with every imaginable argument against the judgment, no matter how weak or far-fetched. Similarly respondents usually have one or two strong arguments, for example lack of prejudice based on the overwhelming weight of evidence that undermines just about any claim of error. Yet they too are prone to filing briefs containing every possible argument—no matter how thin.

Nothing requires (or even advises) a scorched earth strategy of including every conceivable argument in appellate briefs. In many—if not the majority of—cases, an intelligent strategy for the appellant is to argue only the one or perhaps two strongest arguments. Limiting the appeal to the strongest arguments carries the benefit of cost savings by reducing the appellate record and curtailing fees for legal research, brief writing, and preparation for oral argument—without a significant reduction in the odds of success. Thus, the most prudent path forward may be to continue with only *part* of the appeal.

c.   Abandon the Appeal

From the limited perspective that litigation is only a contest resulting in winners and losers, voluntarily dismissing an appeal appears to be irrational surrender. However, from the view that litigation is the quest for a solution to an underlying problem, then dismissal of an appeal makes perfect sense whenever a better solution presents itself. From this latter vantage point, dismissal of an appeal is also logical for an appellant whenever an appeal has negative economic value—that is, whenever all of the effort of litigating does not improve the likelihood of securing a more favorable money judgment. And dismissal of an appeal makes perfect sense from the human perspective when an appellant simply has had enough of the litigation. When the appellate litigation cure is worse than the disease, a party is far better off abandoning the appeal. For example, dismissal of an appeal makes sense when a case has negative economic value, the potential result on retrial is much worse than the current judgment, or continuing negative publicity outweighs the value of continued litigation.

It may not occur to respondents that they have an option to abandon the appeal because only appellants or appellate courts can dismiss an appeal. However, respondents are not required to participate in the appellate court at all.[53] They do not need to file appellate briefs or show up at oral argument. While many parties lose in the trial courts by default judgment after failing to show up or properly contest the legal claims, *most respondents who do nothing in the appellate courts still win*: an appellate court will not reverse—even in the absence of a respondent's brief—absent the appellant's demonstration of

---

53.   Some appellate courts with formal mediation programs may order respondents to participate in a mediation session. Even then respondents have to do very little beyond showing up. They do not have to incur the cost of bringing an attorney. Although it is fraught with peril to show up at a mediation without legal counsel, it *is* an option.

error and prejudice. Thus, counterintuitively, the most intelligent option for a respondent may be to ignore the appeal altogether.

Don't throw money at an appeal with negative economic value. Careful assessment of the odds of success and costs involved to pursue an appeal may reveal that a case actually has a de minimus or even *negative* economic value. We provide an illustration at the end of Chapter 3, with a case that seems to promise a $250,000 verdict on retrial but actually has a negative $5,000 value due to the costs of litigation and odds presented on appeal. When the expected loss exceeds reasonably foreseeable gains, an appellant is best off simply dismissing the appeal to stop expenses from further accumulating. That's not surrender; that's picking the best option.

Seek a legislative or administrative remedy instead of an appeal. Appellate courts have no monopoly on the ability to solve intractable conflicts. An apt illustration involves an appellate judge who sought to challenge California's rule barring post-retirement public (but not private) employment for several years after retirement.[54] While an unfavorable trial court decision was being appealed, legislation to cure the problem was introduced to resolve the problem.[55] Noncontroversial legislation could resolve an underlying problem without the delay and uncertainty involved in the appeals process.[56] Upon passage of the legislation, a lawsuit would be dismissed as moot.

In our tripartite system of government, litigants should consider whether the executive or legislative branches offer more certain, faster, or more universally applicable solutions than an appeal in a single case. For example, the executive branch generally oversees administrative agencies and regulatory bodies that might systemically solve a problem through the administrative rule-making process or by enforcing existing rules or regulations. Similarly, a legislative solution can also provide a better alternative than litigation. For example, after the U.S. Supreme Court declined to grant review of a New York appellate court decision allowing online sales tax collection for a retailer without a physical in-state presence, Amazon.com "urged Congress to act to impose a national solution" to avoid the constitutional uncertainty of the various state sales tax laws.[57] Legislative solutions are not limited to multi-state and multi-billion dollar companies. Even a challenge to a local city ordinance can spur enactment of statewide legislation to address a problem. For example, state legislation resolved a lawsuit challenging New York City's ordinance on electronic waste recycling.

---

54. Gilbert v. Chiang, 227 Cal. App. 4th 537, 540, 173 Cal. Rptr. 3d 864 (Ct. App. 2014).
55. Paul Jones, *Judges Laud Bill to Let Them Take Public Jobs after Retirement*, SAN FRANCISCO DAILY J. A1 (March 5, 2014).
56. *Id.*
57. Adam Liptak, *Justices Pass on Tax Case from Online Merchants*, N.Y. Times, Dec. 2, 2013, http://www.nytimes.com/2013/12/03/business/new-york-ruling-on-sales-tax -collection-by-online-retailers-will-stand.html?_r=0.

Even if a legislative solution is not guaranteed to resolve the underlying dispute before the appellate court issues its decision, the pursuit of a legislative or administrative solution expands a party's options and, depending on the strength of a party's legal arguments, may greatly improve upon the alternative—an appellate court decision. For example, environmental advocacy groups regularly pursue legislative solutions, administrative enforcement actions, and legal cases to increase their bargaining power and likelihood of desired results.[58] In the appropriate case as part of the case evaluation, parties should always explore whether legislative or administrative proceedings are available as a means to expand or improve upon their available options.

d. Declare Bankruptcy

Bankruptcy may seem to be an unattractive option that carries a moral stigma. However, bankruptcy can be a powerful option for a party. Appellants appealing from money judgments can have them judicially erased either by winning on appeal or by having their debts discharged through bankruptcy. Not only can bankruptcy wipe out some debts, but it also has a big effect on pending civil appeals. During bankruptcy proceedings, the underlying civil appeal is stayed. An appellant can seek simultaneous remedies in the appellate court and the bankruptcy court by (1) filing a notice of appeal and then (2) immediately filing for bankruptcy. Not only does this approach give appellant two bites at the apple, but it also forces a delay in the civil appeal that may disadvantage the respondent. On the other hand, bankruptcy can be a complex process, and it cannot discharge every kind of liability. Thus, proper exploration of this option almost certainly requires the assistance of a bankruptcy expert.

e. Comply with the Judgment

When a trial court awards postjudgment interest to the plaintiff, the defendant/ appellant pays an even higher price to appeal. Thus, sometimes paying the judgment while the appeal is pending may actually be the smartest way to continue with an appeal.[59] Postjudgment interest makes a painful judgment agonizing, especially with large money judgments. Statutory postjudgment

---

58. *See, e.g.,* Fiona Smith, *Fracking Opponents Seize on Water Use,* SAN FRANCISCO DAILY J. A1 (March 4, 2014) (reporting that environmental advocacy group is pursuing a ban on hydraulic fracturing ("fracking") by petroleum companies both by litigation and by pursuing legislation in a drought-stricken state to put a moratorium on water being used for such purposes as fracking. The proposed moratorium would remain in effect until administrative agency studies into water use could be completed and administrative regulations promulgated to preserve water supplies.).

59. This option, however, requires care in implementation to avoid surrendering appellate rights by voluntarily complying with the judgment. Usually the solution is to pay the judgment "under protest." However, you should check the case law of your jurisdiction to ensure your compliance preserves your appellate rights.

interest rates are often surprisingly high—up to 20 percent.[60] Thus, statutory interest alone can nearly double the amount owed on the underlying liability if the appeal is protracted. If the money judgment is substantial, the added interest can be especially onerous.

Complying with the judgment eliminates the need for a bond, gets rid of the risk of postjudgment interest, takes away the headache of defending against collection efforts, and leaves only the costs directly related to the appeal.

Respondents, on the other hand, may be wise to leave the judgment alone during the appeal. Very few investments pay a guaranteed return of 10 percent per year. Indeed, from a financial viewpoint, a plaintiff may be better off allowing the judgment to collect a certain and tax-free 10 percent during the appeal (if money damages are for nontaxable tort injuries) than pursuing collection efforts and, if successful, trying to earn enough on an investment to pay taxes and still equal a 10-percent annual gain. The ability to record a judgment as a lien on real property or other assets of the defendant/appellant strengthens the merits of this option.

f. Engage in Mediation or Other Settlement Efforts

You cannot force anyone to negotiate with you. However, extending the olive branch is always a presently available option. You can decide to seek mediation or open negotiations at any time. In Section III, we explore how to initiate and succeed in mediation of civil appeals.

g. An Unacceptable Option Is Not Really an Option

We have explored options that are always available to parties, namely forging ahead with the appeal, continuing with only part of the appeal, abandoning the appeal, seeking a remedy from another branch of government, complying with the judgment, and seeking to negotiate. However, we need to caution that an option that is not at all acceptable to a party is not really an option. Here we discuss a number of commonly unacceptable options.

- **Litigating when you do not have the finances to win, lose, or even continue.** Even though a party may have the legal right to continue litigating, if the party lacks the financial resources to do so, litigation is not a presently available option. Wise would-be appellants do not make down payments on an uncertain remedy they cannot afford. Without sufficient financial resources to fund *all* of the

---

60. Brian P. Miller, *Statutory Post-Judgment Interest: The Effect of Legislative Changes after Judgment and Suggestions for Construction*, BRIGHAM YOUNG U. L. REV. 601, 611 (1994). Often postjudgment rates center around 10 percent. *Id.* When adding pre- and post-judgment interest as well as attorney fees and costs in the trial court and on appeal, a compensatory money judgment can easily be doubled or more.

litigation—including the retrial being requested in arguing for reversal of the judgment—even a winning appeal is worthless. Logically, an appellant who cannot afford the full relief requested on appeal is better off abandoning the appeal. If a respondent cannot afford the cost of retrial, then the outcome of the appeal threatens disaster. Moreover, if the cost of litigation undermines basic living expenses or the resources needed to stay in business, the litigation is ruinous so long as it continues.

- **Litigating when the consequence of losing would mean disaster.** If the judgment (for appellants) or possible judgment on reversal (for respondents) is unacceptable, then the appeal is the legal equivalent of Russian roulette—an uncertain outcome means everything will suddenly be either fine or fatal.

- **Litigating when the emotional stress of the case is paralyzing.** When a party simply cannot endure the emotional turmoil and disruption of further litigation—especially a new trial—then continuing the appeal may well be an unacceptable option.

5. *Step 5: Evaluate the Opposing Party's Appeal*

Knowing the strengths and weaknesses of your client's legal arguments is only part of the preparation necessary before you are ready to proceed. A complete understanding also requires case evaluation from the *opposing* perspective. This means evaluating the opposing party's best case outcome, worst case outcome, and whether the opposing party has any better alternatives to appeal. If, for example, the case evaluation of the opposing party reveals the opposition has an acceptable worst case outcome and a very good best case outcome, you may anticipate that the opposing party will be reluctant to mediate. In such circumstance, you may have to enlist the power of the appellate court to order all parties to appear at mediation in order to have any negotiations occur at all. By contrast, if the opposing party has an extremely unattractive worst case scenario and a very expensive best case scenario, you may find the opposing party much more willing to mediate. A voluntary mediation may make perfect sense in such a circumstance. If the opposing party has excellent alternatives to appeal, your bargaining power will be reduced. By contrast, if you have done a thorough case evaluation for the opposing party and found that the appeal poses for the opposing party a highly problematic drain of financial resources and opportunity costs, you will have prepared a strong negotiating position. With the information you glean from case evaluation of the opposing party's appeal, you will be ready to engage in the negotiations and information exchange we detail in Chapters 6 through 8.

E.   Conclusion

To assess the risks and opportunities on appeal appropriately, appellants and respondents must understand the implications of appellate rules and procedures, which often result in unsatisfactory odds of success, large expenses for fees and costs, and prospects for adverse publicity. Case evaluation is a necessary step once you understand the basics of appeals and before you are ready to negotiate with the opposing party or even determine what your own case is worth. Thus, before engaging in the mediation session, you should carefully evaluate both parties' best and worst case scenarios as well as explore whether your client has any viable alternatives to merely continuing with the full appeal. The information you gain from a thorough case evaluation may enable you to strengthen your bargaining power. Even though case evaluation may not reveal undiscovered strengths of your case, it helps to ensure that you have not overlooked any counterintuitive but effective alternative options to continuing with the appeal (for either side).

Chapter 3
Helping Parties on Appeal Answer the Question "What's My Case Worth?"

A. Introduction

By completing the case evaluation described in Chapter 2, you gain an understanding of the odds and potential outcomes for a civil appeal. With the odds and potential outcomes, you can calculate the dollar value of a civil appeal. This means that you can answer the question "What is this appeal worth?" This question is important to answer *before* negotiating in order to know what settlement offers should be contemplated. In this chapter, we explain how to determine the value of an appeal by using decision tree analysis. Decision tree analysis uses a visual approach to value a civil appeal by drawing the various potential outcomes as branches of a tree. Each branch's value is added to arrive at the *present value* of an appeal.

The present value of a case represents the dollar value of the case *today*. Present value accounts for two important principles of money and risk. First, future dollars—money that will not be realized for quite some time—are not worth as much as present dollars. A bird in hand is worth two in the bush.[1] Thus, decision tree analysis determines the value of the case in present dollars because parties need to know what a case is worth today. Second, the uncertainty of winning and certainty of expenses substantially reduce the present value of possible future gains. A lottery ticket is worth much less than a jackpot.

In addition to providing step-by-step instructions on how to do decision tree analysis, we include worksheets that you can photocopy to help you calculate the dollar value of an appeal. Even after the initial valuation process, you can adjust your estimates of odds and outcomes—such as during a negotiation or when new information comes to light—to update or improve your calculations. With the tool of decision tree analysis, attorneys can explore the case value with their clients, parties can be more confident they are making and accepting rational settlement offers, and mediators can help move negotiations past impasse. Let's get started!

---

1. Used since the 1600s, "[t]his proverb refers back to mediaeval falconry where a bird in the hand (the falcon) was a valuable asset and certainly worth more than two in the bush (the prey)." http://phrases.org.uk/meanings/a-bird-in-the-hand.html. The value of a present asset over a future gain has long been understood.

B.   The Need to Use Real Numbers

No one writes "fair settlement value" as the dollar amount line of a settlement check. Instead, every settlement check contains a specific number of dollars the parties agreed will settle the dispute. Thus, most appellate mediations eventually end up involving offers and counteroffers about the amount of money necessary to settle the case. While there may be terms in addition to money, money usually predominates in the parties' decision whether to accept or reject a proposed settlement.

When bargaining over money, parties must translate discussions about "great" and "weak" arguments on appeal as well as "expensive" or "typical" litigation costs into dollar amounts. Sometimes an estimate of outcome may be precise because it is based on a liquidated damages clause. Much more often, however, the numbers used in decision tree analysis represent estimates. There is nothing wrong with having to "guesstimate" the odds and dollar outcomes possible. And, as research in decision theory has shown, our gut feelings do not provide very reliable estimates of complex and uncertain future outcomes.[2] By contrast, analytic approaches that logically break complex problems into smaller parts—such as decision tree analysis—provide more accurate predictions.[3] Decision tree analysis counteracts emotions that distort and bias the accuracy of our predictions by engaging the parties in an analytic process that does not depend on gut feelings, intuition, or snap judgments. For this reason, decision tree analysis is a highly effective tool for preparing to negotiate in mediation.

Decision tree analysis also works well *during* mediation because it allows for a collaborative process of valuation. Although simple by design, decision trees take into account different possible outcomes (affirmance, modification, and reversal on appeal as well as the consequence of retrial) and different dollar outcomes (preservation of a money judgment and reduction of the money judgment as well as different possible jury awards on retrial). Decision tree analysis also allows parties to engage in a dialogue of the risks and costs that further litigation entails.

Decision tree analysis is also an effective tool for revealing differences in expectations between attorneys and their clients. An appellate attorney might tell a plaintiff/appellant that he or she has a "great chance of winning the appeal," meaning the client's chance of winning is well above the court's historical reversal rate of below 20 percent. By contrast, an optimistic client might hear "great chance" and assume that his or her odds of prevailing are well above 50 percent. Because decision tree analysis requires the parties to use actual numbers rather than generalizations, lawyers and clients are

---

2.   DANIEL KAHNEMAN, THINKING, FAST AND SLOW 20–21 (Macmillan, 2011).

3.   *Id.* at 13; STEVEN D. LEVITT & STEPHEN J. DUBNER, THINK LIKE A FREAK: THE AUTHORS OF FREAKO-NOMICS OFFER TO RETRAIN YOUR BRAIN 51–60, 87–92 (William Morrow, 2014).

able to avoid such miscommunication by revealing hidden but important assumptions.

Moreover, the exploration of possible outcomes facilitated by decision tree analysis makes obvious in most cases that "winning" on appeal usually confers the *opportunity to retry the case* rather than a conclusive correction of the judgment by the appellate court. And the examination of all possible outcomes forces an appellant to confront the stark reality that a financial investment to win an appeal and retry the case may yield a result that is less favorable than the trial court judgment that is the subject of appeal. Defendants on appeal can be surprised to see on a visual diagram that further litigation entails nothing but additional expense with no prospect for improving circumstances. The *process* of engaging in a decision tree analysis can be as important as figuring out the present value of a case.

Mediators may find decision tree analysis to be a remarkably useful tool for breaking impasse when the parties have become glued to their numbers. Decision trees can reveal previously unarticulated assumptions and unrealistic expectations and can help parties break through impasse without feeling as though the mediator attacked the legitimacy of their settlement demands. When working through a decision tree using the parties' own estimates of odds and outcomes, mediators help parties calculate a present value that may be surprising and cause them to reevaluate their demands. In short, decision tree analysis provides a valuable tool for any negotiation in which the money bargaining has become emotional at the expense of rationality.

C.   A Few Things to Know about Decision Tree Analysis before Getting Started

1.   *How Difficult Is Decision Tree Analysis?*

It's no secret that many lawyers went to law school to avoid complicated mathematics. Fortunately, decision tree analysis requires nothing more than multiplication and addition. We have used decision trees in appellate mediations without so much as a calculator. If your math skills are rusty, the simplest calculator now included with every cell phone will amply suffice. Better yet, involve the parties in helping to do the multiplication and addition. As with most aspects of mediation, a collaborative process works best.

Ultimately, decision tree analysis does not require more than a pen and sheet of paper, a whiteboard, or a poster flip-chart. We have made things easier by providing worksheets you can photocopy from this book. The worksheets correspond to each of the four categories of parties you will encounter: (1) plaintiff/appellant, (2) plaintiff/respondent, (3) defendant/appellant, and (4) defendant/respondent. Simply determine which party needs the decision tree analysis and fill out the appropriate worksheet.

2. *What Are the Limitations of Decision Tree Analysis?*

Like any tool, decision trees have inherent limitations. Users of decision trees should understand these limitations before placing unfettered confidence in this type of analysis:

- **Garbage in = garbage out.** Estimating the odds on appeal, especially before thoroughly reviewing the appellate record, is a very difficult task. Assigning percent odds of success to an appeal essentially involves a degree of guesswork. As events stretch out into the future, the degree of guessing increases. Although, there is nothing wrong with employing guesswork, the guesswork of decision tree analysis should be based on complete and accurate information. We simply caution that decision tree analysis is only as good as the quality of the estimate you employ. "We agree with Keynes's observation: 'I would rather be vaguely right than precisely wrong.'"[4] By using the multiple explanation debiasing worksheets provided in Chapter 2, you can improve the accuracy of your predictions of the odds for the outcomes of the case. And using a decision tree analysis itself prods you to use a more accurate system of prediction than over generalizing or simply resorting to gut instinct or limited past experience.

- **Overconfidence.** Parties and attorneys participating in decision tree analysis during mediation routinely offer overconfident estimates. Sometimes the overconfidence may be extreme. Obviously, a decision tree based on overconfident estimates yields an overconfident answer (garbage in = garbage out). Information about historical reversal rates and other challenges appellants and respondents statistically face, which well-prepared attorneys or mediators are able to bring into the conversation, may help parties to be more realistic—and accurate—in their estimates. Again, the case evaluation method provided in Chapter 2 can help improve the accuracy of these forecasts.

- **Not appropriate for joint sessions.** Decision tree analysis is not generally useful in joint sessions with all parties because a single decision tree cannot be used for more than one party. Differences in costs and what it means to win require parties to have their own decision trees.

D.   How to Calculate the Present Value of a Case on Appeal

> "Why," said the Dodo, "the best way to explain it is to do it."
>
> —Lewis Carroll, *Alice's Adventures in Wonderland*[5]

---

4. Lawrence A. Cunningham, *The Essays of Warren Buffett: Lessons for Corporate America,* 19 Cardozo Law Review 185 (1997) (quoting John Maynard Keynes).

5. We cannot help but admire the Dodo, who introduced a game lacking any formal rules but that included every animal that had got wet in Alice's pool of tears. Each

Like any good recipe, decision tree analysis requires specific steps in order to yield the correct result. And, much like a good recipe, decision tree analysis can seem daunting at first. However, once you have worked through two or three decision trees, the process is likely to become familiar and perhaps even intuitive.

We suggest giving the process a few good unrushed tries so you become familiar with it. And, especially at first, we suggest you prepare some practice trees in preparation for mediation in which you plan to create a decision tree "live" with a client or party. Even if you do not end up using them during the mediation session, going through the analysis will give you a good sense of the case.

1. *Identify the Party for Whom You Wish to Calculate the Present Value of a Case*

Because decision trees can be drawn only for one party at a time, begin by identifying the party for whom you wish to calculate the present value of a case. For any civil appeal, there will only be four types of parties: (1) plaintiff/appellant, (2) plaintiff/respondent, (3) defendant/appellant, and (4) defendant/respondent. In multiple party appeals, it will be necessary to draw a decision tree for each party, rather than for all defendants (or all plaintiffs) together, unless all respondents or all appellants are raising the exact same arguments. Thus, if there are two respondents in the same appeal who are defending the same judgment, each respondent will need a separate decision tree analysis. Once you have selected the party for whom you wish to use decision tree analysis, you are ready to identify the possible outcomes.

2. *Identify the Possible Outcomes of the Appeal and Determine Whether Attorney Fee Shifting Applies*

In a civil appeal, the judgment can be **affirmed**, **reversed** for retrial (or at least further proceedings in the trial court), or **modified**. These are the only possible outcomes that emanate from appeal, and we can sketch them at the beginning of our decision tree as in Figure 3.1. Even if you ultimately choose to use the worksheets provided in this book, it is often helpful to make a quick sketch of the applicable decision tree as shown in the figure. This helps you to determine which branches of the tree need to be included in your calculations.

For most appeals, you do not need a branch for modification—the affirmance and reversal branches will suffice. This is because appellate courts modify judgments only in the relatively rare cases in which appellants expressly

---

animal became dry in the process of the chaotic fun—at which point the Dodo declared "EVERBODY has won!" And so it was. They had all become happy and dry despite their wet and dour dispositions at the start. ALICE IN WONDERLAND, ch. 3.

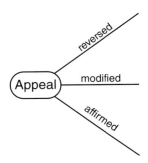

Figure 3.1

request such relief. For example, the appellant might secure a modification by persuading the appellate court to strike the punitive damages part of a money judgment as statutorily unauthorized or constitutionally excessive. Such a request for modification is based entirely on legal argument and not on factual findings or the exercise of discretion in choosing from a range of permissible damages. Modification represents certainty by the appellate court that a particular damage award (or portion of the damages awarded) must be stricken as a matter of law.

If the appellate court reverses and remands for further trial court proceedings, on retrial the judgment may give the appellant all requested relief (**best verdict**) or none of it (**worst verdict**). To account for the possibility of something in between the best and worst cases, the decision tree can include a **mid verdict** branch.

The decision tree in Figure 3.2 represents an appeal that could end with an affirmance, modification, or reversal, and on the reversal branch that indicates the court reversed the judgment and ordered a retrial, we map three potential results—a best, mid, and worst verdict on retrial.

This step culminates in the drawing of an actual decision tree that has two parts: nodes and branches. Nodes represent events that can have multiple outcomes. Here the two nodes are the appeal and the retrial. Each of these events can have good outcomes and bad outcomes. Branches represent the possible outcomes. Thus, an appeal may have branches for affirmance, reversal, and modification. Retrial might have branches for best, worst, and most likely verdicts.

A note on terms we use for describing parts of appellate decision trees:

We use **judgment** for affirmance or modification on appeal. We do so because the judgment being appealed may include damages awarded in the verdict as well as attorney fees and costs awarded by the trial court after the verdict has been rendered. We use the value of the judgment to determine the gain or loss for affirmance and modification on appeal because that is the value that results from these two outcomes.

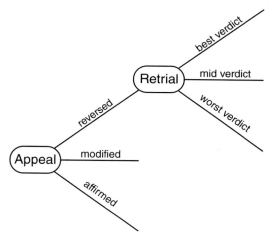

Figure 3.2

We use **verdict** to describe the possible outcomes on retrial. Thus, **verdict** refers to the monetary damages (including compensatory and punitive damages) awarded by the jury or trial judge sitting as the trier of fact, as well as the separate award for attorney fees, if any. Depending on who wins on retrial and whether there is fee shifting, the attorney fees may apply differently for the best case, worst case, and most likely scenarios.

3. Assign Dollar Values and Percentage Odds to Each Possible Outcome

For every possible outcome, it is necessary to ask the following:

- What is the dollar value of the verdict or judgment for each outcome?

- How likely is it for each outcome to occur?

As we have noted, no one knows whether the appellate court will affirm or reverse or whether a jury on retrial will award $10 million, $565,789.88, or nothing. However, it is possible to estimate the probability of outcomes and possible verdicts. And it is necessary to give each possible outcome a dollar value.

The **affirmed** branch reflects the preservation of the dollar value of the judgment being appealed. If the judgment was for $1 million, then the monetary value of the affirmance branch will be $1 million.

The **modified** branch is based on the amount that results if the appellate court grants the appellant's requested relief for modification. For example, if the appellant asked the appellate court to modify a $1 million judgment to eliminate an $800,000 punitive damages award, the monetary value of the modification branch would be $200,000.

The **reversed** branch requires parties to estimate the dollar amounts following retrial—their best and worst verdict scenarios (and, if they so choose, their mid verdict as well).

Once parties estimate the dollar amounts for each outcome, it is time to determine the odds of each outcome. Decision tree analysis requires a percentage number between 1 percent and 99 percent. Estimates such as "good," "bad," and "great" odds of appeal will not work for decision tree analysis. Thus, decision tree analysis not only allows parties to determine a dollar value for an appeal but also, more importantly, fosters a discussion that uncovers hidden assumptions and unwarranted overconfidence. Thus, the value of the analysis lies in parties' revealing their implicit assumptions, hopes, and fears.

We reemphasize the hazard of proceeding with unrealistic estimates of odds and outcomes. If a party uses overconfident numbers, an overconfident product will result. To guard against this danger, we recommend that the multiple-explanations debiasing worksheets in Chapter 2 be filled out before estimating the odds for decision tree analysis.

4. *Multiply the Dollar Value by the Percentage Odds for Each Possible Outcome*

For this step, we calculate the present value of all possible outcomes. As we noted in our introduction, present value reflects the fact that a dollar you have in your hand today is worth more than the possibility that you may gain a dollar sometime in the future. To calculate the present value of the future dollar outcomes on appeal, we take an outcome (such as a $1 million verdict on retrial) and multiply it by the odds of its occurring. A win at retrial will result only if an appellant both wins the appeal (say, a 20-percent chance) and wins at retrial (a 50-percent chance might be a reasonable estimate). Thus, for the appellant in this example, the present value of this possible outcome is $1 million multiplied by 20 percent and then multiplied by 50 percent. This calculation yields a present value of $100,000. Intuitively this makes sense: the value of an unlikely $1 million verdict (here estimated to occur only 10 percent of the time) must be worth substantially less than $1 million "in hand" today. With the estimates used here, the *present value* is thus only one-tenth the possible future gain.

We repeat this calculation for each of the branches—judgment affirmance, judgment modification, and possible verdicts on retrial—to determine the present value of every outcome. We apply this calculation to attorney fees as well.

Don't fear—we give you worksheets for each category of parties on appeal so that you can simply fill in the blanks with estimates of odds and outcomes. You will find them throughout this chapter, beginning on page 71.

5. Add All of the Values to Arrive at the Overall Expected Gain or Loss for the Appeal

Once you calculate the present values for each branch of the decision tree, the next step is to add all the values. Some of the values will be gains—such as favorable verdicts for plaintiffs. Most of the values, however, will be losses, such as unreimbursable attorney fees and—for defendants—any money judgments or verdicts. The sum total of all these present values accounts for all possible outcomes on appeal. For this reason, the sum total is the present value of the case for the party.

We cannot emphasize enough that you must include expected gains and losses from *all* of the branches in the final total. Parties will sometimes want to focus only on outcomes they perceive as favorable. However, it does not work for a party to ignore outcomes and risk that they do not like. Take the example of the miles per gallon that a new car is estimated to achieve. Many consumers focus carefully on the gas mileage of the cars they are considering for purchase. If vehicle manufacturers only included gas mileage occurring when driving downhill or with a tail wind, the reported gas mileage would be inaccurate. Instead, they must also account for *unfavorable* driving conditions when determining the gas mileage to be expected from a particular vehicle. So too decision tree analysis yields the correct result only if we include bad as well as good outcomes. Similarly, because attorney fees can make a large difference in the final total of the present value calculation, they must also be included in the analysis. For many defendant/respondents, it is the present value of possible attorney fees that provides the primary source of loss in a case (even if there is a fee-shifting agreement that applies!).

Or consider the example of an appeal in which the plaintiff/appellant hopes to win a $1 million dollar jury verdict and therefore thinks of it as "a million dollar case." Because the million dollar verdict is a vivid and coveted result, the plaintiff may be ignoring the fact that it is only one possible outcome. The judgment might also be affirmed, thus precluding retrial and therefore the chance to win anything, or reversed with a loss at retrial. Even though the million dollar verdict may be the least likely outcome, so long as the plaintiff ignores the other more likely outcomes, it may seem like a much more valuable case than any objective analysis would suggest. In short, ignoring what you do not like is not a way to determine the dollar value of a case.

E. Decision Tree Analysis for Each Party You Are Likely to Encounter on Appeal

Decision tree analysis for civil appeals will always involve one of four types of litigants: (1) a plaintiff who appeals, (2) a plaintiff who defends the judgment, (3) a defendant who appeals, and (4) a defendant who seeks to preserve the judgment. We examine the situation of each category of appellate litigant in turn and provide a set of three worksheet pages for each type of appellate litigant.

1. *Plaintiff/Appellant's Decision Tree Risk Analysis*

a. *Typical Plaintiff/Appellant Cases*

Decision tree analysis for a plaintiff/appellant generally involves a party that has failed at trial to secure a money judgment, or, if damages were awarded, they were insufficient to satisfy the plaintiff. The plaintiff/appellant who has failed in the trial court now faces an arduous path on appeal in order to achieve any success in litigation. The plaintiff/appellant is highly unlikely to convince the appellate court to provide direct relief from the adverse judgment by, for example, modifying the judgment to specify a greater monetary recovery. Instead, the best the plaintiff/appellant can hope for is reversal on appeal and remand for retrial. Therefore, it is rarely necessary to add a "modify on appeal" branch to the decision tree.

For plaintiff/appellants who mistakenly focus on the amount of damages they requested at trial, decision tree analysis will likely reveal the sobering reality that appeals are worth much less than they think. Even if a favorable jury verdict is highly likely on retrial after the appeal, the case is still probably worth only a fraction of even the best reasonably likely verdict on retrial.

Of all parties, decision tree analysis is likely most beneficial to plaintiff/appellants. It provides them the most useful information in adjusting settlement offers and demands to reflect a logical valuation of the case. It is useful as a tool for attorneys or mediators to employ when plaintiffs are overly optimistic about the case value.

b. *An Example of Decision Tree Risk Analysis for a Plaintiff/Appellant*

Perhaps the best way to learn decision tree analysis is to work through a hypothetical. Let's engage in an analysis for a plaintiff/appellant in the following situation:[6]

PrizeCo v. Cathatrin, Inc.

Riley Brellis, the president of PrizeCo, exclaims, "This is a million dollar case!" PrizeCo provides stuffed-animal prizes to fairs and carnivals nationwide and prides itself on having the latest and greatest prizes. In 2013, a children's television show with very high viewer ratings featured a wide variety of safari-themed animals. Thus, PrizeCo ordered 250,000 stuffed animals from Cathatrin,

---

6. All hypotheticals in this book are fictitious, and any resemblance to real cases or individuals is purely coincidental.

Inc., a large toy manufacturer, and specified in the contract that the stuffed animals should include lions, tigers, elephants, monkeys, hippopotamuses, and giraffes to be delivered by May 2013 in time for the summer carnival season. Cathatrin delivered the following: 10,000 each of lions, tigers, monkeys, giraffes, and hippos; and 200,000 elephants. PrizeCo immediately notified Cathatrin that the order was unacceptable because prizes are valuable only if they are not overly common. PrizeCo asserted that the overwhelming number of stuffed elephants rendered them valueless. Carnivals never purchase prizes out of proportion to the other animals. Carnival goers are a fickle market. In addition, cancellation of the children's show after only one season left safari-themed animals far less valuable.

When PrizeCo's warehouse began overflowing with plush elephants, it sued Cathatrin. Unfortunately for PrizeCo, the jury returned a special verdict that Cathatrin's conduct did not amount to a material breach of the agreement. Thus, the jury never reached the issue of damages. Brellis still adamantly believes Cathatrin caused PrizeCo to suffer $1 million in damages.

PrizeCo is appealing the judgment entered on a jury verdict for the defense. PrizeCo plans to challenge the judgment on grounds that (1) the jury was misinstructed on what constitutes a material breach of contract, and (2) the trial court abused its discretion in precluding PrizeCo from calling as a witness a former vice president of Cathatrin who would have recounted his experience that Cathatrin would change the mix of products whenever it could increase its profit margins even a little. Brellis estimates PrizeCo has a 40-percent chance of winning on appeal due to the strong jury instruction issue for which de novo review applies. PrizeCo has budgeted $30,000 in attorney fees and costs to pursue the appeal and expects Cathatrin will spend $20,000 on the appeal.

If PrizeCo wins the appeal, Brellis believes retrial will cost $50,000. However, Brellis is sure that PrizeCo has a 10-percent chance of winning $2 million, a 60-percent chance of winning $1 million, and a 30-percent chance of another defense verdict. PrizeCo expects retrial will cost Cathatrin $50,000. Cathatrin's litigation spending is important because the contract contains a fee-shifting provision that awards the prevailing party attorney fees and costs.

Using Brellis's estimates of odds, costs, and outcomes, what is the present value of the case to PrizeCo?

Step 1: Identify the party for whom you wish to calculate the present value of a case.

We are calculating the present value for PrizeCo, the plaintiff/appellant in this appeal.

Step 2: Determine the possible outcomes and draw a decision tree.

In this case, the appeal will result in an affirmance or reversal. PrizeCo is not requesting a modification of judgment, and it is not a reasonably likely disposition. Thus, the first node (appeal) has two branches: affirmed and reversed. On retrial, according to PrizeCo, there are three possible outcomes. Thus there are three branches from the second node (retrial): best verdict, mid verdict, worst verdict. When beginning a decision tree analysis, you may find it helpful to make a quick sketch of the decision tree—even if you plan to use the worksheets we provide below. A sketch looks like Figure 3.3.

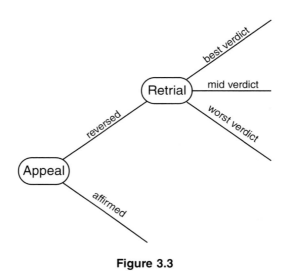

Figure 3.3

**Step 3: Ascertain the odds, awards, and fees
for each possible outcome.**

From our hypothetical, we glean the following applicable estimates of odds of success on appeal and trial. Using the worksheet we provide for plaintiff/appellants, we get the result in Figure 3.4.

Note that the 40-percent estimate of winning on appeal is very optimistic. This is more than twice the rate at which individual appellants win in the U.S. Courts of Appeals. Even though PrizeCo lost the first trial, PrizeCo's president estimates a 70-percent chance of winning at least $1 million on retrial. (Based on Brellis's estimate that PrizeCo has a 10-percent chance of the best verdict on retrial in addition to a 60-percent chance of the mid verdict on retrial.) A certain amount of over optimism is probably inevitable in any analysis that uses a party or attorney's estimates of success. However, the estimates used here likely represent the outer limit of optimism for any reasonable analysis.

A *note on abbreviations for decision tree worksheets*: Whether you use the worksheets we provide or you hand draw the decision tree, you will quickly discover that space is always a premium when doing a decision tree analysis. Thus, we suggest the following abbreviations:

- "M" to signify millions. Rather than $1,000,000.00, you can write $1M.

- "K" for thousands. Instead of $1,000.00, you can write $1K.

- "%" for percentages.

We use these abbreviations for millions, thousands, and percentages in our illustrations.

Decision tree analysis for plaintiff/appellant _____ Prize Co. _____
                                                              (name)

Case Title _____ Prize Co. v. Cathatrin, Inc. _____

Decision tree risk analysis prepared by _____ Brendon Ishikawa _____
Notice: This risk analysis may be protected by mediation confidentiality and/or attorney-client privilege.

Instructions: Estimate the odds, outcomes, and attorney fees for the plaintiff/appellant.

JBA (Judgment Being Appealed) =	$ 0	
JAM (Judgment as Modified) =	$ N/A	(skip if modification not reasonably likely)
OWA (Odds of Winning on Appeal) =	40 %	
OMA (Odds of Modification on Appeal) =	N/A %	(skip if modification not reasonably likely)
OLA (Odds of Losing on Appeal) =	60 %	
These odds must add up to: 100%		
RB (Retrial Best Verdict) =	$ 2M	
RM (Retrial Mid Verdict) =	$ 1M	
RW (Retrial Worst Verdict) =	$ 0	
ORB (Odds of Retrial Best Verdict) =	10 %	
ORM (Odds of Retrial Mid Verdict) =	60 %	
ORW (Odds of Retrial Worst Verdict) =	30 %	
These odds must add up to: 100%		
AFA (Appellant's Attorney Fees for Appeal) =	$ 30K	
AFR (Appellant's Attorney Fees for Retrial) =	$ 50K	
RFA (Respondent's Attorney Fees for Appeal) =	$ 20K	(skip if no fee-shifting agreement or statute)
RFR (Respondent's Attorney Fees for Retrial) =	$ 50K	(skip if no fee-shifting agreement or statute)

Figure 3.4

Step 4: Fill in the outcomes and odds.

Using the worksheet for the plaintiff/appellant gives you a decision tree for PrizeCo that looks like Figure 3.5.

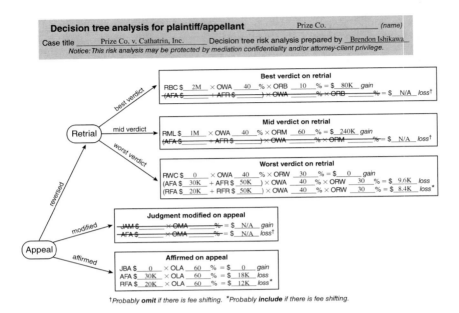

Figure 3.5

Best Verdict and Mid Verdict Branches: The attorney fee lines for these branches are crossed out. Not every line will apply in every case. Here PrizeCo will be the prevailing party if it wins on appeal and then wins a verdict of $1 million or more. Although PrizeCo will have spent money on attorney fees, these fees are reimbursed under the fee-shifting agreement. If reimbursed, attorney fees are neither a gain nor a loss. Because they are neither a gain nor a loss, they can simply be ignored.

Worst Verdict Branch: The situation is different if PrizeCo suffers a defense verdict on retrial. In that outcome, PrizeCo must bear not only the cost of its own attorney but also the cost of Cathatrin's attorney because Cathatrin will be the prevailing party. Thus, there are two lines for attorney fees under the worst verdict branch: one for PrizeCo's own attorney fees and one for Cathatrin's shifted attorney fees.

Modification Branch: The branch for modification is crossed out because modification on appeal is not reasonably likely.

Affirmance Branch: Affirmance on appeal is a losing outcome for PrizeCo. Not only would PrizeCo be stuck with an unfavorable judgment, but it would also have to pay its own attorney fees as well as the attorney fees of the prevailing party, Cathatrin. Thus, the affirmance branch has two lines for attorney fees to account for the fees PrizeCo is likely going to have to pay.

Step 5: Add the values from all of the branches.

Now that we have calculated the present value of each outcome, we must add them together to get the present value of the case. Using the worksheet provided, the calculation looks like Figure 3.6.

Decision tree analysis for plaintiff/appellant _____ Prize Co.
                                                              (name)

Case Title _____ Prize Co. v. Cathatrin, Inc. _____

Decision tree risk analysis prepared by ____ Brendon Ishikawa ____
Notice: This worksheet may be protected by mediation confidentiality and/or attorney-client privilege.

Instructions: Calculate the present value for the <u>plaintiff/appellant</u> by filling in the blanks and adding up the values from all of the branches—both gains and losses.

Best verdict on retrial branch
$ ____80K____ gain (present value of retrial best verdict)
$ ____N/A____ loss, if no fee shifting (present value of retrial best verdict plaintiff's attorney fees)

Mid verdict on retrial branch
$ ____240K____ gain (present value of retrial mid verdict)
$ ____N/A____ loss, if no fee shifting (present value of retrial mid verdict plaintiff's attorney fees)

Worst verdict on retrial branch
$ ____0____ gain or, if defense verdict, zero (present value of retrial worst verdict)
$ ____9.6K____ loss (present value of retrial worst verdict plaintiff's attorney fees)
$ ____8.4K____ loss, if fee shifting (present value of retrial worst verdict defendant's attorney fees)

Modification of judgment on appeal branch
$ ____N/A____ gain (present value of judgment as modified on appeal)
$ ____N/A____ loss, if no fee shifting (present value of plaintiff's attorney fees on appeal)

Affirmance on appeal branch
$ ____0____ gain (present value of judgment being appealed, likely zero if defense verdict)
$ ____18K____ loss (present value of plaintiff's attorney fees on appeal)
$ ____12K____ loss, if fee shifting (present value of defendant's attorney fees on appeal)

= $ __272,000__ **Present value of case to plaintiff/appellant**

Figure 3.6

The present value for PrizeCo in this case is $272,000—or about a quarter of what PrizeCo's president may think of as a million dollar case. This valuation will probably surprise PrizeCo because this is (1) an appeal with much better than average chances of success, (2) for which the most likely outcome is a $1 million verdict on retrial, and (3) for which PrizeCo even has a chance of a $2 million verdict on retrial. The lesson from this decision tree is that cumulative risk, litigation costs, and the potential for fee shifting greatly reduce the value of even a strong case.

Parties, attorneys, and mediators can readily engage in decision tree analysis during a mediation without a computer, worksheets, or a calculator. In the example above, here's how you can do a decision tree analysis for PrizeCo with only a pen and a sheet of paper.

**Step 1. Identify the party for whom you
wish to calculate the present value of a case.**

Again, we are doing the decision tree for plaintiff/appellant PrizeCo.

**Step 2. Determine the possible outcomes
and draw a decision tree.**

We have already determined the basic decision tree for a plaintiff/appellant, as shown in Figure 3.3.

**Step 3. Ascertain the odds, awards,
and fees for each possible outcome.**

We account for possible verdicts and judgments by filling in the dollar values for the outcomes and the percentage probabilities.

Step 4. Fill in the outcomes and odds.

Calculating the outcomes and odds yields a decision tree that looks like Figure 3.7.

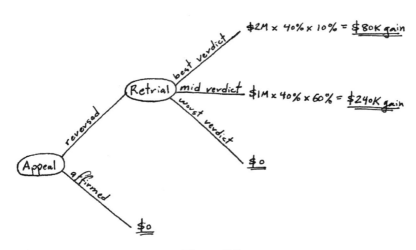

Figure 3.7

Next, we account for attorney fee shifting. We make a note that PrizeCo does not have to pay Cathatrin's fees if it wins a favorable verdict on retrial. And if PrizeCo prevails on retrial, based on fee-shifting, Cathatrin must reimburse PrizeCo's fees. However, for the worst verdict on retrial and for affirmance on appeal, PrizeCo must pay not only its own fees but also Cathatrin's fees. This yields the result in Figure 3.8.

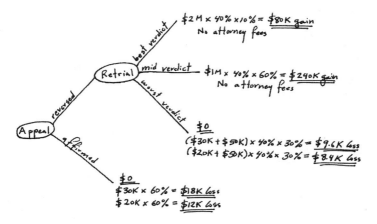

Figure 3.8

Now that we have calculated the values of the possible outcomes, we proceed to step 5.

Step 5. Add up the values from all of the branches.

Simply add the result of every branch to determine the present value of the case to PrizeCo. The result is shown in Figure 3.9.

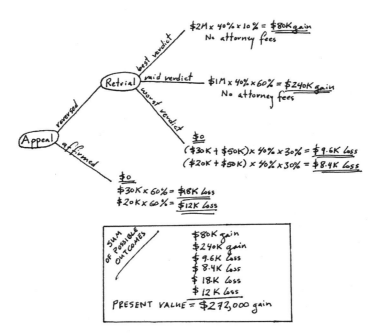

Figure 3.9

Parties, attorneys, and mediators can collaborate to draw this decision tree, which calculates the present value of the case on a single sheet of paper, a whiteboard, or a flip chart.

To help you with valuing cases for plaintiff/appellants, the next pages contain worksheets you can photocopy. If you have access to a photocopier with larger paper, select 11-by-17-inch sheets of paper for easiest use.

Worksheets for a Plaintiff/Appellant

Decision tree analysis for plaintiff/appellant _____
(name)

Case Title _____

Decision tree risk analysis prepared by _____
Notice: This risk analysis may be protected by mediation confidentiality and/or attorney-client privilege.

Instructions: Estimate the odds, outcomes, and attorney fees for the <u>plaintiff/appellant</u>.

JBA (Judgment Being Appealed) = $ _____

JAM (Judgment as Modified) = $ _____   (skip if modification not reasonably likely)

OWA (Odds of Winning on Appeal) =   _____ %

OMA (Odds of Modification on Appeal) =   _____ %   (skip if modification not reasonably likely)

OLA (Odds of Losing on Appeal) =   _____ %

These odds must add up to: 100%

RB (Retrial Best Verdict) = $ _____

RM (Retrial Mid Verdict) = $ _____

RW (Retrial Worst Verdict) = $ _____

ORB (Odds of Retrial Best Verdict) =   _____ %

ORM (Odds of Retrial Mid Verdict) =   _____ %

ORW (Odds of Retrial Worst Verdict) =   _____ %

These odds must add up to: 100%

AFA (Appellant's Attorney Fees for Appeal) = $ _____

AFR (Appellant's Attorney Fees for Retrial) = $ _____

RFA (Respondent's Attorney Fees for Appeal) = $ _____   (skip if no fee-shifting agreement or statute)

RFR (Respondent's Attorney Fees for Retrial) = $ _____   (skip if no fee-shifting agreement or statute)

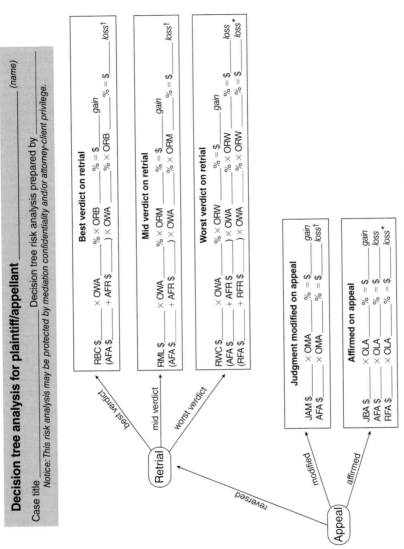

Decision tree analysis for plaintiff/appellant

Case title _____   Decision tree risk analysis prepared by _____ (name)

Notice: This risk analysis may be protected by mediation confidentiality and/or attorney-client privilege.

Best verdict on retrial

RBC $ _____ × OWA _____ % × ORB _____ % = $ _____ gain
(AFA $ _____) × OWA _____ % × ORB _____ % = $ _____ loss†

Mid verdict on retrial

RML $ _____ × OWA _____ % × ORM _____ % = $ _____ gain
(AFA $ _____) × OWA _____ % × ORM _____ % = $ _____ loss†

Worst verdict on retrial

RWC $ _____ × OWA _____ % × ORW _____ % = $ _____ gain
(AFA $ _____) × OWA _____ % × ORW _____ % = $ _____ loss
(RFA $ _____) × OWA _____ % × ORW _____ % = $ _____ loss*

best verdict

mid verdict

worst verdict

(Retrial)

reversed

Judgment modified on appeal

JAM $ _____ × OMA _____ % = $ _____ gain
AFA $ _____ × OMA _____ % = $ _____ loss†

Affirmed on appeal

JBA $ _____ × OLA _____ % = $ _____ gain
AFA $ _____ × OLA _____ % = $ _____ loss*
RFA $ _____ × OLA _____ % = $ _____ loss*

modified

affirmed

(Appeal)

†Probably **omit** if there is fee shifting.   *Probably **include** if there is fee shifting.

Worksheets for a Plaintiff/Appellant

Decision tree analysis for plaintiff/appellant _____
                                                                    (name)

Case Title _____

Decision tree risk analysis prepared by _____
Notice: This worksheet may be protected by mediation confidentiality and/or attorney-client privilege.

Instructions: Calculate the present value for the <u>plaintiff/appellant</u> by filling in the blanks and adding up the values from all of the branches—both gains and losses.

Best verdict on retrial branch

$ _____ gain (present value of retrial best verdict)

$ _____ loss, if no fee shifting (present value of retrial best verdict plaintiff's attorney fees)

Mid verdict on retrial branch

$ _____ gain (present value of retrial mid verdict)

$ _____ loss, if no fee shifting (present value of retrial mid verdict plaintiff's attorney fees)

Worst verdict on retrial branch

$ _____ gain or, if defense verdict, zero (present value of retrial worst verdict)

$ _____ loss (present value of retrial worst verdict plaintiff's attorney fees)

$ _____ loss, if fee shifting (present value of retrial worst verdict defendant's attorney fees)

Modification of judgment on appeal branch

$ _____ gain (present value of judgment as modified on appeal)

$ _____ loss, if no fee shifting (present value of plaintiff's attorney fees on appeal)

Affirmance on appeal branch

$ _____ gain (present value of judgment being appealed, likely zero if defense verdict)

$ _____ loss (present value of plaintiff's attorney fees on appeal)

$ _____ loss, if fee shifting (present value of defendant's attorney fees on appeal)

= $ _____ **Present value of case to plaintiff/appellant**

2. *Plaintiff/Respondent's Decision Tree Risk Analysis*

a. *Typical Plaintiff/Respondent Cases*

A plaintiff/respondent typically has secured a favorable judgment and seeks to defend it on appeal. Although the plaintiff/respondent may not have received as big a verdict as hoped for, he or she is nonetheless sufficiently satisfied to forego appealing the judgment. This party frequently is interested in ending the litigation and settling the case through mediation and may be especially eager to cash in on the judgment when it is a large amount money. Because, as we noted earlier, a judgment is not a check, the plaintiff/respondent may wait years during the appellate process and perhaps during arduous collection proceedings to realize any gain. For the plaintiff/respondent, a quick, certain resolution through a settlement may be a very attractive option. Even so, the plaintiff/respondent may be reluctant to sacrifice any of the judgment's value by receiving a discounted amount in a settlement. Decision tree risk analysis can demonstrate to a reluctant plaintiff/respondent that considerable risks remain if the litigation continues. It can also show that the substantial litigation expenses will mount and possibly double if the plaintiff/respondent loses the appeal.

b. *An Example of Decision Tree Risk Analysis for a Plaintiff/Respondent*

To illustrate the process for a risk analysis for a plaintiff/respondent, let's work through the following hypothetical:

Daven v. Douglas

In this medical malpractice case, a former television newscaster, Carson Daven, sued his plastic surgeon, Reshma Douglas, M.D. Daven sought Douglas's help after a car accident in which Daven suffered nose trauma. As the on-air personality for a popular weekly program, Daven knew he had a problem when his nose began to whistle as he talked. His nasal problems also interfered with proper swallowing. Douglas promised she could fix Daven's whistling nose and swallowing problem. Douglas operated and pronounced the surgery a success. Daven disagreed. He still heard a little whistling whenever he talked and, worse, the shape of his nose was changed! Daven felt a crushing loss of identity. He underwent two more surgeries to correct what he believed to be Douglas's incompetence. But by that time the damage was done, as Daven lost his news program due to lost viewership.

The jury awarded Daven $1 million: $400,000 in compensatory damages and $600,000 in special damages. Compensatory damages were based on Daven's subsequent surgeries and loss of income.

Special damages consisted of a penalty imposed by a new statute on surgeons who fail to secure a signed advisement of risks on the specified form. Although Douglas introduced a signed patient consent form, the form was not identical to the one specified by the statute.

On appeal, Douglas claims (1) the court erroneously permitted extremely inflammatory testimony by Daven's medical expert and extremely inflammatory video footage from Daven's surgery. (2) the special damages should be stricken as a matter of law because the signed form is the functional equivalent of the statutorily required form.

Daven told his attorney, "I was right, and that's why the jury awarded me $1 million! I know about the odds on appeal, and we're going to win on appeal too!" Daven believes he has a 60-percent chance of affirmance, a 20-percent chance that the appellate court will grant Douglas's request for modification of the judgment to strike the special damages as statutorily unauthorized, and a 20-percent chance the court will reverse the judgment. Daven expects to pay $40,000 for the appeal and $80,000 for the retrial (if any), the approximate cost of the original trial. On retrial, Daven estimates a 10-percent chance of winning $1.2 million, a 60-percent chance of the same $1 million verdict, and a 30-percent chance the verdict on retrial will be only $400,000. In this tort action, no fee-shifting contract or statute applies.

Using Daven's estimates of odds, costs, and outcomes, what is the present value of his case?

Step 1. Identify the party for whom you wish to calculate the present value of a case.

Here we are helping plaintiff/respondent Carson Daven determine the present value of his case.

Step 2: Determine the possible outcomes and draw a decision tree.

The appeal node has three branches because the appeal may be affirmed, modified, or reversed. The retrial node also has three branches. These reflect the possible outcomes of a best verdict, mid verdict, and worst verdict. A quick sketch yields the decision tree in Figure 3.10.

Step 3: Ascertain the odds, awards, and fees for each possible outcome.

From Daven's statements, we glean the information that we insert into the worksheet shown in Figure 3.11.

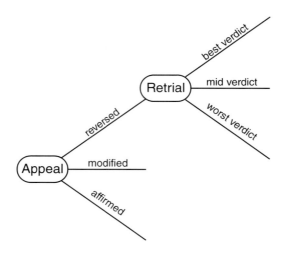

Figure 3.10

Decision tree analysis for plaintiff/respondent Carson Daven
(name)

Case Title Daven v. Douglas

Decision tree risk analysis prepared by Dana Curtis

Notice: This risk analysis may be protected by mediation confidentiality and/or attorney-client privilege.

Instructions: Estimate the odds, outcomes, and attorney fees for the plaintiff/respondent.

JBA (Judgment Being Appealed) = $ 1M
JAM (Judgment as Modified) = $ 400K (skip if modification not reasonably likely)

OWA (Odds of Winning on Appeal) = 60 %
OMA (Odds of Modification on Appeal) = 20 % (skip if modification not reasonably likely)
OLA (Odds of Losing on Appeal) = 20 %
These odds must add up to: 100%

RB (Retrial Best Verdict) = $ 1.2M
RM (Retrial Mid Verdict) = $ 1M
RW (Retrial Worst Verdict) = $ 400K

ORB (Odds of Retrial Best Verdict) = 10 %
ORM (Odds of Retrial Mid Verdict) = 60 %
ORW (Odds of Retrial Worst Verdict) = 30 %
These odds must add up to: 100%

AFA (Appellant's Attorney Fees for Appeal) = $ N/A (skip if no fee-shifting agreement or statute)
AFR (Appellant's Attorney Fees for Retrial) = $ N/A (skip if no fee-shifting agreement or statute)
RFA (Respondent's Attorney Fees for Appeal) = $ 40K
RFR (Respondent's Attorney Fees for Retrial) = $ 80K

Figure 3.11

Note that Daven's estimate of the worst verdict on retrial is still very optimistic. It might be worth exploring with Daven whether his analysis is overconfident in dismissing even the possibility of a defense verdict. On the other hand, it may not be worth the effort because as we shall see, the present value from that branch is only $24,000. In fact, as you become more familiar with decision trees, you'll see that a few values—such as the reversal rate on appeal—make the most difference to the present value calculation. By contrast, retrial outcomes tend to move the needle very little in terms of present value of a case.

Step 4: Fill in the judgment outcomes and odds.

Now we proceed to fill in the blanks on the decision tree, which yields a worksheet that looks like Figure 3.12.

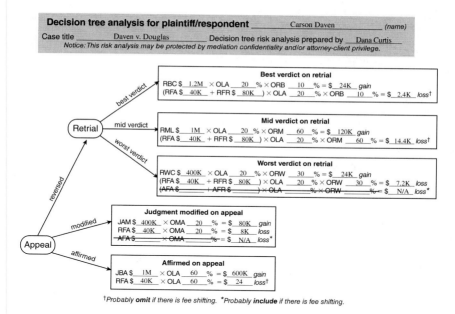

Figure 3.12

Best and Mid Verdict Branches. Even though Daven predicts he will "win" again on retrial, this case demonstrates how the cost of the appeal and subsequent retrial reduce the present value of even a best verdict assumption, sometimes significantly.

Worst Verdict. We cross out the line for Douglas's attorney fees because there is no fee-shifting statute or contract that would require Daven to pay Douglas's fees if he loses.

Modification Branch. Again, we eliminate Douglas's attorney fees because there is no fee-shifting provision.

The remaining values are simply filled in according to the first worksheet. Every value on the first worksheet (Figure 3.11) is labeled with a three-letter abbreviation (such as JBA for judgment being appealed) that corresponds to a blank line on the second worksheet (Figure 3.12) with the same three-letter abbreviation.

Step 5: Add the values from all of the branches.

Now that we have calculated the economic value of each possible outcome, we must add them together to get the present value for the case. Using our worksheet, the calculation looks like Figure 3.13.

Decision tree analysis for plaintiff/respondent _____ Carson Daven _____
(name)

Case Title _____ Daven v. Douglas _____
Decision tree risk analysis prepared by _____ Dana Curtis _____
Notice: This risk analysis may be protected by mediation confidentiality and/or attorney-client privilege.

Instructions: Calculate the present value for the plaintiff/respondent by filling in the blanks and adding up the values from all of the branches—both gains and losses.

Best verdict on retrial branch
$ ___24K___ gain (present value of retrial best verdict)
$ ___2.4K___ loss, if no fee shifting (present value of retrial best verdict plaintiff's attorney fees)

Mid verdict on retrial branch
$ ___120K___ gain (present value of retrial mid verdict)
$ ___14.4K___ loss, if no fee shifting (present value of retrial mid verdict plaintiff's attorney fees)

Worst verdict on retrial branch
$ ___24K___ gain or, if defense verdict, zero (present value of retrial worst verdict)
$ ___7.2K___ loss (present value of retrial worst verdict plaintiff's attorney fees)
$ ___N/A___ loss, if fee shifting (present value of retrial worst verdict defendant's attorney fees)

Modification of judgment on appeal branch
$ ___80K___ gain (present value of judgment as modified on appeal)
$ ___8K___ loss, if no fee shifting (present value of plaintiff's attorney fees on appeal)
$ ___N/A___ loss, if fee shifting (present value of defendant's attorney fees on appeal)

Affirmance on appeal branch
$ ___600K___ gain (present value of judgment being appealed)
$ ___24K___ loss, if no fee shifting (present value of plaintiff's attorney fees on appeal)
= $ ___792,000___ **Present value of case to plaintiff/respondent**

Figure 3.13

The present value to Daven is $792,000, *even though he is sitting on a million dollar judgment that is immediately effective.* (Remember: you can't walk into a bank and cash a judgment.) Even with Daven's tremendous (over) confidence that he will never lose on retrial, he logically should be willing to discount the judgment by more than 20 percent to settle this case.

Alternatively, you can draw the decision tree analysis for this hypothetical on a single whiteboard, poster board, or sheet of paper. A completed decision tree looks like Figure 3.14.

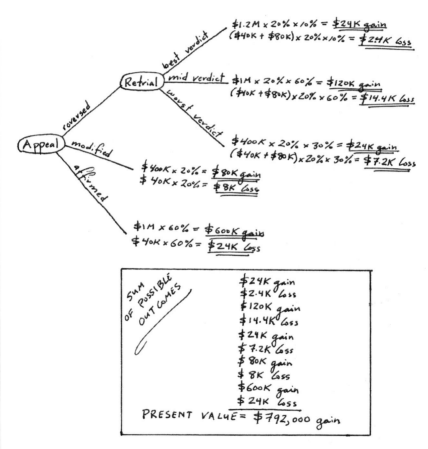

Figure 3.14

To help you with valuing cases for plaintiffs/respondents, the next pages provide worksheets you can photocopy, preferably on 11-by-17-inch paper.

Worksheets for a Plaintiff/Respondent

Decision tree analysis for plaintiff/respondent _____
(name)

Case Title _____

Decision tree risk analysis prepared by _____
Notice: This risk analysis may be protected by mediation confidentiality and/or attorney-client privilege.

Instructions: Estimate the odds, outcomes, and attorney fees for the <u>plaintiff/respondent</u>.

JBA (Judgment Being Appealed) = $ _____

JAM (Judgment as Modified) = $ _____   (skip if modification not reasonably likely)

OWA (Odds of Winning on Appeal) =   _____ %

OMA (Odds of Modification on Appeal) =   _____ %   (skip if modification not reasonably likely)

OLA (Odds of Losing on Appeal) =   _____ %

These odds must add up to: 100%

RB (Retrial Best Verdict) = $ _____

RM (Retrial Mid Verdict) = $ _____

RW (Retrial Worst Verdict) = $ _____

ORB (Odds of Retrial Best Verdict) =   _____ %

ORM (Odds of Retrial Mid Verdict) =   _____ %

ORW (Odds of Retrial Worst Verdict) =   _____ %

These odds must add up to: 100%

AFA (Appellant's Attorney Fees for Appeal) = $ _____   (skip if no fee-shifting agreement or statute)

AFR (Appellant's Attorney Fees for Retrial) = $ _____   (skip if no fee-shifting agreement or statute)

RFA (Respondent's Attorney Fees for Appeal) = $ _____

RFR (Respondent's Attorney Fees for Retrial) = $ _____

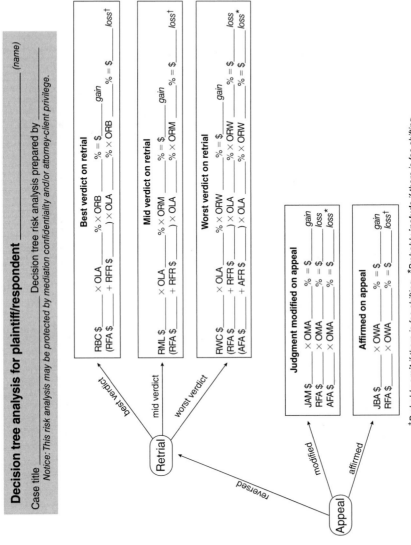

Decision tree analysis for plaintiff/respondent

_____ *(name)*

Case title _____ Decision tree risk analysis prepared by _____

Notice: This risk analysis may be protected by mediation confidentiality and/or attorney-client privilege.

Best verdict on retrial

RBC $ _____ × OLA _____ × ORB _____ % = $ _____ *gain*
(RFA $ _____ + RFR $ _____) × OLA _____ % × ORB _____ % = $ _____ *loss†*

Mid verdict on retrial

RML $ _____ × OLA _____ % × ORM _____ % = $ _____ *gain*
(RFA $ _____ + RFR $ _____) × OLA _____ % × ORM _____ % = $ _____ *loss†*

Worst verdict on retrial

RWC $ _____ × OLA _____ % × ORW _____ % = $ _____ *gain*
(RFA $ _____ + RFR $ _____) × OLA _____ % × ORW _____ % = $ _____ *loss*
(AFA $ _____) × OLA _____ % × ORW _____ % = $ _____ *loss**

best verdict

mid verdict

worst verdict

Retrial

Judgment modified on appeal

JAM $ _____ × OMA _____ % = $ _____ *gain*
RFA $ _____ × OMA _____ % = $ _____ *loss*
AFA $ _____ × OMA _____ % = $ _____ *loss**

Affirmed on appeal

JBA $ _____ × OWA _____ % = $ _____ *gain*
RFA $ _____ × OWA _____ % = $ _____ *loss†*

modified

affirmed

reversed

Appeal

*†Probably **omit** if there is fee shifting. *Probably **include** if there is fee shifting.*

Worksheets for a Plaintiff/Respondent

Decision tree analysis for plaintiff/respondent _____
(name)

Case Title _____

Decision tree risk analysis prepared by _____
Notice: This risk analysis may be protected by mediation confidentiality and/or attorney-client privilege.

Instructions: Calculate the present value for the <u>plaintiff/respondent</u> by filling in the blanks and adding up the values from all of the branches—both gains and losses.

Best verdict on retrial branch

$ _____ gain (present value of retrial best verdict)

$ _____ loss, if no fee shifting (present value of retrial best verdict plaintiff's attorney fees)

Mid verdict on retrial branch

$ _____ gain (present value of retrial mid verdict)

$ _____ loss, if no fee shifting (present value of retrial mid verdict plaintiff's attorney fees)

Worst verdict on retrial branch

$ _____ gain or, if defense verdict, zero (present value of retrial worst verdict)

$ _____ loss (present value of retrial worst verdict plaintiff's attorney fees)

$ _____ loss, if fee shifting (present value of retrial worst verdict defendant's attorney fees)

Modification of judgment on appeal branch

$ _____ gain (present value of judgment as modified on appeal)

$ _____ loss, if no fee shifting (present value of plaintiff's attorney fees on appeal)

$ _____ loss, if fee shifting (present value of defendant's attorney fees on appeal)

Affirmance on appeal branch

$ _____ gain (present value of judgment being appealed)

$ _____ loss, if no fee shifting (present value of plaintiff's attorney fees on appeal)

= $ _____ **Present value of case to plaintiff/respondent**

3. Defendant/Appellant's Decision Tree Risk Analysis

a. Typical Defendant/Appellant Cases

A typical defendant/appellant has lost at trial and now faces an unfavorable judgment, maybe a large adverse money judgment. Not only does a defendant/appellant owe the money in the judgment, but also he or she may feel the need to secure a judgment bond to avoid collection proceedings.

A defendant/appellant may also appreciate that the judgment is getting more expensive each day as postjudgment interest accrues. For a defendant/appellant, decision tree risk analysis can provide a sobering illustration that *no* outcome yields any kind of gain. For almost all defendant/appellants, every branch ends up with a loss. Given the odds against appellate victory, defendant/appellants should have a strong incentive to settle rather than pursue an appeal.

When a defendant/appellant has difficulty figuring out exactly how much to pay to get out of a bad case, as most do, a decision tree can help to determine a reasonable settlement. It bears repeating that the present value calculated by the decision tree process does not account for the emotional distress and opportunity costs the defendant/appellant is likely to experience. Thus, it may make sense for the defendant/appellant to pay more than the decision tree calculated result because peace of mind and freedom from aggravation can be very valuable indeed.

b. An Example of Risk Analysis for a Defendant/Appellant

Let's work through the following hypothetical involving a defendant/appellant:

Jeffener v. Vostferous, LLC

Alex Jeffener sued Vostferous LLC after company owner, Jerri Vost, terminated her following a 30-year history of employment. Jeffener produced evidence of her excellent performance, including testimony that her co-workers sought her help and advice, even though Jeffener worked only on the bag-sealing machines. Jeffener seemed to be able to solve any problem with machinery or materials within a few minutes. Employees also testified that Jeffener "was always there for them" whenever they experienced illnesses or difficulties.

Years ago, Jeffener had been good friends with Vost, but five years ago the relationship deteriorated. The only thing Vost had said to Jeffener in five years was "You're fired!" Employment records showed that no Vostferous employee was employed past the age of 60. Each retiring employee was replaced by someone under the age of 25.

Vostferous records showed Jeffener had been regularly admonished for socializing too much on the job and that co-workers had complained anonymously that Jeffener had invaded employees' privacy by prying into their private lives. Vost testified about the need for greater productivity in light of new, international competition. Vost admitted that his divorce five years ago was so traumatizing that his other relationships simply withered. Vost stated that Jeffener's termination was based only on her lack of productivity due to socializing. Vost explained that a "golden handshake" a few years ago—when profits were still good—was so generous that all employees over 60 accepted the offer. As to the hiring of new, younger employees, Vostferous's expert testified that summer high school student interns skewed the data.

The jury determined that Vost intended to discriminate on the basis of Jeffener's age and awarded Jeffener $1 million. On appeal, Vostferous contends (1) the evidence was insufficient because Vost never gave any indication of discrimination on the basis of age when saying only "You're fired," and (2) the trial court erred in refusing to grant a continuance when Vostferous's expert witness on data analysis of hiring and firing patterns was delayed from flying to testify at trial due to a big snow storm.

Vost is confident Vostferous has a 40-percent chance of winning the appeal. Vostferous is not seeking any modification on appeal. If the case is reversed for retrial, Vost believes Vostferous has a 50-percent chance of winning a defense verdict. But there is a 40-percent chance Jeffener will win again a $1 million judgment and 10-percent chance that the jury will award $1.2 million on retrial.

Vost estimates it will cost $40,000 to appeal and $60,000 to retry the case. There is a fee-shifting clause in the employment agreement, and Vost expects Jeffener to spend $30,000 defending the appeal and $50,000 to retry the case if the judgment is reversed and the case is remanded for trial.

Using Vost's estimates of odds, costs, and outcomes, what is the present value of defendant/appellant Vostferous's case?

Step 1. Identify the party for whom you wish to calculate the present value of a case.

Here we are calculating the case value for defendant/appellant Vostferous LLC based on estimates provided by its company president, Jerri Vost.

Step 2: Determine the possible outcomes and draw a decision tree.

Here the appeal node has two branches because the appeal may result in affirmance or reversal. The retrial node also has three branches. These reflect the possible outcomes of a best verdict, mid verdict, and worst verdict. This yields the decision tree sketch in Figure 3.15.

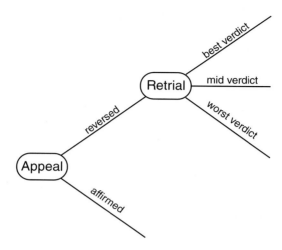

Figure 3.15

Step 3: Ascertain the odds, awards, and fees for each possible outcome.

From Vost, we gleaned the information listed in Figure 3.16.

Decision tree analysis for defendant/appellant _____Vostferous LLC_____
(name)

Case Title _____Jeffener v. Vostferous LLC_____

Decision tree risk analysis prepared by _____Brendon Ishikawa_____
Notice: This risk analysis may be protected by mediation confidentiality and/or attorney-client privilege.

Instructions: Estimate the odds, outcomes, and attorney fees for the <u>defendant/appellant</u>.

JBA (Judgment Being Appealed) = $ __1M__
JAM (Judgment as Modified) = $ __N/A__   (skip if modification not reasonably likely)

OWA (Odds of Winning on Appeal) =   __40__ %
OMA (Odds of Modification on Appeal) =   __N/A__ %   (skip if modification not reasonably likely)
OLA (Odds of Losing on Appeal) =   __60__ %
These odds must add up to: 100%

RB (Retrial Best Verdict) = $ __0__
RM (Retrial Mid Verdict) = $ __1M__
RW (Retrial Worst Verdict) = $ __1.2M__

ORB (Odds of Retrial Best Verdict) =   __50__ %
ORM (Odds of Retrial Mid Verdict) =   __40__ %
ORW (Odds of Retrial Worst Verdict) =   __10__ %
These odds must add up to: 100%

AFA (Appellant's Attorney Fees for Appeal) = $ __40K__
AFR (Appellant's Attorney Fees for Retrial) = $ __60K__
RFA (Respondent's Attorney Fees for Appeal) = $ __30K__   (skip if no fee-shifting agreement or statute)
RFR (Respondent's Attorney Fees for Retrial) = $ __50K__   (skip if no fee-shifting agreement or statute)

Figure 3.16

The defendant/appellant's estimate of a 40-percent chance of winning on appeal is *very* optimistic and probably the highest percentage that can realistically be employed for an appellant's success on appeal in the absence of other information tending to increase chances of success. For example, as we point out in Chapter 2, governmental entities fare better as appellants than other types of parties do. Also, in some instances, optimism such as displayed here may be warranted by a favorable standard of review or limited concession of error by both the appellant and respondent. Especially in the federal appellate courts, estimates exceeding 40-percent odds of an appellant's prevailing on appeal or 50-percent odds of winning on retrial are not realistic. If the litigant has lost the initial trial, any expectation of better-than-even odds of winning during a subsequent trial are probably unrealistic as well.

Step 4: Fill in the judgment outcomes and odds.

If you use the worksheet provided in this book, the result is a decision tree that looks like Figure 3.17.

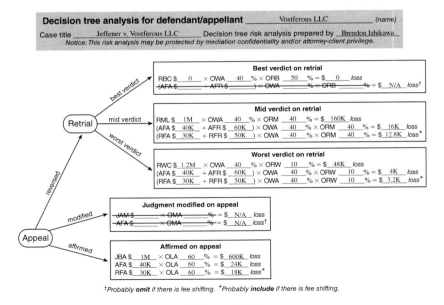

Figure 3.17

Notice that *every* possible outcome results in losses for Vostferous. In other words, there is no real "win" possible. If Vostferous is hoping for some sort of gain, this decision analysis will be, appropriately, disappointing.

Step 5: Add up the values from all of the branches.

If you use the worksheet provided in this book, adding the present value of all possible outcomes yields the result in Figure 3.18.

Decision tree analysis for defendant/appellant _____Vostferous LLC_____

(name)

Case Title _____Jeffener v. Vostferous LLC_____

Decision tree risk analysis prepared by _____Brendon Ishikawa_____
Notice: This risk analysis may be protected by mediation confidentiality and/or attorney-client privilege.

Instructions: Calculate the present value for the <u>defendant/appellant</u> by filling in the blanks and adding up the values from all of the branches—both gains and losses.

Best verdict on retrial branch
$ ____0____ loss or, if defense verdict, zero (present value of retrial best case verdict)
$ ___N/A___ loss, if no fee shifting (present value of retrial best verdict defendant's attorney fees)

Mid verdict on retrial branch
$ ___160K___ loss (present value of retrial mid verdict)
$ ___16K___ loss, if no fee shifting (present value of retrial mid verdict defendant's attorney fees)
$ ___12.8K___ loss, if fee shifting (present value of retrial mid verdict plaintiff's attorney fees)

Worst verdict on retrial branch
$ ___48K___ loss (present value of retrial worst case verdict)
$ ___4K___ loss (present value of retrial worst verdict defendant's attorney fees)
$ ___3.2K___ loss, if fee shifting (present value of retrial worst verdict plaintiff's attorney fees)

Modification of judgment on appeal branch
$ ___N/A___ loss (present value of judgment as modified on appeal)
$ ___N/A___ loss, if no fee shifting (present value of defendant's attorney fees on appeal)

Affirmance on appeal branch
$ ___600K___ loss (present value of judgment being appealed)
$ ___24K___ loss (present value of defendant's attorney fees on appeal)
$ ___18K___ loss, if fee shifting (present value of plaintiff's attorney fees on appeal)
= $ _886,000_ **Expected <u>loss</u> for defendant/appellant**

Figure 3.18

Thus, the present value of this appeal is $886,000 for the defendant/appellant. In other words, *years* of additional litigation reduces the $1 million loss to $886,000, a meager result for the high price of a long period of lost opportunities, stress and uncertainty, and the distraction of litigation (especially if the matter results in retrial). For a defendant/appellant who can afford to pay a judgment right away, it generally makes sense to settle for 90 percent of the judgment today in order to avoid financial and emotional stress.

If you draw the decision tree on a whiteboard or poster, it should look something like Figure 3.19.

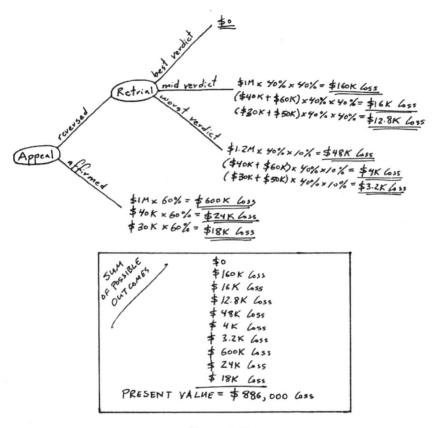

Figure 3.19

To help you with valuing cases for defendant/appellants, the next pages present worksheets you can photocopy. Again, we recommend enlarging them to 11 by 17 inches.

Worksheets for a Defendant/Appellant

Decision tree analysis for defendant/appellant _____
(name)

Case Title _____

Decision tree risk analysis prepared by _____
Notice: This risk analysis may be protected by mediation confidentiality and/or attorney-client privilege.

Instructions: Estimate the odds, outcomes, and attorney fees for the <u>defendant/appellant</u>.

JBA (Judgment Being Appealed) = $ _____

JAM (Judgment as Modified) = $ _____   (skip if modification not reasonably likely)

OWA (Odds of Winning on Appeal) =   _____ %

OMA (Odds of Modification on Appeal) =   _____ %   (skip if modification not reasonably likely)

OLA (Odds of Losing on Appeal) =   _____ %

These odds must add up to: 100%

RB (Retrial Best Verdict) = $ _____

RM (Retrial Mid Verdict) = $ _____

RW (Retrial Worst Verdict) = $ _____

ORB (Odds of Retrial Best Verdict) =   _____ %

ORM (Odds of Retrial Mid Verdict) =   _____ %

ORW (Odds of Retrial Worst Verdict) =   _____ %

These odds must add up to: 100%

AFA (Appellant's Attorney Fees for Appeal) = $ _____

AFR (Appellant's Attorney Fees for Retrial) = $ _____

RFA (Respondent's Attorney Fees for Appeal) = $ _____   (skip if no fee-shifting agreement or statute)

RFR (Respondent's Attorney Fees for Retrial) = $ _____   (skip if no fee-shifting agreement or statute)

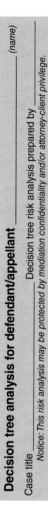

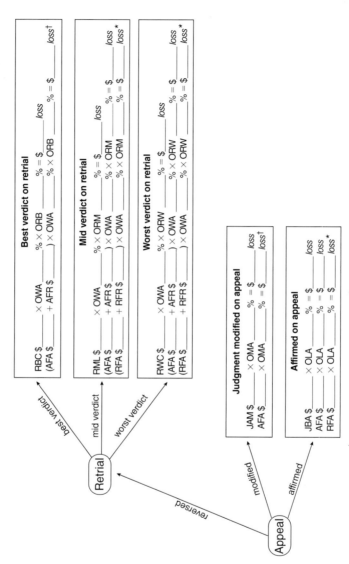

Decision tree analysis for defendant/appellant

Case title _____   _____ (name)

Decision tree risk analysis prepared by _____

Notice: This risk analysis may be protected by mediation confidentiality and/or attorney-client privilege.

Best verdict on retrial

| RBC $ _____ | × OWA _____ | % × ORB _____ | % = $ _____ | loss |
| (AFA $ _____ |) × OWA _____ | % × ORB _____ | % = $ _____ | loss† |

Mid verdict on retrial

RML $ _____	× OWA _____	% × ORM _____	% = $ _____	loss
(AFA $ _____	) × OWA _____	% × ORM _____	% = $ _____	loss
(RFA $ _____	) × OWA _____	% × ORM _____	% = $ _____	loss *

Worst verdict on retrial

RWC $ _____	× OWA _____	% × ORW _____	% = $ _____	loss
(AFA $ _____	) × OWA _____	% × ORW _____	% = $ _____	loss
(RFA $ _____	) × OWA _____	% × ORW _____	% = $ _____	loss *

Judgment modified on appeal

| JAM $ _____ | × OMA _____ | % = $ _____ | loss |
| AFA $ _____ | × OMA _____ | % = $ _____ | loss† |

Affirmed on appeal

JBA $ _____	× OLA _____	% = $ _____	loss
AFA $ _____	× OLA _____	% = $ _____	loss
RFA $ _____	× OLA _____	% = $ _____	loss *

best verdict

mid verdict

worst verdict

Retrial

modified

affirmed

reversed

Appeal

†Probably **omit** if there is fee shifting. *Probably **include** if there is fee shifting.

Worksheets for a Defendant/Appellant

Decision tree analysis for defendant/appellant _____
                                                   (name)

        Case Title _____

      Decision tree risk analysis prepared by _____
      Notice: This risk analysis may be protected by mediation confidentiality and/or attorney-client privilege.

Instructions: Calculate the present value for the <u>defendant/appellant</u> by filling in the blanks and adding up the values from all of the branches—both gains and losses.

Best verdict on retrial branch

$ _____ loss or, if defense verdict, zero (present value of retrial best case verdict)

$ _____ loss, if no fee shifting (present value of retrial best verdict defendant's attorney fees)

Mid verdict on retrial branch

$ _____ loss (present value of retrial mid verdict)

$ _____ loss, if no fee shifting (present value of retrial mid verdict defendant's attorney fees)

$ _____ loss, if fee shifting (present value of retrial mid verdict plaintiff's attorney fees)

Worst verdict on retrial branch

$ _____ loss (present value of retrial worst case verdict)

$ _____ loss (present value of retrial worst verdict defendant's attorney fees)

$ _____ loss, if fee shifting (present value of retrial worst verdict plaintiff's attorney fees)

Modification of judgment on appeal branch

$ _____ loss (present value of judgment as modified on appeal)

$ _____ loss, if no fee shifting (present value of defendant's attorney fees on appeal)

Affirmance on appeal branch

$ _____ loss (present value of judgment being appealed)

$ _____ loss (present value of defendant's attorney fees on appeal)

$ _____ loss, if no fee shifting (present value of plaintiff's attorney fees on appeal)

= $ _____ Expected <u>loss</u> for defendant/appellant

4. *Defendant/Respondent's Decision Tree Risk Analysis*

a. *Typical Defendant/Respondent Cases*

Of all the categories of litigants on appeal, the defendant/respondent is often the party who is most reluctant to make any offers to settle the case. The defendant/respondent may be angry and indignant at being sued. And accusations in the pleadings and motions that cast the defendant/respondent in an ugly light may exacerbate these negative emotions. Moreover, the defendant/respondent has won in the trial court. Especially if the defendant/respondent won on a procedural motion before the matter went to trial, the defendant/respondent may assume an attitude of "nothing to lose" by continuing with the appeal. After all, to suffer an ultimate loss, the defendant/respondent must lose *both* the appeal and the retrial. It will be years before the plaintiff has any chance of success, a reality that often spurs on defendant/respondents.

For defendant/respondents, decision tree risk analysis may shed a new light on the realities of appellate litigation. For one thing, the defendant/respondent may realize that there is no outcome in which he or she gains *anything at all* through litigation. There is only the potential for losses, even if only those due to attorney fee expenses. Even with fee shifting, the best that a defendant/respondent can hope for is to escape with zero loss. In other words, *nothing will improve* for a defendant/respondent by continuing with the litigation. And the possibilities of loss combined with ongoing expenses often make unexpectedly large settlement offers entirely logical for a defendant/respondent.

b. *An Example of Risk Analysis for a Defendant/Respondent*

Let's work through the following hypothetical:

Calorine Construction, Inc. v. Volt & Wire LLP

This case arises out of the construction of a twin high-rise project called Newlett Towers. Calorine Construction, Inc. served as the general contractor for this $200 million project. Calorine subcontracted with Volt & Wire LLP to install the electrical systems. Volt & Wire began work after the foundation had been poured and found that none of the major electrical cables had been installed. Worse yet, no channels had been left for the cables. Construction stopped while Calorine and Volt & Wire argued over who had to pay the considerable cost of cutting the foundation for the main electrical cables. Fearing penalties that would accrue upon delayed project completion, Calorine relented and paid to have the foundation cut and redone to accommodate the electrical cables. Volt & Wire then installed the electrical systems.

Calorine sued Volt & Wire and argued that all electrical systems and cables were the responsibility of Volt & Wire. Calorine further argued the subcontract stated that "any remedial work necessary to install, fit, move, or adjust any cables" was to be "done solely by subcontractor." Volt & Wire defended on grounds that the blueprints showed the foundation to be poured by Calorine was supposed to have deep channels for the main electrical cables.

By the end of trial, there were blueprints and large exhibits everywhere in the courtroom. Expert witnesses flew in from five different states to testify as to the proper interpretation of the blueprints, how much concrete cutting should have cost, and whether there were cheaper alternatives to cutting through the reinforced foundation. About the only thing the parties agreed on was that if a liquidated damages clause in the subcontract applied, damages would be set at $1 million if Volt & Wire were the party responsible for the cost of remedying the faulty foundation.

The trial judge entered judgment for Volt & Wire, and Calorine now appeals on grounds that (1) the trial court should have applied a recently enacted statute excluding "preliminary blueprints" as evidence in disputes over construction, and (2) the trial court erred because the contract specified that Volt & Wire had the duty to move the route for the electrical cables or to remedy the absence of channels.

Volt & Wire estimates a 70-percent chance of securing an affirmance on appeal. However, if the matter goes to retrial, Volt & Wire estimates a 50-percent chance of another defense verdict and a 50-percent chance of losing with a $1 million verdict, a certain worst case outcome due to a liquidated damages clause in the contract. The appeal is expected to cost $40,000. Retrial, however, would not require many witnesses and would likely cost only $50,000. Volt & Wire's owners are driven crazy by how expensive the opposing attorneys' bills have been and expect Calorine to spend $60,000 on appeal and $80,000 on retrial. There is a fee-shifting agreement that applies, much to Volt & Wire's chagrin.

Using Volt & Wire's estimates of odds, costs, and outcomes, what is the present value of the case?

Step 1: Identify the party for whom you wish to calculate the present value of a case.

Here we are doing a decision tree analysis for defendant/respondent Volt & Wire.

Step 2: Determine the possible outcomes and draw a decision tree.

According to Volt & Wire's estimate, this appeal will result in either affirmance or reversal because Calorine has not requested a modification of judgment. Thus, the appeal node has two branches: affirmed and reversed. On retrial, Volt & Wire estimates there are two possible outcomes: a best verdict and a worst verdict. No mid verdict outcome is necessary because Volt & Wire concludes that damages will either be proven or not. Cases with liquidated damages clauses or in which there is no dispute over the amount of damages (but only liability) do not need a mid verdict branch. With a quick sketch, you get the decision tree in Figure 3.20.

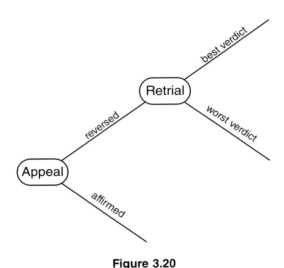

Figure 3.20

Step 3: Ascertain the odds, awards, and fees for each possible outcome.

Using the first worksheet for defendant/respondents yields Figure 3.21.

Step 4: Fill in the judgment outcomes and odds.

Proceeding to the second decision tree worksheet from this book yields Figure 3.22.

As we have noted, this decision tree demonstrates an important concept for defendant/respondent Volt & Wire, namely that no outcome involving continued litigation will improve its situation: continued litigation serves only to risk a worse result for the defendant/respondent.

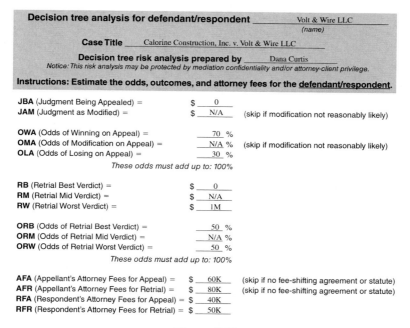

Figure 3.21

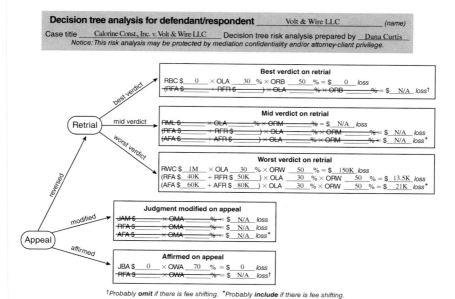

Figure 3.22

Step 5: Add up the values from all of the branches.

Using the third worksheet for defendant/respondents, the calculation of present value looks like Figure 3.23.

Decision tree analysis for defendant/respondent _____ Volt & Wire LLC _____
(name)

Case Title _____ Calorine Construction, Inc. v. Volt & Wire LLC _____

Decision tree risk analysis prepared by _____ Dana Curtis _____
Notice: This risk analysis may be protected by mediation confidentiality and/or attorney-client privilege.

Instructions: Calculate the present value for the defendant/respondent by filling in the blanks and adding up the values from all of the branches—both gains and losses.

Best verdict on retrial branch
$ ___0___ loss or, if defense verdict, zero (present value of retrial best case verdict)
$ ___N/A___ loss, if no fee shifting (present value of retrial best verdict defendant's attorney fees)

Mid verdict on retrial branch
$ ___N/A___ loss (present value of retrial mid verdict)
$ ___N/A___ loss, (present value of retrial mid verdict defendant's attorney fees)
$ ___N/A___ loss, if fee shifting (present value of retrial mid verdict plaintiff's attorney fees)

Worst verdict on retrial branch
$ ___150K___ loss (present value of retrial worst case verdict)
$ ___13.5K___ loss (present value of retrial worst verdict defendant's attorney fees)
$ ___21K___ loss, if fee shifting (present value of retrial worst verdict plaintiff's attorney fees)

Modification of judgment on appeal branch
$ ___N/A___ loss (present value of judgment as modified on appeal)
$ ___N/A___ loss (present value of defendant's attorney fees on appeal)
$ ___N/A___ loss, if fee shifting (present value of plaintiff's attorney fees on appeal)

Affirmance on appeal branch
$ ___0___ loss (present value of judgment being appealed)
$ ___N/A___ loss, if no fee shifting (present value of defendant's attorney fees on appeal)

= $ _184,500_ **Expected loss for defendant/respondent**

Figure 3.23

If Volt & Wire arrived at the mediation prepared to make only a nuisance case offer, this bottom line may be eye opening. When decision trees yield particularly surprising results based on a party's own estimates of odds and outcomes, the party may experience a range of emotions from shock to disbelief or anger. Sometimes the party directs the surprise in the form of negative emotions toward legal counsel. In such circumstances, it is advisable to give parties and attorneys enough time to let the analysis sink in, to have a discussion about the impact of the calculation on their prior assumptions, and to enable them to begin to think about how to approach further negotiations. Although this may take some time during a mediation that has already been going on for many hours, it is a very valuable stage of the process. At its best, it redirects the focus from defending a position to becoming oriented toward settlement.

Also, the decision tree risk analysis might be a vehicle for discussing the emotions and financial stresses that have thus far accompanied the litigation for Volt & Wire. The discussion of the impact of the *process* of decision tree analysis on Volt & Wire may help it realize that avoiding continued litigation is worth a more logical settlement offer than a nuisance case amount.

In this hypothetical, a hand drawn sketch of the decision tree analysis looks like Figure 3.24.

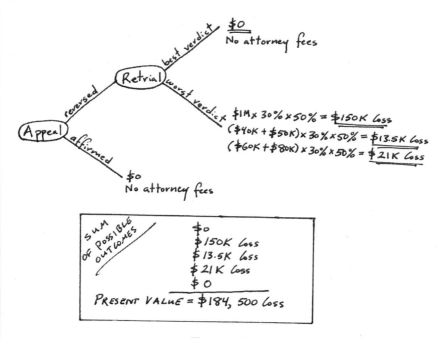

Figure 3.24

Finally, we note that it often makes sense for the settlement offer to exceed the present value of the case as calculated by the decision tree. On the one hand, it's hard to put a price tag on emotion. On the other hand, peace of mind can be priceless—or at least sufficiently valuable to increase the amount offered to end what may be painful and protracted litigation. We explore this in-depth below, in Part F.9 of this chapter.

To help you with valuing cases for defendant/respondents, the next pages present worksheets that you can enlarge and photocopy.

Worksheets for a Defendant/Respondent

Decision tree analysis for defendant/respondent _____
(name)

Case Title _____

Decision tree risk analysis prepared by _____
Notice: This risk analysis may be protected by mediation confidentiality and/or attorney-client privilege.

Instructions: Estimate the odds, outcomes, and attorney fees for the <u>defendant/respondent</u>.

JBA (Judgment Being Appealed) = $ _____

JAM (Judgment as Modified) = $ _____   (skip if modification not reasonably likely)

OWA (Odds of Winning on Appeal) =   _____ %

OMA (Odds of Modification on Appeal) =   _____ %   (skip if modification not reasonably likely)

OLA (Odds of Losing on Appeal) =   _____ %

These odds must add up to: 100%

RB (Retrial Best Verdict) = $ _____

RM (Retrial Mid Verdict) = $ _____

RW (Retrial Worst Verdict) = $ _____

ORB (Odds of Retrial Best Verdict) =   _____ %

ORM (Odds of Retrial Mid Verdict) =   _____ %

ORW (Odds of Retrial Worst Verdict) =   _____ %

These odds must add up to: 100%

AFA (Appellant's Attorney Fees for Appeal) = $ _____   (skip if no fee-shifting agreement or statute)

AFR (Appellant's Attorney Fees for Retrial) = $ _____   (skip if no fee-shifting agreement or statute)

RFA (Respondent's Attorney Fees for Appeal) = $ _____

RFR (Respondent's Attorney Fees for Retrial) = $ _____

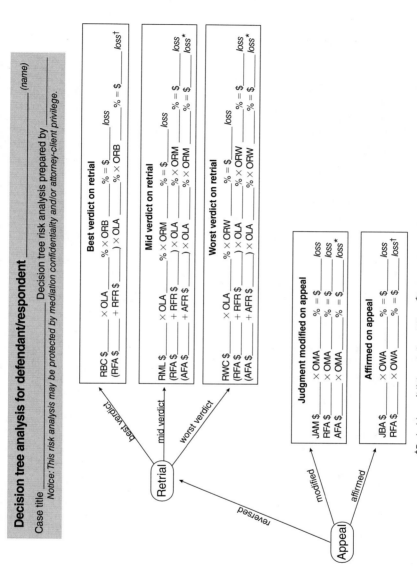

Decision tree analysis for defendant/respondent

Case title _____   _____ (name)
Decision tree risk analysis prepared by _____

Notice: This risk analysis may be protected by mediation confidentiality and/or attorney-client privilege.

Best verdict on retrial

RBC $_____ × OLA _____ % × ORB _____ % = $_____ *loss*
(RFA $_____ + RFR $_____) × OLA _____ % × ORB _____ % = $_____ *loss†*

Mid verdict on retrial

RML $_____ × OLA _____ % × ORM _____ % = $_____ *loss*
(RFA $_____ + RFR $_____) × OLA _____ % × ORM _____ % = $_____ *loss*
(AFA $_____) × OLA _____ % × ORM _____ % = $_____ *loss**

Worst verdict on retrial

RWC $_____ × OLA _____ % × ORW _____ % = $_____ *loss*
(RFA $_____ + RFR $_____) × OLA _____ % × ORW _____ % = $_____ *loss*
(AFA $_____) × OLA _____ % × ORW _____ % = $_____ *loss**

best verdict
mid verdict
worst verdict

Retrial

reversed

Judgment modified on appeal

JAM $_____ × OMA _____ % = $_____ *loss*
RFA $_____ × OMA _____ % = $_____ *loss**
AFA $_____ × OMA _____ % = $_____ *loss**

Affirmed on appeal

JBA $_____ × OWA _____ % = $_____ *loss*
RFA $_____ × OWA _____ % = $_____ *loss†*

modified
affirmed

Appeal

*†Probably **omit** if there is fee shifting.   *Probably **include** if there is fee shifting.*

Worksheets for a Defendant/Respondent

Decision tree analysis for defendant/respondent _____
(name)

   Case Title _____

    Decision tree risk analysis prepared by _____
   Notice: This risk analysis may be protected by mediation confidentiality and/or attorney-client privilege.

Instructions: Calculate the present value for the defendant/respondent by filling in the blanks and adding up the values from all of the branches—both gains and losses.

Best verdict on retrial branch

$ _____ loss or, if defense verdict, zero (present value of retrial best case verdict)

$ _____ loss, if no fee shifting (present value of retrial best verdict defendant's attorney fees)

Mid verdict on retrial branch

$ _____ loss (present value of retrial mid verdict)

$ _____ loss, (present value of retrial mid verdict defendant's attorney fees)

$ _____ loss, if fee shifting (present value of retrial mid verdict plaintiff's attorney fees)

Worst verdict on retrial branch

$ _____ loss (present value of retrial worst verdict)

$ _____ loss (present value of retrial worst verdict defendant's attorney fees)

$ _____ loss, if fee shifting (present value of retrial worst verdict plaintiff's attorney fees)

Modification of judgment on appeal branch

$ _____ loss (present value of judgment as modified on appeal)

$ _____ loss (present value of defendant's attorney fees on appeal)

$ _____ loss, if no fee shifting (present value of plaintiff's attorney fees on appeal)

Affirmance on appeal branch

$ _____ loss (present value of judgment being appealed)

$ _____ loss, if fee shifting (present value of defendant's attorney fees on appeal)

= $ _____ **Expected loss for defendant/respondent**

F.   Frequently Asked Questions about Decision Trees

1.   Question: I Just Did a Decision Tree Risk Analysis and Got a Negative Number for Present Value. Did I Do Something Wrong?

No, you likely did the analysis properly and reached the correct result. *For defendants the present value of a case is always going to be negative.* This is true whether they are defendant/appellants or defendant/respondents. The reason is that defendants stand to gain nothing through litigation. The only question for defendants is how much they will lose before the litigation process is exhausted.

With surprising frequency, a decision tree risk analysis also yields a negative value for plaintiffs. Consider the following illustration:

Vilwek v. Rewarmed-News.com

Charlie Vilwek is a freelance writer who is suing Rewarmed-News .com for copyright infringement. The trial judge dismissed the case before trial based on Rewarmed-News.com's argument that it engaged in parody rather than copyright infringement. Vilwek has taken an appeal and acknowledges that his chances of reversal are no better than the average civil appeal in the federal appellate courts—namely about a 20-percent chance of reversal. But if Vilwek can secure a reversal, he estimates a 50-percent chance of winning $250,000 in damages at trial. There is an equally likely chance of a defense verdict. Vilwek estimates it will cost $25,000 to appeal and $25,000 for trial if he gets a reversal. There is no fee-shifting rule or statute that applies.

We can calculate the present value of the appeal for Vilwek with the decision tree in Figure 3.25.

In other words, this appeal has a negative value of $5,000 for Vilwek. This negative number means that the Vilwek is better off dismissing the appeal than continuing with the litigation. The surprising result of the decision tree risk analysis reveals that the odds of winning are likely too small and the expenses of litigation too great to make it worthwhile from an economic standpoint for Vilwek to continue to litigate the case. For Vilwek, *any* amount of money secured through settlement should be accepted. In such a case, a nuisance offer makes sense both for the offerer and for the offeree.

2.   Question: How Do I Determine Present Value if There Are Both an Appeal and a Cross-Appeal?

When faced with an appeal and a cross-appeal, you need to draw *two* decision trees: one for the appeal and one for the cross-appeal. Then take the products of each decision tree and add them together for the present value of the case. For example, if the plaintiff is appealing the verdict as inadequate and the defendant is cross-appealing the verdict as unfair due to instructional error, you must draw two decision trees for the plaintiff: one for the plaintiff/appellant on the plaintiff's appeal and one for the plaintiff/respondent on the defendant's cross-appeal. Each of these decision trees will yield a value. Add both values to determine the present value for the appeal and cross-appeal to the plaintiff.

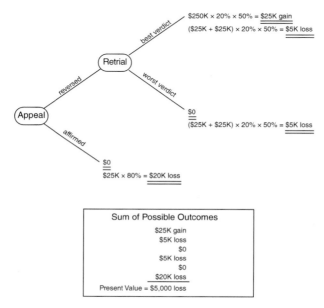

Figure 3.25

3. Question: The Worksheets Have Lines That Predict Who Will Be the Prevailing Party for Purposes of Attorney Fee Shifting. How Do You Know Who Will Be the Prevailing Party?

In formulating the worksheets, we made the following assumptions about which party would be entitled to fee shifting for each outcome:

- If a judgment is affirmed, the respondent will be the prevailing party because the appellant will have lost the appeal.

- If a judgment is modified, the appellant will be the prevailing party because the appellate court has granted the relief—albeit partial—the appellant requested.

On retrial, we can conclude the following for purposes of fee shifting:

- A party is prevailing in its _best_ verdict scenario

- A party is losing in its _worst_ verdict scenario

The mid verdict scenario is more challenging to characterize by category. This scenario most likely means the plaintiff has recovered _some_ money damages from the jury or trier of fact. Even though the verdict fell short of everything requested, the plaintiff has avoided a defense verdict, which likely renders the plaintiff the prevailing party. Our worksheets reflect these assumptions.

We recognize that these assumptions may not be appropriate in a given case. If you believe any of these assumptions are unwarranted, adjust the worksheet accordingly. For example, if an appeal in a case subject to attorney fee shifting focuses only on the punitive damages, the plaintiff/respondent will probably be the prevailing party for purposes of attorney fees for _every_ possible outcome. Thus, in such a decision tree analysis for the plaintiff/respondent, attorney fees could be completely ignored for the plaintiff/respondent because the attorney fees are reimbursed in every outcome. In short, you need to consider adjustments whenever your case has unique considerations that may not be applicable in most appeals.

4. Question: In the Hypothetical for the Defendant/ Appellant, You Mention Postjudgment Interest. Is It Possible to Add the Cost of Postjudgment Interest to the Defendant/Appellant's Decision Tree?

Yes! Many jurisdictions impose statutory postjudgment interest on judgments being appealed. In many jurisdictions, the rate of interest is quite high—often set at 10 percent per year. When a case is pending in an appellate court that averages 18 months to decision and subsequent petition for review or certiorari adds another 6 months to be ruled on, the effect of postjudgment interest is substantial. For the defendant/appellant's hypothetical, you would add postjudgment interest (say, for example, at a 10-percent rate) by adding another line of calculations to the affirmance branch of the decision tree. That line would be the following:

$$(\$1M \text{ judgment} \times 2 \text{ years} \times 10\% \text{ interest}) \times$$
$$60\% \text{ chance losing on appeal} = \$120K \text{ loss}$$

This additional $120,000 loss due to the accrual of postjudgment interest would increase the expected loss from the case for the defendant/appellant from an $886,000-loss to a $1,006,000-loss! In other words, the effect of post-judgment interest means that Vostferous is better off dismissing the appeal and immediately paying the $1 million judgment than continuing to litigate even if its highly favorable estimates of success on appeal and retrial are correct. Figure 3.26 shows the decision tree analysis for Vostferous if postjudgment interest is taken into account.

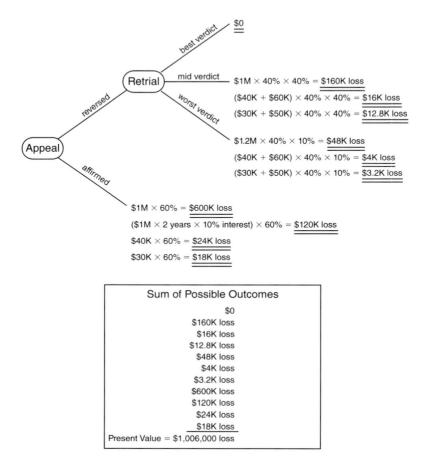

Figure 3.26

Note that the postjudgment interest line is not added to any of the retrial branches because each of those branches depends on the judgment's being reversed by the appellate court; thus, there is no judgment that remains intact to accrue postjudgment interest. If the costs of the appellate bond necessary to stay the judgment pending appeal are substantial, they can be added to the amount of the judgment on the line used to calculate the present value of the postjudgment interest likely to accrue.

5. Question: Why Not Keep Going with More Nodes and Branches?

For each of the hypotheticals and worksheets we provide, we end the analysis at retrial. In other words, we analyze the value of the case as if both parties will give up after the judgment is entered on retrial. After retrial, however, any aggrieved party would have the right to another appeal, hence the question: why not add more nodes for appeal after retrial? The answer is that you can add as many (or few) nodes and branches as you believe to be necessary to properly value the case. However, as the events become more remote in time, they add much more complexity to the decision even though they make little difference in the ultimate calculation of present value. New users of decision trees often have a tendency to make the decision trees too complex. This may be because there are many statistically unlikely possibilities at each turn. For example, on appeal a case could get involuntarily dismissed for lack of justiciability, defective notice of appeal, or inadequate appellate record. However, such outcomes are sufficiently unlikely to warrant their exclusion from the decision tree. Once you complete a few decision tree risk analyses, you will see that additional complexity usually makes a trivial difference in the final number.

6. Question: As an Attorney or Mediator, What Do I Do When an Appellant Wants to Use an 80-Percent Chance of Succeeding on Appeal?

For each of the hypotheticals we presented in this chapter, we attributed very optimistic estimates to the parties, which we find to be commonplace. Dealing with parties who assert even more optimistic odds can be challenging. For example, *any* estimate by an appellant of having an 80-percent chance of success is unrealistic. Due to confirmation bias, it is better not to do a decision tree analysis at all than to use wildly unrealistic numbers. In other words, an unrealistic analysis is likely to do more harm than good in helping parties assess their cases.

7. Question: Why Didn't You Provide a Line for Calculations Pertaining to the Attorney Fees I've Already Spent on My Attorney and That I Still Owe?

Attorney fees already awarded by the court are part of the judgment. Thus, the judgment calculation line for affirmance or modification on appeal already includes them. Attorney fees that are already spent (or still owed) by a party to that party's *own* attorneys and not subject to fee shifting are not included in the judgment because they are what economists call a "sunk cost." Although a party that has incurred the sunk costs probably wishes he or she had not sunk them, these costs are unaffected by future litigation.[7] In other words, they do not affect the present value of the case. Consequently, we exclude them from decision tree risk analysis.

---

7. KAHNEMAN, *supra* note 2, at 342–46.

8. Question: What if There Is a Significant Chance the Appellate Court Will Dismiss the Case for Lack of Jurisdiction, Such as a Late Notice of Appeal, Lack of Standing, or Other Problem of Justiciability?

As a rule of thumb, approximately 5 percent of civil appeals are involuntarily dismissed by the appellate courts because appellants have filed a defective notice of appeal, failed to timely pay filing fees or comply with some other procedural requirement, or filed an otherwise nonjusticiable appeal (such as for lack of standing or in a case that has become moot). Although jurisdictional and justiciability issues are beyond the scope of this book, in certain appeals they are significant issues. When involuntary dismissal is a significant possibility, a decision tree analysis may account for this potential result by adding the percentage odds of an involuntary dismissal to the percentage odds of an affirmance. The reason for the simple addition is that both involuntary dismissal and affirmance on the merits have the same effect: the appellant loses.

9. Question: Does a Decision Tree Analysis Calculate the True Value of a Case?

a. What You Get When Completing a Decision Tree Analysis

A completed decision tree yields the number of dollars representing the present value of an appeal. If a decision tree analysis incorporates a party's own estimates of odds and outcomes, then the present value calculation is the logical settlement value. If we were writing this book for purely logical and emotionless robots, this chapter would be complete. A robot would unhesitatingly accept a settlement offer even one dollar better than that calculated by the decision tree analysis. However, a robot would be unable to answer which is better, enduring years of litigation to pursue a case pegged by a decision tree analysis at $75,000 or immediately receiving a bag containing $75,000 in crisp hundred-dollar bills. To a robot, the value of these options is indistinguishable. We humans know the answer: take the money and run.[8]

The quandary for robots weighing an instant payout against an equal value in prolonged litigation illustrates an important point: decision tree analysis does not ascribe any value to the emotions and stress inherent in litigation. Put another way, decision tree analysis cannot calculate the value of "angry," "vindicated," "dreadful," or "relieved." Because we are not robots, we should

---

8. *Take the Money and Run* (Cinerama, 1969; MGM, 2004). Robots don't understand humor either.

take into account the very real value of avoiding stress, negative emotions, and stigma.

b.   We Gladly Pay to Avoid "Yucky" Stuff. Sometimes We Pay a Lot!

There is value—often a big value—in avoiding emotionally "yucky" stuff. Consider the example of a mansion in Calabasas, California, with six bedrooms and beautiful views that was originally appraised for $2.65 million but ultimately sold at an auction for half price to the only bidder. There was nothing functionally wrong with the mansion. Indeed, the mansion was almost completely renovated when the owners' children, Lyle and Erik Menendez, notoriously shot their parents to death in another house. Even though the murders did *not* take place in the Calabasas mansion, mere connection to the infamous brothers erased $1.3 million of value for the property.[9] Negative emotions can greatly reduce the value of things that otherwise function perfectly and exactly as intended. We often pay to avoid unpleasant emotions or stress—a practice that actually makes sense.

   This example offers a stark reminder that it can make sense to pay a premium to get rid of a bad situation or to accept less than the functional value of a thing to extricate oneself from stress and stigma. Thus, it makes sense for judgment creditors to accept a lower dollar figure and judgment debtors to offer above the decision tree value to account for the avoidance of stresses and negative emotions of the litigation process. So, if you're a plaintiff and the decision tree analysis calculation yields $75,000, the *real* value of the lawsuit to *you* is probably a whole lot less. Why? Emotions have value. Often our emotions have quite a bit of value. The value of avoiding emotional yucky stuff is fully reflected in our legal system. We award money damages for emotional distress, humiliation, pain and suffering, and all kinds of other experiences that we cannot analytically quantify but that *matter* to us.

   "There is an inherent irony in the judicial system in that individuals who bring suit may endure injury from the very process through which they seek redress. The legal process itself is often a trauma. Although many hope—and some find—that it is ultimately restorative, no one brings a lawsuit for his or her health. Justice Learned Hand observed that, 'as a litigant I should dread a lawsuit beyond almost anything short of sickness and death.'"[10] If the plaintiff in a case on appeal dreads every moment of the litigation, then the plaintiff should be willing to accept a lower amount of money to settle than the

---

9.   Alan Abrahamson, *Menendez House in Calabasas Sold for $1.3 million: Courts: Home was Being Finished at Time of Murders*, L.A. Times (Sept. 9, 1994), http://articles.latimes .com/1994-09-09/local/me-36307_1_erik-menendez.

10.   Larry H. Strasburger, *The Litigant-Patient: Mental Health Consequences of Civil Litigation*, 27 J. Am. Acad. Psychiatry & L. Online 203, 204 (1999).

decision tree analysis might suggest. Conversely, if the defendant experiences a great deal of stress dealing with the litigation, the defendant should be willing to pay a premium to get rid of the case.

It is hard to put a value on peace of mind in the abstract. Just remember that litigants often pay for peace of mind. We cannot provide you with a mathematical formula for valuing emotions. However, we can point to research suggesting that although money usually drives litigation, plaintiffs frequently feel better after settling a case, not so much due to receipt of money but seemingly due "to issues besides the money, e.g., not being reminded of the accident, the decreased stress of not having to deal with courts and attorneys and the feelings of vindication or satisfaction."[11]

c. The "True" Costs of Litigation

When we include costs in a decision tree analysis of civil appeals, we are accounting for attorney fees and the expenses of court filings. However, in many cases, there are much larger hidden costs of the litigation. Consider the dispute that arose between Texaco and Pennzoil when each attempted to take over Getty Oil in 1984. After Texaco bought all Getty common stock, Pennzoil sued based on a preexisting contract to purchase almost half of Getty Oil. During the litigation, the combined value of the companies declined by more than $3 billion as Pennzoil stock rose about one-sixth and Texaco stock fell by two-thirds. The combined loss *far* exceeded the litigation costs and caused some scholars to conclude that the market simply became irrational in valuing the companies during litigation.[12] The litigation dragged on as antipathy between company leaders prevented a settlement. Texaco actually declared bankruptcy because the liens resulting from the $10-billion judgment scared away suppliers and dried up the company's access to credit.[13] Eventually the case settled, and the companies regained approximately two-thirds of the loss of their equity.[14] "The Texaco-Pennzoil case demonstrates that legal disputes can impose large costs on a firm, and that the indirect effects of conflict on profitability can be substantially greater than the direct expenses of the litigation."[15]

Of course, litigation costs such as these extend far beyond billion-dollar cases. Individuals too may risk bankruptcy if a worst-case outcome occurs. Businesses may find their lines of credit revoked during litigation. People may not be able to lease new cars while their cases continue to drag on. Even in the corporate context, litigation usually provides enough distress (or at least

11. Renée L. Binder, Michael R. Trimble & Dale E. McNiel, *Is Money a Cure? Follow-up of Litigants in England.* 19 J. Am. Acad. Psychiatry & L. Online 151, 158 (1991).
12. David M. Cutler & Lawrence H. Summers, 19 *The Costs of Conflict Resolution and Financial Distress: Evidence from the Texaco-Pennzoil Litigation.* 19 Rand J. Econ. 169 (1988).
13. *Id.* at 167–68.
14. *Id.* at 157.
15. *Id.* at 170.

distraction) to negatively impact day-to-day operations. Unfortunately, these consequences of litigation often remain unrecognized. They also are not included in the decision tree analysis. However, they are very real costs that often dwarf the costs of litigation if parties consider only attorney fees and court costs.

G.   Conclusion

Decision tree analysis provides an effective process by which parties can begin to answer the question, "What is my case worth?" Rather than relying on hunches, anecdotes, or guesstimates, parties can use decision tree analysis, which represents a logical way to determine the present value of a case. Logic alone, however, fails to account for much of what is important to people, namely their emotional well-being, reputations, and freedom to pursue fulfilling opportunities, in short their happiness. Consequently, the outcome of a decision tree analysis is a dollar value that a stressed-out defendant should be willing to increase in a negotiation. So too a decision tree calculation yields a present value that a plaintiff who is emotionally sick over the case should be willing to discount substantially. Ultimately, the meaningful settlement value of a case should be based on both calculations of present value by decision tree analysis and the hidden emotional and opportunity costs of litigation.

Section II
The Appellate Mediation Process

A.   Introduction

In Section I, we provided an overview of appellate law and procedure that will help advocates and mediators participate effectively in appellate mediation. Thus, Section I provides the background from which all appellate mediations emerge and the context in which the mediation process operates. In describing standards of review, analysis of prejudice, and the basics of case evaluation for civil appeals, Section I also provides information about the language and concepts employed in an appellate mediation.

In Section II, we turn to the appellate mediation process itself. We describe, from beginning to end, the approach to mediating appellate cases we have developed and refined over 20 years of practicing and teaching appellate mediation.

B.   We Offer an Approach to Appellate Mediation that Will Help New and Experienced Mediation Participants Achieve Success

We understand that readers come from various backgrounds and have differing levels of experience in mediation. For this reason, we set forth our approach in a manner that attorneys with no experience in appellate mediation and brand new appellate mediators can use to become competent in this arena. Nonetheless, we anticipate that experienced mediators and attorneys with considerable experience representing clients in mediation will also gain valuable insights from reading this section. Most mediators and lawyers work primarily on cases at the trial court level—and sometimes mediators get involved before a lawsuit is filed. For these experienced mediators and attorneys, we provide insights into what distinguishes appellate mediation from trial court and prefiling mediation.

We also understand that every mediator has a unique style that arises from a constellation of strengths and weaknesses and that attorneys may have strong preferences in how the mediation process is conducted. Nevertheless, we invite experienced mediators and lawyers to expand their skills and understanding in this specialized area of mediation by considering the perspective, approach, and style set forth in this section, which we have found to be effective.

As we explained in the introduction, the appellate mediation process uniquely benefits from a structure that (1) is client-centered, focused on problem solving, and primarily facilitative; (2) includes all necessary activities for achieving a successful outcome; (3) separates the steps into discrete stages so the mediator and participants can understand the focus of activities at the moment; and (4) prevents premature or hasty efforts, such as beginning bargaining over money before exploring whether the underlying problem is even monetary in nature or capable of being solved by one party writing a check. Thus, our approach has the following components:[1]

Premediation

Goals: Learn about the case, lawyers, and parties. Clarify the scope of mediation. Confirm the logistics, approach, confidentiality, and fees (if any).

How to achieve goals: Establish rapport and trust in mediator and process.

Phase 1: Opening the Appellate Mediation

Goals: Discuss mediation and agree on roles, agenda, and procedures.

How to achieve goals: Establish rapport and trust; set an optimistic tone.

Phase 2: Exchanging Information

Goals: Exchange perspectives on what happened, parties' needs, interests, goals, concerns, feelings, and analyses of legal issues.

How to achieve goals: Demonstrate an understanding of all views. Bridge gaps in understanding and create clarity among parties and lawyers.

Phase 3: Defining the Problem and Organizing the Issues

Goals: Identify issues to be addressed and create agenda.

How to achieve goals: Help parties to work together, rather than against one another, to solve problems and to become future oriented.

Phase 4: Developing and Negotiating Solutions

Goals: Explore needs, interests, goals, and concerns as to each agenda item. Create value by exploring, identifying, and evaluating options. Divide value by exchanging settlement proposals. Move past impasses, if necessary.

How to achieve goals: Address obstacles and impasses; assist or coach renegotiation; facilitate case analysis and valuation.

---

1. Dana developed early versions of this outline for her first appellate mediation for the Judiciary of the State of Hawaii. Over the years, it has undergone numerous revisions, for which we thank Richard Birke and Daniel Bowling.

Phase 5: Concluding the Mediation; Postmediation Follow-Up

Goals, concluding the mediation: If parties reach agreement, refine agreements (evaluate them for clarity, completeness, and commitment) and draft and sign memorandum of understanding or settlement agreement. If parties do not reach an agreement, plan timing and strategy for follow-up or next mediation session.

Goals, following up: If parties reach agreement, check in concerning implementation, including dismissal of the appeal; assist with any drafting problems if parties did not sign agreement at mediation; solicit feedback about the mediation; and submit paperwork in court-connected appellate mediations. *If parties do not reach agreement,* follow through with any plan for continuing assistance and contact counsel periodically if appeal proceeds.

How to achieve goals: Communicate your willingness to help and, if the dispute has not been resolved, your optimism that it will still resolve with further effort.

We devote a chapter to each of these phases in Section II. Because some mediators in our appellate mediation training have found this table to be useful to distribute to the parties and lawyers, or to use as their own cheat sheets, we present an example in the Appendix in the form of a mediation agenda for reference by the mediator.

C.   The Advantage of Keeping Each Phase Separate

We acknowledge the somewhat nebulous nature of these phases but nevertheless believe, for several reasons, that a fundamental structure is crucial to an effective mediation process. First, parties want and need a roadmap to resolution. When they have this clarity, they relax a bit. Second, participants also need to know what is expected of them, and when they do they are more likely to participate constructively. Third, when the structure is made clear, the participants also understand there is a time and place for all they need to do and say to get to agreement.

The structure of our approach to appellate mediation provides a large container for the conflict. And within the structure are smaller containers for the conflict conversation. Especially if the parties are highly contentious and the conflict is volatile, organizing the conversation into discrete categories, and encouraging parties to focus discussions on information that is relevant to each, leads to more constructive conversations. That is not to say the parties should not be emotional. We believe emotional expressions are sometimes essential and generally very helpful: they give us an indication of what really matters to people. But when the emotional conversation is for a clearly defined purpose within a structure, it is more likely to be productive than if it occurs randomly.

As an example, in one of her early cases, Dana struggled to help a divorcing couple reach agreement on a number of issues common to this type of mediation: division of personal and real property, including the family home; investments and the wife's business; and support. In the third session, once again the wife began to go into detail about how the husband had left her and its impact on her. The repetition of this story interfered with the parties' ability to move forward. They were stuck in this loop of the wife's story. As Dana began to empathize with the wife, she realized she had done so about five times before and it did not seem to help, even after the wife clearly felt heard and confirmed Dana had understood her.

When she realized the conversation was stuck, Dana excused herself to consult her mentor, Gary Friedman, in the office next door. After she described the experience and asked for advice, Gary said, "The problem is you haven't created a container for the conflict—clearly defined what it is the parties are to be doing. Describe what is happening and ask them if they need to be talking more about how the husband left the wife in order to resolve the issues for their divorce. If they do, you might also want to ask them how this discussion will help them reach their goal. If they choose to go forward with this conversation, then help them to make it more meaningful—expand the discussion to include the husband's perspective and anything else the wife needs to say. If not, ask what they could do that would be more productive or recommend a topic for conversation based on where the parties are in the process. Once you identify that topic, you have a new container. You can then propose a structure, ask if they agree to talk about this topic, and then help them to adhere to it."

Dana followed Gary's advice, and it worked. The wife continued to stray, but when Dana pointed out their agreement to move on to another subject, she returned quickly to the new container and the parties progressed. And the case ultimately settled!

An even more common risk to being off-task is the rush to negotiate over settlement terms. Sometimes from the outset of the mediation, parties or lawyers go straight to negotiation—or, worse, to their bottom line—without taking time to discuss how they will work together, to exchange points of view on the situation and the law, to identify the issues for decision, to explore interests, to pursue creative solutions, or to analyze and value their appeal. Unless the mediator has structured the mediation and defined each particular phase, parties in whom the impulse to rush to solution is strong will continually get in their own way of settlement.

Chapter 4
Premediation

A. Introduction

Premediation preparations and communications are crucial to a successful mediation, so much so that they are a distinguishing feature of appellate mediation. By contrast, with a few exceptions, premediation activities in trial court are limited to arranging logistics such as timing, location, participants, and mediation statements. Instead of interacting with the mediator, lawyers typically inform a case manager of their logistical agreements and the case manager confirms them in a letter. In some large provider organizations, these issues are predetermined, and the letter confirming the mediator's appointment simply spells out the provider's policies. In other words, little is done to set up the mediation for success.

The premediation stage of an appellate mediation invites attorneys, mediators, and sometimes the parties to get ready for the mediation in a thoughtful and deliberate manner. Research suggests a strong attorney preference for premediation preparation, including premediation calls with the mediator.[2] Mediator preparation, including some form of premediation communication with participants, is critical to conducting quality mediation.

Given the critical importance of premediation communications and preparations to the outcome of appellate mediation, we provide a systematic approach that enables the mediator and counsel to address issues that could become problems at the mediation session and design a process uniquely suited to resolving the particular appeal being mediated.

B. Determine Whether a Case Is Amenable to Mediation

The first question is whether the appeal should be mediated at all. If the appeal arises from a criminal conviction or involuntary civil confinement, mediation is probably a nonstarter and may be excluded by the appellate court in which the matter is to be decided.[3] Civil appeals, on the other hand, are fertile ground

---

2. ABA Section of Dispute Resolution Task Force on Improving Mediation Quality 9 (ABA, 2008). Among respondents to a written survey, more than 96 percent indicated premediation preparation by a mediator was important, very important, or essential, and less than 4 percent thought it only somewhat important. All survey participants thought preparation was important.
3. ROBERT J. NIEMIC, MEDIATION & CONFERENCE PROGRAMS IN THE FEDERAL COURTS OF APPEALS 6 (Federal Judicial Center, 2007).

for mediation. Indeed, in many jurisdictions, parties in civil appellate mediation are required by order of the appellate court to participate. For example, all of the federal Court of Appeals circuits have mediation programs—some with full-time, professional mediators on staff.

In courts without formal mediation programs or in instances in which a particular appeal has not been ordered into mediation, parties may choose mediation for themselves. Because of our personal experience with appellate mediation and the impressive settlement rates of appellate mediation programs, we believe counsel and the parties should evaluate the mediation potential of *every* civil appeal.

Whether mediation of an appeal might occur in private mediation or court-connected mediation, the following questions apply to determine whether a case is suitable for appellate mediation.

1. **Is this a test case or a case that should be a published precedent?** Some appeals are brought for the purpose of clarifying an ambiguous law, bringing a constitutional challenge to a particular government action, or securing a published legal precedent to provide guidance for future conduct. There are usually two hallmarks of this type of appeal. First, the case was filed with the express purpose of securing a particular judicial precedent. Second, payment of money damages was either not requested by the plaintiff or irrelevant to resolving the case.

    • As a cautionary note, in many cases parties *say* they want a decision to clarify a point of law in a published decision in their favor, but on closer examination it becomes clear that a party is pursuing the appeal to seek monetary compensation and there are possible settlement options that would be as good or better for the party than a published decision. In most appeals, however, it is factors such as fear of losing, financial cost, time delays, and emotional stress—rather than the particular appellate issues to be presented for decision by the appellate court—that form the basis for the decision to mediate.

2. **Are the parties already on a negotiation track?** If negotiation is proceeding smoothly, through either the parties or their counsel, there may be no reason to initiate a formal mediation. Some appeals successfully resolve without the need for a neutral third party. However, when the parties hit a roadblock, mediation can help them reach their goal. Appellate courts with formal mediation programs often provide assistance to parties who are negotiating independently with a privately retained mediator by staying appellate record preparation or briefing schedules. Court-connected mediation program staff also can help informally to move the negotiations along without ever convening an official mediation session.

3. **Are the parties willing to mediate?** There are two paths to appellate mediation: the parties *agree* to mediate or the court *orders* them to do so. Absent the availability of these paths, mediation will not

happen.[4] Without a clear need for an appellate court decision, a weak commitment to the appeal, or successful ongoing negotiations, the only reason not to attempt mediation is that a party is unwilling to participate. Unlike in the trial court where mediation is ubiquitous, the idea of mediating an appeal may not occur to parties or their counsel. For this reason, we are supportive of court-connected mediation programs, which require parties to consider whether mediation might be useful to them.

C.   Facilitate a Premediation Conference Call

We recommend that mediations begin with premediation telephone communications among all counsel and the mediator shortly after the mediator is appointed or retained. Although separate, confidential calls may follow, convening first with the mediator and counsel *together* has the following advantages:

- **Efficiency.** Making decisions about logistical issues, especially when the lawyers disagree, takes much less time than the back-and-forth of separate calls to resolve logistics.

- **Understanding lawyer dynamics.** In a joint call, communication dynamics may become apparent, allowing the mediator to anticipate potential problems and help address any challenges before the mediation.

- **Development of a team.** This call enables the lawyers and mediator to form a professional team that will support the parties in reaching agreement.

- **Development of trust.** As a mediator works with all lawyers together, the lawyers gain confidence in the mediator to be impartial, which is especially important if the mediator has worked previously with one lawyer and not the other.

The premediation phone conference is an important tool that helps lawyers to communicate and the mediator to understand the numerous distinctive features of each case and to account for these differences as the mediator customizes the mediation process. In fact, this premediation contact is a fundamental feature of appellate mediation in a number of court programs.[5] For example, shortly after appeals are filed in selected cases, circuit mediators for the U.S. Court of Appeals

---

4. In Sections III and IV, we provide some suggestions about bringing refusing or reluctant parties to the mediation table.
5. *See* Brendon Ishikawa, *Appellate Mediation*, in Norman Piatt, ed., California Civil Appellate Practice § 15A.33 (CEB, 2014) (surveying California courts); http://www .cafc.uscourts.gov/sites/default/files/Dec-2013-Revision/mediation%20guidelines_

for the Ninth Circuit schedule mandatory 30- to 60-minute settlement assessment conferences with counsel, and sometimes parties, to determine whether mediation is appropriate and, if so, how to design the mediation given the parties' goals and the difficulties presented by the parties or the legal issues.[6]

D. Address Important Issues in Premediation Discussions

As a best practice, we suggest mediators provide counsel with an agenda for the premediation call. Typically, this agenda includes the following topics:

- Introductions of participants (including roles in the mediation and an explanation of the purpose of the call—to enhance the possibility of resolution)

- Confidentiality (of the premediation call and the mediation, including the confidentiality agreement)

- Disclosures of any potential conflicts

- The nature of the dispute

- The parties to the dispute (their relationship to one another and their goals for the mediation)

- Scope of the mediation (whether there are disputes other than the appeal the parties would like to resolve in the mediation)

- Information parties require in order to be prepared to mediate

- Date, time, and location of the mediation

- Participation in the mediation (and whether participants will have the authority required to resolve the dispute)

- Opportunities for and obstacles to resolution

- Ideas to improve the effectiveness of the mediation or matters that could pose impediments

- The approach to mediation and the role the mediator will play

---

effective_12-6-2013.pdf (Federal Circuit); and http://www.tenthdistrictcourt.org /information/mediation.cfm (Ohio's Tenth Circuit).
6. *See* http://www.ca9.uscourts.gov/mediation/view.php?pk_id=0000000669

- Mediation statements (the content, length, timing, and exchange)

- Amount and allocation of mediator fees and any requirement of deposit of fees

- Mediator suggestions (including for client preparation)

- Additional topics, suggestions, or questions

- Next steps (including scheduling additional joint or separate calls or meetings)

For the benefit of less experienced appellate mediators, we include a script of a sample premediation telephone conference in the Appendix.

E.   Conclusion

Abraham Lincoln is credited with saying "Give me six hours to chop down a tree and I will spend the first four sharpening the axe."[7] This wisdom expresses the rationale underlying the premediation stage of appellate mediation: thorough preparation results in a smooth approach toward a successful outcome of the mediation process. Successful mediators use premediation joint and separate calls to deepen their understanding of the dispute, the views of the lawyers and parties, and the dynamics of the conflict.

---

7.   http://www.brainyquote.com/quotes/quotes/a/abrahamlin109275.html.

Chapter 5
Opening the Appellate Mediation in Phase 1

A. Introduction

This first phase of the mediation session is usually brief in comparison to the other phases. Phase 1 can take as little as 10 minutes to complete, while Phase 4 (focusing on solutions) can take 10 hours—or several days. Nevertheless, this first phase constitutes a potent 10 minutes! If the parties and mediator achieve the goals of this phase, they set a positive tone for the mediation and launch the process on a trajectory for collaboration and creativity. A perfunctory Phase 1, on the other hand, deprives the parties of this opportunity or, if not handled well, allows the parties (and lawyers) to erect unnecessary barriers that must be overcome during the remainder of the mediation. Just as oral argument in front of the appellate court is considered to be "the most important 15 minutes of the appeal," so too is the opening phase of appellate mediation (in which we structure the mediation) the most important few minutes of the mediation.

B. Goals for Phase 1

Although the exact form of this phase varies from mediator to mediator, a successful Phase 1 ensures the participants understand and agree on how they will work together during the mediation, sets a respectful and optimistic tone for the mediation, and begins to engage the participants in a collaborative process.

The goals of Phase 1 are to:

1. Understand and agree on the purpose of the mediation, the roles of the mediator and participants, and the plan for the day;
2. Establish guidelines for confidentiality and, perhaps, communication; and
3. To begin to create an atmosphere of collaboration and rapport between the mediator and the parties.

Participants arrive at a mediation session with varying degrees of preparedness. Most lawyers are experienced in mediation, but if they have not worked with the particular mediator, they do not know what to expect from the mediator or what the mediator expects from them and their clients. Even if the mediator and lawyers discussed the mediation in the premediation telephone conference, it helps to start the mediation session with a clear understanding of the goals, the roles, and the structure of the day. It serves as a reminder to lawyers, and—if the lawyers have not described the procedures to their clients—it orients the parties to the process.

Likewise, parties are not always equally prepared when they arrive at mediation. Some lawyers do a great job of preparing their clients, including discussing the clients' participation. Others do not. When parties, lawyers, and mediators align their expectations of one another and of the mediation process, the tension can lessen and the mediation can go more smoothly.

In addition to understanding what is expected of the participants, what the participants can expect from the mediator, and how the mediation is likely to unfold, it is important to set the atmospheric stage for the mediation. In Sections III and IV, we discuss how lawyers and mediators can contribute to the development of a constructive atmosphere during Phase 1.

C.   How to Accomplish the Goals for Phase 1

1. Confidentiality

By the time of the mediation session, participants have usually reviewed the confidentiality agreement prepared by the court, if the case is within a court-sponsored program, or by the mediator, if not. As the mediation opens, the mediator typically asks the participants to sign the agreement if they have not already done so and reiterates the parameters of the agreement. Three levels of confidentiality are relevant to mediation, and it is important that the parties understand and agree on all of them:

- **Mediator confidentiality**, as to the entire proceedings and the rest of the world and as to information learned in separate session(s);

- **Evidentiary protections** or exclusions related to mediation communications and documents prepared for or in the course of mediation; and

- **Confidentiality as to third parties**, or the parties' expectations concerning what they may reveal about the mediation and to whom.

Except in the jurisdictions that have adopted the Uniform Mediation Act, mediation confidentiality regulations vary widely. It is beyond the scope of this book to give mediation confidentiality the full attention it deserves, but it is important for appellate mediators and lawyers representing clients in mediation to be familiar with the statutes and rules of court regarding confidentiality.

In addition, standards of practice in numerous jurisdictions dictate a mediator's obligations to address particular confidentiality issues. For example, California requires court-appointed mediators at or before the first mediation session to "provide the participants with a general explanation of the confidentiality of mediation proceedings."[1]

---

1.   Cal. Rules of Court, rule 3.854(b). Other states are in accord, such as Alaska (http: //courts.alaska.gov/mediation/),   Colorado   (https://colorado.feb.gov/programs

2. Logistics

Mediators also handle housekeeping matters that can help put the parties at ease, such as the time schedule for the session and the participants' availability throughout, the location of restrooms, access to the Internet and computers, and the mediator's practice regarding breaks and lunch.

3. Explanation of the Roles of the Mediator and Participants

Typically, mediators explain that they are impartial and objective, they have no stake in the outcome, and they will assist parties to find resolutions that best meet their needs and interests rather than making a decision for them. Mediators also may reiterate any agreements participants have made about their roles or make recommendations about how they can participate. Some mediators, ourselves included, strive to cover much of this information in a conversational style, rather than a monologue. In this approach the mediator might initiate the conversation with well-chosen questions about the parties' experience or understanding of mediation—or about the parties' goals and how they might most effectively achieve them. In general, effective participation of parties includes the following:

- Willingness to enter into an agreement that works both for themselves and for the other party,

- Openness to learning something new about their dispute in the mediation, and

- Willingness to change their minds if the circumstances warrant their doing so.

Lawyers participate effectively when they do the following:

- Educate their clients, the mediator, and the other party and lawyer about the legal risks and opportunities on appeal;

/alternative-dispute-resolution/), and Hawaii (http://hawaii.gov/jud/selmed.htm). Likewise, the private mediator and arbitrator firm JAMS has adopted mediator ethics guidelines requiring its neutrals to explain mediation confidentiality to the parties (http://www.jamsadr.com/mediators-ethics/). And the Air Force Alternative Dispute Resolution Program emphasizes the following: "Of particular importance is the need for the mediator to review the confidentiality of the process. While confidentiality should already have been addressed during case intake, the mediator must ensure the parties understand what can and cannot be held in confidence." http://www.adr .af.mil/factsheets/factsheet.asp?id=7362

- Learn about and integrate the other lawyer's perspective and educate their clients about it;

- Help their clients to explore their interests and those of the other party;

- Assist their clients to negotiate to resolution; and

- Draft and review any mediated settlement agreement.

4. *Communication Guidelines*

Some mediators establish basic ground rules, such as parties must be respectful or refrain from interrupting. We tend to assume people will be civil and prefer to deal with problems if and when they occur either in the premediation calls or at mediation. Other mediators think of communication guidelines more broadly and either elicit from the participants or coach them in how to ensure the mediated discussions will be productive.

5. *Agenda for the Mediation Session*

If, as we suggest, the mediator has conducted a premediation telephone conference and perhaps additional follow-up in which the lawyers and parties have agreed on the approach to the mediation, the mediator generally summarizes the procedural arrangements and invites any suggestions for modification. We provide a sample agenda based on our approach in the Appendix.

    If not, it is even more important that the mediator describes the agenda for the mediation and seeks feedback and, ultimately, agreement from the participants before moving on.

D.   Conclusion

As the mediation opens in Phase 1, the mediator establishes a working relationship with the participants. The mediator has the opportunity to connect with everyone in the room, to set an optimistic tone for the mediation process, and to demonstrate the ability and commitment required to help the parties resolve their dispute. In addition to the personal qualities the mediator brings that build rapport and trust, Phase 1 also allows the mediator to demonstrate process competence in helping the participants achieve the primary goal of Phase 1: to create a strong foundation for the mediation. By the end of this phase, participants understand and agree on the purpose of the mediation and the roles of the mediator and participants. They have established guidelines for confidentiality and communication. And they have a picture of how the mediation session can lead to resolution.

Chapter 6
Exchanging Information in Phase 2

A.   Introduction

Phase 2 of the appellate mediation process focuses on the exchange of information. Frequently, Phase 2 of an appellate mediation begins with a skeptical audience. Parties, attorneys, and even mediators might question whether the exchange
of information is even necessary, especially after lengthy trial court proceedings
and the submission of mediation statements. Thus, it comes as a surprise to
the participants when a fruitful Phase 2 yields new and important information,
which it almost always does. Indeed, constructive giving and receiving of information is a hallmark of a successful and productive appellate mediation process.

Notably, Phase 2 is where the *appellate* mediation process differs most from
trial court mediation and settlement efforts. Because no new evidence can be
admitted on appeal and the parties have presumably revealed their best strategies in trying to win in the trial court, participants tend to be more open in
sharing information because they have little or no incentive to withhold information during mediation. Moreover, the guarantees of mediation confidentiality that most jurisdictions provide further support the free and frank exchange
of information. Consequently, Phase 2 is the right time for participants to
answer the question "What do we need to understand—and what do we need
to say—in order to resolve this appeal to the benefit of the parties?"

In short, Phase 2 is the most underappreciated phase of appellate mediation.
Rather than being a regurgitation of trial court arguments and evidence, this phase
represents a key step in laying the groundwork for later problem solving, including brainstorming and evaluating options and negotiating the terms of an agreement. The exchanges in Phase 2 allow parties to better understand the people and
what matters to them, the legal and practical issues, and the current problems to
be solved—groundwork that is essential for building an agreement later.

B.   Address Each Topic Related to the Appeal and the
Underlying Problem in a Separate Conversation

The Phase 2 information exchange encompasses topics that fall into two
broad categories: (1) the legal and procedural issues arising in the appeal
and (2) everything else. Everything besides the appeal typically includes
information about the parties' interests and needs regarding settlement. It
may also encompass the parties' perspectives on the situation that led to litigation and, especially where the parties' had a personal or business association, how the conflict affected the relationship, and their feelings about it.

Because these two conversations cover such different material and serve divergent purposes, we believe segregating the topics into separate conversations is crucial to the successful exchange of information. Discussions about the law tend to magnify or exaggerate differences of perspective and if not carefully facilitated can devolve from information exchange to argument, a dynamic that often polarizes the parties.

Legal discussions also tend to dominate the conversation in appellate mediation. If the legal discussions occur alongside discussions about the parties' perspectives on what happened or their interests, the legal discussions easily eclipse the more subtle, but sometimes most important, conversations about what matters to the parties, the transaction costs or other consequences of pursuing an appeal, or the often-neglected analysis of what a prevailing party actually gets with a win.

1. Discussing the Legal Merits of the Appeal

In an appellate case, mediation necessarily occurs in the context of a legal dispute that is currently subject to appellate law and procedures. Moreover, the value of a case is usually greatly dependent on the strengths and weaknesses of the parties' arguments on appeal. Consequently, the attorney participants tend to contribute the bulk of the discussion on this topic. Legal arguments are, of course, the stock in trade for the attorneys who represent clients during the mediation. Therein lie the seeds of peril and opportunity for the remainder of the process.

The peril. If the lawyers dominate the conversation, elevate the importance of the legal arguments above all other considerations, and posture prematurely in anticipation of the negotiation phase, the discussion becomes adversarial and distributive. By distributive, we mean the tendency of legal analysis to see solutions as dividing an available set of money or resources in a zero-sum game. Distributive analysis and bargaining create "winners" and "losers" who must scrabble for each gained mote. Any potential for collaboration that generates additional value, understanding, and healing remains untapped in a distributive discussion. If the discussion of the merits of the appeal devolves into a right-wrong, win-lose argument by the lawyers, the mediation begins on a sour note that is nearly impossible to harmonize later.

Smart attorneys reassure their clients before the mediation that they will strive to get the best possible deal for their clients and will be strong advocates for them throughout the mediation. They also explain the difference between advocacy before the court and advocacy in mediation. And during mediation the mediator can remind parties that effective advocacy during a mediation will likely appear dramatically different from advocacy during trial or in open court. If both lawyers and mediators adhere to the proposition that clients' best interests are most effectively advanced during mediation by listening, learning, and collaborating, not by arguing, clients will not expect—and be disappointed not to find—the same lawyers that represented them at trial. Ceaseless argument and attacks on the other side are counterproductive and unnecessarily lengthen a process already likely to be quite tiring by the end.

The opportunity. Attorneys can accomplish much in their discussion of their appellate arguments and analyses. First, an attorney who demonstrates a keen understanding of the appellate process and how a client's arguments are best framed for the appellate court inspires confidence. By cogently explaining the legal analysis we covered in Chapter 1, the attorney can frame the client's legal position within the context of the standards of review, legal merits, and analysis of prejudice. By explaining other legal alternatives such as those we covered in Chapter 2, the attorney can demonstrate that the client has additional options besides the appeal. Especially if the attorney represented the party at trial, a clear, thoughtful presentation can demonstrate competence and commitment to zealously represent the client if the case does not settle. These demonstrations of mastery over the case also educate the opposing party and show that the opposing counsel is well prepared and able to analyze and assess the merits of the case during mediation.

Attorneys' presentations of their clients' legal case are usually argumentative and sometimes even blustering. When attorneys bring the zeal that fuels this behavior to mediation, as they often do, it will not suffer being ignored forever. If the attorneys are not allowed to express their perspectives and "demonstrate their worth" early in the proceedings, they may never make the shift from the competitiveness with which they present their case to collaboration, which is essential later in the process to preserve any fragile progress toward harmony.

Second, an attorney who can clearly articulate the strengths of a client's case and problems of the opposing party's case—without alienating others or without being pompous or combative—can sow doubt into the minds of opposing parties and counsel. As we explained in Chapter 2, most people end their analysis as soon as they imagine a way to reach their desired result. Thus, they never continue the analysis to consider what might derail or deny their success. Consequently, an attorney who can explain succinctly how an opposing party's position on appeal is problematic or subject to a poor standard of review or difficult law can cause the opposing party to reevaluate the merits (and thus value) of its case. Although attorneys seldom convince opposing parties they are right, a thoughtful and well-communicated legal analysis is likely to sow uncertainty. Fresh information frequently affects the settlement value of a case and can motivate parties to find previously hidden options for settlement. In short, the exchange of information about the law during the mediation may well change assumptions, inspire parties to re-evaluate their case, and ultimately lead to greater flexibility in settlement.[1]

---

1. *See* especially Chapter 3, in which we present an approach to risk analysis, which if followed often leads to results that surprise parties and their lawyers because the outcomes are at odds with the conclusions they have drawn about the logical settlement value of their case.

Third, an attorney can educate the other side about the legal and practical *context* of the controversy. The fact that a case is one among other collateral actions may heavily influence the negotiation and explain why, later, a party is so insistent on a confidentiality clause. A lawyer might also address other circumstances of the case, such as whether the case is subject to a stay of the appeal or a bond on appeal and, if so, whether the parties must anticipate and deal with what will occur once the stay or bond is dissolved—or whether attorney fees and costs will be an issue in the negotiation.

As we have emphasized, we recommend that absent compelling reasons not to do so, Phase 2 occurs in joint session. When lawyers address each other and the parties directly, they can communicate their legal analysis with a full understanding and appreciation of the case, rather than trusting the mediator, who is not as well acquainted with the issues, to carry important information to the other side. By separating the legal discussion from information exchange about other issues and by setting a context in which the purpose is to educate and to learn from one another, the mediator helps the attorneys to assist parties to analyze their opportunities and risks on appeal more effectively. Addressing the legal points of the appeal early in the process frees the participants to discuss what gave rise to the litigation and the underlying problem unencumbered by the win-lose paradigm of a lawsuit.

2. *Discussing the Underlying Problem and Parties' Current Circumstances*

Eliminating an appeal is easy, requiring only a request for dismissal by the appellant. Resolving the underlying controversy is the hard part. It requires parties to find solutions to problems that have eluded them throughout the litigation. We have been consistently amazed at how much new information comes to light during appellate mediations. This seems counterintuitive given the often-lengthy history of the feud and resulting lawsuit. However, many lawsuits start where the parties' discussions ended. And trial usually leaves parties dissatisfied about their day in court. Rather than being able to finally tell their stories, parties have found themselves cross-examined. Answers they wanted to give were often stricken by the trial judge as nonresponsive. Thus, parties often have a lot to get off their chests when they arrive at an appellate mediation. Their spouses and friends have suffered through many rehearsals of their stories, and Phase 2 is the time for a party to finally have his or her say.

Humans are storytellers, and the act of describing how things happened to us, how we felt, and what we wanted to result is itself cathartic. Mediations often reach a palpable tipping point when an angry party has finally been able to tell the opposing party and attorney about the disappointment, bewilderment, and difficulties underlying the case. A previously frustrated party suddenly becomes able to move beyond the story of the past to become future-oriented toward solutions. Thus, the parties' perspectives, rather than the lawyers' views, are the focus of this aspect of Phase 2. If possible, parties *themselves* should communicate directly with the other participants and learn directly from them.

Mediation confidentiality contributes to the free flow of discussion possible in an otherwise restrictive legal environment.[2] Especially in light of confidentiality, it is important for the attorneys to let clients who want to talk, talk. In trial court mediations, clients tend to be relegated to exhibits as their attorneys want to show how good they will look at trial. "I will have a compelling client on the stand" often serves as a proxy for "You should settle this case."

By contrast, appellate mediations invite a larger and more important role for clients. *This is the parties' best opportunity in the entire litigation to tell their stories.* Thus, clients should be prepared to participate fully in the mediation—beginning with telling compelling stories of their perspectives on the case. Often, clients can humanize the loss and difficulties underlying their legal claims. They can also garner sympathy for their circumstances in a way that makes later negotiations more productive. As Dana has observed, "With the exception of the bad case, which even a perfect client can't make better, over the years I have seen [defendants] become more flexible in mediation when they judge a client to be a good person."[3]

The parties benefit from exchanging perspectives on the situation that led to litigation and its impact, as well as their needs and interests—or what is important to them—in joint sessions.[4] In cases where the parties are interested in repairing their personal or business relationship, direct conversation with each other may be the only way to make inroads toward this goal. If there is no ongoing relationship, the parties may nevertheless want the emotional

---

2. "Virtually all state legislatures have recognized the necessity of protecting mediation confidentiality to encourage the effective use of mediation to resolve disputes. Indeed, state legislatures have enacted more than 250 mediation privilege statutes." UNIFORM MEDIATION ACT editors' notes (2003) (discussing the need for candor in mediation). Since space does not allow us to examine each of these confidentiality statutes, we leave to it counsel and mediators to understand the applicable laws. However, we note that under the Uniform Mediation Act, confidentiality is protected with exceptions only for "threats made to inflict bodily harm or other violent crime; parties' attempt to use mediation to plan or commit a crime; the need for information to prove or disprove allegations of child abuse or neglect; or the need for information to prove or disprove a claim or complaint of professional misconduct by a mediator." http://www.uniformlaws.org/Narrative.aspx?title=Why%20States%20Should%20Adopt%20UMA. Even so, counsel and mediators should counsel participants that matters deemed secret should be kept secret. Just because information cannot thereafter be admitted in court does not mean that it cannot be used in the real world. Trade secrets, highly sensitive information, and strategic plans are often best not shared.
3. Dana Curtis, *Getting More for the Plaintiff in Mediation*, THE TRIAL LAWYER 30 (Spring 2004).
4. In Section IV we provide practice tips for lawyers and mediators about how to work effectively in joint session during Phase 2.

satisfaction of communicating their perspectives on what happened and what is important to them in resolving the dispute to the other party directly.

These opportunities should not be lost.

C.   The Value of the Mediator in Phase 2

Appellate mediation should be more facilitative than evaluative when compared to trial court settlement conferences. A facilitative process involves the mediator as a neutral party who ensures that the parties communicate effectively and achieve greater clarity about the issues on appeal and surrounding the case. The mediator plays a key role in keeping the exchange of information free and frank—and ensuring that the legal analysis is thorough and complete, covering all of the relevant issues and arguments. This is an especially important role for the mediator to play while the participants remain in joint session.

Thus mediators have the role of keeping participants from alienating the other participants by insulting, disparaging, or threatening comments. In the end, negotiated agreements often require all parties to make reluctant concessions in order to settle. Mutually acceptable solutions usually require all parties to make uncomfortable sacrifices to reach an agreement. Reducing antagonism among the parties increases the chances that negotiations will proceed successfully.

Effective mediators also help the participants to listen effectively—for understanding. If parties can demonstrate their understanding of the other party's views, and if lawyers can do so regarding the law and what else matters to them to the satisfaction of the speaker, they ensure they have not missed or misunderstood anything of importance. They also have demonstrated respect for the other side and thus contribute to a more positive atmosphere.

D.   To the Extent Possible, Conduct Phase 2
in Joint Session

Given the important work and value of information exchange between the attorneys and the parties, we believe the virtues of remaining together outweigh any downside risk of alienating the other party. The opportunity to clarify and elaborate on matters they believe to be important to their negotiation has value in all areas of their discussions.

The joint session offers an excellent forum for value creation. At its best, value creation involves creativity and results in advantages to the parties that cannot be awarded by courts. Although inexperienced negotiators often start by focusing on who will pay money and in what amount, in most cases there are often additional options to be explored. These additional options may include some that are more valuable to the recipient than costly to the offerer. For example, tax characterization of a settlement can be much more valuable to the plaintiff than costly to the defendant.

Although participants may start off thinking of mediation as nothing more than a lengthy negotiation about money, the process encompasses much more than mere division of dollars. Thus, counsel should avoid rushing out of a joint session and the opportunity for candid exchange that it provides. Although parties are often eager to split into private caucuses to start the "real work" of negotiating, such myopic focus on value division should be avoided as short sighted.

E. It's Not Yet Time to Negotiate

Phase 2—especially during the first joint session of the mediation—is best reserved for listening and learning rather than digging into an entrenched position. Parties cannot tell their stories and bargain over money at the same time. For these reasons, negotiations properly occur during a later phase of the mediation.[5] Because appellate mediations need time to unfold, it is helpful for parties to understand that bargaining can be undertaken too early in the process. Starting a mediation by declaring a bottom line or proceeding to distributive bargaining does not portend a successful resolution of the appeal. Were the parties able to engage directly in productive negotiations, the case would already have settled. Thus, parties should accept that the process works well but that it is a *process*—precisely because not everything connected with a negotiation can happen all at once.

F. People Get Angry; It's Okay

In Section I, we covered appellate procedures, substantive law governing review, outcome statistics, and quantitative risk analysis. If humans were entirely rational, nothing more than the information in Section I would be needed to resolve an appeal with a settlement agreement. Humans, however, are marvelous mixtures of cold logic, hot anger, icy avoidance, giddy hope, brilliant ideas, and unfounded assumptions. Thus, any effort at resolving disputes should account for the rational *and emotional* aspects of mediation participants.

Anger is a frequent hallmark of an *effective* mediation! We have found a surprising number of appellate mediators whose primary goal is to keep parties from becoming angry, displaying anger, or angering each other. In this view, anger is bad and to be avoided. When attorneys and mediators encounter emotions standing in the way of a settlement—or even active negotiation—they often believe the obstacle of irrationality improperly stands in the way of getting sensible agreement. Attorneys are also usually more comfortable with the logic of legal arguments than the outpouring of strong feelings by parties. But

---

5. *See* Chapter 8, where we discuss Phase 4, in which appellate mediation mediation participants develop and negotiate solutions.

emotions are powerful and essential because we all need to hope, dream, and love in order to live full lives!

In the Kübler-Ross model of grief, there are five stages: denial, *anger,* bargaining, depression, and acceptance.[6] In this model anger is not superfluous, bad, or even avoidable. Instead, it is an integral step in the process toward acceptance. For many parties in an appellate mediation, their anger is also a step in their own personal journey toward acceptance and resolution. To avoid this or any other emotion sometimes amounts to avoiding resolution.

Joint sessions in Phase 2 often provide a good forum for addressing the strong emotions that may be the reason why the case has been protracted enough to arrive at the appellate stage. Don't rush to avoid anger or joint sessions. They may be necessary stepping stones on the way to successful resolution. We know it is not easy to manage conversations that are charged with emotion, so we provide guidance for mediators on how to work with strong emotions in joint sessions in Section IV.

G.   It Is Crucial to Listen for Understanding of One Another's Views during Phase 2

It is one thing to *listen,* but it is another to *understand.* Generally, when we are in conflict we listen for what we can use when it is our turn to talk. Effective mediators know how to listen differently, to empathize, which is much less difficult for someone who is not a party to the conflict. They also demonstrate their understanding by restating what they hear, seeking feedback about the accuracy of their understanding, and correcting any misunderstanding.

H.   Private Caucuses Provide the Opportunity for "the Rest of the Information" to Be Exchanged—Even If Only with the Mediator

A private caucus is limited to people on just one side of the case, such as the appellant and appellant's counsel. Most often private caucuses include everyone associated with a side: the parties, attorneys, insurance representatives, spouses, accountants, and so on. In a case with multiple appellants or respondents, each party may have a private caucus when their positions do not coincide with another party's.

Compared to joint sessions, private caucuses are more likely to include activities that lie on the evaluative end of the mediation model spectrum. Specifically, private caucuses can be used to assess how the mediation process is going and to reformulate the negotiation strategy after new information has come to light during the joint session. Private caucuses offer an opportunity

---

6.   *See generally* ELISABETH KÜBLER-ROSS, ON DEATH AND DYING (Scribners 2003).

to give the mediator additional information that the mediator might use with other parties to evaluate their positions on appeal or to suggest new avenues for settlement without risking rejection simply because an opposing attorney is the source of the idea.

Another type of private caucus that is sometimes useful is a meeting with the mediator and the attorneys—without clients. This kind of private meeting can be useful when forging consensus on how the mediation should proceed, discussing matters without embarrassing counsel in front of clients, helping an attorney with a difficult client, or discussing the legal details of a settlement.

Private caucus offers more than an opportunity to speak without the opposing side listening in. Sometimes it gives counsel a chance to help a client move beyond barriers of emotion or attitude that stand in the way of settlement. A private caucus can also be used by counsel to enlist the mediator's help in breaking bad news to counsel's own client. Mediators with good rapport and empathy skills can help clients come to terms with the difficulties they may face with continued litigation. And sometimes clients benefit from having the mediator deliver, in a different style, the same message that counsel is attempting to convey to a client whose emotions or outlook remain stuck.

I.   Conclusion

Phase 2 offers wonderful potential in the appellate mediation process. Participants can learn from one another important information about the appeal and underlying problem. Attorneys can demonstrate their value to their clients. Everyone can get a better sense of what is at stake both in the appeal and in the mediation. And parties can achieve the catharsis that comes when they finally get to tell their stories with all of its emotions and be understood by the other party or at least the mediator. Skipping any part of Phase 2 omits part of the foundation upon which a later agreement can be built.

Chapter 7
Defining the Problem and Organizing the Issues in Phase 3

A. Introduction

Once participants understand one another's legal arguments and the parties' perspectives on the problem underlying the litigation, they are ready for Phase 3. Phase 3 involves identifying the issues the parties must resolve. The issues on which the parties will seek agreement are different from the legal issues to be decided by the appellate court if the case does not settle. Although parties are extremely unlikely to agree on the legal issues, nevertheless they usually are able to resolve issues necessary to settle the appeal. Most often, an agreement on payment of money conclusively resolves the case, even though the parties will never agree about who will prevail in the appeal. Thus, the parties might agree to a narrow scope of issues necessary to settle the case. At other times, parties might decide to include collateral legal actions that might not yet be ripe for appeal but should be addressed in a global settlement.

In short, Phase 3 involves the mediation participants' exploring this question: "What issues do the parties need to resolve during this mediation session to reach an agreement?" The goal for Phase 3 is to include all issues that are necessary for a settlement agreement and exclude any issues that are not necessary to resolve the appeal. Phase 3 marks the transition between focusing on the past and focusing on the future to seek a resolution of the problem.

B. The Value of the Mediator in Phase 3

In Phase 3, the parties determine whether the settlement will encompass only the matters on appeal or also other matters. They also identify the issues they need to resolve to achieve a settlement. An effective mediator applies to Phase 3 the same skills used in Phase 2 to facilitate a free and frank discussion that arrives at a complete list of issues, a clear and shared definition of each issue to be resolved, and an agreement about the order in which the parties will address them.

C. Determine the Scope of the Problem to Be Solved

Decisions about the scope of the appellate mediation include whether the parties hope to achieve settlement among all parties or just some and whether they wish to resolve only the appeal or additional disputes as well. If the dispute involves parties to a former or ongoing relationship, the parties may wish to expand the concept of resolution beyond settlement of a lawsuit to include reconciliation. If the mediator and the lawyers are aware of this more expansive scope of resolution, they are able to help the parties reach a more comprehensive agreement and more complete closure of the dispute that precipitated litigation. This potential to address all aspects of a conflict is one of the great benefits of mediation over litigation because the latter must be focused only on issues that fit within a narrow legal framework or within a particular court's jurisdiction, while the mediation process can expand to include solutions that meet the parties' interests. Common issues to be resolved during mediation include the following:

- Payment of money by one party to another for damages arising out of the problem underlying the case.

- Payment of attorney fees. Will each party bear its own fees? Will one party pay another's fees? Will fees be apportioned according to a formula?

- Payment of court costs. Especially in cases requiring extensive expert testimony and expensive exhibits, court costs can loom large.

- Do the parties need to take future action apart from the payment of money? If the judgment grants injunctive or declaratory relief, parties may wish to build into a settlement an agreement to hand over documents, provide letters of reference, refrain from specifically defined conduct, file a joint motion to vacate the trial court's judgment, cooperate on a clearly defined task, sell particular property and divide the proceeds, and so on.

- Will the settlement in this appeal affect other pending cases?

- Will the terms of the settlement be subject to a confidentiality clause?

- In a marital dissolution case, parties may need to resolve questions of custody and visitation, child and spousal support, the family residence, or personal property and other assets.

- In an employment case, parties may need to address the future status of the plaintiff's employment, the amount of any financial settlement, the terms of any payment, references or recommendations, changes or additions to the employer's policies or procedures, confidentiality of the agreement, or release language.

In a complex business dispute or a dispute among family members about the care and financial matters of an ailing parent, the list of issues may be several pages long. In other cases, the list may be very short and include only payment of money, and attorney fees and court costs or perhaps confidentiality of the terms of the settlement agreement.

D. Organize the Issues and Create an Agenda

Phase 3 also includes discussion about the order in which the parties will address the issues. In some cases, logic dictates this order. For example, in an employment dispute, the parties must first answer questions about whether the employee will return or remain in the employ of the defendant. Until they decide that issue, even if only tentatively or hypothetically for the purpose of discussion, the parties do not have a sufficient reference point from which to consider monetary issues, nor can they know whether to include nonmonetary considerations on the list such as job references or recommendations.

In terms of ordering the issues, some mediators like to prime the process for success by tackling smaller and easier issues first. Early successes inspire hope that even the difficult issues can be resolved. After years of failure to reach any agreement, this quick success on a small issue enables the parties to experience a collaborative working relationship and builds momentum for successful resolution of the more challenging issues.

In some cases, it is necessary to decide tough threshold issues before moving on to easier ones. In such instances, resolution of the difficult issues means that it hopefully will be easy downhill sledding toward finishing with a settlement agreement. Sometimes this approach also makes sense because the threshold issues will determine the success or failure to reach an agreement because of the minor nature of all other issues. In such an instance, it makes sense to work on the dispositive issues and avoid wasting time on more trivial matters if the case ultimately cannot be settled. In any event, the organization of the issues must fit the particular appeal being mediated.

By determining the scope of the mediation and developing an agenda that encompasses all issues the parties must discuss and agree upon to resolve their dispute, the parties begin negotiations with an explicit and shared understanding of the task they face in creating an agreement. In addition, by jointly developing an agenda, they have engaged in collaborative problem solving about procedural matters that can serve as a model for resolution during the remainder of the mediation.

E. Work in Joint Session in Phase 3 to the Extent Possible

In addition to the tangible outcomes of Phase 3—clarifying the scope of the mediation and listing and organizing the issues the parties must decide—this phase also serves an important procedural purpose. It requires the parties to work collaboratively toward a common goal: to define the mediation's scope and create an agenda that contains all of the issues they need to resolve in order to move on. Parties can certainly accomplish in separate caucuses the *substantive* task of developing a list of issues and ultimately agreeing on an order in which to consider them. However, in doing so they forfeit the *procedural* advantage of working together if they simply retreat to caucus. In meeting together they have the felt experience of turning away from the problem to the solution that cannot happen when they are separated. In joint session, they also get to interact collaboratively on a common task, perhaps for the first time, which can have carry-over benefits later when they are negotiating a solution.[1]

---

1. The exercise of creating a list is akin to brainstorming, a form of induced cooperation, which we discuss at length in Chapter 15. *See* James H. Stark & Douglas N. Frenkel, Changing Minds: The Work of Mediators and Empirical Studies of Persuasion 266, 328–42 (2013), for a discussion of how this exercise can lead to greater cooperation in other aspects of the mediation.

Chapter 8
Developing and Negotiating Solutions in Phase 4

A. Introduction

Having laid a foundation by exchanging information, defining the issues to be resolved, and setting an agenda for the remainder of the mediation, the participants are ready to begin identifying possible solutions to their problem and the litigation. Phase 4 encompasses the work of developing and negotiating solutions. In Phase 4, participants consider this question: "Are there options we can all agree are better than continuing with the appeal?" The activities that occur in Phase 4 help parties to answer this question by providing a forum in which to (1) explore their interests; (2) identify and evaluate available opportunities, options, and solutions; and (3) negotiate a mutually agreeable settlement that meets their interests better than continuing with the appeal.

This is a phase that parties, and especially attorneys, are eager to start. Indeed, the main danger is that attorneys will prematurely begin Phase 4 bargaining during the information exchanging phase by declaring a bottom line or tossing out an offer to settle. Even if the participants have held off on negotiation in prior phases, once they arrive at Phase 4, they may tend to rush into the volley of offers and counteroffers. This is a mistake.

As we explain next, Phase 4 is most valuable when parties attend to each task of this phase, beginning with an exploration of the parties' interests. Once parties understand what matters to each of them—what interests the settlement needs to address, at least in part—they are ready to explore potential value-creating options for settlement. By this we mean that the participants should start by creating options and solutions, both those that are obvious and those that require a bit of brainstorming to imagine. But it's called "creating" for a reason: this work of imagination creates value. Mediators create a space within which the participants look for ways to add value for themselves in a way that the appellate court cannot and in a way that simple division of obvious resources (usually just money) cannot. Once parties have generated options and possible solutions, mediators can work with them and their attorneys to formulate a negotiation plan even before the first offer is conveyed. Phase 4 culminates with parties' negotiating and reaching a settlement agreement.

Phase 4 is also when careful preparation by the participants pays off. The thoughtful selection of a mediator, the premediation communications and planning, the preparation of the mediator and the parties, the exchange of information, and the clarification of the scope of the mediation and the issues establish a strong foundation to support the parties' negotiation. In Section III, we offer suggestions for lawyers about how to prepare for and participate effectively in these discussions. And, in Section IV, we offer suggestions for mediators about how to facilitate constructive discussions in each phase of the mediation.

B.   What Are Parties Trying to Accomplish through Negotiation?

Before we launch into the practical aspects of Phase 4, we pause to identify exactly what the parties should try to accomplish. The glib answer that many parties and their attorneys might give reflexively is "More money for our side." In our view, mediators and participants should examine this assumption because it shrinks the pool of potential solutions and, with it, the likelihood of a successful outcome.

The very reason to engage in mediation—rather than blindly continue with litigation—is to improve on options presently available to each party. Basic negotiation theory dictates that "[t]he reason you negotiate is to produce something better than the results you can obtain without negotiating."[1] In Chapter 2, we examined how each side can compare the value of its present circumstance (the appeal) to other options available without compromise (such as dismissing the appeal, filing a different lawsuit, pursuing an administrative remedy, or seeking a legislative change in the law). Against this background of what can be done *without* agreement, parties are ready to examine what can be done *with* an agreement. In essence, Phase 4 requires an honest and open appraisal of the question "Are there options that we can all agree are better than continuing with the appeal?"

C.   The Secret Sauce of Great Appellate Mediations Is to Begin Negotiations by Generating Options and Solutions that Expand the Pie and Potentially Address the Parties' Interests

Participants engage in the valuable work of Phase 4 by identifying options that work better for them than pursuing an appeal, namely a settlement agreement whose terms are more acceptable than loss on appeal and perhaps even better than the result of winning on appeal. Therein lies the "secret sauce" for a great appellant mediation: identifying better options to an appeal by first engaging in *integrative negotiation* and then, if necessary, *distributive negotiation*.

Parties generate value for themselves by beginning with integrative negotiation. Integrative negotiation focuses first on understanding what is important to the parties—their interests—followed by an effort to generate solutions

---

1. ROGER FISHER, WILLIAM L. URY & BRUCE PATTON, GETTING TO YES: NEGOTIATING AGREEMENT WITHOUT GIVING IN 100 (Penguin, 2nd ed. 2011).

that "expand the pie" and address the parties' interests to the greatest extent possible. In this process, although issues can be addressed one by one, the agreement is kept open until the parties resolve all issues, thereby allowing the parties to revisit earlier tentative agreements and, if appropriate, to negotiate trades that reflect their priorities.

In contrast to integrative bargaining in which parties strive to create value, *distributive negotiation* involves dividing or distributing a limited or fixed resource—usually money. To the extent one party *gains* something, the other party *loses* something. Distributive negotiations typically include discussions about who is right or wrong—who will win or lose on appeal—that are designed to convince the opposing party to make concessions. This second type of negotiation is typically characterized by haggling and hard-bargaining tactics designed to "win" in negotiation. Unless carefully managed by the mediator and the lawyers, distributive bargaining can be polarizing and cause parties to lose much of the good will they established earlier in the mediation.

Appellate mediations that consist solely of integrative negotiations are rare. Almost all mediations include both integrative and distributive negotiations. If one of the issues identified for resolution in Phase 3 involves money, then no matter how large the amount of money, the parties need to divide it at some point. Nevertheless, to the extent the parties create value by enlarging the pie through interest-based negotiations and address at least some important issues by interest-based, nonmonetary solutions, a carefully managed distributive negotiation to divide the pie can be made less divisive.

The mediation process we propose encourages opportunities throughout to explore the potential for interest-based solutions that create value for the parties, beginning in premediation with discussion of the parties' goals for the mediation and a preliminary exploration of their interests or what matters to them that needs to be reflected by their agreement. In Phase 2, exchanging information, interests are also among the topics for discussion. And in Phase 4, as the parties seek resolution to the issues one by one, interests again become a focus for discussion.

Mediators vary in their approaches to integrative negotiations. The approach we suggest begins with a brainstorming exercise, in which the mediator facilitates a discussion to generate options for solutions that helps the parties address their interests to the greatest extent possible.

The process we suggest consists of the following steps.

D.   Brainstorm for as Many Options as Possible— Especially Options with Asymmetric Gains

1.   *Generate Options*

Before arriving at mediation, parties usually have taken opposing positions on issues, and so potential solutions are severely limited. The exercise of creating options can be challenging and requires the assistance of a skilled mediator, but it is crucial to optimal interest-based negotiations. To make the most of option generation, mediators encourage parties to create as many potential solutions as possible and to separate the development of options from the evaluation and the claiming or negotiation of them.

Even when the issue under discussion is money, it can be helpful to explore options that meet the parties' interests and thus "expand the pie," such as timing or manner of payment and how the settlement will be characterized for tax purposes.

Expanding the pie is a favorite metaphor of mediators and negotiation theorists because it aptly and colorfully illustrates the goal of this part of Phase 4. But *how* do you expand the pie? In reality, pie pans do not expand magically when put into an oven, and mediation participants who are used to distributive bargaining may believe that expanding the value of solutions to the appeal is equally unlikely. Let us help clarify. Expanding the pie happens when participants can identify some option or potential agreement term that causes one party to gain substantially more than another party loses. In other words, one side gets a whole bunch even though it costs the other side relatively little. It is not quite win-win, but it is win-and-lose-only-a-little. We can think of these as asymmetric gains.

Thus, this part of Phase 4 should bring out the thinking caps and be a creative exercise in identifying potential settlement terms with asymmetric gains. To spark the imagination, we provide a list of frequently available options in Table 8.1.

Table 8.1: Potential Settlement Options with Gains that Outweigh Losses

Settlement Possibility	Advantage to Receiver	Disadvantage to Offerer
Tax characterization of settlement award	Substantial money savings to injured plaintiff who may receive settlement proceeds tax free or at lowered rates if characterized as tort damages	No disadvantage to the defendant in how settlement funds are characterized for tax purposes
Confidentiality provision to keep settlement terms private	Potentially large economic advantage to company or insurance company facing many collateral legal actions or similar cases in avoiding an expensive precedent	Minimal disadvantage to individual plaintiff who needs money, not publicity
Apology	Important to injured party who wants to have his or her suffering, pain, and loss of dignity acknowledged	No economic disadvantage, and actually advantageous for party who is genuinely sorry*

Settlement Possibility	Advantage to Receiver	Disadvantage to Offerer
Agreement to seek stipulated reversal of the judgment	Valuable to a defendant, especially an institution cast in a bad light in the judgment, to have an unfavorable judgment erased	No disadvantage to plaintiff because a settlement renders the judgment moot
Dividing assets by type rather than by percentage	Possibly large gain because a party gets more of the type of property (or unique item) that he or she wants	Possibly small or no loss to a party who does not want the particular type of property and may conversely gain another type (or item) he or she actually wants
Sale with right of first refusal	Immediate satisfaction to giver of the right but who immediately gets the property he or she desires	Reassurance to the party receiving the right of refusal that he or she can safeguard the property from being lost (especially valuable in cases where the property has sentimental value)
Profit-sharing	Preserves an investment of time or resources with future stream of money; allows the receiver to share in the risk and rewards of the venture; allows productive capital to remain productive	Allows the offerer to avoid dissolution of the company, segregation of productive assets, processes, or products; offerer surrenders only the part of profits due to another's investment
Licensing agreements	Allows receiver to use the valuable product or process to generate profits	Offerer may lose exclusive use but gains an income stream and potentially greater adoption of the product or process
Changes in company or institutional policy	Provides receiver the satisfaction that his or her perseverance has made the world a better place	Perhaps no loss at all because company policy may need to change under the law or to avoid liability for future misconduct of the sort at issue in this case
Agreement to provide positive job references in the future	May make the difference between being able to continue working in a chosen profession or field and having to abandon a previously enjoyed profession	No economic cost and may be a way to make things right for a prior employee who did nothing wrong or only violated internal policy or procedure

(continued)

Settlement Possibility	Advantage to Receiver	Disadvantage to Offerer
Restructuring the business	May preserve tremendous value because a live company is worth more than one sold for book value or parts	Each party may end up with a viable part of a company or a single going concern that gives every party an acceptable role in it
Agreement to cooperate on a task or to share a future cost	May make an endeavor or project possible where neither party has the resources to pursue what is a shared goal	Will require the contribution toward the cost being shared or task undertaken but promises greater reward than can be achieved by one party alone
Rotating custody or possession	Rather than cutting a beloved dog in half or forcing football fans to sit next to each other at every game, rotating custody, possession, or use allows periodic enjoyment	Avoids the pain of the total loss of a possession that is not divisible—or the forced sale of the asset, where only money (and not future enjoyment) remains
Sell and lease back	Allows seller to immediately realize value of the property while continuing to use it into the future	Allows buyer to gain the desired property and a future stream of income from the property
Noncompete agreement	Receiver of the promise can make plans based on greater clarity about the competition[1]	Offerer of the promise not to compete may not want to continue working in the field anyway
Free or discounted advertising	Receiver of the new or increased advertising may see dramatic gains in revenues and sales	Cost of advertising may be cheaper for the offerer of the promise or the offerer might already be paying for a great deal of advertising and the inclusion of the other party in part of the ads may cost little or nothing more
Structured settlement	Because income is constructively received by a taxpayer when it is made available, receiver avoids a big one-time tax hit	May reduce borrowing costs and avoid financial jeopardy with payment of entire settlement all at once
Buy-sell agreements	Creative agreements can push asset division into the future, include optionality, and structured sales so that the receiver gets the desired property; may overcome an obstacle that blocks an immediate sale	May reduce obstacles to seller who might not otherwise be able to make the sale or even afford to keep or maintain the asset

Settlement Possibility	Advantage to Receiver	Disadvantage to Offerer
Release of known and unknown claims	Receiver may gain peace of mind and the ability to plan for the full cost of the problem being litigated	Offerer may not be surrendering anything if the release of liability ultimately describes all of the loss

* However, beware that an insincere, bad, or half-hearted apology can make things much worse rather than a little better. *See* Lee Taft, *Apology Subverted: The Commodification of Apology*, Yale L.J. 1135–60 (2000).

† Caution: Noncompete agreements are governed by numerous varying statutes in the United States and may be prohibited in whole or in part in a particular jurisdiction.

In addition to these possible settlement terms, we note that the very act of settling a case on appeal is asymmetrical in gain. Because appellants usually bear the entire cost of producing the appellate record and longer and more costly briefs, appellants stand to gain more in savings by a settlement than respondents do. This practical reality in addition to the long odds that they face explains why appellants typically discount their settlement demands more than respondents do.

2. Clarify the Options

Mediators should ensure that participants reach a common understanding of each brainstormed option. The goal is to *understand* each option, and especially any nuances, not to evaluate or begin horse trading options.

3. Evaluate the Options

Once the parties' common definitions have been achieved for each option, they must evaluate them to test the most promising options against the criteria of their interests. Ultimately, they negotiate to resolution of the issue by selecting the mutually agreeable option or combination of options that best address their interests. Using their underlying interests, as well as the practical reality of their situation, as criteria, the parties evaluate their options. Generally the parties focus most of their attention in this evaluation stage on the most promising options. As they discuss the criteria and options, they sometimes modify them and generate new options.

Some cases are obvious candidates for interest-based negotiation, such as divorce cases in which there are numerous issues that can be traded according to the parties' interests; if the parties have children, their agreements will be more satisfying, particularly in the long term, if they consider the interests of both the parents and the children.

In other cases, the application of interest-based negotiation may not be so obvious. A commonly cited example of a case where integrative bargaining makes no sense is the personal injury case in which the parties have no ongoing relationship and the negotiation is just about money. We encourage lawyers and mediators not to underestimate the value of exploring interests in any case, even one that is just about money. Questions such as "What will the money do for you?" or "What would be the result of your paying/receiving that sum of money?" may not lead immediately to a creative solution other than money, but the foundation of understanding that is laid by the identification of interests can form the basis for creative ways to bridge gaps later in the distributive negotiation about money. In an employment case, for example, a plaintiff might explain that the money represents the ability to meet her expenses until she is reemployed. Knowing this underlying concern, the parties might consider ways to hasten her reemployment such as making placement services available to her, perhaps at a rate that is lower than it would be if she paid directly. They might also explore ways to remove obstacles to employment, such as a retroactive resignation that removes her termination from the record and enables her to answer truthfully that she resigned her employment with the defendant.

In other seemingly distributive negotiations about money, discussions might reveal that time has value to a party. The defendant, for example, may be willing to pay a larger monetary settlement if payments can be made over time. A plaintiff might also benefit from positive tax consequences made possible by payments over a number of years or characterization of damages resulting in more favorable tax treatment.

Most mediation participants want to go immediately to distributive negotiation, especially when the settlement appears only to involve the payment of money. However, it is in the parties' interest to delay this aspect of negotiation until they have exhausted integrative negotiations. Although integrative negotiations rarely lead directly to full resolution, the information they exchange may lead to creative possibilities that become important during the money negotiation, particularly at the end of the negotiation when the parties are searching for a way to close the gap between their negotiating positions. By defining the issues, identifying and clarifying options, and developing criteria by which to evaluate the options before exchanging proposals and counterproposals, the parties lay the foundation for more effective negotiations and for reaching agreement.

E.   After Exploring Integrative Solutions, Negotiate Distributive Issues

Let's be clear: there is nothing bad about distributive negotiation, especially if it follows concerted efforts at integrative negotiations. Indeed, as we noted above, whenever there is a fixed sum of money or pool of resources, the negotiations necessarily must be distributive at some point. Unfortunately, claims for money addressed by distributive negotiations "are usually settled with prolonged bargaining consisting of numerous rounds of painful concessions."[2] And these drawbacks may be inherent in the process.

At the start of the distributive negotiation there is usually a large gap between the parties' positions, leading to pessimism about the outcome. Also typically, there is uncertainty about how to begin—whether the plaintiff or defendant will make the first offer or demand—and questions about what the opening settlement positions actually mean.

F.   Negotiations Using Joint Sessions and Private Caucuses

Different types of negotiations require different approaches. Integrative negotiations are usually best conducted in joint sessions where everyone can contribute to the brainstorming of creative options and participate in discussions about how well the options address their interests.[3] But there are times when it is more skillful to discuss potential options in private caucus. If the mediator wishes to inquire about a potential solution that, if rejected by the party required to perform, would offend the other side, it may be better to discuss the solution in private caucus. The issue of continuing employment or re-employment of the plaintiff in an employment dispute is an example. Some mediators choose to communicate settlement proposals as if the proposal came from the mediator in order to avoid the cognitive trap of reactive devaluation.[4] Reactive devaluation is triggered when the antagonism between parties is so pronounced that they cannot hear the merit of any proposal from the other side. They instinctively believe that a proposal that is acceptable to the other party must be bad for them. Coming from the mediator, rather than from "the enemy," a party will likely evaluate the proposal more objectively and, in fact, may immediately recognize its benefit. Although this approach may be effective to overcome reactive devaluation, it does require the mediator to misrepresent, or at least obscure, the truth, a practice that may offend your sense of ethics. As with all such decisions, we urge you to examine whether expedient practices

---

2. J. ANDERSON LITTLE, MAKING MONEY TALK: HOW TO MEDIATE INSURED CLAIMS AND OTHER MONETARY DISPUTES xii (ABA 2007). On the topic of distributive negotiations, we highly recommend this excellent book.

3. "Integrative bargaining benefits from more, rather than less, communication. The likelihood that parties will discover solutions that meet one party's needs at little cost to the other party is enhanced when the parties convey their true needs and concerns—their underlying interests . . . —and if they remain engaged with each other, exchanging information and exploring options. Thus, being aggressive and self-focused is not productive." Bruce Barry and Raymond A. Friedman, *Bargainer Characteristics in Distributive and Integrative Negotiation*, 74(2) J. OF PERSONALITY & SOCIAL PSYCHOLOGY 348 (1998).

4. *See generally* Lee Ross, *Reactive Devaluation in Negotiation and Conflict Resolution*, in KENNETH ARROW ET AL., EDS., BARRIERS TO CONFLICT RESOLUTION (1995).

such as this one are congruent with your values and the ethical principles of the profession of mediation.

Distributive bargaining usually occurs in private caucuses with the mediator engaging in shuttle diplomacy by conveying offers between the separate rooms. Private caucus offers parties the opportunity to evaluate proposals and formulate counterproposals without revealing information they are uncomfortable disclosing. Sometimes these caucuses occur without the mediator. Other times the parties want the mediator to assist them to evaluate proposals and formulate counterproposals the opposing party may find acceptable. Private discussions with the mediator can also be used to plot out a series of moves and countermoves when the bargaining comes down to money.

In some cases, the difference between offers and counteroffers spans only a narrow gap even though the parties are rational and able to communicate effectively with each other through the mediator. In such cases, even distributive negotiations may productively occur in joint sessions. When they work, joint session negotiations often work amazingly fast. We might remind readers that most distributive bargaining in the world occurs face to face. So viewed, mediation is a rare instance of private caucuses with a neutral that can always avail itself of a more direct type of interaction.

G. The Moment of Decision

At some point during Phase 4, a party will decide whether the better option is to continue with the appeal or to accept terms of a proposed agreement. When a party measures an available settlement offer against the prospects of continued litigation, the result is likely to yield a truly successful mediation—*regardless of whether it settles the case.*[5] If the proposed agreement is better than pursuing the appeal, a party should accept the agreement. Conversely, if the proposed agreement is not better than the appeal, a party should reject the proposal and continue with the appeal. Or, for cases with negative economic value, no matter the chances of prevailing on appeal, a party should abandon the appeal unless the litigation is brought as a test case to secure a published decision of widespread legal significance or for other unique, noneconomic reasons.

Even if a settlement proposal is not as favorable as offers made in the trial court, a party should not reject a good settlement offer only because it compares unfavorably to a past, but now unavailable, settlement proposal. Neither should a party spurn an offer just because a previous offer serves as an anchor to prior negotiations.[6] Parties are better served by careful analysis of their prospects on

---

5. Roger Fisher, *Negotiating Power: Getting and Using Influence*, 27(2) Am. Behavioral Scientist 149, 156 (1983).
6. *See* Daniel Kahneman, Paul Slovic & Amos Tversky, eds., Judgment Under Uncertainty: Heuristics and Biases 17 (1982) (noting that for the anchoring effect "[t]his bias is common to naïve and to sophisticated subjects").

appeal. Appellants should heavily discount the possibility of ultimate victory in the face of an unfavorable judgment. Respondents need to confront the reality that vindication by the trial court has now given way to uncertainty and prolonged litigation on appeal and, possibly, the return to trial court.

The decision of which of the available options is better should also include an honest consideration of the emotional costs of uncertainty and loss that inhere in appeals. Chapters 2 and 3 provide participants with an analytic framework for valuing an appeal and determining whether there are other presently available options, even in the absence of an agreement. The analysis we suggest in these chapters will help parties avoid decisions based only on vague estimates, approximate rules of thumb, or nebulous hopes.[7]

H.   The Value of the Mediator in Phase 4

Skilled mediators can make a real difference in Phase 4. In particular, mediators can serve the following purposes:

Help parties develop and carry out a negotiation plan. Unless parties have a plan for the negotiation, they negotiate reactively, not proactively; that is, they make decisions about each move based on their reaction to the other party's proposal, not based on a well-considered plan designed to get them to their goals. A mediator can urge them to develop such a plan that plots steps in terms of several movements during the bargaining process, without prescribing what those numbers should be.

In addition, because the language of distributive negotiations is numbers, an indirect and—until the end when a negotiator stops moving—an unclear means of communicating, a mediator can help parties communicate more directly or help them to interpret the meaning of numbers.

Help parties move from a focus on the past to the future. Mediators can help parties move from nursing past wounds to focusing on solutions. An example of how they can help is sunk costs. As a consequence of focusing on the past, parties are often motivated to continue litigating because they have spent so many resources—sunk costs—fighting the other side that they do not want to quit. Although sunk costs tend to make the reason for the spending seem too important to abandon,[8] they are an unsound reason to continue with litigation. Even though it feels right to parties to continue the fight because they have

---

7. DANIEL KAHNEMAN, THINKING, FAST AND SLOW 3–20 (Macmillan 2011).

8. Hal R. Arkes & Catherine Blumer, *The Psychology of Sunk Cost*, 35 ORGANIZATIONAL BEHAVIOR & HUMAN DECISION PROCESSES 124 (1985). ("The prior investment, which is motivating the present decision to continue, does so despite the fact that it objectively should not influence the decision."). Rather than lamenting sunk costs, "decisions should be based on the costs and benefits that are expected to arise from the choice of each option." *Id.* at 127. Yet, the effect of sunk costs regularly influences decision making six months after a prior expenditure (*Id.* at 128)—well within the time frame between conclusion of a trial and an appellate mediation.

put so much into it, sunk costs do not make irrational plans for future litigation somehow rational. Mediators can encourage parties to think through this decision rather than fall prey to this or other psychological traps.

Help parties evaluate the merits of settlement offers and options, despite their emotional reactions. If parties decide to continue with litigation rather than to settle, it is often because the option available to them in the mediation did not provide sufficient emotional satisfaction—vindication, enough money to change their lives or businesses for the better, or a sense that justice was achieved.

Parties often need assistance in evaluating a proposed settlement based on what it *does* provide them and how it compares to the alternative of continuing with the appeal even though it *may not* satisfy them emotionally. The assistance we suggest is not the heavy-handed pressure to make a deal. It is the support to enable parties to consider all available information in order to ensure informed self-determination. In the end, counsel or the mediator may not agree with a party's ultimate decision, which may be to accept a deal they judge to be unfavorable or to reject a seemingly advantageous offer. Of course, parties are free to make irrational choices. But mediators *can* make sure that along with the emotional response to a proposed settlement parties have also considered the information necessary to evaluate proposals rationally.

Some mediators during Phase 4, if they conclude parties are not acting rationally in rejecting proposals, will try to convince—or even coerce—them to settle, a strategy that is profoundly misguided. There are more effective and ethical ways mediators can help parties to make good decisions in Phase 4. One example is decision trees, which we explained in Chapter 3. The decision tree analysis worksheets we provided allow mediators to work with participants to determine if their best numbers reflect irrational hopes or gut feelings that logic cannot support.

Self-determination means parties are entitled to make their own decisions, even bad ones. But mediators can see to it that they do so fully informed about the alternatives, including litigation, and the consequences of these choices.

I.   Conclusion

Many people might think all of Phase 4 can be summed up in the phrase "OK, let's talk dollars." However, Phase 4 offers an opportunity to both expand the pie and make sure everyone gets an acceptable slice. Although there is often a rush toward the end of Phase 4's distributive negotiation about dollars, wise participants and skilled mediators first ensure that integrative negotiations have allowed the parties to explore other potential value.

Chapter 9
Concluding the Mediation and Postmediation Follow-Up in Phase 5

A. Introduction

Important, and sometimes extensive, work remains after the moment a party says, "I accept the settlement offer." The parties should evaluate the terms of the settlement agreement for clarity, completeness, and commitment. Under the laws of most jurisdictions, settlement agreements must be reduced to writing and signed by the parties and/or their attorneys. Of course, the appeal must be dismissed. Thus, we provide a few thoughts on how to answer the question "How do we make sure the parties' settlement agreement works and is enforceable?"

As important as Phase 5 is for a final and lasting conclusion of the case, this phase often gets short shrift. At the end of a long and arduous day, when the participants are tired and eager to go home, they may lack the patience, energy, and focus required to conclude the mediation in a thoughtful manner. If the dispute did not settle, they may be discouraged or angry or be unwilling to spend more time and money on the mediation process. Because the tasks of concluding vary depending on whether the parties reach agreement at the end of Phase 4, we provide guidance as to both possibilities.

If the case settles, participants may minimize the importance of this phase out of optimism that they share a common recollection and understanding of the agreements and they will be able to work out any differences easily. Until the parties have a written and signed agreement, they do not have an agreement. Thus, Phase 5 encompasses (1) the documentation of settlement in a formal settlement agreement or a less formal memorandum of understanding, (2) dismissal of the appeal along with any necessary accompanying motions, and (3) enforcement of the settlement agreement (especially if the terms of the agreement are to be fulfilled before the trial court[1] loses jurisdiction). Settling parties need to preserve the progress they made and minimize the opportunity for future disputes that cost the parties time, money, and perhaps good will and, in the worst case, unravel the settlement.

If the case does not settle during the mediation session, all is not lost. Our experience at the Third District California Court of Appeal is that about one-third of cases referred to mediation simply do not settle, another third settle at the mediation session, and *a third settle after the mediation session with the continued*

---

1. Yes, the *trial court.* If this strikes you as counterintuitive, we urge you to carefully study our advice in Part B.1 ("Compliance Checkpoints"). An excellent discussion may also be found in *Lyons v. Booker,* 982 P.2d 1142, 1999 U.T. App 172 (Utah Ct. App. 1999).

efforts of the mediator and the attorneys. In other words, if everyone gave up after an unsuccessful mediation session, the Third District's program would go from overwhelmingly successful to overwhelmingly unsuccessful. Thus, participants in an appellate mediation that does not settle during the mediation session should take time to understand why they were unable to resolve their dispute. They should then appraise whether and, if so, how and when they will resume their negotiations and what the mediator's role might be going forward. Mediators can be enormously helpful in generating this analysis and discussion.

B.   When the Mediation Session Ends with an Agreement

Once the parties reach agreement, especially if it is late in the day or in the wee hours, they may be tempted to leave—and leave documentation of the settlement to tomorrow. But until they have a written, signed agreement and the case is dismissed, they remain litigants, subject to orders of the appellate court (including procedural requirements) so long as the appeal continues to pend.

In refining the agreement, crafting enforceability provisions, and recording the settlement in writing, attorneys play one of their most important roles in the appellate mediation. Attorneys are used to the concepts of contract law that apply to settlement agreements and owe their clients a duty to ensure that an agreement does not dissolve into a tangled web of ambiguity and enforceability problems.

1.   *Reaching Agreement Happens Only When Parties Address Every Essential Issue and Agree on Every Term*

As the parties reach interim or tentative agreements during the mediation, the mediator or the lawyers are usually recording them in their notes. As the final missing piece falls into place and the settlement is assured, it is important for the lawyers or the mediator to review *all* of the terms of the settlement as they understand them. This step enables parties to uncover any latent misunderstandings and to ensure that the parties' interpretations of the terms of the agreement are aligned.

Of course, a written agreement must include the case name and number of the lawsuit that is being settled and sufficient detail to make it a binding contract: the names of the parties to be bound, the dollar amount of the settlement or other consideration, the scope of the release, and other terms appropriate in the case. However, the parties probably do not yet have an agreement until they have considered whether the following issues apply to their case and, if so, how their agreement will resolve them:

- **What is the scope of the release of liability?** Many settlements involve the release of claims by one party in exchange for payment of money by another. If so, the parties must agree on exactly what is being released. Will the release cover even unknown claims or only the claims contained in the plaintiff's complaint or petition? And are there any other collateral legal or administrative actions that are included or excluded from the settlement agreement? Remember that a settlement agreement can resolve fewer than all of the issues on appeal or can encompass other cases not connected in a formal legal sense.

- **Who will pay for attorney fees and costs?** An agreement silent as to costs and fees allows the parties to bring motions to seek them.[2] A settlement agreement that fails to mention how costs and fees are to be allocated allows the parties to seek those sums in the trial court even after dismissal of the case.[3] As the U.S. Supreme Court has noted, "A request for attorney's fees should not result in a second major litigation. Ideally, of course, litigants will settle the amount of a fee."[4] Especially in vigorously contested cases, these sums can be quite large. Often the parties will specify that each side is to bear its own costs and fees. Once again, however, it is the prerogative of the parties to decide for themselves how they wish to allocate fees and costs.

- **Language necessary to make the mediation agreement enforceable under the governing law.** This can be unexpectedly tricky. For example, California requires agreements reached in mediation to state that they are binding and based on a present intent to settle, with the effect that "[p]arties overlooking this requirement may inadvertently enter into a written settlement agreement that is unenforceable because it is inadmissible."[5]

- **Compliance checkpoints prior to dismissal of the case from trial court jurisdiction.** For example, an agreement should specify the timing of payments or delivery or execution of documents by specified dates occurring before the time designated for dismissal of the case by the court. If money is to be paid as part of the settlement, the failure to specify the manner and timing of payment may render the agreement unenforceable for lack of agreement on a material term.[6] Will the agreement specify that the trial court will retain jurisdiction

---

2. In our experience, there are a surprising number of lawsuits that remain alive only because the matter of fees and costs has not yet been resolved. As a consequence, an agreement silent as to costs and fees may leave open a very important issue. While the parties are agreeing on how the causes of action should be resolved in a settlement, they might do well also to reach agreement as to costs and fees in writing.
3. Folsom v. Butte County Assn. of Governments, 32 Cal. 3d 668, 671, 652 P.2d 437 (Cal. 1982).
4. Hensley v. Eckerhart, 461 U.S. 424, 437, 103 S. Ct. 1933, 76 L. Ed. 2d 40 (1983).
5. Fair v. Bakhtiari, 40 Cal. 4th 189, 147 P.3d 653 (Cal. 2006).
6. *E.g.*, Lindsay v. Lewandowski, 139 Cal. App. 4th 1618, 1622–23, 43 Cal. Rptr. 3d 846 (Ct. App. 2006).

and the case be dismissed only after all of the settlement conditions are fulfilled? *Why the trial court and not the court of appeal?* Because the question of whether a party has complied with terms of a settlement agreement is a *factual* question that the appellate court—which does not find facts but only reaches questions of law—cannot answer. Consequently, *the enforcement of all settlement agreements occurs in the trial court* even if the settlement is reached during an *appellate* mediation. Once the appeal is dismissed, the trial court usually regains jurisdiction,[7] at which point motions for attorney fees and costs are ordinarily heard in cases in which the settlement agreement does not specify who bears fees and costs. Once the trial court dismisses the case, there is no court with remaining power to enforce the terms of the settlement. Of course, this circumstance does not render the settlement agreement void. The problem is merely one of efficiency in enforcing the terms of a settlement. Enforcement must be through the filing of a new lawsuit for breach of contract rather than a motion to enforce the settlement agreement. What a pain, but a pain that can easily be avoided with smart settlement agreement drafting.

- **Will consent of the insurer be necessary?** In many cases in which the insurer has provided for the legal defense of a party, that insurer's consent is necessary to settle the case. Many standard insurance policies give insurers the right to control the defense and to determine whether to settle. Indeed, these insureds have no right to consent to a settlement under the terms of many policies.[8]

- **Are there tax characterizations and implications?** Merely reaching an agreement on the sum total to be paid for a release of claims can leave the important question of tax consequences unresolved. Depending on how payments are characterized in family law and personal injury cases, one side may bear the burden of taxes that it did not anticipate. Or one side may find that the settlement counts toward income on which child or spousal support may be premised.[9] The settlement agreement's terms can greatly influence the tax liabilities of the parties, for better or for worse. If agreements characterize damages for tax purposes, the parties who are paying the settlement amount frequently

---

7. *See, e.g., Lyons,* 982 P.2d at 1143 (as to the "Motion to enforce settlement agreement," the "court of appeals does not hear or consider new evidence, as granting appellant's motion would require.").

8. *E.g.,* Mitchum v. Hudgens, 533 So. 2d 194, 196 (Ala. 1988).

9. *E.g.,* Marriage of Heiner, 136 Cal. App. 4th 1514, 1521, 39 Cal. Rptr. 3d 730 (Ct. App. 2006) (characterization of settlement proceeds determined whether the funds could be considered for support obligation purposes); *see also* Stephen G. Mehta, *Lasting Agreements: Carefully Drafted Settlement Terms Are the Key to Ensuring That an Agreement Does Not Unravel,* L.A. Law. 31–32 (Sept. 2007) (discussing tax consequences arising out of constructive receipt of settlement proceeds and the taxability of confidentiality clauses to the extent that they are valuable to only one party).

insist on provisions indemnifying them for any adverse tax consequences should taxing authorities not accept the characterizations.

- **Is there a stipulation to seek reversal of judgment?** The law governing stipulated reversals of judgment is arcane, a bit baffling, and does not arise very often.[10] In a nutshell, a settlement on appeal may resolve the issues between the parties but does not itself vacate the judgment entered by the trial court. Some defendants do not like the idea that there is a judgment against them—even if it has been rendered toothless by a written settlement agreement. These defendants insist on bargaining for a stipulation by all parties to reverse the judgment as part of the settlement. Unless the parties intend their settlement to evaporate if the court does not reverse the judgment, they should not condition settlement on the appellate court's reversal of the judgment. Such a settlement will automatically fall apart if the appellate court denies reversal. If parties intend their settlement to be durable, the better option is for the agreement to require the party defending the judgment to join in the stipulation to reverse the judgment with the burden to prepare and file the motion resting with the party that is attacking the judgment on appeal.

- **Do contractual confidentiality provisions apply?** Statutory mediation confidentiality may not suffice to safeguard trade secrets, intellectual property, or personal information.

- **Is there a cooling off period imposed by law on settlement agreements?** In most jurisdictions, there is no cooling off period within which parties may change their minds about the settlement agreement.[11] However, some jurisdictions do impose cooling off periods of 3 days and sometimes as long as 30 days![12]

- **Who will sign the agreement?** Usually a settlement agreement is binding on the parties if their attorneys sign on their behalf.[13] However, the better practice involves the parties' signing for themselves. Statutes and case law of the jurisdiction in which settlement agreements are executed dictate whether the parties themselves, rather than

---

10. Its exotic and abstruse nature, however, makes it a natural magnet for the attention of appellate specialists and authors of appellate mediation guidebooks.

11. Facebook, Inc. v. Pacific Northwest Software, Inc., 640 F.3d 1034, 1040 (9th Cir. 2011).

12. *E.g.*, State *ex rel.* Jones v. Conrad, 92 Ohio St. 3d 389, 390, 750 N.E.2d 583 (Ohio 2001). Although likely unwise, it may be possible to put a cooling off period into the settlement agreement. McNamara v. Tourneau, Inc., 464 F. Supp. 2d 232, 241 (S.D.N.Y. 2006) (contractual agreement granting plaintiff seven-day right of rescission in otherwise fully enforceable settlement agreement).

13. I.M.A., Inc. v. Rocky Mountain Airways, Inc., 713 P.2d 882, 888 (Colo. 1986) (holding that parties' agreement on essential terms of a contract as required to establish a contract can be inferred from their conduct or oral statements).

their attorneys on their behalf, may bind parties. The authority of parties to bind public or private entities likewise may be governed by special rules or requirements contained in statutes or case law.[14]

Every mediation is unique and may require additional terms to carry out the intentions of the parties in their agreement. Unfortunately, every jurisdiction is also unique: "over 2,500 separate state statutes affect mediation proceedings in some manner."[15] Thus, in drafting and executing settlement agreements, counsel must conduct sufficient research into applicable laws that apply to the case being settled. Fortunately, the extreme variability of the laws applying to mediations and settlement agreements may be reduced as more states adopt the Uniform Mediation Act, which has been enacted in 11 states and the District of Columbia as of 2015.[16] For now, however, counsel must check on the laws and rules applying to the appeal being mediated.

2. *Signing the Agreement* at *the Mediation Session*

If the parties settle their dispute at the mediation, the best practice is to sign an agreement at the mediation. Before the parties adjourn, one of the lawyers or the mediator generally reduces the terms of their agreement to writing. Sometimes lawyers have prepared and circulated a blank long-form settlement agreement in advance of the mediation. At the mediation, they add the agreed terms and the parties sign the final agreement before leaving mediation. This practice eliminates the possibility of protracted negotiations at the mediation concerning terms that can reasonably be anticipated, such as the scope of a release or the inclusion of a confidentiality provision.

If not, a lawyer or the mediator will draft a memorandum of understanding containing the essential terms. If the parties wish this document to be an enforceable contract, the document must so indicate. In very simple cases, the memorandum of understanding may include all the terms of the parties' agreement in final form. Usually, the memorandum signed at the mediation is a temporary document that the attorneys will replace after drafting a more formal and longer document prepared after the mediation.

Mediation confidentiality statutes in some jurisdictions require that any agreement to settle contain specific language if the parties intend it

---

14. *See generally* LAWRENCE E. SUSSKIND, SARAH MCKEARNEN & JENNIFER THOMAS-LAMAR, EDS., THE CONSENSUS BUILDING HANDBOOK: A COMPREHENSIVE GUIDE TO REACHING AGREEMENT 511 (Sage Publications 1999).

15. http://www.uniformlaws.org/ActSummary.aspx?title=Mediation%20Act. "More than 250 of these deal with confidentiality and privileges issues, alone." http://www.uniformlaws.org/Narrative.aspx?title=Why%20States%20Should%20Adopt%20UMA

16. www.uniformlaws.org/LegislativeFactSheet.aspx?title=Mediation%20Act.

to be enforceable and admissible in a later enforcement proceeding.[17] The memorandum should also include the case name and number of the lawsuit that is being settled and sufficient detail to make it a binding contract: the names of the parties to be bound, the dollar amount of the settlement or other consideration, the scope of the release, and other terms appropriate in the case.

Although it is rare, occasionally the parties record the terms and sign a memorandum of understanding indicating that they do *not* intend to be bound but want to have a common memory of their tentative agreement, such as when a party representative for a city or county does not have the authority to commit the party to a settlement and must seek approval from a governing body.

Some mediators will draft the memorandum of understanding or provide a form for some of its terms. Others are willing to draft the formal agreement, believing it facilitates settlement. And others refuse to draft or even to serve as the scribe of agreements because doing so exceeds the scope of their responsibility, could violate mediator neutrality and party self-determination, or constitutes the practice of law, which may not be covered by mediator malpractice insurance policies. We choose to leave the drafting of agreements to the lawyers.

3. Drafting the Written Agreement after the Mediation Session

If the parties have merely signed a memorandum of understanding at the conclusion of mediation, shortly after the mediation ends the lawyers will draft a formal written settlement agreement. Many mediators follow up with lawyers as they convert the memorandum of understanding into a formal agreement and make themselves available in case the drafting process bogs down because of disagreements regarding language or unresolved issues. And lawyers may also call on mediators to help them overcome obstacles to the completion of the agreement.

4. Testing the Agreement for Clarity, Completeness, and Commitment

Once the agreement is reduced to writing, we suggest the parties test it for clarity, completeness, and commitment. This step ensures the terms are *clear* and accurate—that the agreement says what the parties intended. It also ensures

---

17. *See, e.g.,* Cal. Evid. Code § 1123, which provides that a written settlement agreement reached in mediation is *inadmissible* to prove the terms of the agreement *unless* the agreement expressly "provides that it is admissible or subject to disclosure, or words to that effect," "provides that it is enforceable or binding or words to that effect," or "[a]ll parties to the agreement expressly agree in writing, or orally . . . to its disclosure."

completeness. A complete agreement includes not only the terms required to create a legally binding contract and to resolve the issues parties identified in Phase 3, but also the terms necessary to address the most significant interests of the parties. A final goal of testing the agreement is confirming the parties' individual *commitment* to it. Will they follow through with their promises? The agreement should be explicit about deadlines and dates for fulfilling obligations. Leaving room for misunderstanding about the timing of an obligation can be as damaging to a fragile truce as being unclear about the substance of the obligation itself.

5. *Implementing the Agreement*

After the parties sign the formal agreement, either at the mediation or thereafter, many mediators continue to follow up during the implementation phase and are available to assist with any problems that arise during this period. In a simple case, checking in may consist of a brief e-mail or phone call to confirm that the matter has been concluded and that the promised money has been paid and the appeal dismissed.

If the parties have entered into ongoing obligations, early and consistent mediator monitoring, especially initially, may encourage the parties to follow through; when they do not, mediator involvement early on can help the recalcitrant party to get back on track or assist the parties to restructure their agreement.

C.   Disposing of the Appeal

Under the rules of the appellate court in which the appeal is pending, the appellant usually has the duty promptly to inform the appellate court that a settlement has been achieved. Even if an appellate court has been informed that a settlement has been achieved, there may still be a requirement to file a formal notice of abandonment of the appeal. Or sometimes the case is actually dismissed in the trial court. And to make matters more complicated, the question of whether an appeal must be abandoned in the appellate court or dismissed in the trial court depends on the procedural posture of the appeal, such as if the appellate record has been completed and filed with the clerk of the appellate court.[18]

Counsel may also need to give additional notices. For example, if a deposit has been given for the trial court to prepare the reporter's and clerk's transcripts for the appellate record, notice should be given that the record is no longer needed

---

18.   For example, in California, a case that settles *prior* to the filing of the appellate record requires a motion to abandon the case *in the trial court.* Cal. Rules of Court, rule 8.244(b)(1). However, if the case settles *after* the appellate record has been filed in the Court of Appeal, the appellant must request dismissal *in the appellate court.* Cal. Rules of Court, rule 8.244(c)(1). These sorts of procedural rules can be traps for the unwary.

and that any unused portion of the deposit be refunded to the parties. This prevents the trial court clerk and reporter from preparing unneeded transcripts.

D.   When the Mediation Session Ends without an Agreement

We often encounter cases in which the parties do not reach agreement during the initial mediation session but that ultimately resolve in agreement. Agreements often result from the mediators' continuing efforts to keep discussions going.

1.   Analyze Why the Parties Did Not Reach Agreement

Before abandoning settlement discussions, in an effort to restart the negotiations, mediators should explore why negotiations have stalled and how they might be restarted. Even if this effort is unsuccessful and the mediation ends without a settlement, the dispute may still settle, particularly if the parties, lawyers, and perhaps the mediator engage in a thoughtful exploration of the obstacles to resolution and options for overcoming them.

The first step toward an after-mediation settlement is to understand why the parties failed to reach agreement. Beyond the usual glib conclusion that the other side was unreasonable, lies an important analysis of the obstacles to settlement. Reasons for failure to settle at the mediation include the following:

- Walking away too soon, before exploring all of the possibilities for resolution;

- Misperceiving the legal issues on appeal or incorrectly evaluating the risks and opportunities on appeal;

- Employing a mediator whose approach is inconsistent with what the case or the parties require;

- Incomplete or inappropriate party representatives attending the mediation;

- Inadequate exploration of the parties' interests and options for addressing them in the resolution;

- Failure to acknowledge and allow for the parties' emotional obstacles to settlement; and

- Lack of clarity about the distinction between the parties' positions and their underlying interests.

2. *Plan the Next Steps*

When the parties understand the reasons behind a frustrated settlement, they are better able to plan the next steps in their negotiation. For example, if the parties did not come to mediation with the right representatives, they can reconvene the mediation with the right ones. If the mediator's approach was not what the parties needed, they can reconvene with a new mediator. If insufficient attention to interests is the obstacle, the lawyers and the mediator can explore interests and ideas for addressing them with the parties separately or reconvene the mediation for this purpose.

Perhaps a failed mediation was not a failure at all but just the first step in a longer process of the parties' becoming more fully informed about the legal issues and more adequately reflective about their interests and their needs for closure. Although they were not able to shift their perspectives on the spot, with time and continuing discussions, they may be able to do so. Sufficient mediator attention to Phase 5 in a "failed" mediation enhances the probability of settlement after the parties leave the mediation.

Following a mediation that did not result in settlement, the parties have numerous options, including the following:

- **Parties can continue to negotiate directly or through their lawyers.** Attorneys may decide to continue settlement negotiations after the parties have failed to reach agreement in mediation. The attorneys' analysis of why the case did not settle may provide information about whether, when, and how to resume negotiations. As parties reflect on information they gathered at the mediation and reconsider settlement proposals, the simple passage of time may make them more amenable to settlement.

- **Parties can continue to work with their mediator.** If appropriate given the reasons why the case did not resolve in mediation, attorneys and parties may welcome the mediator's continued involvement. A subsequent mediation session, when the parties may be more open to settlement, may resolve the appeal, although the first mediation did not.

- **Parties can agree on a binding process.** When parties fail to reach agreement, arbitration may be an effective follow-up to mediation. Disagreements about legal—or, with interlocutory appeals, factual—issues present an insurmountable barrier to settlement and may best be addressed through an alternative, binding process. In cases where resolution depends on the valuation of real property, as in a divorce mediation, or of a business, and the obstacle to settlement is the inability to agree on a price, parties may agree to delegate the issue to an arbitrator with appropriate expertise or to be bound by an appraisal by an agreed-on expert.

3. Follow Up to Achieve Agreement

Experienced mediators understand the value of following up with the lawyers after the mediation, whether or not mediation resulted in settlement. If the appeal settled and the parties signed a memorandum of understanding intending that the lawyers draft a formal written settlement agreement later, mediator assistance may be helpful. The preparation of the settlement agreement usually requires back and forth between lawyers that may reveal misunderstandings between the parties or issues the parties failed to address at the mediation that require further discussion and, perhaps, negotiation.

After the parties sign the formal settlement agreement, either at the mediation or thereafter, the mediator may continue to follow up during the implementation phase and be available to assist with any problems that arise during this period. In a simple case, checking in may consist of a brief e-mail or phone call to confirm that the matter has been concluded and that the promised money has been paid and the appeal dismissed.

If the parties have entered into ongoing obligations, early and consistent mediator monitoring, especially initially, may encourage the parties to follow through. If they fail to do so, a mediator may be able to influence the recalcitrant party to perform. Sometimes due to problems in implementing the agreement, the parties realize the agreement must be modified, in which case the mediator may be helpful or even necessary.

E. Conclusion

Insufficient attention to concluding and following up, even in mediations that were impeccably facilitated from the premediation discussions to a successful negotiation, can result in failure to reach agreement. Many circumstances work against the skillful management of the concluding and following-up phase. Everyone, including the mediator, may be emotionally and physically exhausted, especially if the mediation has lasted the entire day, and thus participants may be resistant to spending additional time on the tasks of clarifying or recording agreements. Parties may be reluctant to pay the mediator to follow up. Mediators may resist follow-up calls because of their busy schedules or because, when cases do not result in agreement, they are reluctant to start a conversation about what they might have done differently or better.

We urge mediators and lawyers to appreciate the importance of this phase, to overcome these obstacles, and to stand strongly for respecting this final phase of concluding and following up. Doing so will allow the parties to make the most of their mediation opportunity and in some cases save an agreement.

Section III
Practice Tips for Appellate Attorneys
Overview

In Section III, we help attorneys fulfill their obligations to clients during the appellate mediation process. Whether the appellate mediation is court-connected or voluntarily initiated, lawyers have a special role to play as agents and advocates of the parties. In contrast to the rigid procedural constraints of appeals, attorneys perform a wide range of interesting tasks in mediation. They can help design the process of mediation, select the mediator, explore their clients' interests, help their clients calculate the economic value of a case on appeal, contribute creative ideas and solutions that lie beyond the power of an appellate court but address their clients' interests, encourage and support their clients to persevere in negotiations, evaluate the merits of proposed settlements, and ensure agreements meet the requirements of legality and enforceability.

The collaborative approach of mediation—and its informality and creative aspects—may take attorneys out of their adversarial comfort zones. Legal analysis may take a backseat to nonlegal considerations as the parties identify the interests they hope to satisfy in a settlement agreement. Rather than having an unapproachable set of appellate judges, attorneys have a mediator with whom they are able to engage in ex parte contacts to prepare for mediation, to keep the negotiations from derailing, or to assist them in helping their clients come to terms with the realities facing them in connection with further litigation.

As in every other aspect of legal representation, in mediation an attorney owes the client a duty of loyalty, zealous advocacy, and competency. To this end, this section offers attorneys an overview of duties attending the appellate mediation process along with practice tips for increasing the chances of a successful resolution. Chapter 10 addresses the start of the appellate mediation process, from initial contacts with a court-connected mediation program or mediator in a voluntarily initiated mediation up until the start of the actual mediation session. Mediation entails its own necessary skills such as listening, brainstorming, and negotiating. Just as attorneys are duty-bound to become familiar with the areas of law being litigated, so too they have an obligation to acquire necessary skills and understanding to be able to participate effectively in appellate mediation.

As Aristotle noted, "Well begun is half done."[1] For mediation, this aphorism is especially true. Appellate mediations involve difficult disputes that have evaded resolution—sometimes for years. In order to resolve them in one

---

1. ARISTOTLE'S POLITICS 195 (Oxford Press 1908).

day-long session, which is the usual approach, parties and counsel must be well prepared. There is simply no time for counsel, or a client, to make up for omitted preparations once the mediation session begins. We designed Chapter 11 to help lawyers effectively participate in what can be a fast-paced journey toward a successful resolution by the parties in an appellate mediation. And, in Chapter 12, we provide tips for attorneys to help them successfully conclude the mediation by crafting an effective settlement agreement or adopting a strategy for reaching an agreement after the mediation session ends. And, we briefly note some of the continuing professional obligations that attorneys have even after a settlement agreement is signed.

The good news is that attorneys regularly find appellate mediation to be challenging, thrilling, and rewarding. So, come along as we explore an attorney's role in the appellate mediation process.

Chapter 10
Tips for Attorneys Preparing for the Mediation Session

A. Begin to Prepare as Soon as Possible

Ideally, an attorney begins planning for the possibility of appellate mediation even before filing the notice of appeal. One of the biggest advantages of mediation is the cost savings to parties if they can settle before incurring the expense of preparing the appellate record or briefs. The earlier the appellate mediation takes place, the greater the potential cost savings. For this reason, many court-connected mediation programs are designed to schedule mediation sessions before the appellate record or briefs are completed.[2] Parties who file appeals in courts with formal mediation programs must be prepared to enter the mediation process within a few weeks of filing an appeal.

Following the filing of the notice of appeal, the appellant's counsel may be inclined to put off work on the appeal because the first appellate brief (and the legal research it requires) is months away. And counsel for the respondent may not expect to work on the case until the appellant files the opening brief. However, clerks in courts with formal mediation programs send out forms and questionnaires at the outset of the appeal in order to gather information for evaluating whether the court will order a case into mediation. These mandatory questionnaires usually have short deadlines. Yet they can be filled out by appellate counsel only after discussing the issues with trial counsel and clients, conducting an initial review of trial court documents, and engaging in preliminary legal research and analysis of arguments likely to be raised on appeal.

In addition, if the appeal is referred to mediation, all counsel may be required to prepare mediation statements long before the briefs would be due. Although mediation statements tend to be shorter and less formal than appellate briefs, they still require substantial time and care to prepare. Given the tight time constraints in appellate mediation programs, counsel for all parties should take the following steps as soon as the notice of appeal is filed, in order to be adequately prepared for mediation.

---

1. Robert J. Niemic, Mediation & Conference Programs in the Federal Courts of Appeals (Federal Judicial Center 2007) (noting "[a]n underlying assumption by some program designers is that parties' incentives for settlement often decrease as their briefing and oral argument preparation progresses. Early scheduling is intended to give parties the opportunity to settle before they incur the major expense of filing briefs and appendices.").

B.   Gather the Key Documents That Were Filed in the Trial Court

Regardless whether the attorney who will attend the mediation is a newly retained appellate specialist or a trial attorney continuing with the litigation, counsel should assemble important documents at the outset of the appellate mediation process, especially if the appellate court has a formal mediation program. The local rules may require counsel to attach the judgment or order being appealed. Thus, counsel should prepare for both the appeal and possible mediation by assembling the following documents:

- The judgment and any orders being appealed;

- The trial judge's statement of decision supporting the judgment and any objections filed by the parties in response;

- Any written order of the court to be challenged on appeal, including awards of attorney fees and costs;

- The contract or any other writing (such as the description of an easement in a real property case) upon which the case depends;

- General and special verdict forms of the jury;

- Postjudgment motions and oppositions—especially if granted, even in part; and

- Trial briefs submitted by the parties to the trial court, along with any pretrial motions likely to be challenged on appeal.

From these documents, counsel can begin to determine potential issues on appeal, the applicable areas of law, and the standards of review the court will likely employ. Conversely, the absence of any of these documents—as occurs when a party fails to request or object to a statement of decision—can reveal issues of waiver or failure to preserve issues for appeal. Even a cursory review of documents related to the case—or noticing missing documents—can inform counsel's assessment of strengths and weaknesses of an appeal that will be part of the mediation briefs and discussions at the mediation session itself. Newly retained appellate counsel should promptly request these documents from trial counsel in order to allow sufficient time to review them.

Accurate assessment of some issues—such as challenges to trial evidentiary rulings, arguments made by counsel in front of the jury, or sufficiency of the evidence—almost always requires a reporter's transcript. Because the court usually reviews these issues under an abuse of discretion standard of review, they tend to be among the weaker appellate arguments.

By contrast, assessment of the *strongest* appellate issues, which the court reviews de novo, may not require a reporter's transcript, because they are generally supported by documents that are already available, such as the trial court's statement of decision and the parties' last moving papers.

C. Talk to Trial Counsel and Clients about Potential Appellate Issues

Especially if appellate counsel is new to the case, it is important to discuss the lower court proceedings with trial counsel and the clients early, even before the reporter's transcript has been prepared. This discussion should go well beyond trial counsel's mere identification of issues to be raised on appeal. To this end, it is especially helpful to invite trial counsel and the client to describe the moment when they believed the outcome in the trial court became clear. This narrative by trial counsel and clients is an excellent source of insight into appellate issues before the reporter's transcript is completed. In addition, the trial attorneys' legal analysis often provides invaluable insight into the appellate issues.

Equally useful is a similar dialog with respondents and their counsel. Clients and trial counsel should be asked if there were any surprising omissions in the lower court proceedings as a way to identify arguments regarding waiver and failure to preserve issues for appeal. This information is important for adequate preparation for the mediation session and even for the initial decision of whether to seek mediation in a district in which mediation is voluntary or initiated by the parties themselves.

In discussing the lower court proceedings, appellate counsel should also inquire about any prior settlement offers, mediations, settlement conferences, or negotiations, in particular why any prior efforts at negotiation failed to achieve a settlement. Usually, such information cannot be gleaned from any source other than the client and trial counsel, even after the appellate record is completed. So it's a good idea to have an in-depth conversation with both trial counsel and clients. In addition to giving broader context for the appeal, such information may be required on court-connected mediation questionnaires.

D. Analyze the Strengths and Weaknesses of the Appellate Case

To persuade the opposing side to accept a proposed settlement during mediation, you must demonstrate how the benefits of an agreement outweigh the risks of appeal. Doing so effectively requires appellate counsel to identify the applicable standards of review to determine if the trial court erred and to analyze whether the error was sufficiently prejudicial to compel reversal of the judgment.[3] Attorneys who understand error and prejudice analysis can play a pivotal role during the appellate mediation session in educating the mediator and the opposing parties and counsel regarding prospects for success on appeal.

The postjudgment motions and the parties' trial briefs often are a fertile source for identifying appellate issues and the law governing them. Even so, additional research is almost invariably necessary to assess the prospects of an issue on appeal. And, for institutional clients, early research may be necessary to determine whether mediation is even appropriate. If the appeal involves a matter of first impression that regularly affects the party, an appellate decision may be preferable to a mediated agreement. Conflicts among appellate courts on key issues of law are also important to identify.

Finally, attorneys are not ready for an appellate mediation until they can help their clients evaluate settlement offers in the context of their needs and interests and the risks and opportunities of their appeals. In Chapter 2, we described in detail our suggested approach for evaluating a case on appeal.

E.   Initiate the Mediation

Although most appellate mediations are either initiated or governed by court mediation programs and rules, the increasing prevalence of appellate mediation means that, more and more, appeals are being mediated voluntarily. We suggest how attorneys can participate effectively in both court-ordered and voluntary appellate mediation.

1.   Understand the Case-Screening Process for Court-Connected Mediations

Court-connected mediation usually begins with a case-screening process conducted by a court clerk or mediation program coordinator. The case-screening process almost invariably involves a standard court form or questionnaire that parties are required to file. Usually these forms or questionnaires are not considered confidential, and thus counsel should not use them to disclose confidential or privileged information about the case. Instead, counsel should merely provide a brief summary of the case, issues they expect to raise on appeal, and any nonconfidential information about the case that renders it particularly suitable or unsuitable for mediation.

Once the parties have submitted the case-screening forms, many courts permit counsel to speak informally and confidentially with the mediation program coordinator or court staff who schedules mediations. And, often, the program coordinators call counsel to discuss the nature of the case and probable

---

3. *See* Chapters 1 and 2 for guidance on how to analyze the strengths, weaknesses, and alternatives to an appeal.

issues on appeal as well as the attitudes of the parties toward mediation. These telephone discussions tend to be informal and relatively brief. Even so, the substance of the conversations can greatly influence the chances of an appeal's inclusion in the mandatory mediation process. The mediation program coordinator or staff often have substantial input on the final decision as to whether to order mediation.

While it is rare for a case to be ordered to mediation when a party professes to be absolutely against negotiation, mediation often involves at least one party who is reluctant to negotiate. For this reason, appeals are sometimes selected for mediation even if a party is hesitant or leery of mediation. We suggest counsel and parties, despite their reluctance to negotiate, engage wholeheartedly in mediation as an opportunity for appellate advocacy. In our experience, even skeptics settle cases once the mediation begins and momentum for settlement gathers.

Unlike cases in which a party is simply reluctant to negotiate, appellate courts recognize that some appeals are not appropriate for mediation because they require the precedent-setting authority of a published decision. Counsel should let the program coordinator know during the case-screening process if the appeal is being pursued as a test case or to secure a published appellate decision on an issue of law that is unsettled.

2. If the Appellate Court Does Not Have a Mediation Program, Explore Voluntary Mediation

Even in the absence of a court-connected appellate mediation program, you can help your clients by exploring the option of voluntary mediation. Not long ago, an attorney proposing appellate mediation would be seen as signaling a terminally weak case. Because many appellate courts now have mediation programs, parties and attorneys increasingly expect mediation to be part of the appellate process.

When proposing appellate mediation, you may encounter resistance from the opposing side. If so, have a conversation with opposing counsel about the source of the other party's hesitancy to mediate, and once you understand its source, explore ways to address the concerns. For example, if the other side lacks confidence in your client's willingness to negotiate in good faith, make an effort to demonstrate your client's desire to negotiate. Offer to stipulate to mediation—indicate that your client is willing to share in the cost of a mediator, explain options for settlement that you and your client are willing to explore, or simply express confidence that mediation appears promising at this stage. If past failed attempts to negotiate or mediate have left a residue of frustration and resentment, stress the context of a "new day" following appeal or otherwise explain why there is reason to be optimistic about a mediated settlement.

Most importantly, you can provide opposing counsel a convincing rationale for mediation. For example, point out the value of mediation when time is an issue, when parties have a continuing business or personal relationship, when a creative solution is available, or when the costs of litigation outweigh any likely relief from the appellate court. It is also helpful to describe successful appellate mediations, especially those in which the parties entered into the process reluctantly.

F.   Consider the Effect of Mediation on a Pending Appeal

Once it appears an appeal is slated for mediation, you should consider whether, in the meantime, a successful mediation requires you to address the procedural posture of the case:

- **Should you seek a stay of the appellate process?** Some appellate court rules provide for automatic stays of the appeal once a mediation has been scheduled, saving parties the costs of preparation of the appellate records or briefs. In courts without such rules, counsel should consider seeking a stay to accomplish the same cost savings.

- **Should you request that *part* of the appellate record be prepared for the mediation session?** Some errors can only be demonstrated with a transcript of the trial court proceedings, such as erroneous trial court rulings on the evidence or misinstruction of the jury. If the issue is pivotal, counsel may need the portion of the appellate record to demonstrate the error prepared for the mediation session to better convince the other side of the strengths of your client's position on appeal.

- **Is it too late to prevent a decision by the appellate court?** In some cases, it takes the parties a long time to reach a settlement. Negotiations may drag on after the mediation session. Or parties may delay settlement efforts until after completion of the briefing or even after oral argument. Sometimes settlement occurs at a time the appellate court is ready to issue a decision. In such circumstances, appellate counsel should inform the court that negotiations are ongoing and may soon settle the case. Even so, appellate courts will sometimes refuse to dismiss the case or delay a decision in light of the negotiations. However, the appellate court's refusal to stay the issuance of a decision need not derail the settlement process. Parties can contractually agree to a settlement and specify that the terms of the contract are binding on the parties regardless of the subsequent decision of the appellate court.

G.   Select and Work with a Mediator

A good mediator can shepherd even a contentious and emotionally charged appeal through a productive mediation process. A mediator can also be enlisted to help with the occasional difficult problem of client control. Sometimes a determined client may persist in desiring to litigate even when it would be wiser to settle—whether to avoid unfavorable odds or to secure timely payment of the judgment. Despite the best efforts of legal counsel, a client may not yet have taken the advice to seriously consider an end to the case. A good mediator with empathy and persistence can help parties rethink their dedication to win at all costs and focus on what is best for them under the circumstances. Thus, selection of a mediator is an important part of counsel's duty of advocacy. Moreover, selection of a mediator—no less than the hiring of any expert witness—reflects directly on the quality of representation provided by an attorney.

For these reasons, counsel should devote thought and care to the process of selecting a mediator. The ideal mediator for any case has both substantive expertise, which is necessary when an arcane area of law is implicated, and the skills and understanding required to work with strong emotions when parties have become irrational about the litigation. If you are not able to agree on a mediator who excels in both arenas, you may wish to opt for expertise and a strong reputation in appellate law if your opposing counsel seems mired in the legal analysis suited to the trial court but not the appellate court. A mediator who has appellate expertise may also be a good choice when a party—for any side—needs to hear and understand bad news about the prospects for success on appeal. If you must choose between a mediator with expertise in a particular substantive area of law or appellate gravitas and a mediator skilled in conducting the negotiation process, in most cases, the mediator with process expertise may be the better choice.

In many legal communities, there is often a short list of the most sought-after appellate mediators. Sometimes, counsel may simply decide to "let the other side pick the mediator" when the list of potential mediators comprises a pool of competent neutrals. Indeed, such a strategy may be sound if it increases the legitimacy of the mediator with the opposing attorney and party. At the end of the day, when negotiations are greatly helped by the parties' trust in the mediator, the parties' selection of the mediator can help acceptance of the mediator's guidance and/or evaluations.

Even when mediation is mandatory as part of a court-connected program, many appellate courts allow parties to provide input that can greatly affect the selection of a mediator. In courts having mediation programs that rely on volunteer mediators, the court mediators tend to have primary expertise either in mediation or in appellate representation. Thus, you should still view mediator selection as a process requiring due diligence even in cases being mediated by order of the appellate court. For example, you may still decide to pay for a private mediator to get a particular experience or expertise even when a volunteer mediator is available. Especially when the pro bono time will not be sufficient to resolve the case because preparation is expected to be extensive and/or settlement will require several mediation sessions, it may be a good idea to pay for a private mediator if doing so will increase the chances of achieving a settlement agreement.

H.   Communicate with the Mediator before the Mediation Session

Premediation communications—usually by telephonic conference call—are a tremendously helpful way to prepare for the mediation session. Indeed, the rules of some court-connected mediation programs require premediation conference calls, for good reason. Premediation communications introduce the mediator to the case and the mediator and counsel to each other so they can address logistics, such as timing, location, number of sessions, and other issues related to preparation for mediation, such as mediation statements and additional calls with the mediator.[4] If appellate counsel has been newly retained, premediation calls may provide the first opportunity to interact with opposing counsel. Most often, the only participants to the call are the mediator and counsel. The primary tasks to be accomplished are the following:

- **Select the date, time, and location for the mediation session.** For some court-connected mediations, the mediation program coordinator will schedule the mediation session even before the appointment of the mediator. Otherwise, the date, time, and even location for the mediation session can be established during a premediation conference call.

- **Agree on the participants.** Who will be present at the mediation? Will they have authority to settle? Will they possess sufficient information about potential creative solutions? Are there objections to the proposed participants? Are there any requests for additional participants? In a court-sponsored mediation program, do the proposed participants meet the requirements of local rules?

- **Agree on preparation for the mediation session.** Is there information the parties need from each other in order to be prepared for the mediation? Will they also submit mediation statements? Will they be subject to page limits? Will the mediation statements be submitted only to the

---

4.   We provide an example of a premediation telephone conference in the Appendix that illustrates how helpful to the mediation participants the initial communication with the mediator can be.

mediator or also exchanged with opposing counsel? Will they submit *confidential* mediation statements? Are there other matters requiring the attention of the mediator to ensure the mediation session begins well?

- **Agree on fees, if any, to be charged by the mediator.** Shortly after the parties select the mediator, you should ensure that arrangements regarding the mediator's fee are clearly set out in writing. This allows you to communicate the nature of the fees to be charged by the mediator to the client. Many mediators provide parties with written agreements for mediation services that describe fee arrangements in detail. If your mediator does not do so, you should inquire about the mediator's fee policies—for example, whether there are administrative fees or other hidden charges in addition to the mediator's daily rate or hourly fee, whether the mediator requires a deposit of estimated fees, and whether the mediator imposes forfeiture penalties for cancellation or rescheduling of mediation sessions. You should also discuss and agree on the allocation of mediator fees. If the parties cannot agree on allocation, it may be helpful to call on the mediator to assist you in reaching agreement.

- **Request confidential calls with the mediator.** The mediator or counsel may also want to request separate, confidential communications with the mediator in advance of the mediation session. Some mediators routinely initiate separate calls with counsel, usually after they review the parties' mediation statements, to explore counsel's legal analysis or to address concerns or procedural questions about the upcoming mediation. Although there are advantages to bringing up challenges in the joint call, where counsels' perspectives can be shared—or aired—and, with the help of the mediator, collaboratively addressed, it may be more appropriate to discuss some challenges privately with the mediator. A confidential call before mediation to problem solve how to deal with issues you do not want to reduce to writing or raise in a joint telephone conference, such as difficult clients, attorneys, or other participants, can be the least problematic way to prevent the mediation from becoming unproductive.

I.   The Mediation Statement

The rules of many court-connected mediation programs and most private mediators require counsel to submit mediation statements (sometimes called mediation briefs) before the mediation session. Far from being an empty exercise, a concise and insightful mediation statement educates the mediator about the legal issues and arguments and provides the mediator with additional information to allow for structuring the mediation session in a manner that fosters a productive dialogue. A good mediation statement also demonstrates to the mediator that counsel is prepared and able to serve a useful role in advancing the analysis and negotiation of the case toward a successful resolution. Accordingly, attorneys should craft mediation statements with care.

1. Practice Pointers

Mediation statements are informal. They do not have to conform to the same stringent rules governing style and format for appellate briefs. Some mediators, and some court programs, provide outlines for mediation statements. If not, you can request a suggested form or outline.

Mediation statements tend to be shorter than appellate briefs. Effective mediation statements *cogently* present the background information and an analysis of the appellate issues, including the strengths of your client's contentions and the weaknesses of opposing party's.

The most effective mediation statements include the practical implications of the appeal in addition to the legal argument. Pointing out the *practical* impacts of an appeal, such as postjudgment interest, costs of an appeal bond or an immediately effective, collectable judgment, or the implications for reversal of the judgment may cause the opposing party to think more deeply about the consequences of a failed settlement.

Mediation statements should be exchanged. Insist on receiving the other party's mediation statement and be willing to share yours. The more information parties have before mediation, the better able they will be to prepare—and the better decisions they will make. In the absence of compelling reasons to the contrary, a mediation statement should be shared with the opposing party as well as the mediator.

Regarding form, content, and timing of mediation statements, consult your private mediator or court rules in court-connected cases. Mediators usually have protocols regarding timing and submission of mediation statements or if asked will provide mediation statement outlines. Court-connected appellate mediation programs often prescribe mediation statement protocols regarding timing, exchange, and content of mediation statements.[5]

In contrast to trial court mediation, where parties virtually always exchange mediation statements simultaneously, in appellate mediation it may be useful to begin with the submission of the appellant's statement, which apprises the respondent of the issues, followed by the respondent's statement a week or so later and, possibly, a reply brief several days after that.

Ensure the mediation statement contains essential information, including the following:

- **The identity of the participants.** Provide the names and titles of the parties, their attorneys, and any other persons anticipated to attend the mediation (such as insurance representatives, spouses, and so on).

---

5. *See, e.g.*, U.S. District Court N.D. Cal. ADR Local Rules 6–7(a), (c); *Preparing for Mediation* (9th Cir.), http://www.ca9.uscourts.gov/mediation/view.php?pk_id=0000000673.

- **Relevant procedural background, including a brief description of the judgment being appealed.** In addition, include copies of the statement of decision, order, or judgment being appealed for the benefit of the mediator.

- **The context in which the litigation is occurring and the interests of the parties to be served by any agreement.** In other words, include the underlying "human problem" the litigation was intended to remedy. In a family law context, the parties' interests may include allowing children to spend enough time with each parent, having a stable living situation for the parties or their children, being able to fund a realistic budget, or getting education to allow for future and ongoing income. Parties to business litigation may have interests in recovering financially from losses believed to be caused by the other party, in recovering from negative publicity that has tarnished the business, or in repairing a previously beneficial business relationship. Plaintiffs in the personal injury context may have interests in having the ability to pay medical bills, in securing future care for a permanent physical impairment, or avoiding unnecessary tax consequences. A defendant in personal injury cases may have interests in restoring a good reputation, ensuring financial solvency, or avoiding bankruptcy.

- **An analysis of the issues on appeal, including the strengths of your arguments and the weaknesses of the opposing side's.** Because the mediation occurs in the context of an appeal, reference to the standards of review and a brief analysis of prejudice (or lack thereof) and waiver is vital. See the appendix for sample mediation statements illustrating how to present this information effectively.

- **Issues needing to be resolved to settle the case.** For example, will the defendant need a release of all known and unknown claims? Is consent of an insurer necessary to settle? Is confidentiality of a settlement agreement of vital importance?

Err on the side of giving information rather than guarding it. Giving and guarding information can be quite tricky at the trial court level of negotiations. By contrast, most appellate mediations take place after each party's best evidence and arguments have actually been produced at trial. Consequently, there is little strategic reason for withholding best arguments or emphasizing the strongest evidence of the client's claims. Additionally, mediation statements are confidential.

Consider whether trade secrets or other especially sensitive information require an additional agreement to prevent unwanted disclosure. Determine whether the mediation confidentiality rules related to mediation statements are sufficient to meet your client's needs. Mere exclusion from admission into evidence in court does not mean that your client's trade secrets or sensitive personal or business information are adequately protected by the applicable mediation confidentiality statutes or rules of court. If your client requires enhanced confidentiality protections, negotiate changes to any form confidentiality agreements the court or the mediator provides, or seek a protective order if necessary.[6] In securing added confidentiality protection of a mediation statement, we advise doing so in a manner that allows the other party—not just the mediator—to receive it.

Attach copies of one or two documents that support your legal analysis. Attach any documents that establish your client's position or clearly illustrate the gravamen of the appeal. For example, respondents should include the special verdict when redundant findings support the judgment on multiple grounds; appellants should include documents that demonstrate the error of the lower court, such as faulty jury instructions or daily transcripts showing the occurrence of error at trial. Always include the statement of decision or order being appealed not already provided to the mediator as part of a court-connected screening procedure. Remember, however, that a mediation statement is not a formal appellate brief. Thus, not every factual assertion must be supported by a citation to the record. To the contrary, avoid drowning the mediator and opposing counsel in documents when only the judgment or appealable order will suffice.

2. *Make Sure the Necessary Persons Attend Mediation with Full Settlement Authority*

An underappreciated but critical step toward mediation success is securing the attendance of all parties with authority to settle the case.[7] Few things are as irritating and futile as mediations in which it is discovered, after much negotiation, that an essential party either does not have full settlement authority or is missing from the mediation. For court-connected mediations, almost invariably the rules of court will require parties to attend with "full settlement authority" without defining what constitutes full settlement authority.[8] And there does not seem to be a universally accepted definition of the term, although mediators

---

6. No matter what kind of confidentiality applies to mediation, do not confuse "confidential" with "secret." For a cautionary tale, *see* Facebook, Inc. v. Pacific Northwest Software, Inc., 640 F.3d 1034, 1041 (9th Cir. 2011) (holding that a confidentiality agreement "merely preclude[d] both parties from introducing evidence of a certain kind" but did not prevent parties from using the underlying information for other purposes).

7. Parties may have a duty "to notify insurance carriers with potential insurance coverage that appellate mediation has been ordered and that the carrier must have a representative attend all mediation sessions in person, with full settlement authority." Campagnone v. Enjoyable Pools & Spas Service & Repairs, Inc., 163 Cal. App. 4th 566, 574, 77 Cal. Rptr. 3d 551 (Ct. App. 2008).

8. The only court rule defining full settlement authority seems to be Florida Rule of Civil Procedure 1.720, which provides the following in pertinent part: "A 'party representative having full authority to settle' shall mean the final decision maker with respect

often define full settlement authority as the ability of the participants present at the mediation session to completely and finally resolve an appeal without resort to phone calls, e-mails, or follow-up meetings with persons not personally present at the mediation.

In both court-connected and private mediations participants often have differing assumptions about the meaning of full settlement authority. In cases involving money damages, plaintiffs often assume full settlement authority is the prerogative to settle at an amount between zero and the full face value of the judgment (including attorney fees, costs, and postjudgment interest), while defendants assume it means the most the defendant is willing to pay to settle the case. In cases involving insurance coverage, full settlement authority is sometimes assumed to be the ability to offer full policy limits.

Given the lack of a common understanding of the meaning of full settlement authority, if the mediator does not raise the issue during premediation communications, counsel should do so. A premediation conference call provides the best opportunity to ensure that opposing counsel is present with everyone necessary to settle for the other party. During the premediation conference call, the best practice is to articulate expressly who will participate and with what authority, by stating something such as, *I understand that you will be attending with an insurance representative with full settlement authority up to and including the policy limits.* If there is no premediation conference call, counsel should address the issue in some manner with the mediator and opposing counsel well before the start of the mediation session.

a. When It Is Not Possible for a Representative to Attend with Full Settlement Authority, Be Clear about What Can Be Accomplished at Mediation and the Procedures and Timeline for Approving Any Settlement

The requirement of full settlement authority can be a challenge when one of the parties is a public entity governed by an elected board, a private entity controlled by a large board of directors, or any organization in which a settlement must be approved by vote of numerous members or shareholders. The problem in these circumstances is that it is impossible, or at least impractical, to fit everyone into the mediation conference facility. Moreover, in the case of public entities, any approval of settlement may have to comply with notice and open-meeting requirements set forth in state or federal law. Lawsuits involving city councils, county boards of supervisors, and certain governmental agencies fall into this category.

---

to all issues presented by the case who has the legal capacity to execute a binding settlement agreement on behalf of the party."

The best way to resolve this problem is to ensure the attendance of party representatives on both sides who possess the requisite influence to persuade the party they represent to accept the settlement terms tentatively agreed at mediation. General counsel or the attorney normally representing that entity may also be a good choice to send to the mediation session.

Even prior to the mediation, the agenda for the entity's next meeting after the mediation should already reflect a time for discussion of proposed acceptance or rejection of the settlement terms. For cases of great importance to the entity, or if the decision making body meets infrequently, a special meeting should be considered for a date shortly after the scheduled mediation session. By planning for full consideration of the proposed settlement before the mediation session begins, the parties can ensure that mediation retains its promise of quick and cost-efficient resolution of the appeal, even though it is not possible to conclude the settlement on the day of mediation.

3. Consider Whether Parties, though Required to Attend, Are Not Essential to the Settlement and Should Be Excused from Attending

In private mediations, it is clearly up to the parties to decide who needs to be present at the mediation. In court-sponsored mediations, even though rules may require an individual's attendance, it is nevertheless important to consider whether attendance is *necessary*. In many court programs, parties may be excused by agreement of all parties and the mediator. In others, the parties may need to request relief from the rule from the court.

Following an analysis of full settlement authority, counsel may conclude that an individual may serve no useful role at the mediation even though technically named as a party to the appeal. For example, where an insurer has provided the legal defense of a party and the insurer's consent is not required to settle the case, the defendant and the insurer may agree that attendance of the carrier representative is not necessary.

Standard insurance policies routinely give insurers the right to control the defense and to determine whether and how to settle, with the effect that the insured individual or entity actually serves little role in settling the case.[9] Although it is important to consider whether the attendance of the insured might be important for other reasons—for example, the insured's interest in influencing the carrier's decisions, the ability to address the other side directly, or to contribute to creative solutions not available through the insurance company. Absent a reason why the insured needs to participate, individual plaintiffs or named defendants may serve little function in a case other than to fulfill standing requirements necessary to preseve the appellate court's jurisdiction

---

9. *See, e.g.,* Hurvitz v. St. Paul Fire & Marine Ins. Co., 109 Cal. App. 4th 918, 930, 135 Cal. Rptr. 2d 703 (Ct. App. 2003).

over the case. If all parties agree, such persons may simply be excused from attending, depending on the court rules.

Conversely, sometimes the attendance of nonparties can be very helpful or even essential. In both private and court-connected mediation, the decision to include additional participants is up to the parties, with the help of the mediator if they are not able to agree. Minors need to be represented by a parent or guardian. Spouses or significant others can be a real source of support to injured parties or parties that rely on them for decision making. Finally, it is occasionally wise to have an expert attend when technical expertise is necessary to devise terms of the agreement—as with structured settlements calculating Medicare set-asides, the rewriting of property boundaries, or even an interpreter if language might be a challenge for any participant.

If possible, all necessary persons should attend the mediation for the entirety of the session. Many court-connected mediation programs require in-person attendance because it enhances the quality of communication and makes a successful settlement more likely. Allowing persons with settlement authority merely to participate by telephone toward the end of the session invites rejection or quibbling over an agreement that may have required herculean efforts to achieve. Although sometimes necessary, telephone participation is a poor substitute for personal participation in the mediation process. If telephone participation is unavoidable, we strongly recommend that any telephone participants remain on the phone throughout the mediation.

J.   Prepare the Client to Participate

Explain the mediation process. Most clients have never attended an appellate mediation session and may therefore be nervous about this unknown process. Counsel can reduce their anxiety by explaining mediation, including the following:

- **Mediation confidentiality.** Help the client to understand the implications of confidentiality statutes or the confidentiality agreement the client must sign and ensure it is sufficient for the client's purposes.

- **The role of the mediator.** In the usual case where a party is participating in appellate mediation for the first time, a discussion of the mediator's role in general is a good idea.

- **The structure of the mediation process.** If, as we suggest in Chapter 4, the mediator and lawyers (and perhaps the parties) have engaged in premediation discussions, they most likely have agreed on an approach to mediation. Counsel should describe this agreed-upon structure, with the proviso that mediation is a flexible process. Section III describes this process in detail. The appendix also provides a one-page summary of our approach to appellate mediation. Counsel may wish to explain how a settlement conference with a trial judge differs from an appellate mediation for parties accustomed to settlement conferences. An analysis of those differences is included in the detailed discussion of the appellate mediation process in Section II. Counsel may also want to describe how the appellate mediation process will differ from any previous mediations in the case.

- **Prepare clients to participate effectively.** In many trial court mediations, the client has little or no opportunity to speak to the other side in joint session. In our suggested model of appellate mediation, clients play a central role and therefore need to be prepared to fully participate. Their participation may include telling a compelling story of their perspectives on the dispute, thereby enabling them to humanize the loss and difficulties underlying their claims. An impressive client can garner sympathy in a way that makes later negotiations more productive. With the exception of the bad case, which even a perfect client can't make better, over the years we have seen, for example, insurance adjusters become more flexible in mediation when they judge a client to be a good person.

  Because appellate mediations need time to unfold, it is helpful for clients to understand that bargaining too early in the process is counterproductive. Starting a mediation by declaring a bottom line or proceeding immediately to distributive bargaining does not portend a successful resolution of the appeal. Were the parties able to engage directly in productive negotiations, the case would already have settled.

  It is also important to educate clients inexperienced in mediation about the tensions inherent in mediating, particularly as they negotiate about money. In the end, negotiated agreements often require all parties to make reluctant concessions in order to settle. A well-worn mediator adage advises that 90 percent of the negotiation occurs in the last 10 percent of the time in mediation. Normalizing this tension beforehand helps clients survive this last 10 percent of the time and stick with the negotiation even though it seems hopeless.

  Finally, be alert for clients whose emotional state signals they are likely to insult, disparage, or threaten the other party. Caution against such behavior and help them find a way to express their perspectives and their feelings that will not alienate the other participants. Reducing antagonism among the parties increases the chances that negotiations will proceed successfully.

- **Educate clients about the differences between trial and mediation.** The timing of appellate mediation soon after the filing of the notice of appeal means that clients will often have fresh memories of trial and postjudgment proceedings. Mediation, however, is not a trial. For one thing, mediation is not bound by rules of evidence or trial procedure. In contrast to preparing clients for testimony, cross-examination, and interrupted testimony, mediations require a different sort of preparation of clients for the process.

It is also important for the client to understand that effective advocacy during a mediation may appear dramatically different from that of trial or open court. By describing effective representation in mediation—and reassuring the client that you will attend the mediation with the intention to reach the best possible agreement for the client—you can avoid client concerns during mediation that you are not being tough or aggressive or that you do not have confidence in their case. Your client's best interests are most effectively advanced during a mediation when you listen, learn, and collaborate. By contrast, ceaseless argument and attacks on the other side are counterproductive and unnecessarily lengthen a process already likely to be quite tiring by the end.

- **Explore the possibility of creative solutions.** Educating your client about the opportunity mediation provides to craft a better, cheaper, wiser solution than proceeding with the appeal is essential. Discuss creative ideas with your client and if a promising option emerges suggest your client investigate the idea prior to mediation and be prepared to discuss it. Is it possible? Practicable? What would it take for approval? Implementation? Who should participate in person or by phone to develop the idea should it gain momentum and should questions arise?

1. Special Concerns to Discuss with Appellants before the Mediation Session

Attorney-client tensions. Counsel for the appellant—especially if counsel also served as trial counsel—may face a delicate task in preparing the client for mediation. An appellant, by definition, is a party that is disappointed by the trial court's judgment. That client may assign at least part of the blame for the lack of success in the trial court to the attorney. Appellant counsel's challenge may thus be to regain trust and confidence ahead of the mediation. Appellants may not yet understand that even a "great" appeal may have less than a 50/50 chance of success. However challenging the conversation about prospects for the appeal may be before the mediation, it will be much more difficult if undertaken for the first time *during* the mediation by an evaluative mediator. Consequently, you should educate an appellant about the strengths and weaknesses of the appeal before the mediation session. You will undoubtedly find it more pleasant to inform your client of the risks before the mediator or the opposing lawyer surprises your client with statistics indicating low reversal rates in the appellate court where your case is pending.

2. Special Concerns to Discuss with Respondents before the Mediation Session

Winners rarely attribute their success to chance. Respondents, having prevailed in the trial court, may thus begin mediation in an overconfident manner. If appeals, with an 80-percent chance of succeeding, are stacked against appellants, then why would a respondent ever want to settle? We discuss the reasons respondents may be better off settling at length in Chapter 1. You can help your clients avoid the overconfidence trap by guiding them through the debiasing exercise we present in Chapter 2. Appeals are expensive, stressful, and time-consuming. Even 20-percent chance of losing may be unacceptable. A respondent who has endured the expense, emotional turmoil, and disruption of a trial may conclude that a retrial constitutes an unacceptable option. When faced with the prospect of loss, respondents tend to be risk-averse.[10] A negotiated appellate settlement can preserve a victory and avoid an uncertain and unacceptable result.

Finally, if a case is on appeal, the respondent has already failed to achieve the initial, hoped-for result—a quick, inexpensive victory—despite the fact that the respondent was the "winner" in the trial court. Unless a respondent is excited to bring a test case, ending up in the Court of Appeal or the Supreme Court is not something parties to litigation look forward to. The original goal to secure a favorable result as quickly, easily, and inexpensively as possible remains foremost on appeal.

K.   Formulate a Negotiation Plan and Be Ready to Settle

Before attending the mediation session, you and your client should develop a negotiation plan. A good negotiation plan is based on a realistic, well-researched analysis of the risks and opportunities on appeal that includes the considerations we cover in Chapter 2. It also includes, to the extent possible, creative ideas for settlement. To prepare to negotiate, we suggest you and your client engage in the following steps:

1. **Identify issues to be negotiated.** What we mean by "issues" are the topics parties need to discuss and reach agreement about in order for the appeal to go away and the specific problems to be addressed. Issues are the headings for various negotiated provisions of the settlement agreement—for example, in addition to boilerplate terms (an integration clause, the admissibility of the agreement, and an attorney fee provision), a mediated employment agreement might include the following paragraphs:

    - Waivers and releases of liability,
    - Payment of moneys,
    - Re-employment,
    - Protocols upon inquiry of potential employers, and
    - Confidentiality of settlement terms.

---

10.   John Toker, *Appellate Mediation in California*, Plaintiff Mag. 1 (September 2007).

Most appeals resolve during an initial mediation session. That means negotiations proceed quickly. Parties who identify, define, and prioritize the issues that matter to them in advance of mediation are in a good position to plan the negotiation and do not risk leaving for the end—or perhaps ignoring—issues that matter to them. For example, raising the issue of confidentiality of the agreement *after* the other issues are decided reduces the chances of success on that issue, and, if the issue is a deal breaker for either side, it may even unravel an otherwise great settlement.

2. **Identify your client's needs and interests.** Perhaps the predominant reason parties are unable to resolve disputes without mediation is that they adopt positions, they persist in arguing over which position is more justified, and they refuse to move away from them. Usually they have not given sufficient consideration to their *interests* or what really *matters* to them. They have not thought about the *reasons* they hold onto particular positions. By delving beneath positions to interests, a party may be able to address an issue in multiple ways. If a party sticks to a position, there is only one way to address the problem.

3. **Anticipate the other side's interests.** In addition to you and your client's understanding your client's interests, it is equally important to anticipate what might matter to the other party. Foreseeing the other party's interests allows you to reflect ahead of time on ways an agreement might address those interests, sometimes at little or no cost to your client. This pie-expanding exploration allows you to come to mediation with options for settlement and information about how they might be implemented. It also allows you to consider whether the parties' interests are *independent*, that is different from each other but not in opposition so that the parties' interests can be met without colliding with each other; *shared* so that addressing a common interest can satisfy both of the parties because they care about the same thing; or *conflicting*, so that addressing one party's interest inhibits the possibility of addressing the other party's interests.

4. **Identify options that address interests.** Once parties identify their interests, the next step is to help them to identify options for settlement that address those interests. The options we are referring to are in addition to the payment of money or terms one party may need to agree to pay in order to settle the claims. For example, plaintiff's counsel should discuss with the plaintiff the likelihood that a defendant will settle only if plaintiff signs a release of all known *and unknown* claims. Counsel might also strategize with clients as to concessions and trade-offs that might be acceptable, targets for a settlement agreement, and approaches to negotiating over specific terms. In addition, counsel should consider the following:

   - Consulting with a tax expert as to whether a particular characterization of settlement proceeds is advantageous to the client.

   - Identifying who will pay for the parties' attorney fees and costs—especially if the case is subject to attorney fee shifting.

- Researching the law governing the requirements for preserving trial court jurisdiction to enforce the settlement agreement.[11]

- Calculating the cost savings or penalty resulting from structured payments.

- Drafting confidentiality clauses for inclusion in a settlement agreement if necessary to protect trade secrets or other sensitive information.

- Checking with an insurer as to whether the insurer's consent is necessary for a settlement agreement. If an insurance representative will be present at the mediation, counsel should be sure to communicate with the representative before the mediation session.

- Researching whether applicable law requires any particular language to make a settlement agreement binding or admissible. Sometimes the inclusion or omission of particular terms can render the settlement agreement invalid or unenforceable.[12]

5. **Bringing a draft settlement agreement to the mediation.** At the end of most mediations, participants are often tired, and some may be emotionally drained. Having done some prethinking about interests will help counsel ensure that the important points of a settlement agreement are properly addressed in an agreement. To ensure the benefit of the preparations, counsel should consider bringing a draft settlement agreement to the mediation. Specifics, such as the settlement amount, may be left blank for filling in during the mediation. It is even more efficient to work with the opposing attorney to negotiate an agreed form for the settlement agreement to avoid doing so at the mediation. Alternatively, counsel may bring a laptop computer with a draft agreement in order to complete the agreement during the mediation session. Many mediator offices and mediation facilities have ready access to printers.

---

11. Even when a case settles during an *appellate* mediation, enforcement of the resulting agreement is almost invariably handled by the *trial* court. Appellate courts are not suited to fact finding and therefore cede the factual questions of whether a party has breached or complied with the terms of an agreement to the trial court. *See* Chapter 15.

12. For example, in California, "arbitration clauses, forum selection clauses, choice of law provisions, terms contemplating remedies for breach, and similar commonly employed enforcement provisions typically negotiated in settlement discussions do not qualify an agreement for admission" to prove terms of the settlement agreement in court. Fair v. Bakhtiari, 40 Cal. 4th 189, 199–200, 147 P.3d 653 (Cal. 2006). Moreover, if money is to be paid as part of the settlement, the failure to include the specifics of payment may render the agreement unenforceable for lack of agreement on a material term. Lindsay v. Lewandowski, 139 Cal. App. 4th 1618, 1622–23, 43 Cal. Rptr. 3d 846 (Ct. App. 2006).

Chapter 11

Tips for Attorneys During the Mediation Session

A single mediation session often resolves a case that has taken up years of the parties' lives and substantial amounts of their resources. Thus, lawyers would do well to think of appellate mediations as fast-paced opportunities to demonstrate their abilities, educate the other party, advocate for their client's viewpoint, analyze, console, bargain, and craft agreements. Even so, the day of an appellate mediation session can be as exhausting as it can be exhilarating. Just as premediation legal research, client preparation, and communications with the mediator all increase the likelihood of a successful mediation session, having a game plan during the session can mean the difference between an enjoyable session and an aggravating one. To this end, we offer a few tips to bear in mind for the day of the mediation session.

A. To the Extent Possible, Have a Clear Calendar for the Day

Before the start of the mediation session, it is impossible to predict how long it will last. Sometimes sessions end before lunch, and sometimes they go late into the night.

While it is often possible to respond to other matters by cell phone or e-mail during breaks, that is not a certainty. Everyone may need to remain fully engaged in an extended joint session. Even if the parties meet separately in caucuses, there may be little downtime; some clients require continual attention throughout the mediation, or it may be necessary to do additional research, draft agreements, or talk with others about the negotiation. Mediation is hard work and requires sustained focus. Attempting to do other work—especially remotely—may be problematic. Mediation is your client's chance to end the litigation, and this opportunity deserves the undivided attention of both of you.

B. Be Mindful of Your Physical Needs

The reality of a litigator's life often rudely collides with the ideal of taking good care of yourself. Paying attention to physical needs allows you to be more fully present for your clients and otherwise enhances your performance as a lawyer. Here are a few ways taking care of your physical needs can enhance your performance at mediation:

- **Arrive rested.** Participating in mediation and supporting your client in the process requires energy and focus, which are much easier to maintain throughout a long day of mediation if you have had a good night's sleep.

- **Don't starve.** Eat a good breakfast. Although mediators often provide food during the session, we suggest you bring your own low-sugar, high-protein, energy-dense items such as trail mix or power bars to help you and your client sustain energy. A thermos of water, coffee, or tea can also be a much-appreciated companion to a mediation session. Finally, a quick check beforehand on nearby places serving food can prevent a mad scramble if the mediation session breaks for lunch or dinner.

C.   Tips for an Effective Opening in Phase 1

Aristotle's maxim "Well begun is half done" applies to Phase 1. A thoughtful mediator will begin the mediation on a positive note and utilize the initial session to discuss how the participants will work together to start the parties on a path to resolution. Lawyers, too, have a role in setting the tone of mediation from the outset. Here are some ideas about how you can contribute positively to this phase:

- **Begin with a positive statement about your intention for the mediation.** The first words out of your mouth should assure the participants and the mediator that you hope the day ends with resolution and that you intend to work as hard as you can to make it happen.

- **Declare you are there to learn something.** Admitting that you do not know it all is disarming and, by the way, an effective tool of persuasion.[1]

- **Encourage your client to begin with a statement of positive intention as well.** And prepare your client to do so. A statement of commitment to the process does not cost your client anything but is of great value in getting the mediation off to a good start. Many parties enter mediation skeptical of the other side's willingness to settle, and your client's statement to the contrary, and later actions that demonstrate commitment to resolution, can dispel that view.

D.   Tips for Exchanging Information in Phase 2

The overarching goal of Phase 2 is for the parties to exchange information—to assert their perspectives on what happened and what they expect will happen in the future if they fail to achieve a settlement and to understand the perspectives of the other participants. Effective information exchanges increase momentum toward settlement and allows the parties to make better-informed

---

1. STEVEN D. LEVITT & STEPHEN J. DUBNER, THINK LIKE A FREAK 19–48 (HarperCollins 2014) (exploring the difficulties talented professionals have in saying "I don't know" even though it is certainly true that "[t]he key to learning is feedback. It is nearly impossible to learn anything without it."). *Id.* at 34.

decisions. Both lawyers and clients play a role in listening to understand. And they each play a role in asserting the client's perspective.

Contributing to a positive atmosphere in Phase 1 is easy. Doing so in Phase 2 can be much more difficult. Above we addressed ways to prepare your client to participate and, where appropriate, to assert the client's perspective. Below we suggest how you can be more effective in this phase as well. If you can master effective representation in Phase 2, in our experience you will set yourself apart from 90 percent of lawyers. The following are some ideas that will help you achieve that mastery in the tasks of asserting your and your client's perspectives and in listening to learn about the other party's point of view.

1. Consider Joint Sessions to Be a Powerful Opportunity to Advance Mutual Understanding in a Way that Trial and Appeal Cannot

Sadly in our view, in many if not most jurisdictions, joint sessions are no longer fashionable among lawyers. Even more distressing is the trend toward the outright rejection of joint meetings altogether, even for the limited purpose of introductions or discussions of procedural matters at the beginning of the mediation. When asked the reason for refusing joint sessions, lawyers express concern that frank and open discussions of opposing points of view may negatively affect settlement. With an effective mediator to help shape conversations, participants can minimize the downside and maximize the upside of meeting together. Joint sessions offer the promise of a direct and candid exchange of information not possible in the courtroom. Such information exchange greatly increases the mutual understanding of the parties and prospects for a settlement agreement.

2. Present a Great Case on Behalf of Your Client

In discussing the merits of your client's case, approach the task as an opportunity to *educate* the opposing party and lawyer about your case, not *argue* about it. The distinction between education and argument is a subtle but important one. Education involves providing information and explaining it; it is making your perspective clear to the other side. Argument focuses on why you are right and, more significantly, why the other side is wrong. A desire to educate, well executed, engenders curiosity and engages the other party in analysis and reflection. Argument, on the other hand, engenders defensiveness and engages the other party in debate. Here are some tips on how to further your goal to educate the opposing side and the mediator about the legal risks and opportunities of the appeal:

- **Avoid fire-and-brimstone lectures and inflammatory statements directed at the opposing party or counsel.** At best, these diatribes cause an unnecessary setback that requires substantial effort to over-come before the mediation session can be productive. Attorneys often feel the need to demonstrate that they are knowledgeable, capable, and determined to get the best deal possible for their clients. However, it is not necessary to be irritating to be effective. To the contrary, you can demonstrate confidence without being intimidating and show zeal-ous advocacy without attacking the other party. You can be confident, knowledgeable, and capable without being threatening or overbearing.

- **Explain how a case will appear to the judges on the appellate court rather than try to defeat the other side's argument.** An attorney's most effective opening remarks are likely to focus on the law appli-cable to the case. Thus, you may begin with something like, *I may not be able to convince you that we have the stronger position on appeal, but here's how we believe the appellate judge, who will decide our case without learning anything about it that lies outside the appellate record, will view the case. When the judge looks at the record using applicable standards of review and applying the law, he or she will conclude . . .* This approach allows you to demonstrate vigorous and effective legal representation without unduly antagonizing the other party by denigrating their point of view. It also reassures your client to know, later in the day as the parties exchange settlement proposals, that the other side has heard a clear analysis of the strengths of his or her case and the weaknesses of the opposing party's.

- **Resist the urge to dredge up personal animosities; instead, focus on the legal issues and arguments that matter on appeal.** In cases where the other side has been uncooperative or offensive, it may be tempting to retaliate or to refer to case history with each new insult. Even though it feels good to respond in like kind, we all know there is nothing to be gained by recounting the slights, delays, and difficulties that inherently attend the contest in the trial court. They are irrelevant to educating the other side about why you will prevail. And there is everything to lose. The other side inevitably has its own laundry list of more egregious but also irrelevant slights that can bring any forward momentum to a screeching halt.

- **Become future oriented in analyzing the drawbacks of continued litigation for the opposing party—without fanning the flames of indignation and anger.** Surprisingly, appellants fail to consider obvi-ous downsides to pursuing an appeal, including the time it will take to decision, the costs, and, most commonly, the truth that an appeal will almost certainly lead to further trial court proceedings regardless of which side prevails in the appellate court. This message is best deliv-ered in a conversation, not a barrage of threats, which tend to generate denials and defensiveness. Counsel can invite this conversation simply by introducing the topic—*Let's talk about what happens if you win.*—or *with curiosity* asking a hypothetical question—*Let's say the court agrees* *with you and you win. What relief will the appellate court likely give you? Is that relief what you really hope to get out of this case?*

- **Articulate a willingness to engage in a reasonable negotiation process and work toward a deal.** In short, counsel can demonstrate zealous advocacy *and* advance negotiations by explaining how parties can work together toward settling the case.

E.   Allow Your Client to Speak

If parties take the opportunity to speak freely and, with the help of a skilled mediator, express strong emotions in Phase 2, their intense negative emotions usually dissipate. This clears the way for a more productive negotiation, including the exploration of options, that follows. Unexpressed anger and quiet sulking are incompatible with open exploration of settlement possibilities. Often something surprising and helpful that even the parties' own attorneys have not yet heard may emerge.[2]

Although courtroom conditioning may make some attorneys cringe at the thought of their clients' speaking without the direction of carefully crafted questions, this is the time to take advantage of mediation confidentiality by allowing a client to speak freely. Not only is it likely to humanize the client, but also it often adds a helpful perspective. And if the client demonstrates a readiness to engage in reasonable negotiations, the mediator can refer back to such olive branch statements in a private caucus to remind the other side that settlement is well within reach. Finally, and perhaps most importantly, the client may feel much more engaged after being able to tell his or her story.

Good client preparation is essential to an effective client presentation or dialogue in joint session. If your client naturally makes a good impression, preparation may be minimal. Clients who are not particularly likeable require more work. You may have perfect clients, but if you do not prepare them adequately, you may lose the value of their inherent integrity, presence, and spirit—or, worse, reduce the value of their presence to the other side. Thorough preparation can reduce clients' anxiety, allowing them to be more themselves. It also allows you to avoid your own anxiety produced by the uncertainty of turning your clients loose. The following are some guidelines for client preparation:

---

2. "It is not uncommon that understanding the problem to be solved involves a revelation that the reasons for litigation are not what they seem." JOHN A. TOKER, CALIFORNIA ARBITRATION & MEDIATION PRACTICE GUIDE: COURT-CONNECTED ADR 176 (Dana Curtis ed. 2008 Supp.).

- **Allow sufficient time.** In our view, insufficient preparation is one of the top three mistakes lawyers make in representing clients in mediation. Client preparation should take at least as long for mediation as for a deposition.

- **Educate your clients about what to expect when speaking in joint session.** Lessen your clients' anxiety by discussing what to expect in this phase in general and what to expect from the mediator in particular. Be detailed and specific. Tell stories about other mediations, especially those with happy endings.

- **Determine how active your clients are willing to be.** Encourage and motivate your clients to be as participatory as possible, but do not push them beyond their comfort level.

- **Identify topics for your clients to address, and then practice addressing them.** Discuss appropriate areas for your clients' participation and prepare them for when and how to enter into the discussion during joint session. Share the outline of your opening, indicating where you would like your clients to speak. If you decide your clients should respond to questions from the other side, anticipate those questions and discuss the responses. Anticipate questions the mediator might ask in joint session as well. You can also check with the mediator in advance of the mediation about likely mediator questions. It is also essential to discuss with your clients whether there are topics they are uncomfortable discussing in the presence of the other party—or any topics you believe would be addressed more effectively by you, rather than your clients. Be clear about topics your clients should avoid and give them a graceful way to defer questions to you.

- **Avoid over-rehearsing your clients.** If you script your clients' presentations and responses and practice them excessively, you will likely shroud their inherent qualities of integrity, authenticity, and presence.

- **Avoid premature bargaining or commitment to positions.** Parties sometimes wish to announce, at least to the mediator, their bottom line for a settlement. This early commitment may reflect (1) nervousness about reaching a result that they will later regret, (2) a desire to ensure the mediator's help in steering the process aims toward their goal, (3) a hope to avoid the nail-biting tension inherent in the offer and counteroffer stage of negotiations, or (4) uncertainty at how mediation works or when the appropriate time is to extend an offer. Premature declaration of a bottom line or even an offer to settle is almost always a mistake. Commitment to a position is an emotional trap that can freeze parties into a stance that should be reevaluated as part of the mediation process.[3] In many mediations that resolve disputes, both sides must accept an agreement that is far outside the zone they were willing to accept at the outset of the mediation.[4]

F.   Use Private Caucuses Effectively

As we discussed in Section II, private caucuses have a number of important functions during the mediation process. They offer an opportunity to give the mediator additional information that the mediator can use with other parties to evaluate their positions on appeal. Although we believe lawyers are best served by discussing the risks and opportunities on appeal frankly and openly in joint session in Phase 2, there are instances in which you may want to discuss the case privately, such as to get a mediator's view on a novel legal theory or to hear a mediator's frank, direct feedback about your client's case outside earshot of the other side. Or, if your client is uncomfortable discussing the weaknesses of the case in the presence of the other party, meeting alone with the mediator may be the only option.

Private sessions can provide a forum in which to test novel avenues for settlement without risking rejection—reactive devaluation[5]—simply because the idea came from the opposing side. Private discussions about options for settlement also avoid the risk of raising the other party's hopes about an idea only to dash them if, following careful examination of the idea, it turns out to be unworkable.

Although you should be candid with the mediator, be sure to tell the mediator if you have revealed information that you do not want shared with the opposing parties or anyone else not in the room with you.

---

3.   "Once we make a choice or take a stand, we encounter personal and interpersonal pressures to behave consistently with that commitment. Those pressures will cause us to respond in ways that justify our earlier decisions." ROBERT CIALDINI, INFLUENCE: SCIENCE AND PRACTICE 53 (4th ed. 2001).

4.   Commitment decisions, even erroneous ones, have a tendency to be self-perpetuating because they can "grow their own legs." That is, people often add new reasons and justifications to support the wisdom of commitments they have already made. As a consequence, some commitments remain in effect long after the conditions that spurred them have changed. *Id.* at 96.

5.   *See generally* Lee Ross, *Reactive Devaluation in Negotiation and Conflict Resolution,* in BARRIERS TO CONFLICT RESOLUTION (Arrow et al., eds. 1995).

Chapter 12

Tips for Attorneys on Concluding the Mediation and Appeal

> "It ain't over 'til it's over."
>
> —Yogi Berra

A. Reduce the Agreement to Writing *before* the Mediation Session Concludes

When an appeal settles at the end of a mediation session, how can counsel help the parties *finally* resolve the case? The short answer is that counsel should make sure everyone agrees on all provisions of the agreement, and once the agreement is clear, help them to record their agreement in writing. A written agreement, crafted and signed during the mediation session, can reduce the risks of unnecessary delay, loss of focus, and unraveled consensus. The following are tips on reducing agreements to writing at the end of the mediation session:

- **Ensure your client understands the implications of the terms of the settlement agreement.** Quite often new terms may emerge during the negotiations, and at the last minute parties may agree to clauses to make the agreement possible. Although everyone will be impatient to conclude the agreement at the end of the day, take sufficient time to discuss any last-minute terms with your client and allow your client to reflect on whether the added terms will work for the client into the future.

- **Make sure *everyone* agrees on *every* part of the settlement agreement.** Because contract law principles apply to negotiated settlement agreements, there needs to be a meeting of the minds on all terms.

- **The best practice is to bring a form settlement agreement to the mediation that your client and the other lawyer have reviewed and approved.** This practice allows time for you to explain—and for your client to understand and to reflect on the implications of—the terms of the settlement agreement in advance of mediation. Although it will be necessary to fill in blanks and perhaps add new terms toward the end of the negotiations in order to make an agreement possible, having a basic form agreement that you can complete, refine, and print—and that the parties can sign—saves considerable time and controversy at the end of a long, trying day.

- **If you decide not to prepare the formal agreement, a handwritten agreement can be a satisfactory substitute.** A handwritten agreement

can work provided it (1) contains the essential terms, (2) is signed
by the parties themselves or duly authorized party representatives,
(3) includes a statement of the parties' intent to be bound, (4) clari-
fies whether the parties intend to create a more formal agreement to be
signed later, and (5) states the parties' intention that the agreement be
admissible for the purpose of enforcement. There is no need for perfectly
formatted, spell-checked, laser-printed agreements. Once the parties have
set forth their agreement in a handwritten document, photocopies can be
made, and the parties can sign the identical copies. For this reason, if the
parties achieve settlement after they have completed the briefing, it is prudent to include a provision in the settlement agreement indicating their
intent to be bound notwithstanding a decision by the appellate court.

- **Have clients themselves sign the settlement agreement.** As the California Supreme Court has aptly observed, "The litigants' direct participation tends to ensure that the settlement is the result of their mature
  reflection and deliberate assent. This protects the parties against hasty
  and improvident settlement agreements by impressing upon them the
  seriousness and finality of the decision to settle, and minimizes the
  possibility of conflicting interpretations of the settlement."[1]

- **If a memorandum of understanding is the best that can be accomplished at the mediation session, make firm and specific plans to
  follow up with a formal settlement contract.** Realize that a memorandum of understanding itself may not be binding or enforceable
  as a settlement agreement,[2] and by substituting a memorandum of
  understanding for an agreement you may have snatched continued litigation from the jaws of settlement.

Usually the solution to these challenges is to have the mediator conclude
the mediation in joint session to allow all participants to hammer out the specific terms of the agreement and sign the agreement to make it binding.

Courts view settlement agreements as contracts and construe them by
applying contract law. You have a duty to your client to craft an agreement that
remains enforceable even under attack by a party that later changes its mind. As
Edna Sussman has written on enforcing settlement agreements, "The question
of whether the facts support mutual consent to all material terms as necessary

---

1. Levy v. Superior Court, 10 Cal. 4th 578, 585, 896 P.2d 171 (Cal. 1995).
2. "Even in circumstances when commercial parties draft a term sheet that is intended
    to serve as a template for a formal contract, the law of this state, in general, prevents
    the enforcement of the term sheet as a contract if it is subject to future negotiations
    because it is, by definition, a mere agreement to agree." Certainteed Corp. v. Celotex
    Corp., 2005 WL 217032, *14 (Del. Ct. App. 2005). *But see* Bar OK Ranch, Co. v. Ehlert,
    308 Mont. 140, 151, 40 P.3d 378 (Mont. 2002) (holding that the memorandum of
    understanding "was not merely an agreement to agree, but rather was an uncondi-
    tional resolution of the parties' claims.").

to form an enforceable contract is the area of potential attack that has been most successful in defeating efforts to enforce mediation agreements."[3] Writing settlement agreements demands care to ensure that all necessary terms are included in the agreement because parole evidence and the mediator's testimony are unlikely to fill in the blanks.[4]

B.   After the Parties Sign the Settlement Agreement

Once the parties have signed a settlement agreement, counsel—at least for the appellants—still has duties remaining. Most obviously, someone must inform the appellate court that a settlement has been achieved. This task should be promptly fulfilled, not only as a courtesy to the court but also because the court may refuse to cancel oral argument or dismiss the appeal once the justices have written an opinion. Although it may be possible to craft a settlement agreement so that it survives the issuance of the appellate court's decision, why take an unnecessary chance?

Regardless of the specific terms of the agreement, completing the settlement will require your assistance after the mediation session ends. If the settlement involves payment of money or exchange of property, you will need to calendar all of the compliance dates so that you can check that the conditions of the settlement agreement are properly fulfilled. If you represent the appellant, you may need to dissolve the appeal bond in a timely manner to free up the collateral your client was required to deposit. Ensuring fulfillment of all terms of the settlement agreement represents the culmination of the successful representation of your client.

C.   If the Case Does Not Settle on the Day of the Mediation Session

Sometimes a case that comes tantalizingly close to settling during the mediation session does not result in agreement despite everyone's best efforts. Even in such circumstances, parties should not give up hopes of reaching a settlement. Sometimes a party or insurance representative has not attended the mediation with sufficient authority to immediately settle the case but has been convinced that an agreement makes sense. On occasion a party needs more time than allowed in a mediation session in order to come to terms with the idea of letting go of the case. In any event, appeals regularly settle in the weeks after a mediation session has concluded "unsuccessfully."

---

3.   Edna Sussman, *A Brief Survey of US Case Law on Enforcing Mediation Settlement Agreements over Objections to the Existence or Validity of Such Agreements and Implications for Mediation Confidentiality and Mediator Testimony*, IBA LEGAL PRACTICE DIVISION MEDIATION COMMITTEE NEWSLETTER 32 (2006).

4.   N.L.R.B. v. Joseph Macaluso, Inc., 618 F.2d 51, 56 (9th Cir. 1980); Fackler v. Powell, 891 N.E.2d 1091, 1097 (Ind. Ct. App. 2008).

Counsel should follow up with the mediator, who in turn should follow up to see if anything has changed for the opposing party. The mediator can work with both sides to seek monetary concessions or to explore other resources to facilitate a settlement. Counsel can also enlist the mediator to keep the dialogue open and proceeding in a productive manner.

Finally, the completion of the appellate record or briefing presents a natural opportunity to reconsider settlement with your client, as the additional information sheds light on the issues. Sometimes parties realize, in the process of preparing the appellate brief, that their positions on appeal are more vulnerable to loss than they believed during the mediation session. In short, it's never too late to explore a negotiated solution that can give the parties a better solution than a decision by an appellate court can.

D.   Conclusion

The skills necessary to fulfill an appellate attorney's obligations to a client differ dramatically between the rigidity of appellate briefing and the informality of the mediation process. In Section III we have shown that mediations offer attorneys a rare opportunity to improve the circumstances facing their clients quickly and conclusively. Attorneys can do so by being collaborative rather than combative, exploring options rather than cross-examining, employing creativity in seeking solutions rather than flaws in legal assertions, and helping parties negotiate a deal that is a win for everyone. To fulfill these duties, appellate attorneys must prepare themselves, their clients, and the mediator to ensure a productive mediation session.

Regardless of their views of the settlement potential of their case, attorneys should prepare for a session that culminates in a settlement—especially given the rate of success of appellate mediations throughout the country. Settlement agreements are subject to myriad rules depending on the jurisdiction in which they are made. Thus, counsel not only must prepare for the negotiation that occurs in mediation but also be prepared to craft an enforceable settlement agreement that will result in the complete resolution of the dispute. Although mediation sessions can be long and tiring, they often result in the exhilarating feeling that comes with having a client finally, conclusively, and acceptably resolve the dispute. That sense of satisfaction is one to celebrate and for which attorneys deserve congratulations for representing their clients with skill and purpose.

Section IV
Practice Tips for Appellate Mediators

This section provides guidance and practice tips for appellate mediators based on the unique considerations in settlement negotiations after a trial court has entered a judgment or appealable order.

Appellate mediators tend to come from two backgrounds. The first is mediators with *process* expertise gained in prelitigation and trial court mediation. Experienced mediators have valuable skills to help estranged parties communicate, to assist with integrative and distributive bargaining, and to create an environment within which the mediation process can unfold productively. However, without knowledge of appellate procedures and terminology, even very accomplished mediators may be baffled by concepts such as analysis of prejudice, de novo review, or stipulated reversal of judgment. And if appellate mediators help the parties to evaluate the risks and opportunities on appeal, as most do,[1] then to meet the ethical obligation of competence, they must be well schooled in appellate law and procedures. Strictly facilitative mediators must also understand appeals in order to manage (or to follow) the parties' discussion and facilitate thoughtful case analysis. If you are not conversant in the language, law, and procedures of appeals, we urge you to read Section I, where we provide a crash course on these topics.

The second category of appellate mediators that will benefit from studying this section consists of appellate attorneys who are expert in the legal arena but usually lack the background and skills necessary to conduct a productive mediation. Unlike trial attorneys who regularly attend mediation, most appellate specialists have little or no exposure to mediation or involvement in negotiating settlements on behalf of their clients.

Brendon's experience prior to becoming a member of an appellate court mediation panel illustrates the contrast between the world of mediators and the world of appellate attorneys. When he maintained a full-time private practice limited to civil appeals, he would regularly go for days without any contact with clients. Indeed, he never had a face-to-face meeting with a substantial number of them because the trial attorneys frequently served as co-counsel and maintained responsibility for client communications. If your experience is similar to Brendon's, we recommend reading Section II, where we delve into the

---

1. Dwight Golann, *Variations in Mediation: How—and Why—Legal Mediators Change Styles in the Course of a Case*, J. OF DISPUTE RESOLUTION 42 (2000), n.24 ("legal mediators spend a good deal of time privately assessing the strength of the parties' legal arguments and underlying interests").

mediation process for appeals. We also recommend additional mediation skills training.[2]

Regardless of background, this section has something for every appellate mediator. Chapter 13 concerns the premediation and opening phases of mediation and offers advice about setting the appellate mediation on a path to success with thorough preparation and an effective opening session.

Chapter 14 focuses on the phases during which the parties exchange perspectives on what happened to lead to litigation, the legal risks and opportunities on appeal, and the interests that must be taken into account in any interest-based negotiation. It encourages mediators to extend the time they spend in face-to-face discussions, or joint sessions, and provides suggestions for maximizing the benefits of direct conversation. It also offers guidance on conducting separate sessions—or caucuses—during these phases.

Chapter 15 concerns the end of a mediation session and provides ideas about how both to expand the pie and to divide it, including negotiating interest-based solutions and monetary settlements. It also addresses the often-overlooked but crucial task of documenting and refining agreements the parties reach. And it provides suggestions about following up after mediation when the parties reach agreement and when they do not.

Finally, Chapter 16 offers insight and advice to appellate mediators about professional development—how to become a more effective appellate mediator—and business development—how to grow an appellate mediation practice.

---

2. In particular, we recommend that appellate attorneys who are new to the role of mediator read the following: ROGER FISHER, WILLIAM L. URY & BRUCE PATTON, GETTING TO YES: NEGOTIATING AGREEMENT WITHOUT GIVING IN (Penguin 2011) (a readable classic on integrative negotiation); J. ANDERSON LITTLE, MAKING MONEY TALK: HOW TO MEDIATE INSURED CLAIMS AND OTHER MONETARY DISPUTES (ABA 2007) (a fantastic guide to distributive bargaining); DOUGLAS STONE, BRUCE PATTON & SHEILA HEEN, DIFFICULT CONVERSATIONS: HOW TO DISCUSS WHAT MATTERS MOST (Penguin 2010) (exploring a skill that may be underutilized given the solitary and erudite nature of appellate work); and GARY J. FRIEDMAN & JACK HIMMELSTEIN, UNDERSTANDING CONFLICT: MEDIATION THROUGH UNDERSTANDING (ABA Section of Dispute Resolution and Harvard Program on Negotiation 2008) (an elaboration of understanding-based, noncaucus mediation foreign to most lawyers, in which the parties are in the foreground and focus on their interests, as well as the risks and opportunities going forward if they do not reach agreement). In the appendix, we provide a more comprehensive list of our favorite books and articles that can help any appellate mediator.

Chapter 13
Premediation and Phase 1, Opening the Mediation

A. Overview

No matter how much you prepare, nothing guarantees a satisfying appellate mediation process or a process that will end with an agreement. But, *failure* to prepare thoroughly jeopardizes your credibility and risks an unsatisfying process and outcome for participants—and for you. Among frequent participants of mediation, more than 96 percent consider premediation preparation by the mediator to be "important, very important or essential."[3] Regular consumers of mediation services uniformly believe it is essential for mediators to know the case and read the key documents.[4]

Appellate mediation demands more preparation than trial court mediation because the history of the litigation is more extensive and the legal arguments are likely to be more complex and more fully developed, especially if appellate lawyers are involved. Additionally, the parties may be more pessimistic about settlement given past failed efforts and the reality that the trial court has declared a winner and a loser. The premediation phase presents opportunities for appellate mediators and attorneys to begin to deal with these challenges and to set the mediation process on a track toward success, despite previously unsuccessful settlement efforts and a judgment declaring a winner and a loser.

Preparation begins in the premediation phase, sometimes referred to as the "convening" phase, when you first speak with the lawyers.[5] This early contact allows you to get a snapshot of the background, scope, and legal issues in the case; ensure the right people participate and are well prepared for discussions about the legal issues and other matters that are important to them; and make arrangements for mediation statements that provide everyone involved with the information needed to be well prepared. Preparation continues until the mediation session begins, as you read mediation statements, study and reflect on the legal issues, and prepare your opening remarks and agenda. Often, preparation includes further telephone calls with lawyers after you review the mediation statements. Thorough and thoughtful preparation is key to a successful

---

3. AMERICAN BAR ASSOCIATION TASK FORCE ON IMPROVING MEDIATION QUALITY, FINAL REPORT 5, 7 (2008) [hereinafter ABA MEDIATION QUALITY].
4. *Id.*
5. For ease of discussion, we assume premediation contacts will be with lawyers. Although it rarely occurs in our practice, we recognize that in self-represented cases, mediators will be working with parties, not lawyers.

mediation, as we demonstrate in this section. It is also fundamental to your own enjoyment of and respect for the mediation process.

B.   The Premediation Phase

1.   *Conduct a Premediation Call as Soon as Possible after You Are Hired or Appointed*

An American Bar Association study recently concluded that the "desire for substantive and procedural pre-mediation discussions indicates a real evolution in the field and implies that a higher level of process design and substantive pre-mediation collaboration between mediators and users is a trend for the future."[6] We agree. Soon after you become the mediator in an appellate case, it is essential to talk with the lawyers. We suggest your first premediation contact be a telephone conference rather than separate calls. A joint call allows you to assess the relationship dynamic between the lawyers, address logistical decisions efficiently, and, in the best cases, engage counsel in collaborative decision making about the process, as practice for later collaboration on substantive issues. The premediation telephone conference is an efficient and effective means to do the following:

- Understand the *nature of the dispute* and learn about the *parties*. This call may be the mediator's first chance to learn anything about the case.

- Make any *disclosures* of previous relationships or other potential conflicts, such as past mediations conducted with any of the participants.

- Determine who will participate in the mediation and ensure party representatives will attend with *full settlement authority*. Few things are as irritating and futile as mediations in which it is discovered, after much negotiation, that one of the essential parties either does not possess full settlement authority or is simply missing from the mediation. Conversely, the parties may agree that unnecessary individuals (such as insureds under policies in which the insurer retains sole settlement authority) may be excused from attending the mediation.[7]

- Cover the basics of *confidentiality* with attorneys or self-represented litigants who may not know the contours of mediation confidentiality in your jurisdiction. Many attorneys do not know when mediation confidentiality begins or ends in the appellate process. If you do not help them understand the duration of confidentiality, discussions may be unnecessarily inhibited.

---

6. ABA Mediation Quality, *supra* note 1, at 9.
7. We do not mean to suggest that an insured who has no say in the final resolution is irrelevant to the process. Sometimes insureds want to participate or their participation is important for reasons specific to a case.

- Discuss *mediator fees* and how the parties intend to allocate them. Some court-connected mediators do not charge for their services. If you intend to bill the parties, we advise you to raise the issue and secure agreement on fees during this call. Sadly, we know of mediations that derailed when the court-connected mediator brought up fees for the first time during the mediation session. If you are conducting a court-connected mediation, be sure to check that your billing practices conform to the local rules of court.[8] Finally, your jurisdiction may require that any fee agreement be made in writing.

- Coordinate the *logistics*—that is, when and where to meet for the mediation session and for how long.

- Request *mediation statements* along with any key documents that can help you understand the parties' views of the legal and practical realities of the case, determine the due date, and decide whether the parties will exchange them.

- Get a sense of the level of acrimony or cooperation among parties and lawyers and start *building rapport* with the participants.

We suggest you follow this call with a letter or e-mail to confirm the agreed-upon arrangements. We include a sample of this follow-up letter, as well as a more detailed description and a sample script for the premediation telephone conference call, in the appendix.

2. Review Mediation Statements and Key Trial Court Documents

A definitive assessment of the issues on appeal requires a review of the entire appellate record and all applicable law. Especially following a long trial in complex litigation, the record and law can be far too voluminous for any mediator reasonably to review. For mediation purposes, it is possible to gain an efficient, adequate understanding of the case from the parties' mediation statements and a few key trial court documents.

Request the key trial court documents. If they exist, ask the lawyers to send you the following documents:

- The order or judgment being appealed,

---

8. *See, e.g.*, Cal. Court of Appeal, Third Dist., local rule 1(h) (prohibiting court-appointed mediators from charging for the first four hours of mediation or for premediation preparations except in "exceptional cases").

- Any written order of the court to be challenged on appeal,[9]

- The trial court's statement of decision explaining the basis for the appealed order or judgment, along with any party's objections filed in response,

- The contract (if the appeal focuses on a contract's meaning), and

- The special verdict form completed by the jury (if tried to a jury).

Although it may be necessary to have a reporter's transcript of trial to assess some issues—such as challenges to evidentiary rulings or the sufficiency of the evidence or statements made in arguments by counsel—these issues tend to be among the least likely to lead to reversal.[10] The strongest appellate issues often do not require review of the transcript; they are discernible from the trial court's statement of decision and the parties' last moving papers. It is generally wise to request that these documents be sent to you right away.

From these few documents, you can begin to understand the potential issues on appeal, the applicable areas of law, and the standards of review likely to be employed. The absence of any of these documents may signal forfeiture of the issue on appeal or indicate that the issue played a minor role in the trial court.[11] A review of these documents prior to the mediation can facilitate your understanding of the issues as well as the strengths and weaknesses of an appeal.

Request and review mediation statements. The easiest way to learn about the appeal is for the lawyers to tell you. Thus, most mediators request—and many court-connected mediation program rules require—mediation statements. Most parties have identified and can clearly articulate their legal arguments. If they have not analyzed the legal arguments in-depth, the exercise of preparing mediation statements helps to ensure they do so by the time of the mediation. Mediation statements also encourage parties to consider additional circumstances surrounding the appeal, including the rate of postjudgment interest and the status of any appeal bond, judgment collection efforts, or collateral litigation and other realities not readily apparent from an examination of trial court documents.

---

9. Often an appealable order or judgment is not itself the focus of the appellate challenge. Instead, the appellant seeks to focus on an earlier error committed by the trial court, such as an evidentiary ruling before or during trial. In such instances, you should request any trial court order that explains the challenged ruling.

10. This is because many of these issues occurring during trial are subject to the very deferential abuse of discretion standard of review that applies to such issues as errors in admitting or excluding evidence. See Chapter 1, part C.

11. See Chapter 1, part F, for a discussion of how failure to argue an issue in the trial court likely forfeits (i.e., precludes from argument in the appellate court) the issue on appeal.

The sample mediation statements in the appendix suggest topics you may want the parties to discuss in their mediation statements, such as the legal issues, their best arguments to be raised on appeal, the practical consequences of the litigation on the underlying problem, any areas of agreement (even if only regarding the facts or law governing the case), and any ideas parties might have regarding options for resolution.

We strongly recommend parties also *exchange* mediation statements. Reviewing the opposing argument helps parties assess their own appeal and be better prepared to discuss the law and to negotiate at the mediation. If parties are reluctant to provide their statements to the other side, we suggest you encourage them to do so and help them explore the benefits of sharing their statements. This discussion may motivate them to do so. Some of the benefits of exchanging mediation statements are as follows:

- The parties have the opportunity to evaluate their own appellate arguments more fully and accurately when they understand the counterarguments better.

- The parties are better able to formulate a negotiation strategy, including proposals that meet all parties' interests, if they know how the other side is viewing the case and, for plaintiffs, especially if the statement contains a demand supported by a rationale for it.

- The parties come to mediation better prepared to discuss the appellate issues in-depth with the other party or the mediator.

If lawyers remain reluctant to exchange statements, find out why, discuss their concerns, and help to address them so the exchange can occur. For example, if they are worried about exacerbating the conflict or polarizing the parties with inflammatory briefs, you can help them agree on ground rules to address the fear, such as eliminating accusations against or characterizations of the other party or, more generally, approaching mediation statements as an opportunity to *educate*, not to *debate*, the other side.

If parties do not want to exchange briefs because they may contain sensitive or private information, you might suggest they submit separate, confidential statements containing the sensitive information or speak with you separately and confidentially prior to mediation.

Be clear about the due date. A week before the mediation is customary, although parties do not always adhere to the deadline. Some mediators prefer to limit the length of mediation statements. Unless the case is unusually complex, parties can articulate the gravamen of the appeal and the surrounding circumstances in 5 or 10 pages.

Conduct your own research, if necessary. Usually the mediation statements and documents you receive from the parties will suffice to prepare you sufficiently to discuss legal issues with the parties. However, appeals can delve into procedural and substantive complexities that can stymie any casual reader. In order to bolster your confidence or to help you grasp the arcane or complex arguments that appellate cases sometimes involve, you may need to consult your favorite appellate specialist colleague or conduct a bit of your own legal research. We do not typically charge the parties for the time it takes us to bone up on appellate law or think through the appeal with an expert. If you plan to charge the parties for your research, we suggest checking with the parties first to see if they are willing to pay for the extra preparation.

Consider making an outline of the issues. As she reads mediation statements, Dana creates, for her own use, a timeline of events, an outline of the issues, and a summary of each party's perspective. A digest of the information enables you to enter mediation with a command of the issues and demonstrates to the parties that you are well prepared. It also gives you easy access to important facts and law during mediation that are impossible for most of us to retain without such aids.

3. Design the Mediation

In Section II we set forth a recommended phase-by-phase approach to appellate mediation. Although this basic structure forms the skeleton of most appellate mediations, we oppose the idea of a one-size-fits-all structure. Because no two cases are alike, we believe an individualized approach to mediation allows parties the best opportunity to resolve their disputes. Each case presents unique parties and circumstances that bring them to mediation. The interplay of issues in each case is also distinctive, as are the context, timing, facts, and emotions. If you mediate long enough, you recognize the emergence of common themes, scenarios, and characters, but in fact no two mediations are ever identical.

The phases we outline in this section allow us to introduce new mediators to the various tasks of mediation and the usual way they unfold to help parties reach agreement, but we do not mean to suggest that you need to adhere to them rigidly to be effective. In fact, we believe effective appellate mediation requires mediators to understand the dispute and to work with the lawyers to tailor the process to the needs of the parties. The premediation telephone conference call (along with any necessary separate calls to counsel) gives you information necessary to design an appropriate process. In tailoring the process, consider the following:

- **The parties' relationship.** Other than the relationship as litigation opponents, have they had a previous or ongoing business or personal relationship? Do they hope or need to preserve or restore it as a result of the mediation? What is the present state of the relationship? Is there high emotion, such as resentment or anger? Where important relationships are at stake, the task of designing the mediation is most challenging—and potentially most rewarding.

The instinct of many mediators is to conduct mediation with highly conflicted parties entirely in separate sessions to calm the waters, to curtail disruption, and to avoid further damage to the relationship that would interfere with settlement. Although separate sessions may be the better approach, for example in a sexual harassment case in which the plaintiff strongly objects to being in the same room with the defendant, if the parties have an interest in bettering the relationship even in a modest way, joint sessions are preferable. If the mediator can help the parties have a constructive conversation, perhaps for the first time since the dispute arose, they may begin to understand one another and to gain skills that enable them to continue to strengthen their relationship after the mediation ends. Later in this chapter, we provide additional information about structuring and facilitating constructive joint sessions.

- **The parties' goals.** If parties come to mediation voluntarily, it may be safe to assume they want to resolve the pending appeal. However, until you ask whether there are additional objectives that an optimal resolution would satisfy, you may miss information essential to design a process that will give them the chance to achieve important goals. For example, does one party have the process goal to express his or her perspective—or to hear another party's viewpoint—before settlement can occur? Once you are aware of the goals, you can structure the mediation to provide opportunities for the parties to achieve them. If the court has ordered the parties to mediate, it is not safe to assume they are there to settle the appeal. Sometimes they just want a published decision in a test case. Brendon was counsel in exactly such a case. He had to explain to the mediator that his clients did not pursue the appeal for money or a settlement. They were there for a published decision on behalf of *all* similarly situated plaintiffs. The design of a mediation process in this case will look quite different from one in which the parties want to settle or mend a relationship. An effective mediator in Brendon's case might have inquired premediation about his client's goals, and upon learning about the desire for a decision might have explored *interests* that underlay this *position*. The resulting conversation might have been useful for two reasons. It would have helped the mediator understand how firmly committed Brendon's client was to going the distance on appeal, and, knowing this, allowed the parties to decide whether mediation was worthwhile.

- **Cultural differences.** Are there cultural issues to consider in designing a mediation process, such as ethnic or religious differences that should be accounted for or that may even form the basis of the conflict? When organizations or governmental bodies are parties, have their cultural differences contributed to the conflict, and do they need to be addressed for the mediation to be successful? If so, you can inquire further about how these differences might affect the mediation and what needs to occur before or during mediation to address any potentially disruptive effects.

Designing the process is a joint effort among the mediator, the lawyers, and the parties. Although you take the lead in suggesting an approach based on the premediation conversations, you should seek feedback from the lawyers. If you were also in contact with the parties, it would be important to hear from them as well.

4. Secure Agreement on Mediator Fees

Confirm your fee agreement in writing prior to the mediation. In the appendix, we provide a mediator fee agreement as an example of how you might structure a fee arrangement and the terms you may wish to consider for inclusion.

C. Phase 1: Opening the Mediation

As a mediator, you are in charge of opening the mediation. For some mediators the opening phase is perfunctory, limited to the transmission of preliminary data such as the introduction of the participants, the sequence of events for the session, and logistics such as restrooms and breaks. This information is important.[12] Indeed, the one-page mediation checklist of the mediation phases we include in the appendix includes these topics. Well conducted, Phase 1 is much more: an opportunity to create a collaborative atmosphere and influence the quality of the participants' interaction and discussions for the remainder of the day. In this section, we provide some ideas about how to do so.

Another problem with perfunctory openings is that they are lectures, not conversations, and as such they miss the opportunity for you and the other participants to learn from one another. Although there is information the mediator should convey, we prefer for it to become part of a discussion rather than be delivered as a lecture.

Orient the participants to the appellate process and appellate mediation. Parties and lawyers commonly lack experience with appeals and come to appellate mediation skeptical about whether it will work. We think it is important to talk about these concerns and provide participants with information that will help them to better understand the process, but in a conversational way,

---

12. We cover the basics of Phase 1 in Chapter 5. In addition, a good general overview of opening a mediation session may be found in Dwight Golann, Mediating Legal Disputes: Effective Strategies for Lawyers and Mediators 15–21 (ABA 2009).

not a lecture. Assuming discussion is *how* you orient parties to appellate mediation, below we address *what* you might want to talk about.

In most ways, mediating appeals is not much different from mediating other cases, and the procedure we describe in Section II for Phase 1 applies universally to all types of cases. However, there *are* night-and-day procedural differences between trials and appeals. Especially if the participants are not experienced in the appellate process, it is useful at the outset to discuss these differences.

Parties often view these differences as obstacles. "After all," they say, "we couldn't settle the case before, so why would we be able to do so now, when we have a winner and a loser?" It may also be helpful to acknowledge their skepticism and seize the opportunity to educate the parties about appellate mediation. Most of the differences parties assume to be drawbacks, are actually advantages. As you work with parties to analyze the upsides and downsides of appellate mediation, you help them to move beyond their skepticism. Even better, you help them to see that some apparent downsides in fact enhance the possibility of settlement.

Table 13.1 lists the most significant differences between appeals and other cases and provides examples of how you might explain these special considerations in an encouraging light during the opening or at another appropriate time.

Table 13.1: Differences between Trial Court Cases and Appeals

Difference	Mediator Comment
There has been a winner and a loser.	*You come to mediation as a winner or a loser. Some people believe it is impossible to resolve cases where there has been a decision about who is right and who is wrong. I understand that perspective. After all, the respondent has convinced a jury (or judge) of the correctness on his or her position. There is good reason to believe the appellate judges will agree with the trial court: most of the time they do. But sometimes they do not, and for this reason prevailing parties are often willing to compromise rather than take a chance they will lose an appeal.*
A decision by the appellate court probably will not end the dispute.	*Here, the parties have a final judgment. True, but until the highest court—the Supreme Court—rules in a case, it is not over. This case demonstrates that fact: it has a continuing life because a party appealed. But in the court of appeal, it is highly likely that if the court disagrees with the trial court decision, this case will not end with the appellate decision. Instead, the judges will send the case back for retrial. You start over. For this reason, winning parties often settle. They did not like paying for a trial and risking a loss the first time. They do not want to do so again.*

(continued)

Table 13.1: (*continued*)

Difference	Mediator Comment
The rules and procedures are different from those in the trial court.	*Unlike the trial court's task, which is to determine who is right on the facts and the law, the court of appeal's responsibility is to determine whether the trial court erred as a matter of law and, if so, whether the legal error made a difference to the outcome. It applies prescribed standards of review as it looks at what happened in the trial court to make its determination. The court does not hear testimony and in many cases does not hear oral argument from the attorneys. Nor do the judges ever communicate directly with the parties. These differences sometimes frustrate the losing party, who would like another day in court to tell his or her version of the case, but these differences may help the case to settle. Of course, if appellant prevails, there will likely be a new trial. If so, the parties once again look to the jury or trial judge to determine factual issues. But until and unless the court grants a new trial, the parties are no longer guessing, like in trial court mediation, which version of the facts a jury will believe.*

You can also help to relieve participants' concerns that cases cannot settle on appeal by pointing out the settlement rate of local state and federal appellate mediation programs, or the numerous reasons why even the winner at trial would be better off to settle, or reasons unique to each side that motivate settlement rather than continuing litigation. For a discussion of the many reasons why a party who prevailed at trial would be better off settling an appeal, see Chapter 2 and part F.9 of Chapter 3. For information about settlement rates, see Chapter 2 and Chapter 10.

Create a positive emotional climate. Dealing with the parties' skepticism about mediating at the appellate level and, as we discussed earlier, being organized and knowing *what* to talk about—and *when*—are important to your preparation, but even more important to the success of the opening phase is *how* you approach it—that is, the personal qualities[13] you bring into the room, such as your commitment to working with the parties to achieve an agreement, optimism about their ability to reach a mutually acceptable agreement, competence to create a safe and productive space for the communications and negotiations, and, more importantly, presence with an ability to connect with all of the participants.

As the mediator you are the leader of the process and can effectively set the tone of the mediation. Social psychologists describe this as "emotional contagion," which refers to the phenomena that (1) the moods of individuals in a group tend to converge as they spend time together, and (2) the group leader's emotions and mood are contagious and tend to disseminate to the other

---

13. For a nuanced exploration of mediator personal qualities and how to develop them, see DANIEL BOWLING & DAVID HOFFMAN, BRINGING PEACE INTO THE ROOM: HOW THE PERSONAL QUALITIES OF THE MEDIATOR IMPACT THE PROCESS OF CONFLICT RESOLUTION (Jossey-Bass 2003).

participants.[14] In other words, if you radiate optimism and confidence, partici- pants will be pulled subconsciously into the same positive affect.[15] The benefits for the remainder of the mediation are significant: "positive emotional con- tagion group members experienced improved cooperation, decreased conflict, and increased perceived task performance."[16]

Later in the process, a mediator's positive affect tends "to increase conces- sion making, stimulate creative problem solving, increase joint gains, increase preferences for cooperation, reduce the use of contentious tactics, and increase the use of cooperative negotiation strategies. [But n]egative affect has been shown to decrease initial offers, decrease joint gains."[17] Because we create a pos- itive emotional environment primarily with nonverbal cues such as our facial expressions, body language, and tone of voice, consider *what you say* during the opening phase to be only part of what you are communicating.[18] Perhaps the most important work you do is accomplished not by doing anything in particu- lar but by *being* positive, confident, and empathetic. Don't rush![19]

Develop rapport and trust. There are as many ways to develop rapport as there are mediators. As with most attributes of a successful mediator, rapport develops not by what a mediator *does*; it develops because of who the media- tor *is*—in other words, the personal qualities of the mediator. Qualities that contribute to rapport building and allow parties to be at ease with and develop confidence in the mediator include the following:

- Presence—the ability to focus attention fully on the present moment, especially on the people in the room.

- Curiosity—an attitude of openness and eagerness to learn about the parties and their perspectives.

---

14. Sigal G. Barsade, *The Ripple Effect: Emotional Contagion and Its Influence on Group Behav- ior*, 47 ADMINISTRATIVE SCIENCE QUARTERLY 645, 669–70 (2002).
15. *Id.* at 645.
16. *Id.* at 644.
17. Gerben A. Van Kleef, Carsten K.W. De Dreu & Antony S.R. Manstead, *The Interpersonal Effects of Anger and Happiness in Negotiations*, 8 J. OF PERSONALITY & SOCIAL PSYCHOLOGY 57 (2004), citations omitted; *see also* Robert A. Baron, *Environmentally Induced Positive Affect: Its Impact on Self-Efficacy, Task Performance, Negotiation, and Conflict*, 20 J. OF APPLIED SOCIAL PSYCHOLOGY 368–84 (1990).
18. Barsade, *supra* note 12, at 647.
19. The rush toward solutions before developing rapport and trust permeates the world of negotiations. For example, the Federal Bureau of Investigations reports that for its hostage negotiators, "[t]he most common mistake negotiators make is trying to hurry the process by rushing into problem solving before establishing a measure of trust. This is typified by negotiators who ceaselessly press subjects to surrender before they are ready. Negotiators should not drone the mantra, 'When are you coming out?' Only after they have established rapport and earned the right to do so can negotiators begin to influence the subject by suggesting resolution options." Gary W. Noesner, *Negotia- tion Concepts for Commanders*, 68 FBI LAW ENFORCEMENT BULLETIN 10 (1999).

- The *party's* trust—that the mediator is competent and well-prepared to lead the mediation process and understand the subject matter of the dispute, especially the appellate context; and that the mediator cares about the parties' predicament and is committed to helping them find resolution.

- The *mediator's* trust—in the process; in the parties and their lawyers; and in the mediator's own ability to guide the parties to a mutually satisfying resolution.

Likable mediators settle cases more effectively because "[p]eople really do say 'yes' more to people they like."[20] As a practical matter, if the mediation involves caucusing, much of the negotiation in later stages of the mediation actually passes through the mediator by shuttle diplomacy. In addition, many procedural agreements are made through the mediator—for example, whether to continue negotiating, searching for additional solutions, or even trying something new at the mediator's suggestion. Thus, rapport and trust are the stock in trade of the mediator and should be cultivated—and deserved—from the outset of the mediation.

Ask good questions. In the opening phase, you can also encourage shared ownership of the mediation process by engaging the participants in conversation with good questions. After all, "It is not the answer that enlightens, but the question."[21] The quality of discussions in mediation largely depends on the quality of the questions the mediator asks. We find that most mediators, but especially less experienced ones, could use some help with forming appropriate questions at each phase. It is in this spirit that we offer questions that elicit the reflection and response necessary to initiate and enrich the conversation. The subject matter and nature of questions differ depending on the stage of the mediation process. Thus, we suggest questions that work well for us in each phase.

Questions can help establish a positive tone. We mentioned the importance of establishing a positive emotional climate early in the mediation and how to do so, including by monitoring and managing your own attitude and emotional state. You can also incline the attitude and emotional states of others in the room with good questions designed to do so. If you intend to ask questions that can affect the mood of the room positively, we suggest you alert the lawyers to the nature of the questions and your purpose in asking them so they can be prepared and prepare their clients to offer constructive answers. Questions like the following have worked for us: *What would you like to be able*

---

20. Richard Birke, *Neuroscience and Settlement: An Examination of Scientific Innovations and Practical Applications*, 25 Ohio State J. on Dispute Resolution 497 (2010).
21. Stuart Wells, Choosing the Future: The Power of Strategic Thinking (1997), quoting Eugène Ionesco, Découvertes (1970).

to say at the end of the day about how the mediation went? What is your fondest hope for the day? What do you hope can happen today? What would it mean to you to walk out of here today with an agreement that truly works for you/for your business?

Questions to initiate discussion about the appellate process. Launching into a lecture on the appellate law and procedure can defeat the mediator's purpose to connect with the parties and can instead bore them. Beginning with a question about whether they are interested helps to engage them. And if you preface the question with an explanation of why it might be useful to describe the appellate process, even better. Here is one of a series of questions we have used successfully for this purpose: *Although attorneys understand how the appeal process works, I thought you [the parties] might be interested to know what will happen procedurally if the appeal does not resolve in mediation. Would it be helpful for me to give you a brief description of that process?*

Questions to initiate discussion about the "settle-ability" of appeals. There is often an undercurrent of pessimism or skepticism as appellate mediations begin. We find that raising the issue can help the parties set these attitudes aside or, at least, move them to the background. Here's one way to start this conversation: *Parties and lawyers usually have difficulty understanding how mediation of an appeal can possibly work, given the trial court has declared a winner and a loser. How about you? Does this concern you? Any other concerns about mediating on appeal?* These questions—and their answers—naturally lead to discussion about the differences (and advantages) mediating cases at the appellate stage, which we describe in Table 13.1.

Questions to initiate discussion about working together in the mediation. Especially if the mediation involves face-to-face discussions, which we recommend, parties need guidance and support to have constructive conversations. Some mediators lay down the law about conduct in mediation. We do not endorse that approach. Instead, we presume the participants will be well behaved. If the communication becomes problematic during mediation, we help the parties deal with it and formulate ground rules as necessary. Sometimes, though, we know from the premediation discussions that the parties are communication-challenged and they have been in trouble before they come to us. In those cases, if you are not a lay-down-the law kind of mediator, you can help the parties have a good conversation about how to deal with their difficult communication dynamic, beginning with an appropriate preface: *Before we got here today, we all agreed it would be helpful, or even essential, for you to be able to talk with each other directly about the situation that gave rise to this litigation. I understand from your lawyers that you have not had much success doing this in the past. Before we begin, I'd like to talk with you about how to make the most of this opportunity and what you—and I as your mediator—can do to ensure that it works really well.*

From here, the questions can take different forms. The following ones work for us: *What agreements would you like from the other party that would help you have a good conversation? What can you do to ensure this conversation is constructive?* If the parties attempted mediation previously, you might say the following: *I know you had a previous mediation. Did you try to communicate directly with each other in that process? What worked? What didn't work so well? How can we avoid that problem from derailing your conversation here?*

To humanize the participants. Some mediators begin every mediation by inviting participants to introduce themselves not just by stating their names and roles in the mediation but also by sharing something personal about themselves. When they do so, the participants begin mediation by seeing the "enemy" as a person. Almost always, these exchanges lead people to discover shared interests and experiences that contribute to greater friendliness and collaboration throughout the day. You may consider using this approach with a preface such as the following: *I like to begin mediation with each of us saying something personal about ourselves that we are comfortable revealing in this setting. I find that when we do so, we experience each other as real people, not just as our roles—of attorneys, mediator, parties to litigation, or in some cases as enemies. I find it helps us to have a more respectful and interesting conversation throughout the rest of the day.*

Here is an additional way to kick off this introduction: *Would you please tell us something about yourself that we are unlikely to know that you feel comfortable mentioning in this group? I'll begin and then move to my right. If you need to pass because you need more time to think of something, just say so, and I will come back to you. If you want to pass because you don't want to say anything, that is OK, too.*

To head off behavior that may disrupt the conversation. It does not happen often, but sometimes you have reason to anticipate that conduct of a participant may disrupt the discussions, either because you have experienced the problem firsthand or because a lawyer has warned you about it. Fortunately, with the right questions you can head it off at the pass. All it takes is a little conversation to encourage the challenged parties to (1) reflect on their own communication challenges, (2) take responsibility for those challenges, and (3) monitor and manage their own conduct. Here is one very simple question that has worked over and over for us (and requires no preface): *What would you like to tell your friend or loved one at the end of today about the way you conducted yourself in this mediation?*

If you like, you could also preface this question with the following: *It is not easy to work out conflict, especially by the time a dispute gets to the appellate court—after years have gone by and litigation has likely made it worse. It will take all of us to be at our best in order to make settlement possible. What is your "best" you can bring to this enterprise?*

These questions elicit the participants' commitment. We know from decision-making research that when we say we will do something, we are far more likely to do it. Commitment and consistency bias compels us to do so.[22]

---

22. Barry Goldman, The Science of Settlement: Ideas for Negotiators 108–13 (ALI-ABA 2008) (describing the "consistency trap" we tend to fall into).

D. Transitioning from Phase to Phase

Before we move to Phase 2, we want to address an unappreciated topic that relates to all phases: how to move from one phase to another, or how to end one phase and begin another. If the mediator moves to Phase 2 before the parties have achieved the goals of Phase 1, the parties will have failed to lay the proper foundation for a productive Phase 2. Thus, we suggest that when mediators think it is time to move to the next phase, they first do the following:

1. **Remind the parties of the goals of the current phase.** You might say: *For the past 20 minutes, we have been discussing how we will work together throughout the mediation session today, each of our roles, confidentiality in the joint and separate sessions and outside the mediation, guidelines for communication, and the basic agenda for the day.*

2. **Ask if the goals have been met.** For example, you might inquire: *Do you have any questions related to this phase? Are you clear about all of our roles? Are there questions about the agenda, or changes you would suggest? Are we ready to move on to the next phase, where we work to gather more information about each of your perspectives?*

3. **Answer questions or discuss issues the participants raise until they are ready to move on.** At times, one party might be ready to move on to the next phase before another party seems ready to wrap up the task at hand. In such circumstances, even if the mediator thinks it is time to conclude a phase, it is important to stay in the conversation to see what the objecting party thinks is missing. The decision about whether the task is complete resides with the parties, not the mediator. Although it might challenge the mediator's and the other party's patience, it is important to stay with the task. Rushing to the next phase over the objection of the party risks loss of that party's trust and may foreclose discussion that needs to take place for the case to resolve.

As we explain elsewhere, mediation seldom progresses in the strictly linear adherence to this model. Although our approach to the transitions between phases assures that the parties are ready to move on, it does not ensure that they are finished with a phase *forever*. You can acknowledge this reality by stating before you move to the next phase: *It looks like we are ready to move on. However, if at any time you want to discuss how we are working together feel free to raise issues related to this phase.*

Chapter 14
Phase 2, Information Exchange, and Phase 3, Identifying and Organizing the Issues

A. Introduction

In this chapter, we celebrate the unsung heroes of the mediation phases: Phase 2, in which the parties exchange information, and Phase 3, in which they identify the issues to be resolved and develop an agenda for addressing them. Especially in appellate mediation, these phases tend to get short shrift. Many participants wrongly assume long-pending litigation has brought to light all there is to know about the case. Similarly, participants often arrive assuming the only settlement option is the payment of money by one party to the other. The processes explored in this chapter are as important as they are unappreciated. Your job as mediator is to encourage participants to lay the necessary groundwork before they begin to negotiate solutions, especially about money.

Because participants in appellate mediation wrongly assume they already know everything there is to know about the case and that an appellate negotiation is just about money, they often want to move immediately from a joint opening session to private caucuses with the mediator—or eliminate joint session altogether—to begin discussing settlement proposals. The rush to private caucuses is usually a mistake. It ignores the important foundation that must be laid before a settlement agreement can be built to everyone's satisfaction. If settling the appeal required no more than isolated parties sending negotiation offers back and forth, the case would almost certainly have settled before mediation. Instead, what is needed is something extra. This something extra frequently surfaces during Phase 2's exchange of information. The parties learn how each other recalls the underlying events, what those events mean to each of them, and the impact of those events. They learn about their interests—what matters to themselves and to the other party—and begin to form ideas about how the settlement might address them.

B. Facilitate the Exchange of Information

1. Shift from Debate to Dialogue

If the appellate court decides the case, there will be a winner and a loser.[1] By contrast, mediation does not crown a winner or declare a loser. Rather, it presents

---

1. Quite often no one feels like a winner following an appellate court decision. Having spent a large sum of money on attorney fees and court costs and waited for a long

an opportunity for party self-determination and a joint search for a solution. When the parties persist in a win-lose framework, they erect a major obstacle to communication and a successful Phase 2. Instead of listening and speaking to develop understanding, they argue about who is right and who is wrong, a well-worn groove they have dug—sometimes for years.

A major challenge in Phase 2 is to help the parties have a productive exchange of information about their perspectives on what happened and on the legal arguments. Typically, if they are willing to talk directly to each other, the conversation consists of debate rather than dialogue that is necessary to lead to understanding.

In cases where the parties' (or the lawyers') communication is compromised, you may wish to start Phase 2 by distinguishing between debate and dialogue, as set forth in Table 14.1.[2]

Table 14.1: Shifting from Debate to Dialogue

Dialogue Is	Debate Is
Assuming many people have pieces of the answer	Assuming there is a right answer and you have it
About finding common ground and making good decisions	About winning
Listening to understand and to find meaning and areas of possible agreement	Listening to find flaws for counter-arguments
Being open to learning	Defending your view
Revealing assumptions for reevaluation	Defending assumptions as truth
Revealing and exploring underlying interests	Defending positions
Listening to understand, find meaning and discover areas of possible agreement	Listening to find flaws for counter-arguments
Working side by side to achieve a shared understanding of the issues	Talking at each other

The stark contrast of these two approaches demonstrates to the parties and lawyers what constitutes a constructive conversation—and an unconstructive one. Especially when the contrast is accompanied by an effective introduction, such as the one below, it creates a productive atmosphere for the mediation.

time for the decision, even the prevailing party may wondering whether "winning" was worth the time, money, and emotional energy. With surprising regularity, in his role as an attorney in an appellate court, Brendon reviews petitions for rehearing from *both* parties to an appeal in which they seek reconsideration of a decision that all of the parties believe to be incorrect.

2. Adapted from Public Conversations Project & Mark Gerzon, Mediators Foundation.

Moreover, dialogue fosters effective communication and sets the mediation on the path toward a successful resolution. As UCLA School of Law Professor Russell Korobkin has observed, "A settlement proposal that might be acceptable to a litigant who feels personally validated and fairly treated by her opponent, despite the legal dispute, may be unacceptable to a litigant who feels ignored, unheard, or invalidated by her opponent."[3]

2. Employ Empathy by Listening for Understanding

If there is such thing as a magic wand for appellate mediators, it is not a world-class command of appellate law or even a charming personality (though it does not hurt to possess either). It is the ability to be empathic, to listen to learn about another person's feelings, thoughts, or experiences. Empathy, as we intend it, has three components. The first is *understanding* another person's perspective. The second is *demonstrating that understanding* by stating in words what we understand the experience of another to be: the external situation, the feelings, and the personal meaning. The third is *caring* about the other person's experience, genuinely wanting to understand it.

When most professionals, lawyers included, listen to their clients, they do so only to the extent they think is necessary to figure out how to solve the client's problem. By contrast, mediation calls for empathic listening in which the parties experience foremost that you care about their predicament. As Maya Angelou is attributed with stating, "People will forget what you said. They will forget what you did. But they will never forget the way you made them feel."[4] When you listen wholeheartedly, parties feel respected and more connected to you. They experience your understanding and care. When you demonstrate you have fully heard parties, you earn their trust. As therapist and empathy trainer Dr. Tony Roffers puts it, "They emotionally hire you." That trust enables you to guide parties through the mediation process as they explore their own interests and understand what matters to the other party. It allows you to help parties and their lawyers better understand their own appellate case and, more importantly, the other party's perspective on the law.

Empathic listening also encourages people to talk. When they believe you are listening with your entire attention, they share information more fully and freely. It is surprising how often you hear something unexpected and helpful that even the attorneys have not yet learned—even after a long trial—as a result of skillful listening. "It is not uncommon that understanding the problem to be solved involves a revelation that the reasons for litigation are not what they seem."[5]

---

3. Russell Korobkin, *Aspirations and Settlement*, 88 Cornell L. Rev. 17 (2002).
4. Bob Kelly, Words Worth Repeating: More Than 5,000 Classic and Contemporary Quotes 263 (Kregel Publications 2003).
5. John Toker, California Arbitration & Mediation Practice Guide 176 (Lawpress 2008 Supp.).

In addition to expanding the mediator's and the other parties' understanding, empathic listening allows those who "own" the problem to understand *themselves* better. When they articulate their perspectives to you, they also listen to themselves. As they do so, they may gain insight into their situations, better understand their relationship to it, and develop, refine, and perhaps revise their perspectives and positions. As a result, they become better equipped to solve their own problems.[6]

Thus, careful and attentive empathic listening accomplishes several crucial purposes: (1) it helps you understand what the dispute is about factually, legally, and emotionally, what matters to the parties—their interests, what motivates them to continue on appeal, and what they need and hope to avoid; (2) it gives the parties the satisfaction of describing their experience—telling their stories—to someone who sincerely wants to understand them and cares about their situation, how it has affected them, and how they feel about it; (3) it provides a safe forum early on in which parties can express their feelings, allowing strong emotions to dissipate before emotional reactivity derails later efforts to explore creative options and develop an agreement; and (4) as parties listen to you demonstrate in your own words your understanding of "the enemy's" perspective, they are able to understand the other side, perhaps for the first time.

a. Empathy's Undeserved Bad Reputation

In some circles, empathy is considered the domain of the psychologist and criticized as being too "touchy-feely" or overly emotional to be useful or even relevant to a serious lawyer mediator in commercial or civil mediation. Our experience as mediators and mediation trainers has demonstrated to us the failure of this bias. In trainings, even if judges and lawyers exhibit initial resistance based on empathy's undeserved bad reputation, they inevitably embrace it and incorporate it into their practice—and personal relationships. This conversion occurs as a result of training exercises in which they both give and receive empathy. Once they are on the receiving end of empathy, they experience its *intellectual* power that enables them to examine their viewpoint, on the law and otherwise, more fully. They also realize empathy's *emotional* power. They see what it is like when another person is fully present and open to learning about them, and they realize how rare that experience is. They feel respected by the mediator, and they respect the mediator for it. We hear comments like this: "I have never been listened to in this way before!"; "Empathy can really clarify the nature of a problem and the relative desirability of possible solutions."; "I understood the problem much better and began to explore what to do about it, rather than just complain about it."

In addition to allowing them to have a positive experience with empathic listening, empathy training helps participants to respect empathy as a complex

6.   Gregory E. Billikopf, Helping Others Resolve Differences (UC Press 2004).

skill, not just a "soft skill." "Far from being a mysterious, intuitive process, empathy requires a high level of cognitive and emotional maturity."[7] It requires close attention, analysis, synthesis, and a rich vocabulary, abilities good lawyers possess, especially appellate lawyers.

b. What We Usually Do Instead of Empathizing

The humanistic psychologist Carl Rogers observed, "[Empathic understanding] is extremely rare. We neither receive it nor offer it with any great frequency. Instead we offer another type of understanding which is very different."[8] In the name of being a good listener, if you are like most people, especially lawyers, you engage with clients in ways that are anything but empathetic. You merely state the conclusion "I understand." Although you might actually understand, when you do not *demonstrate* your understanding, you forego the positive benefits of empathy: establishing rapport and trust; correcting our own or the other parties' misunderstanding; encouraging further exploration; or lowering the emotional temperature.

You might also respond to what you hear with questions without first empathizing. You listen attentively and craft relevant and perceptive—even brilliant—questions based on what you hear. Incisive questions are an important mediator tool, but they are limiting, particularly in the early stages of mediation in which understanding differing views is critical. The main problem with substituting questions for empathy is that your questions change the direction of the discussion and thus preclude a party's exploration into territory that could prove important, or even critical, to the resolution. Finally, if the questions are leading—and lawyers are masters at formulating leading questions—a party may feel manipulated or, worse, demeaned by being led down "the primrose path."

Instead of empathizing, you might be tempted to offer a solution or advice—to fix the problem. Fixers are often surprised to learn their efforts to solve a problem may offend the speaker. If you are listening empathically, you are not giving advice, trying to fix anything, or solving a problem. You are just listening. In fact, jumping to the solution before you fully understand the problem is an act of arrogance, not competence. How can you, with your limited understanding, possibly know in just a few minutes how to solve a problem that has evaded a solution for the many years it has taken to get to appeal? Although it might be appropriate to offer solutions at a later point in mediation after you learn far more about the background and practical realities of the problem and the parties' interests in resolving it, doing so before truly understanding both parties' perspectives is highly problematic.

---

7. JOYCE L. HACKER & WILLIAM W. WILMOT, INTERPERSONAL CONFLICT 39 (1991), quoting M.S. PECK, THE DIFFERENT DRUM: COMMUNITY MAKING AND PEACE (1987).

8. CARL ROGERS, ON BECOMING A PERSON: A THERAPIST'S VIEW OF PSYCHOTHERAPY 62 (HOUGHTON MIFFLIN HARCOURT 2012).

Another common substitute for empathy is sympathy, especially if the communication concerns the speaker's suffering. Sympathy, which is often confused with empathy, involves your *own* feelings, not the feelings or experience of the speaker. For example, a party's sadness at the loss of a job may elicit your own feelings of sadness for the party. A sympathetic response would be "I am so sorry you lost your job and your livelihood." An empathetic response, on the other hand, eliminates your feelings and focuses on the *party's*: "Losing your job and your livelihood was a blow." By responding empathically, rather than sympathetically, you demonstrate understanding while maintaining the appearance of neutrality. Not so if you sympathize, especially in a joint session. Your sympathy may be interpreted as alliance or favoritism. When you are too much in the experience of your own feelings, you might also miss the opportunity to understand the experience of the speaker by confusing your feelings with those of the other person.

Finally, particularly if you want to help parties or lawyers understand each other, it is important to distinguish between empathy and agreement. Empathy is *understanding*, not agreement. It is possible for a party or lawyer to hold a point of view and still articulate that of the opposition. When parties realize they can listen to and demonstrate their understanding of an opponent's perspective without creating an impression that they adopt it, they are much more willing to practice empathic listening themselves.

As mediators listen and engage in these non-empathic responses, they do so with the best intentions to connect with the parties or to be helpful. But when they employ responses other than empathy, they do so at the expense of empathy and miss one of the most important opportunities in mediation: to help the parties understand each other.

c. *What It Takes to Listen Empathically*

We are all capable of listening well when we are motivated to do so, but most of the time we are lazy listeners. The first ingredient of effective listening is *appreciation* of how important and how powerful the art of listening actually is. The second is the *intention* to understand the experience of the other person.

The stronger your intention is, the more focused you will be on the task of listening and the more successful you will be in incorporating the third ingredient, *attention*. To achieve the quality of attention required to be an empathic listener, you must attend to both the internal and external conditions that enable you to give the speaker your full attention. The *external* conditions are straightforward: a private environment free from distractions and the physical comfort necessary to allow you to focus.

Achieving the *internal* conditions for listening with full attention is more elusive and challenging. It depends on your ability to detect when your thoughts and emotions divert your attention from fulfilling your intention to understand another person. Your thoughts can be more or less benign distractions, having little emotional association with the other person, such as what you are having for dinner or the argument you had with your partner last night. Your mind just meanders.

Other distracting thoughts are more problematic. You are put off by a party or lawyer. You are self-conscious about your performance. You are preoccupied by the desperate thought that the mediation must end with a settlement or your career is doomed. These sorts of thoughts, usually associated with strong emotions, hijack your mind in a more troubling way. When thoughts like these intrude, not only do they interfere with your listening, they also negatively affect the negotiation by shifting the entire atmosphere. As we discussed in Chapter 13, a mediator's emotional state is contagious.

d. Five Internal Barriers to Listening

We all have our unique combinations of thoughts and feelings that interfere with our ability to listen empathically, but we find that they fall into one of five categories: attachment, aversion, low energy, doubt, and anxiety and worry.[9]

Attachment is a strong attraction to someone or a strong need or desire for something in particular to happen. Attachment may manifest in liking one party more than another, which can make it difficult to empathize equally with the parties. It is much easier to empathize with the preferred party, especially if the preference is strong. Attachment also is evident when you feel a strong need for a case to settle. When you are attached to settlement, you may listen selectively for information that enables you to solve the problem later and be so preoccupied with how to fix it that you filter out valuable information that is not directly relevant to this task.

Another form of attachment is the desire to look good or to be liked. If you are attached to looking good, you may be more focused on *yourself* than on the participants and their problems. If you are trying to get the other person to respond more positively to you, you are occupying mental space that you need to be able to listen fully.

Finally, you can be attached to your style or approach to doing things a certain way. When parties do not comply with your requests or you fear they are messing up your process, the brainpower you expend to get them to do what you want robs your attention.

Aversion is the flip side of attachment. When you experience the internal barrier of aversion, you are repelled by, rather than attracted by, a person or what is going on in mediation. You do not want what is happening to be happening. As you hear a point of view you do not like or do not agree with, you are not just listening and empathizing, you are also judging and resisting what is.

---

9. The ideas presented in this discussion are the product of collaboration between Dana and Daniel Bowling related to an advanced mediation workshop they presented together.

Aversion involves negative judgments. You do not like or trust one of the participants, or you conclude he or she is not very bright. In extreme cases, you may harbor ill will or become angry or contemptuous. At its worst, aversion can lead to aggression. When aversive thoughts intrude on your effort to empathize, you become disinterested in the speaker because you already "know" him or her to be undesirable in some way. If you listen through the lens of your negative opinion, you seek and overweigh evidence that confirms your hypothesis and ignore or undervalue evidence that contradicts it.[10]

A particularly insidious form of aversion is negative self-assessment, or judgment of *yourself*. The voice in your head says, "I am a terrible mediator," "I am not a good listener," or "If I were a better person, I would not be judging this party." When this self-judgment operates in tandem with the attachment to being liked, you become paralyzed. The person you are listening to fades into the background, because suddenly, *it is all about me*. And the *me* I see is not a pleasing sight to behold.

Low energy, relative to aversion, is rather benign. When your energy is low, you lose the ability to focus on the other person; you are distracted by thoughts of how tired you are or how you do not want to be there. Your mind wanders because you are not interested in the other person or engaged in the conversation. In the worst cases, you are bored or begin to nod off.

Doubt is a form of fear, a nagging lack of confidence—that the case can settle, that the parties can overcome significant barriers to resolution, that you are a good enough mediator. Like aversion and attachment, doubt deprives you of precious mental space necessary to understand the speaker's experience.

Anxiety and worry is the fifth category of internal barriers to listening. Like doubt, the predominant emotional state associated with anxiety and worry is fear. You do not trust the parties and lawyers to be able to settle the case. You do not trust the process to help them solve their problem. You do not trust yourself to be able to mediate effectively. You are pessimistic about most everything in mediation when flooded with anxiety and worry. This emotional state is challenging to manage because it can be so subtle. Unless you pay attention to the butterflies in your stomach or constriction in your chest, you may not be aware of its undercurrent of fear that preoccupies you and, like a magnet, pulls your attention away from the person you are listening to.

e.   Addressing Internal Barriers to Listening

We suggest a four-step process (the four As) to address our internal impediments to listening:

---

10. PAUL BREST & LINDA HAMILTON KRIEGER, PROBLEM SOLVING, DECISION MAKING, AND PROFESSIONAL JUDGMENT: A GUIDE FOR LAWYERS AND POLICYMAKERS 278 (Oxford University Press 2010).

1. **Awareness.** Bring your attention to your internal state and behavior, and notice any thoughts that distract you from listening. Identify the category of the barrier.
2. **Acceptance.** Be okay with whatever you observe: note it, breathe, and allow it to be there. Do not criticize yourself for your distracting thoughts.
3. **Analysis.** Consider the options available to you for addressing the barrier by following these three steps:

   - **Recall** your intention to understand the experience, thoughts, and feelings of the speaker.

   - **Reflect** on the situation and what caused the barrier to arise.

   - **Review** the options for removing or addressing the barrier.

4. **Action.** Implement the appropriate option(s) and return to listening.

The first option to exercise with any barrier is simply to breathe. After that, you can address many barriers with the first two As—awareness and acceptance—or by bringing your *attention* back to your *intention* to listen.

Thoughts involving strong emotions or recurrent thoughts, such as the negative judgments of aversion, may require you to do something more to be able to focus on the speaker. Table 14.2 is a list of options for addressing the five categories of barriers when the simpler interventions do not work.

Table 14.2: Overcoming Barriers to Listening

Barrier	Options for Addressing Barrier
Attachment	Remember the inevitability of change and the consistent nature of all things.
	Do not take what is going on personally.
	Become curious about what will happen.
	Remember that it is not your job to solve the parties' problem.
	Let it go.
Aversion	Be kind.
	Be compassionate.
	Reignite your curiosity—about the circumstances that led the object of your aversion to be so difficult, or why you are reacting so negatively.
	Focus on the good in the person or situation.
Doubt	Develop comfort with uncertainty.
	Reignite your curiosity.
	Trust your past experience.
	Trust in the ability of the participants to resolve their own problems and release personal responsibility.
	Trust in life.

(*continued*)

Table 14.2: (*continued*)

Barrier	Options for Addressing Barrier
Low energy	Eat or drink. Reignite your curiosity. Consider whether you missed something or got hooked by something that caused you to lose your focus. Take a personal break to investigate what happened or what hooked you. Give everyone a break. Take a walk. Notice if you are responding to the energy of the participants—examine what made them lose their focus.
Anxiety and worry	Breathe, especially with this barrier. Reignite your curiosity about what will happen. Remember that it is not your job to solve the parties' problem. Recite this phrase: "Everything works out in the end, and if it hasn't worked out, it's not the end."[11]

As you pay attention to your internal barriers to listening, you will become aware that mediation is not the only time they interfere with your ability to understand another person. And as you become better at empathizing with mediation participants, you will notice you are better at doing so in your life generally. It is likely this experience that led a judge who participated in our appellate mediation training to comment that mediation training also happened to help improve his marriage.

Mediation and life constantly present opportunities for you to practice the skill of empathic listening. As you practice empathy, you will appreciate its power to change attitudes and minds, not the least of which is your own.

3. *Work Effectively with Lawyers*

When presented with difficult legal representatives during a tough mediation, even the kindest and most empathetic mediator will resonate with William Shakespeare's line, "The first thing we do, let's kill all the lawyers."[12] We understand the frustration of mediators who decry the negative effect they perceive lawyers can have on negotiations.

One antidote to aversion to difficult lawyers is compassion. Some attorneys are surprised to find themselves engaged in a process in which the familiar adversarial tactics that work in trial are not effective—and they lack the skills and understanding to enable them to shift gears. To enhance your compassion, we invite you to consider the following unique challenges lawyers (especially those who also served as trial counsel before the appeal) encounter that take them out of their comfort zones when representing clients in an appellate mediation.

---

11. From *The Best Exotic Marigold Hotel*. DVD. Directed by John Madden. Fox Searchlight, 2012.
12. William Shakespeare, Henry VI, Act IV, Scene II.

- Clients get to talk. When clients talk—especially in front of opposing counsel—attorneys become nervous. It is hard to let go of the vigilance necessary to object to improper cross-examination or prepare for redirect, even when there is no trial going on. Moreover, attorneys like to (or are at least taught to) speak for their clients. The unfamiliar role of silent listener may make them uncomfortable or feel lost.

- Attorneys want to demonstrate to their clients that they are needed during the mediation. Clients are much happier paying fees when they feel they have received vigorous representation.

- Some attorneys seem to need to bluster and strut a bit in front of opposing counsel. Trial attorneys are not known as shrinking violets, and attorneys who pride themselves on their litigation skills frequently need to demonstrate their confidence and skill.

- Appeals can generate substantial income for an attorney, but, if the case settles, counsel's source of income evaporates. Moreover, if an award for attorney fees is part of the judgment, lawyers may see their livelihoods being used as bargaining chips.

- An attorney may not have good client control. Clients can be temperamental and abrasive. They are, after all, drivers of a lawsuit that persists even to appeal. Not only do attorneys have the challenge of dealing with the opposing party and opposing counsel, but they may also have difficulties getting along with their own clients.

- The appellant's attorney may have been the trial attorney who lost the judgment or order being appealed and thus has an independent interest in seeking the vindication a reversal on appeal would provide.

- More generally, some studies suggest that due to the stress of practicing law depression and alcoholism are more prevalent among lawyers than in the general population.[13]

Thus, developing the ability to experience and express empathy for the attorneys goes a long way in helping a mediator to develop rapport with them and to work with them in a positive manner during the hard parts of negotiations. We also offer the following ideas for dealing with "difficult" attorneys.

- **Let them bluster a bit.** Perhaps it is an unthinking familiarity with the adversarial process or some deeply ingrained primate need to show one's stature, but some counsel can't help but bluster or strut a bit. Usually, they run out of steam pretty quickly. For this reason,

---

13. "Depression," ABA Lawyer Assistance Program website, http://www.americanbar.org /groups/lawyer_assistance/resources/.html.

it is sometimes best simply to listen—and to allow this initial barking.

- **Acknowledge them.** Want to know the fastest way to stop counsel from barking? Help them look good in front of their clients. Pay attention to what they have done or are doing well, and acknowledge them for their expertise or accomplishments. A little genuine praise can satisfy the overly zealous attorney's need to demonstrate to the client how tough the attorney is. Caution: such praise should be saved for caucus! Do not compromise the appearance of impartiality by praising one side for its trial court victory (even if just a minor one) or a job well done in front of the other party and counsel.

- **Expressly acknowledge attorneys' difficulties.** Empathize with their defeats while noting how professionally they handled the matter. Pity the poor attorneys: they are probably tired from a recent trial, posttrial motions, and all of the other work that piled up on them while they were at trial. Worse, the losing attorney now has to spend the day with a client who is sorely unhappy about the outcome at trial and may have grave doubts about the attorney.

4. Encourage the Expression of Feelings and Manage Emotional Discussions Effectively

In Section I, we explored appellate procedures, substantive law governing review, statistics regarding reversal in courts of appeal, and decision tree analysis. If parties were entirely rational, nothing more would be needed to help them analyze their appeals and alternatives to appeal in order to reach settlement agreements. Humans, however, are marvelous mixtures of cold logic, hot anger, icy avoidance, giddy hope, brilliant ideas, and unfounded assumptions. Experienced mediators also understand that "emotions are inherent to negotiation and social conflict."[14]

Appellate attorneys new to the mediation role may believe strong emotions stand in the way of a settlement—and sometimes in the way even of productive negotiation. To the appellate expert used to winning or losing on the merits of the legal arguments, it may seem that emotional irrationality should not be allowed to obstruct a sensible and "obvious" settlement agreement. Thus, the

---

14.   Gerben A. Van Kleef, Carsten K.W. De Dreu & Antony S.R. Manstead, *The Interpersonal Effects of Anger and Happiness in Negotiations*, 8 J. OF PERSONALITY & SOCIAL PSYCHOLOGY 57 (2004). "[E]motions are communications to both oneself and other people conveying information about how one feels about things, about one's social intentions, and about one's orientation toward other people. Because emotions only arise in response to events that are appraised as relevant to some concern, they provide important information to observing individuals. In the context of a negotiation, emotions may signal what value one attaches to the different issues and provide critical feedback about one's mood and willingness to agree." *Id.* at 58, citations omitted.

appellate mediator may be tempted to brush aside the feelings of a party or preempt a party's expression of frustration and move directly to the negotiation phase. However, we strongly caution that it is a serious mistake to give short shrift to the strong emotions underlying just about every legal dispute that is protracted enough to arrive at the appellate stage.

Rather than ignoring the strong emotions, feelings, or "irrationality" of the parties during a mediation, mediators should consider that in the end participants' emotions count at least as much as—and probably more than—logical analysis of appellate law. Indeed, the skillful handling of the parties' emotions is a *necessary step* in the mediation process because "[i]f two parties have a difference of opinion but neither has an emotional reaction, there will be no negotiation."[15] In short, any effort to resolve disputes must account for both the rational and the emotional aspects of mediation participants. Being a good appellate mediator requires developing the skill and confidence required to be present with people who are very angry or sad. Thus, we recommend a reflective practice in Chapter 16 to help you remain calm and productive when others are distressed.

5. Make Full and Best Use of Joint Sessions

Discomfort and inexperience in dealing with strong emotions (by both mediators *and* participants) explains why "most active mediators prefer the simplicity, comfort, and confidentiality of a short opening and a quick move to caucus" in which the opposing sides are isolated from each other.[16] For mediators and for parties too, "[t]his may be a terrible tactical choice."[17] As Professor Richard Birke explains, "Parties cite confidential information and bad feelings as reasons to go into caucus, but mediations conducted in caucus often become exercises in mistrust. The lack of visual confirmation that words match affect causes listeners to distrust speakers' intent."[18] In other words, instead of enabling resolution, a rush to private caucus often interferes with it by guaranteeing more of the same suspicion and antagonism that prevented the case from reaching a settlement in the trial court. For these reasons, and others we discuss next, we encourage you to develop skills to manage joint sessions effectively and to encourage parties to meet together whenever appropriate, which we believe to be most of the time.

If you want a different and better result, you generally have to do something different and better. A face-to-face exchange of information is different from most trial court mediations and in our view a better approach for several reasons. Despite depositions, settlement conferences, and trial, a joint session in appellate

---

15. *Id.* at 57.
16. Richard Birke, *Neuroscience and Settlement: An Examination of Scientific Innovations and Practical Applications*, 25 Ohio State J. on Dispute Resolution 502 (2010).
17. *Id.*
18. *Id.* at 506.

mediation is likely to be the *first* chance for all attorneys, parties, insurance representatives, and other stakeholders to meet together for constructive, candid discussions. Parties, in particular, are often disappointed by trial and frustrated that their day in court did not allow them to articulate their side of the story. Instead, they were constrained by rules and statutes governing the admissibility of testimonial evidence. On cross-examination, their views were overly simplified, and they were limited to answering manipulative yes-or-no questions. The judge struck from the record as nonresponsive the parts of their narratives they considered to be at the heart of the problem. Attorneys too have had little opportunity to interact without a judge present or for more than a few minutes before or after a hearing. No wonder the participants mistrust each other!

To take full advantage of the opportunity for all participants to share what is most important to them, a mediator must create a space for productive face-to-face conversation, a place where no one (such as a judge or an overbearing attorney or party) dominates the discussion. To facilitate effective joint sessions, we offer the following suggestions.

Invite the parties and lawyers to explore whether and, if so, how they might benefit from face-to-face exchange of perspectives. Although you may see the value in such discussions, if the parties themselves appreciate the opportunity, they are more likely to take full advantage of it. Questions such as "Do you think the other participants understand your perspective?" followed by "If they did, would that be helpful to you? How so?" allow parties to find their own motivation to participate constructively in this conversation.

Explain why you are a fan of the joint session. Do not be afraid to be transparent in asking the parties to help you try something new and better by sharing their perspectives, concerns, and hopes in joint session. In describing the value of face-to-face information exchanges, you can relate success stories from other mediations in which the parties agreed to stay together. You can also explain why you encourage their use. Here are a few reasons why we advocate so strongly for joint sessions in appellate mediation:

- **Appellate mediation may just be the best chance parties will ever have to tell their stories *fully* to one another.** Human beings are naturally storytellers.[19] Supporting participants to share their experiences and points of view about the dispute with one another gives them the potential for catharsis. They are finally free to express what matters to them and experience the satisfaction of being heard and understood, maybe for the first time. They also have the benefit of an expanded understanding of the situation and what matters to the other parties, which can help them later to figure out how to resolve the dispute.

19. Jonathan Gottschall, The Storytelling Animal: How Stories Make Us Human 18, 102 (Houghton Mifflin Harcourt 2012).

- **The appellate stage, when there is no point in holding anything back for trial, is especially hospitable to joint discussions.** At trial the parties have presumably introduced their best evidence and arguments in an effort to win. And because the appellate record is closed and what happens at mediation will not influence the outcome of the appeal, attorneys need not fear their clients' talking freely could sink the lawsuit.

- **In highly emotional cases, constructive joint sessions enhance the parties' opportunity to repair their relationship or achieve closure.** Kenneth Cloke describes the degrees of closure of conflicts: (1) stopping the fighting, where the outcome is ceasefire and the degree of closure is de-escalation; (2) settling the issues, where the outcome is settlement and the degree of closure is ending the fight; (3) resolving the underlying reasons for the dispute, where the outcome is resolution and the degree of closure is completion; (4) forgiving others and self, where the outcome is transformation and the degree of closure is closure; and (5) reconciling, where the outcome is transcendence and the degree of closure is disappearance of the conflict.[20]

  When an important relationship is at stake, if the parties want to achieve a more enduring and meaningful level of resolution, they need to talk to each other. If they do not do so, there is little chance to achieve such closure in a mediation Likewise, although they might settle the dispute or make a deal that ends the legal fight, significant personal emotional closure is unlikely to be fostered in a purely caucus mediation.

6. Questions for Phase 2

Good questions in this phase are open-ended and elicit information that expands understanding of the problem. They seek perspectives the parties wish to express or to understand. Beginning with Phase 2, we suggest such questions for each phase of mediation and propose ways to introduce and structure each of these conversations.

The conversation in Phase 2 may be the first opportunity the parties and lawyers have had to educate one another about their views on the law and everything else that matters to them. Good questions at this point can encourage the exchange of information that leads to collaboration. Bad questions can invite debate that leads to competition. We present some questions to pose to lawyers about the law and to parties about everything else that enable effective information exchanges and lead to greater understanding and cooperation.

---

20. KENNETH CLOKE, THE CROSSROADS OF CONFLICT 168–69 (Janis Publications 2006).

We suggest you begin Phase 2 with a brief statement about the purpose of the discussions that will follow and the roles that each of the participants will play in it, such as the following:

> We have agreed to take time now to explore the legal landscape of this case and how each of your lawyers is analyzing the dispute from a legal point of view. By the time we finish this conversation, you will have more information about this legal landscape than you do at this moment. Having this more complete picture will help you later on figure out whether a settlement that is available to you today is better for you than taking your chances on appeal. The more information you have to assess the strengths and weaknesses of your case, the better job you will do of figuring out what will likely happen if you keep litigating the case.
>
> To make the most of this opportunity, I have two suggestions. First, when you present your point of view, do so for the purpose of educating the others, not persuading them. You can resolve a dispute without agreeing about the law or what happened. The exercise is to understand, not necessarily to agree.
>
> Second, listen—not in the way we usually do in a dispute, which is to formulate what we will say to counter the other's perspective when it is our turn, but simply to understand.

Good questions to kick off discussions of the law encourage lawyers to present their perspectives on the law in a manner that *educates* rather than *debates*. In other words, good questions encourage dialogue, not debate, as we described earlier. You might introduce legal discussions with this statement: *We have agreed to hear from the lawyers about their legal analyses. This discussion provides the opportunity for counsel to educate each other—and the rest of us—about their perspectives on the law. This discussion will provide insight into how the lawyers are advising their clients. It also allows you to expand your own analyses of the appellate issues, as you discover a new and different way of thinking about them. All of this information helps you to be more effective in negotiation and more accurate in analyzing your own case and the opportunities and risk you face on appeal.*

After the introduction, you can initiate the discussion with a broad, open-ended question, such as this one: *Ms. Kendall, would you please tell us what you think we need to understand about the law from the appellant's perspective?* In most trial court mediations, this approach will work fine. It also works well with experienced appellate lawyers or appellate specialists who are sure to present each issue they intend to raise on appeal and identify and explain the standard of review and, where relevant, waiver and prejudice. Except in the rare instance where both parties are not represented by lawyers, broad questions about the law generally work to elicit all of the information parties need to be able to analyze their appeals.

In those cases in which lawyers are not as experienced with appeals, a more structured invitation will likely result in more complete information. One approach is to structure the legal discussion to occur iteratively as to each issue. Here is an example of how you might structure this discussion and a sequence of questions that serve this purpose, beginning with the appellant's counsel: *I understand from your mediation statement and our premediation discussions that you intend to raise three issues on appeal. It would be most helpful to discuss the elements of each of these issues one by one beginning with the appellant's perspective and following with the respondent's perspective. As to the first issue—that the trial court erred in refusing to admit the testimony of your expert—would you please tells us your analysis of the standard of review?*

After the appellant's counsel has addressed this question, we suggest you invite the respondent's counsel to ask any questions. Once those questions are answered or if there are none, you might ask the following: *What is the respondent's perspective as to the standard of review for this issue?*

After you invite the appellant's counsel to ask any questions, you can resume the analysis of the first issue with the appellant with a series of questions about other discrete aspects of the appeal, including the following: *What points will you make to convince the court that there was error under the applicable standard of review?*

Many mediators—ourselves included—summarize the legal analysis after the lawyers' presentations of each issue, a practice that ensures you grasped the analysis accurately and sufficiently. It also serves as a translation of the presentation. Because the mediator version is generally more succinct and less argumentative, it may be easier for the opposing side to digest.

In addition to or instead of your own summary, you may ask the lawyers to demonstrate their understanding of the other point of view: *Could you please summarize the other perspective on issue number one?* This exercise exposes the lawyers' mistaken or incomplete understanding of the opposing argument and has the added benefit of self-persuasion. Self-persuasion enhances the ability of lawyers to analyze the case more accurately by including an opposing perspective along with their own.[21]

In addition to the previous discussions, if the lawyers are willing to do so in each other's presence, you can encourage them to dig a little deeper with their analysis to explore their vulnerabilities. You might preface with this statement: *Everyone has lost the sure thing, and every attorney has been surprised to win a case he or she expected to lose.* To encourage greater candor in exploring the unthinkable scenario, we like to start this discussion with this question: *If the unthinkable happens and your client loses on the first issue, what reasoning will the appellate judges have used to support such a conclusion?* We also encourage you not to stop with the first answer: *What is another reason the judges might have ruled against your client? And another?*

---

21. James H. Stark & Douglas N. Frenkel, Changing Minds: The Work of Mediators and Empirical Studies of Persuasion 352, 273–81 (2013).

It also helps, as with any request, to explain why you are asking these questions. A good reason to explore the hypothetical loss is that parties will arrive at a more accurate assessment of their case if they explore multiple alternatives rather than curtailing their exploration once they figure out how to win. We explore multiple alternatives analysis in depth in Chapter 2.

You can structure the discussion of everything else similarly to how you structured the legal discussion. The questions differ, of course, and tend to fall into several categories. The first is a very general, open question that permits parties to answer it in a way that has the most meaning for them: *What would you like us to understand about the situation that led to this litigation that you believe would be helpful resolving this dispute?* Remember to empathize—reflect back your understanding of the situation, what it means to the party, and how the party feels about it.

If you are interested in starting a conversation about the underlying dispute, you might ask this: *What happened that made litigation seem necessary?*

You may also wish to follow up with an invitation to talk about a particular event: *Could you say more about the initial contract negotiations? Or: I understand that being sued was upsetting to you in ways we might expect, but being a defendant seems to have affected you very personally. Could you please tell us about that?*

As we suggested above, it can be very useful for the parties, like the lawyers, to stand in the other person's shoes and describe the other's experience: *You have just heard each other describe the situation from two different perspectives. To make sure you really understand each other, could you please summarize what you just heard?* Again, follow up with a question to the other person: *Did he/she get it right? Is there more? What did he/she miss?*

This approach, which is known as counter-attitudinal advocacy, is another form of self-persuasion. In fact it is among the most effective tools available to mediators to help parties and lawyers change their minds about their case. It works so well because to articulate an opposing point of view, a party or lawyer is forced to engage personally with a conflicting perspective he or she is not otherwise psychologically predisposed to take in.[22]

7. Encourage the Participants to Remain in Joint Session as Long as They Are Learning

Those of us who have participated in mediation, as mediators or attorneys, have all experienced what happens when people *finally* listen and understand one another. We recall the end of a trust and estate mediation in which a brother and sister *really* listened to each other. As she left, she confided, "I have never felt so close to my brother as I did today." Some call it the magic of

---

22.   Stark & Frenkel, *supra* note 20, at 277.

mediation, when parties locked in conflict shift. Although it seems truly magical when such moments occur, it is not magic at all. The shift is a result of hearts opening. And hearts open when people listen empathically—or when their experience tells them the other person has heard them.

Author Wendell Berry describes the moment one of his characters let go of a deeply held belief because he for the first time understood the opposing point of view as "feeling under his breastbone the first pain of a change."[23] If parties do not talk with one another, they can never experience a profound shift in perspective that comes from understanding—that "pain of change." They may make a deal, but they will never, as a result of a caucus mediation focused on dollars, have a change of heart. If parties can stay together and if mediators can ask questions that go to the heart of the matter, then magical moments are possible.

Encourage participants to remain in joint session as long as they are learning something new. Because so much good comes out of the underappreciated joint session, we adhere to Professor Dwight Golann's rule of thumb that he prefers not to "mov[e] out of joint session until one-third of the expected time for mediation has gone by."[24]

An effective joint session accomplishes more than the catharsis of storytelling; it also sets the dynamic for effective communication, reduced suspicion, and an atmosphere of greater cooperation. Although the parties will not reach agreement at this stage (nor should they), you help them to begin cooperating by taking turns in listening to each other with the goal of achieving greater understanding. This cooperation will likely persist, even if only in subtle ways, to make the rest of the mediation far more productive.[25]

If parties are well prepared to meet together and if the mediator is skilled in helping the participants communicate constructively, remaining in joint session through Phase 3 is possible and worthwhile. Our rule of thumb is to remain in joint session as long as the parties are *learning* something new, *working* on the problem, and *willing* to stay together.

8. Help the Parties Stay on Task

a. Manage the Communication

Avoid the incompatible activities of speaking and listening from occurring at the same time. People cannot do two things at once. Certainly, they cannot do

---

23. *Id.* at 133.
24. DWIGHT GOLANN, MEDIATING LEGAL DISPUTES: EFFECTIVE STRATEGIES FOR LAWYERS AND MEDIATORS 21 (ABA 2009).
25. *See* Michael W. Kramer, Chao Lan Kuo & John C. Dailey, *The Impact of Brainstorming Techniques on Subsequent Group Processes beyond Generating Ideas,* 28 SMALL GROUP RESEARCH 222 (1997) (noting that structured group activity rules persist in affecting subsequent group processes and communications).

two things at once well.[26] For this reason, participants at a mediation cannot accomplish two things at once. When interruptions make it impossible for you or the other participants to listen, you have a choice about how to address the problem.

Mediators seem to be of two minds about dealing with this problem. One is to set and enforce ground rules that help create order out of chaos. These mediators look to basic guidelines—perhaps ones they set in the beginning— for example insisting that participants not interrupt one another. The other mediators prefer to engage the parties in setting the ground rules by first inquiring whether they are understanding each other, or letting them know if they are having difficulty doing so themselves; then seeking their input about whether their interactions are getting them closer to their goal of settlement; and, if not, engaging them in a problem-solving discussion in which they can figure out how to get back on track to a more constructive process.

In either case it helps to understand why parties in conflict have such difficulty separating listening from speaking and address the problem quickly and straightforwardly. Interruptions are born of fears that there will not be enough time for everyone to tell their stories or the worry that they might forget an important point by the time there is an opportunity to speak. You can invite participants to jot notes to themselves for the latter worry, and for the former, make it clear that you will listen as long as someone has something new to add to your understanding of the case. In structuring things in this way, parties feel safe separating listening from talking.

A final word of caution: conflict is very challenging and often messy. Particularly if parties have not had a real face-to-face conversation about the problem since it arose, the initial foray into that territory may result in interruptions and be difficult to follow. But inserting yourself as the "heavy" too soon and too authoritatively risks cutting off the conversation before it gets started. Managing these conversations well takes training, skill, and experience. It also takes emotional intelligence and the ability to recognize and manage your own emotional reactions, which we address in Chapter 16.

b. Be Aware of the Distinctions between the Phases

Similarly, parties cannot tell their stories and formulate their negotiating strategy at the same time. Give them a roadmap to the mediation that shows that understanding and negotiations are separated into different phases of the mediation. Because of the importance of paying attention to the task at hand, it is important to create clear boundaries between one task and the next. Thus,

---

26. As Lord Chesterfield observed long ago, "There is time enough for everything in the course of the day, if you do but one thing at once, but there is not time enough in the year, if you will do two things at a time." Quoted in Christine Rosen, *The Myth of Multitasking*, 30 THE NEW ATLANTIS 105 (2008).

it helps to delineate clearly between the phases. If you move from one phase to the next before the parties have achieved the goals of the phase, you may not lay the proper foundation for the tasks to follow. Thus, we suggest the following when moving from one phase to the next:

1. **Remind the parties of the goals of the phase.** *For the past 20 minutes we have been discussing how we will work together throughout the mediation session today, each of our roles, confidentiality in the joint and separate sessions and outside the mediation, guidelines for communication, and the basic agenda for the day.*

2. **Ask if their goals have been met.** *Do you have any questions related to this phase? Are you clear about all of our roles? Are there questions about the agenda, or changes you would suggest? Are we ready to move on to the next phase, where we work to gather more information about each of your perspectives?*

3. **Finish discussing issues only partially addressed.** At times, one party might be ready to move on to the next phase before another party seems ready to wrap up the task at hand. In such circumstances, it is important to stay in the conversation to see what the objecting party thinks is missing. The decision about whether the task is complete should be left to the parties. Although it might challenge your and the other party's patience, it is important to stay with the task. Rushing to the next phase, over the objection of a party, risks loss of that party's trust and may foreclose discussion that needs to take place for the case to resolve.

C. Help the Parties Define and Organize the Issues

Immediately after the exchange of information in Phase 2, participants usually are in a rush to negotiate about money, believing the only question to be resolved is how much money will change hands.

The exercise of Phase 3, which we discuss in Chapter 7, helps the parties to realize there is more to their negotiation than arriving at the appropriate settlement number. Even if money is the main currency of a settlement agreement, the parties must also negotiate additional issues such as timing of payment, enforceability, scope of the release of liability, and perhaps whether the terms of the agreement will be confidential. A premature and myopic focus on money, before the parties identify other issues for resolution, may cause them to overlook important points until the last minute after the monetary issue is decided. If these issues are critical, raising them at the last minute may delay or even destroy what is otherwise a perfectly good settlement.

Thus, Phase 3 presents a chance to plan ahead to resolve all issues, to identify issues that can lead to creative solutions, and to enhance cooperation. Your job is to carve out the space in which Phase 3 can occur.

1. *Identify Issues to Be Resolved*

We suggest parties engage in Phase 3 in joint session, where all participants can work together to identify the issues that must be addressed in a settlement agreement. Not every conceivable issue has to be resolved in mediation. Thus, the participants can decide to ignore collateral litigation and unripe legal actions. Conversely, a settlement agreement will be incomplete if it fails to capture agreement on all of the terms necessary for a certain and enforceable settlement. Necessary terms of an agreement tend to fall into five categories:

1. **Money and property transfer.** When the judgment involves payment of monetary damages, attorney fees, or court costs, a settlement agreement will include the same topics. If the judgment involves division or transfer of real or personal property (as is often the circumstance in probate or family law cases), the parties will need to determine how to distribute it.

2. **Timing of transfers.** Agreements to pay a certain number of dollars tomorrow, 100 years from now, or in equal parts for the next 10 years are very different. Thus, to have a complete settlement the parties must agree on the timing of payments and how the payments will be made.

3. **Future actions.** If the judgment being appealed includes injunctive relief (whether imposing a duty to do something or to refrain from doing something), the parties must agree about any required or disallowed future actions.

4. **Enforceability provisions.** An unenforceable contract is a worthless agreement. Thus, parties and attorneys should be prepared to discuss milestones, enforceability provisions, and whether to include terms to allow verification of another party's compliance with the settlement agreement.

5. **Confidentiality.** A quick way to derail a settlement is for one party to mention the need for a confidentiality provision in the agreement for the first time after the drafting of the agreement has begun. Confidentiality is valuable. And if a party wants to include that term, everyone should know this before negotiations begin.

In short, Phase 3 is the stage in which you help participants develop a shared understanding of the issues they need to agree upon in order to reach a settlement.

As straightforward as this task seems, it can be quite tricky, unless you structure the discussion by doing the following:

- Explaining the task. *Let's take a few minutes to make a list of the topics that are essential to discuss and make decisions about in order to resolve your dispute fully. Think of these topics as headings in your settlement agreement. So far, I have heard mention of the following issues: (list the ones you noted, such as money).*

- Reframing positions or interests to issues. *You said you want an apology (a position), so it sounds like you need to find a way to address issues concerning your reputation. Would it be accurate to put "reputational issues" on the list?*

- Asking the right question to initiate a discussion.

Good questions for Phase 3 with which to identify the issues. The ease of this phase lies entirely with the quality of the questions the mediator asks to generate a list of issues. We know this because we have experienced what happens when you ask the wrong questions. If you want to identify the issues—or what it is the parties need to reach agreement about—you need to structure the conversation: *Now let's create a list together that will form the basis for our agenda in the next phase when you search for solutions.* Then, ask questions that elicit this information: *So far, I have heard you say you need to figure out whether Alex will regain her employment at Vostferous LLC and how much, if any, compensation she will receive based on her claim. Am I correct? Are there additional issues you need to address in order to resolve the appeal? To leave here today with a complete resolution to this dispute, what issues will you have agreed upon?*

2. Create an Agenda

Once the parties have identified the issues to be resolved, you can help them decide the order in which to address them. There is no best order. Sometimes the parties decide to start on the easy issues to gain momentum toward success. Sometimes they decide to address the make-or-break issues first to avoid wasting time on other issues if an agreement ultimately cannot be reached. And sometimes the problem they are trying to solve dictates the order in which they address issues. In any event, facilitating agreement on the issues to be decided and the order in which to decide them is the beginning of crafting an agreement that finally settles the case.

Good questions for Phase 3 to organize the issues. Unlike the task of generating a list of issues, helping the parties figure out the order in which to address them is fairly straightforward. One way to structure this discussion is to say the following: *If this list captures all of the issues, let's talk about where to start.* Some simple questions will get the conversation going: *Do you have any ideas about where to begin? And then what should we turn to after that?*

D.   Use Private Caucuses Effectively

In most mediations, if someone has not requested a private caucus by the end of Phase 3, he or she will do so during the interval between creating the agenda and beginning to negotiate. Whether the idea to separate comes from one of the participants or from you, you should employ care when transitioning from joint to separate sessions.

1. *Manage the Transition to Separate Sessions*

Skillful facilitation of the transition from joint to separate meetings is critical to preserving any spirit of collaboration and forward momentum created in the initial joint session. Be deliberate and thoughtful as you make the transition. Mark the end of the information exchange phase by asking a clean-up question to make sure this phase is complete, such as this: *Is there anything else you would like the other party to understand or you would like to understand from the other party?* And remind the parties that they are always free to revisit this phase if something occurs to them later.

Also mark the beginning of the next phase. At this point, the mediator has the opportunity to influence the effectiveness of separate meetings. These meetings allow the parties to reflect on and integrate what they learn in the joint session and consider how the dispute might be resolved.

Once participants exchange perspectives on the background and legal aspects of the dispute and identify and organize the issues, they usually want to convene separately, with or without you, as they transition from exchanging information to negotiating the resolution. Private caucuses can give participants a chance to cool down after highly emotional storytelling in joint sessions. However, if private caucuses only represent a chance to get away from the other side and to begin the shuttle diplomacy of offers and counteroffers, they lose most of their value.

2. *Avoid Premature Bargaining*

Especially if you are a results-oriented mediator, at the first opportunity in separate sessions, you, like the parties and lawyers, may be tempted to jump to problem solving. Resist the urge. The best and highest use of the first private caucus is to learn more from the participants about their experience and the emotional aspects of the lawsuit. Parties may be more willing to talk openly with you if they are not afraid of the other side's reaction.[27] Thus, your empathic listening skills should remain fully engaged because parties and their attorneys may feel compelled to express their outrage or other strong emotions or reveal what's really going on in the case. By listening attentively, you immediately convey the sense that they are being heard, and you gain information that may prove relevant to settlement later in the mediation.

Instead of launching into narrow questions, we suggest you begin the initial caucus with empathetic comments that demonstrate how carefully you listened in the joint session and acknowledge any positive contributions of the others in the caucus: *Even though it must have been hard to hear what Joe had to say, you stuck it out and really listened. Thank you.* Although you may want to follow up on particular topics raised in the joint session, we suggest instead that

---

27. Birke, *supra* note 15, at 510.

you begin more broadly by asking a general question: *Is there anything else you would like me to know that you did not talk about in our joint session?*

Mediation sessions frequently involve more than one private caucus. After the first caucus, you have the opportunity to elicit more information so that you *and the participants* can gain a better understanding of their situations. In this sense, private caucuses represent a safe learning environment. In this spirit, you can ask questions to explore the needs, interests, hopes, and anxieties of the parties. By summarizing and reflecting back, you can help parties to hear what their attorneys have to say and enable them to be more reflective in considering their personal stance to the negotiation.

Good questions for subsequent caucuses focused on the legal analysis, asked with a sense of curiosity, might include the following:

- *What do you win if you win on appeal?* Appellants who win on appeal usually gain no more than the opportunity to spend more money and time on a retrial or further trial court proceedings. Respondents win no more than to have the judgment already entered not be any worse.

- *What are your odds of winning?* Appellants usually face poor odds of success on appeal.

- *What are the consequences to you of losing?* Respondents who lose on appeal can face dire consequences when all the attorney fees get shifted to them and they now have to go to a retrial with binding case law that may have eviscerated their best argument or evidence. Appellants who lose on appeal probably face a worse judgment due to post-judgment interest accruing during a lengthy appeal.

- *What are the prospects for collecting on the judgment?* There's a maxim among attorneys that says winning is only half the battle, and collecting is the harder part.

- *What alternatives to appeal do you presently have?* Only when parties understand their alternatives to a negotiated agreement can they properly assess the value of the appeal compared to the value of other options such as settlement.

- *What do you need to be able to address the underlying problem?* Rather than reciting a litany of *wants*, it is helpful for a party to articulate the *interests* that must be addressed in order to solve (or begin solving) the problem for which the litigation is being waged.

If you come from a strong litigation background, it may be easy for you to slip into cross-examination mode, asking questions to elicit intended answers. We encourage otherwise. If you ask questions, make sure you are asking them because you are genuinely curious. That way you cannot possibly convey the message that there is a right answer.

Conversely, be prepared for the fact that most participants (even the attorneys) will arrive at the mediation without having fully examined the consequences of winning or losing on appeal or their immediately available alternatives to the appeal. You can be fully prepared to explore these issues with the participants by studying Chapter 2, in which we cover case evaluation for civil appeals.

E.   Discourage Premature Commitment

As an appellate mediator, at some point you will encounter participants who pull you aside right before a mediation session to tell you their bottom line. And in nearly all mediations somebody will let you in on the bottom line very early in the negotiation phase. There are a variety of reasons why participants do so: (1) nervousness about reaching a result that they will later regret, (2) a desire to enlist the aid of the mediator in making sure the process aims toward their goal, (3) the wish to hasten settlement in order to avoid the nail-biting tension attending the numerous offers and counteroffers inherent in negotiations, or (4) lack of experience in mediation and uncertainty about the appropriate time and procedure for making an offer.

These early declarations are problematic. The reason is that commitment is a psychological trap that can fix parties into positions they should be re-evaluating throughout the mediation as new information comes to light and they begin to analyze the situation in greater depth and detail. "Once we make a choice or take a stand, we encounter personal and interpersonal pressures to behave consistently with that commitment. Those pressures will cause us to respond in ways that justify our earlier decisions."[28] "Commitment decisions have a tendency to be self-perpetuating because they can 'grow their own legs.' That is, people often add new reasons and justifications to support the wisdom of commitments they have previously made. As a consequence, some commitments remain in effect long after the conditions that spurred them have changed."[29]

In most mediations that successfully resolve the dispute, both sides ultimately accept an agreement that crosses the bottom lines they drew earlier in the mediation. Unfortunately, premature commitment to a number by either side—but especially by both—works against the possibility of sufficient movement and dooms a mediation unless premature commitment is avoided or overcome. Here are some ideas for dealing with this problem:

- Just ignore it: *I see.*

---

28.   ROBERT B. CIALDINI, INFLUENCE: SCIENCE AND PRACTICE 53 (Allyn & Bacon, 4th ed. 2001).
29.   *Id.* at 96.

- Listen and reframe the statement to focus on the present moment: *Right now you are thinking $1 million is what it will take for you to resolve this case at the end of the day. Is that right?*

- Listen and reframe the statement from bottom line to aspiration: *I appreciate your candor so early in the process. It is good to know what you are hoping for at the outset.*

- Use humor: *If I had a nickel for every time a party settled for something other than their bottom line, I would be a wealthy retiree.*

- Do a little negotiation coaching: *I appreciate your letting me know. In my experience, in most mediations the best negotiators continue to re-evaluate their bottom lines throughout the mediation and adjust them if the information they learn along the way warrants it. I assume you are a smart negotiator and will likely do the same. Am I right about that?*

- Set the expectation that as a responsible mediator you may ask the party to revisit that decision: *I see that you decided before coming here to draw the line at $1 million. That may be the right number to hold. But it may not be, if a thoughtful and thorough analysis of the legal risks and opportunities on appeal does not support that much or if a settlement you create here is below your bottom line but nevertheless is more attractive to you than the bottom line you came in with. I may encourage you to re-evaluate this bottom line. Otherwise, I don't think I would be serving you very well. I want to make sure you think through this important decision and are making a well-informed decision throughout the day—not just before you got here. What do you think about that?*

F.   Conclusion

In this chapter, we explored the most underappreciated phases of appellate mediation. However, these phases in which parties exchange information and identify issues represent the difference between a successful appellate mediation and all of the previous unsuccessful settlement efforts in the trial court. As the mediator in Phases 2 and 3, you bear the responsibility for ensuring that parties have an opportunity (1) to educate each other about their perspectives on the law and whatever else matters to them, including the background of the case and their interests and (2) work together to set the agenda for the remainder of the mediation.

Chapter 15
Identifying and Finding Solutions in Phase 4, and Concluding the Mediation in Phase 5

A. Introduction

In this chapter, we explore how mediators can be most helpful during the final two phases of mediation. In Phase 4, mediators assist parties as they negotiate. In Phase 5, parties who reach agreement benefit from mediators who help facilitate the process of documenting their settlement. We also explore how mediators can help parties keep the possibility of settlement alive when there is no resolution during the mediation session. We also offer ideas about how, once the mediation session ends, mediators can continue to serve parties who do not resolve their disputes during the mediation. Many lawyers and mediators see the value of a facilitative process up to this point in the mediation, but when it comes time to negotiate a resolution they expect the process to shift into high-gear evaluation. They subscribe to the maxim that mediators are facilitative in the morning and evaluative in the afternoon. Or they believe that all of the preceding phases are merely warm up for the "real work" done during the negotiation and crafting agreement phases. Some attorneys may tolerate joint sessions early during the mediation but expect to remain in private caucus for the remainder of the day. Such binary views overlook the reality that "professional legal mediators in fact use a variety of styles, and that they change their approach constantly during a single mediation, even within a single meeting with a disputant."[1] Moreover, an effective mediation requires the flexibility to move between private caucus, joint sessions, and meetings with only the attorneys, or other ad hoc strategies to help parties reach their goals.

Almost all appellate mediations involve both (1) integrative and value-creating (interest based) efforts, *and* (2) distributive or value-dividing (zero-sum) discussions. These activities involve different processes and different types of assistance from the mediator. We advise you to begin with interest-based negotiation.

---

1. Dwight Golann, *Variations in Mediation: How—and Why—Legal Mediators Change Styles in the Course of a Case*, J. OF DISPUTE RESOLUTION 42 (2000).

B.   Identifying and Finding Solutions in Phase 4

1.   Facilitate Integrative Bargaining

a.   *Begin by Exploring Interests*

For parties to find an interest-based solution, they must first identify and explore the interests they hope to satisfy. We chose to introduce the topic of exploring interests here, although we might easily have done so when we discussed Phase 2 in Chapter 14, in which the parties exchange other information. In reality, parties might express their interests in every phase. The mediator's skill is in knowing how to listen for interests when they come up spontaneously and how to ask questions that prompt parties to think about and articulate their interests.

Parties do not always resonate with the term "interests." So introducing a conversation about interests requires you to help them understand what you are asking them to do. Unlike positions (what people *demand*) that can be satisfied in one way, interests can be satisfied in a variety of ways. Unlike needs (fundamental, universal requirements such as safety and respect) that are so general they are not very helpful to problem solving, interests reveal what matters to people personally. Mediator and trainer Gary Friedman defines interests as possessing the following additional qualities:

- Of personal importance.

- Capable of being satisfied in multiple ways.

- Tangible.

- Capable of being described as a present or future benefit, rather than as a cost to the other party.[2]

Good questions to elicit interests. Some mediation teachers suggest that one question—"Why?"—is all that is required to elicit the parties' interests. *Why do you want an apology? Why do you want to stay in the house, rather than sell it and split the proceeds?* We shy away from that question out of concern that parties might experience it as challenging them to justify their points of view or positions. Although you can ask the question "Why?" in a tone and demeanor that convey genuine curiosity, other questions help to generate conversations about interests without the downside risks of "Why?" Additionally, we find it far more interesting to inquire about interests with a wide variety of questions and we imagine the parties do, too.

Some questions that reliably lead parties to communicate and explore their interests are: *What interests of yours do we need to be aware of and take into*

---

2. Gary Friedman, *Advanced Training: Working with Interests*, a workshop held in Sausalito, CA, April 18, 2014.

account in order to create an agreement that works for you? What is it about staying in the house that makes it so important to you? If the agreement you reach really works well for you, what interests of yours does it need to address?

Sometimes when you ask about interests, parties answer with positions, such as "What matters most is that I get to stay in the house." In response to this answer or other answers that do not describe the parties' interests, just keep going deeper until parties get to their interests. Here are a few ways of prompting this exploration: *Could you please say more about what staying in the house would mean to you? What interests of yours would be met by staying in the house? If your interest in staying in the house could be met here, how would that change things for you? What would that give you that you do not have now?*

A great discussion about interests accomplishes a number of important goals. It helps to create or expand knowledge of what matters to people simply for the sake of understanding; in the best cases, it helps estranged parties to re-establish connection; it stimulates thinking about potential solutions; and it forms criteria by which the parties can evaluate any potential solutions. Speaking of solutions, we now turn to how to go about generating them.

b. Generate Options for Settlement in a Brainstorming Exercise

Once the parties identify their interests, they are ready to explore an interest-based resolution, which, as Professor Dwight Golann points out, "remains one of the most valuable concepts in dispute resolution."[3] If parties focus on the amount of money to be paid and do not explore other ideas for resolving their dispute, they miss the opportunity to address their interests, particularly emotional interests such as restoring a reputation or repairing a relationship. Studies show that even in commercial disputes—the kind of conflict for which one might expect money to be the only ingredient in the settlement—an integrative approach often uncovers additional, nonmonetary options that the parties ultimately adopt as part of their solution. One study of commercial mediations concluded, "[c]ounting repairs [of previously strained relationships] as an integrative term, at least one such term appeared in settlements of 47 percent of the surveyed cases. The nature of these terms was notable, however, few appeared to be central to the settlement" of the dispute.[4] In other words, although creative solutions and options for restoring some sense of relationship do not usually constitute the central aspect of the settlement agreement, they occur with sufficient frequency to be worth exploring. Thus, even in cases in which

---

3.   Dwight Golann, *Beyond Brainstorming: The Special Barriers to Interest-Based Mediation, and Techniques to Overcome Them*, 18(1) Disp. Resol. Mag. 22 (2011).

4.   *Id.* at 23. Although not focusing on appellate mediations, the commercial context of the survey suggests that integrative solutions should not be ignored just because a case is on appeal.

creative solutions do not form the centerpiece of resolution, they can nevertheless enhance the value of a settlement as an add-on to money.[5]

A brainstorming session is an effective way to go about generating options
for settlement. Most mediators are familiar with brainstorming steps:

1. Generate options.
2. Clarify the meaning of the suggested options.
3. Evaluate the options on the basis of how well they meet the parties'
   interests.
4. Create packages that give parties the greatest share of what they value
   most.

In introducing brainstorming, you can help the parties understand that the
creative formulation of options can endow mediations with the promise of a
better solution than the appeal offers. You might mention other positive effects
of brainstorming. Properly facilitated, people tend to find group brainstorming exercises to be pleasant and worthwhile.[6] Moreover, group brainstorming
appears to produce greater group cohesion and positive attitude change.[7] The
process may also reduce egocentrism and increase the ability to take the perspectives of others. It also allows the party that did not formulate an option
more readily to accept an idea generated in a collaborative setting.[8] And group
brainstorming can break the stranglehold of the prevailing belief that mediation is nothing more than a dollar-division contest.

In addition to pointing out the advantages of brainstorming, it is important to structure the exercise effectively. The success of brainstorming depends
on the parties' adherence to the following simple principles:[9]

- All options are welcome. Sometimes even crazy or totally unacceptable
  options stimulate thinking and lead to new ideas that will work. And
  sometimes ideas that first appear to be crazy actually do work.

- Suggesting an option does not mean you would agree to it. If parties
  are evaluating their ideas and editing out ones that do not advantage
  them because they would never agree to them—or for other reasons—
  they are interrupting the creative process.

- Parties participate as equally as possible. A brainstorming session in
  which one party dominates the exercise does not work. Participants

---

5. *Id.* at 26.
6. James H. Stark & Douglas N. Frenkel, Changing Minds: The Work of Mediators and Empirical Studies of Persuasion 332–33 (2013).
7. Michael W. Kramer, Chao Lan Kuo & John C. Dailey, *The Impact of Brainstorming Techniques on Subsequent Group Processes beyond Generating Ideas*, 28 Small Group Research
   236 (1997).
8. Stark & Frenkel, *supra* note 6, at 331 n.242.
9. *See generally* Corinne Faure, *"Beyond Brainstorming: Effects of Different Group Procedures
   on Selection of Ideas and Satisfaction with the Process."* Journal of Creative Behavior 38
   (2004): 21; *see also* Kramer et al., *supra* note 7, at 223 (noting that untrained groups
   without a facilitator or leader typically involve criticism and participation inequality).

need to be equally committed and engaged in the activity. If they are not, it will fizzle, or, worse, the possibility of creating an atmosphere of collaboration will be frustrated.

- Separate option generation from option evaluation. Parties need first "to capture [ideas] . . . and evaluate later. A big mistake people make is to start visualizing the criticism or the feedback while they're still generating. That can shut you right down."[10] Research in this area consistently shows that "[a]s the idea quantity increases, so does the idea quality."[11] Thus, you want to facilitate a process in which the participants can generate as many options as possible whether they seem promising or not.

Mediators often wonder whether it is appropriate for them to offer options during a brainstorming exercise. Experienced mediators and appellate specialists often have ideas that can help solve the underlying problem. We see no reason not to share them, but we do adhere to the conventional wisdom that if you are going to offer any ideas, offer them last and offer more than one. Interestingly, when surveying sophisticated mediation participants, the American Bar Association found that 100 percent want the mediator to "suggest possible ways to resolve issues."[12]

Once they exhaust the possibilities option-generation, the next step is to determine whether the parties understand the options in the same way, for example with this question: *Are there any of these options that you don't understand or would like additional information about?* If you, as mediator, don't understand a suggestion, ask the party who suggested it to clarify it.

After generating options and clarifying them, the next step is evaluating how well they address the parties' interests. Unless the parties' list of options is short, they will need to narrow the options before evaluating them. This task can begin in many ways, such as by eliminating ones that seem unworkable or obviously unacceptable or by categorizing and then prioritizing the options in order of most to least promising. Trainers Robert Mnookin and Gary Friedman suggest asking the parties to rank the options as A (most promising, which the parties discuss), B (somewhat interesting, which they discuss if the A options do not lead to solutions), and C (nonstarters, which the parties seldom discuss).

Instead of the Mnookin-Friedman approach, you might begin this discussion with one of the following questions: *Shall we put these ideas into categories? What might they be? Do any of these look more promising than others? Do any jump out at you? Do any of these seem to meet your interests or goals better than others? Which of these ideas would you like to explore first? Are there any you want to eliminate?*

Reaching agreement on creative solutions occurs in many ways. Sometimes the solution is obvious to the parties very early in the process of generating

---

10. Mariette Dichristina, John Houtz, Julia Cameron & Robert Epstein, *Let your creativity soar*, 19 Sci. Am. Mind 29 (2008).
11. Kramer et al., *supra* note 7, at 220.
12. American Bar Association Task Force on Improving Mediation Quality, Final Report 14 (2008) [hereinafter ABA Mediation Quality].

options or during the process of evaluating them. Other times it takes further discussion and perhaps further brainstorming.

When the parties face decisions on multiple nonmonetary as well as monetary issues, we suggest a further brainstorming guideline: the parties keep all decisions tentative to allow flexibility at the end to trade among the issues. Doing so gives the parties the freedom to trade among the issues and create packages that give them what they value most—or that address their most important interests as best they can.

A Cautionary Note about the Option of Apology

It is not uncommon for someone to raise the possibility of an apology in mediation, either because a party wants to *get* one or, less commonly, because a party wants to *give* one. If the party who committed the harm accepts responsibility and is willing to apologize, mediation provides an ideal forum in which to make a full expression of remorse because the parties have the benefit of your assistance in facilitating this important and sensitive conversation.

Although some writers extol mediation as an ideal forum for apology because it can be made without adverse legal consequences, others point out that a "protected" apology frustrates an essential element of apology: the offender must be willing to accept the consequences of wrongful actions. This debate is only one of the fascinating and nuanced issues that come to light as you investigate apology in-depth.

A genuine apology facilitates closure and opens the door to forgiveness and reconciliation. It can be a powerful event that allows parties to settle their legal war. However, a botched apology—one that is ill-timed, half-hearted, or motivated solely to achieve a more favorable settlement—can derail the mediation and worsen the conflict. For this reason and others, before you tinker with apology in mediation, we recommend you read about it and consider getting advanced training.[13]

Given the delicate and potentially high-stakes nature of apology, we caution you to tread lightly. If you intend to orchestrate an apology, you should be prepared to allocate the time and effort required to educate yourself about it and ensure the apology will be a full one that accepts responsibility for the harm and expresses remorse.[14] Some researchers of apology believe that a statement of intent to change may also be necessary.[15] An apology is strong medicine: it can be very healing or very harmful. Plan accordingly.

---

13. We highly recommend reading Lee Taft, "Apology Subverted: The Commodification of Apology," *Yale Law Journal* (2000): 1135–60 (in part on the elements of genuine apology and the moral dimension of apology) and James H. Stark and Douglas N. Frenkel, *Changing Minds: The Work of Mediators and Empirical Studies of Persuasion* (2013): 352, 281–97 (on the opportunities and risks of orchestrated apologies).
14. Stark & Frenkel, *supra* note 6, at 287.
15. *Id.* at 288.

2. Facilitate Distributive Bargaining

Be prepared to spend substantial time and energy on the distributive bargaining phase. "Although integrative negotiation and the search for additional value are important and worthwhile, they rarely completely resolve the dispute. "Eventually . . . one comes to bargaining in which added benefits to one impose corresponding significant costs on the other."[16] The reality of appellate mediation is that virtually every civil appeal comes down to distributing some resources, usually in the form of money. Often there is a money judgment to address. And there is always the issue of court costs and, frequently, attorney fees. Occasionally there is a judgment involving title or possession of property. Allocating responsibility for payment or entitlement to money or property involves the distributive negotiations that parties and attorneys expect to be the real work of the mediation.[17] And, it *is* real work. Be prepared to spend the bulk of your time and effort in facilitating a productive distributive negotiation.

Realize that mediating about money is largely facilitating a problematic form of communication. For many parties negotiating over money via the "shuttle diplomacy" of having a mediator go back and forth between private caucuses is like winking in the dark: you know what you are doing, but no one else does.[18] Every proposal to settle for a dollar value is a communication. Initial offers, which parties often intend to be moderately unreasonable.

Parties communicate with numbers throughout the distributive negotiation. The movements between subsequent offers are crude signals of the parties' desired range of final settlement. Parties respond to proposals they do not like with miniscule counteroffers—or none at all—to signal their disgruntlement. They make more generous counteroffers in response to offers they consider to be appropriate. They stall in conveying new offers or present a succession of offers with no meaningful movement to signal when they reach their best numbers or are frustrated with the way negotiations are developing.

In addition to using numbers to communicate about the *substance* of the negotiation, parties also express their *feelings* through numbers,[19] particularly if they have not had a satisfying joint session in which they discussed the underlying dispute and its impacts.

---

16. James J. White, *The Pros and Cons of "Getting to Yes,"* 34 J. Legal Education 115, 116 (1984); J. Anderson Little, Making Money Talk: How to Mediate Insured Claims and Other Monetary Disputes 27 (ABA 2007).
17. Golann, *supra* note 3, at 23.
18. With apology to Steuart Henderson Britt, who originally said, "Doing business without advertising is like winking at a girl in the dark. You know what you are doing but nobody else does." Steuart Henderson Britt & Harper W. Boyd, Marketing Management & Administrative Action (1968).
19. Little, *supra* note 15, at 63.

The language of numbers is inherently imprecise. As J. Anderson (Andy) Little puts it in his excellent book about mediating disputes about dollars, *Making Money Talk: How to Mediate Insured Claims and Other Monetary Disputes*, "The parties communicate indirectly and, as a result, they often miscommunicate."[20] The first step to mediating distributive issues, which mostly concern money, effectively is to understand that this negotiation is a mode of communication. The next step is to acquire some tools to employ when mediating these issues. Listed next are a few that have helped us.

Help the parties to anticipate and prepare for the tension and emotional intensity of distributive bargaining. When the parties understand the distributive negotiation dance, they tend to react less personally to proposals they do not like. When they can anticipate and prepare for the boldly exaggerated first steps of opening offers and demands, the irritatingly slow rhythm in the beginning, the expectations of reciprocal movements, the sometimes halting progress, and the threat of premature ending, they will have a less frustrating experience.

You can help them to be more effective under the pressure of this phase if you let them know what to expect:

- Almost every negotiation about money is a tug of war in which tension builds and people feel frustrated and, perhaps, despondent. If you warn them about the challenges they are about to face, they do better. If you can also reassure them with authority and conviction that despite this intensity, almost all cases settle, they are even better prepared to weather the storm.

- Be even more precise about *how* the tension builds. As our friend and colleague San Francisco mediator Jerry Spolter says, "Ninety percent of the negotiation occurs in the last ten percent of the time." Knowing this, parties will be more inclined to hang in there when the going gets tough because they recognize that there is not so far to go. A little humor later in the moments of highest tension helps, too. We have quoted Jerry early in our mediations, and later, when parties are about to give up, we say, "I told you so! Perhaps we are close to a resolution."

Encourage parties to develop a negotiation plan. As surprising as it sounds, rarely do people come to mediation with a well-developed plan—or *any* plan for that matter—for negotiating about money. If they have planned at all, it was only to come up with their bottom line. The absence of preparation is particularly prevalent in appellate mediation. Typically parties have not negotiated at all after entry of judgment or an appealable order. Unfortunately, parties who do not have a plan tend to respond to the other side's proposals

---

20. *Id.* at 67.

reactively—influenced by their emotional response—rather than proactively according to a plan designed to enable them to reach their goal.

You can encourage parties to plan for their negotiation during the premediation phase in the following ways:

- Inquire about the parties' settlement history postjudgment. *What has occurred?* If there have been no discussions, ask why not. The answer will give you insight into how to help them begin the process.

- If the plaintiff has not made a demand, determine whether the defendant needs one to prepare for the mediation. If so, discuss timing and how the plaintiff will communicate it. You may also want to offer premediation assistance with this exploration.

- Encourage the lawyers to come to mediation with a plan for negotiating about money, being concrete about what it might include. We suggest at a minimum parties plan their tentative reservation or walkaway point, which is based on information they have developed to date about their legal case, including chances of prevailing on appeal and a concrete case valuation based on this analysis (see Section I, which sets forth our approach to these tasks). Encourage them also to determine their tentative "target price," or the point at which they will resist further movement (Andy Little calls this their "best numbers");[21] their opening moves; and a plan for making concessions.

Negotiation planning is the subject of numerous texts and articles. We are partial to Richard Shell's *Bargaining for Advantage: Negotiation Strategies for Reasonable People,*[22] If you and counsel have read it before coming to the mediation, you will share a common negotiation language and understanding of the process that helps the negotiation proceed more smoothly, enhances rapport among you, and makes the process a lot more fun for you.

Even when the parties are unprepared to negotiate distributive issues, you can still make a difference by helping them think through a plan at the mediation. If you invite, rather than impose, the suggestion to create a plan, you will be more successful in engaging parties in a meaningful exercise. And if you are a student (or teacher) of negotiation and are willing to be more hands-on with the exercise, your input and guidance can be extremely useful to the process. A note of warning, though: some mediators are not comfortable in this role, fearing that coaching the parties will compromise mediator impartiality or at least the perception that they are impartial. Offering assistance to both sides helps to alleviate this concern. Some mediators are also uncomfortable with interjecting advice of this sort for

---

21.   LITTLE, *supra* note 15, at 87.
22.   RICHARD SHELL, BARGAINING FOR ADVANTAGE: NEGOTIATION STRATEGIES FOR REASONABLE PEOPLE (Penguin Books 1999).

fear that they are influencing the outcome, compromising the standard not only of impartiality but also of self-determination. Although we do not share these concerns, we do pay attention to these potential ethical problems and encourage you to do so as well. And, of course, we respect these other views and encourage you, as with all our suggestions, to consider your own values and decide for yourself.

a. Follow These Tips for Effective Distributive Bargaining

Stay optimistic and flexible. Mediated negotiations succeed where direct negotiations fail in part because mediators stay optimistic about the prospects for agreement when the parties have given up hope.[23] Mediators are also willing to try something new while the parties might be mired in only one or two strategies. Observations of experienced mediators show that mediators try several different approaches even in the same interaction with a party.[24] Optimism and flexibility are important ingredients for success, and you bear responsibility for adding them when no one else can.

Encourage the parties to evaluate whether the proposal they are about to make is consistent with the message they intend to convey. And if it is not, you can help them decide whether to change the number or express the message directly, explaining why the number is at odds with the message.

Help parties to translate the language of distributive negotiation: money. Because the language of numbers is so imprecise, we suggest you encourage parties to send explicit, direct messages even when the numbers and the messages they intend to convey seem consistent. However, in advising that parties articulate a clear message, we do not mean to suggest, as some negotiation teachers do, that the message must include a justification or rationale for the new number it represents. During most of the mediation, parties do not reveal their true negotiation positions. They do not know for certain what the other party is thinking until the very end—and only then if the parties settle the case. So for most of the mediation, parties must infer a message through the language of numbers. As a result, they often draw negative conclusions or take personal offense in response to settlement proposals they do not like—which is *most* of the time in *most* of our cases.

This propensity to be personally affronted has the power not only to confuse the situation but also to destroy any good will the parties may have created during Phase 2 as they exchanged perspectives and worked to understand each other. If you appreciate the destructive potential of distributive bargaining and have a few tools for managing it—and managing yourself in the process—you can increase the probability that the parties will come through it relatively unscathed. The following ideas have worked well for us:

---

23. *Id.*
24. Golann, *supra* note 3, at 23.

Help parties to communicate clear messages with their numbers. Regrettably, in extending counterproposals, parties usually just *react*. They do not *reflect* before they respond. If they like a proposal, they respond in kind. If they do not like a proposal, they retaliate with a proposal they believe to be equally offensive. If they communicate any message directly, it is usually limited to anger or indignation at an insulting proposal. You can help parties address the limitations of the language of numbers by helping them to determine the message they want to convey to the other party and explore their options for doing so.

Keep calm in the storm. When tension is high, you may be the only person in the mediation who can remain calm and present. As we discussed earlier, due to the effects of emotional contagion, if you remain calm and relaxed the other participants are more likely to do so. Remaining calm requires emotional intelligence, first to be self-aware, to notice your physical and emotional tension and troubled thoughts. You need to be able to hear your internal voice, especially the one that joins the chorus of doubt and pessimism about settlement (*I don't think this case is going to settle*), self-doubt (*I am such an incompetent negotiator/mediator*), worry (*If this case doesn't settle, these people will never hire me again* or *Oh, no, that is a really bad idea and I think they are about to run into an oncoming train*), and negative judgments (*They're bad negotiators/lawyers/communicators*). And you need to be able to manage that voice, to relax your body, to shift your emotions and unhelpful thoughts and ultimately to be fully present in the mediation.

b. Provide Analytic Input

First, we address "a topic that is something of a land mine in the field of mediation"[25]: whether and, if so, when a mediator should become *evaluative* by injecting an opinion, analysis, or prediction of the outcome rather than remaining *facilitative* by keeping communications open and productive. Dare we even mention the possibility of becoming *directive* (by telling the parties what they should do)?

We value self-determination. We firmly believe this principle enables mediation to be a rare (and likely the only) chance parties will have to take control of the appeal's outcome rather than ceding it to an external authority. Unlike some, we believe that most appellate mediators can properly engage in an evaluative style at some point in the mediation without violating the principle of self-determination. We also believe evaluative and facilitative mediation can coexist in the same mediation and that mediators can be both facilitative and evaluative in the same mediation. In fact, as the mediation literature demonstrates, "the use of evaluative techniques is . . . frequent, even among those mediators who favor a broad, facilitative approach."[26]

---

25. ABA MEDIATION QUALITY, *supra* note 12, at 15.
26. Golann, *supra* note 1, at 42.

When we refer to the evaluative role of the mediator, we do not mean as a coercive force or as a superior expert. An evaluative mediator, in our view, provides "analytic input," a term the American Bar Association uses to describe the help an evaluative mediator can provide.[27]

Rather than resenting analytic input, "many reasonably sophisticated mediation users in civil cases want mediators to provide certain services, including analytical techniques. A substantial majority of survey participants (80%) believe some analytical input by a mediator to be appropriate."[28] Moreover, 95 percent of sophisticated mediation participants *want* the mediator to "give [an] analysis of case, including strengths and weaknesses."[29]

Understanding the strengths and weaknesses of an appeal is critical because a settlement represents the party's conclusion that the terms of the agreement are better than the prospects of continuing with the appeal. For the most part, parties derive this information from the mediation statements and from discussions the mediator facilitates during mediation. In facilitating discussions about the law, the mediator provides analytic input in a number of ways, such as structuring a discussion to help the parties digest legal information; ensuring they listen to each other's point of view; and organizing or summarizing the issues.

At times the parties want the mediator's perspective on the strengths and weaknesses of their arguments—another form of analytic input. When parties (and even attorneys) lack understanding of appellate law, mediators can help parties evaluate their appeal by clarifying appellate concepts and legal principles and providing input about the strengths and weaknesses of the case, if the parties invite it. Only with an accurate understanding of appellate rules can parties make a realistic comparison between continuing with the appeal and accepting a negotiated settlement.

In addition to helping the parties understand appellate law and procedure and appreciate the risks, opportunities, and costs of their appeal, during a distributive negotiation, you can provide analytic input in the form of a reality check concerning the parties' *interests*.[30] For example, you can remind them that

---

27. *See* ABA MEDIATION QUALITY, *supra* note 12, at 15. We agree that "[i]f mediation is to become fully professionalized, it needs to overcome its squeamishness about the topic of persuasion. It needs to base its best practices and ethical norms on more than folklore, opinion or the official imprimatur of dispute resolution organizations. It needs reliable, evidence-based knowledge about what kinds of mediator interventions work in producing settlements, and how they are experienced by people in disputes." Stark & Frenkel, *supra* note 6, at 352.

28. ABA MEDIATION QUALITY, *supra* note 12, at 14.

29. *Id.* Moreover, "users thought the listed activities would be helpful in about half or more of their cases: 95%—ask pointed questions that raise issues; 60%—make prediction about likely court results; 84%—recommend a specific settlement; and 74%—apply some pressure to accept a specific solution." *Id.*

30. A review of the psychological foundations for negotiation advises negotiators that "[f]or an agreement to stand the test of time, you should persuade opposing counsel

they mentioned being depressed about the litigation, anxious about the effects of losing on appeal, or perseverating on the past at the expense of considering how to create a better future. Sometimes a reminder of what really matters strikes a chord with parties and inspires broader perspective taking.

Analytic input comes in many forms, from expressing your view about the merits of the appeal to helping parties to revisit and explore their interests. You must find a comfort zone within this arena that is consistent with your expertise, values, and sense of your role. We believe there is a significant role for mediators in the analytic function of mediation, and we encourage you to reflect on and ultimately determine the size and shape of that zone in light of your preferences *and* the value to the parties of a truly self-determinative mediation process.

If you are comfortable providing analytic input, the question becomes one of choosing the most effective approaches to make the contribution. Although we lack space in this book to elaborate on all approaches to helping the parties better understand their circumstances on appeal, we offer this brief overview to get you started.

Multiple explanations exercise. When parties or attorneys are certain about an uncertain outcome or even overly optimistic in light of objective indicia of case weaknesses, an exercise that reduces bias can be just the right thing. Research suggests that a multiple explanations analysis is one of the most effective ways to reduce unwarranted optimism or pessimism.[31] In Chapter 2, we describe how to conduct a multiple explanations exercise and provide four worksheets to use with the parties and attorneys to come up with multiple plausible explanations for how the appeal might turn out. Done collaboratively with a party and attorney in private caucus, this exercise can prompt a much more realistic appraisal of the strengths and weaknesses of a party's position on appeal.

(and the party they represent) that the settlement is in some sense optimal in terms of satisfying their interests." Donna Shestowsky, *Psychology and Persuasion,* in Andrea Kupfer Schneider & Christopher Honeyman, eds., The Negotiator's Fieldbook 366 (ABA 2006). Unless the parties have analytically grappled with advantages and disadvantages of a particular settlement agreement, "[b]uyer's remorse is likely to be the product." *Id.* This advice applies not only to negotiators but also to mediators who want to minimize day-after regret for the parties.

31. Edward R. Hirt & Keith D. Markman, *Multiple Explanation: A Consider-an-Alternative Strategy for Debiasing Judgments,* 69 J. of Personality & Social Psychology 1084 (1995). A closely related version of this exercise is sometimes called role reversal, counterattitudinal advocacy, or consider the opposite, which requires the participant to articulate the arguments, feelings, or positions of an opponent. *See* Stark & Frenkel, *supra* note 6, at 273–80. Although effective, parties may be more resistant to role reversal than a multiple explanations analysis exercise in which you can begin by asking them to consider an *even better* outcome than the one they have already seized upon.

Two-sided refutational statements. Although quite firmly on the evaluative spectrum of mediator efforts, the two-sided refutational statements approach is very effective way to convey a persuasive message by (1) articulating in detail the arguments of *each* party and (2) providing detailed, explicit reasons why in your view one side is more likely to prevail. If you are inclined to enter the evaluation arena, this approach is a most effective way to do so. Research confirms that "explicit arguments—arguments that state explicit reasons for a conclusion and describe those conclusions in detail—are much more persuasive than arguments with implicit reasons and/or implicit (or no) conclusions."[32]

If you provide analytic input in the form of two-sided refutational statements, we suggest you do so in the spirit of expanding the parties' understanding of the law. Most parties and lawyers are interested in your legal analysis. If, on the other hand, you offer two-sided refutational statements to coerce a settlement—or to force particular negotiation moves—you risk offending them and, in our view, offending the ethical principle of self-determination. As Andy Little notes, "Many people say that a mediator should not be evaluative when what they really mean is that a mediator should not be directive."[33]

Rhetorical questions and cross-examination. We warn you to steer clear of rhetorical questions. Anyone who has endured or inflicted cross-examination in a deposition or at trial undoubtedly recalls how unpleasant it is to have answers extracted in this manner—and if you were the recipient of rhetorical questions how much you resented the questioner. Not surprisingly, rhetorical questioning and cross-examination are poor ways to get people to change their minds or even consider new information. Moreover, they are highly problematic for a mediator who depends on rapport and empathetic listening skills to ask questions not intended to be answered or genuinely to elicit information.[34]

Using fear and guilt. Before dismissing the idea that you would ever intentionally try to instill fear or induce guilt to persuade someone in a mediation, consider whether you believe a mediator may ever sow doubt into the mind of a party to encourage the acceptability of a great settlement offer. Also consider this question: Should a mediator ever tell parties they "owe it to themselves" to follow through on their commitment to accept a logical solution to a problem that has worried them to the point of depression?

---

32. Stark & Frenkel, *supra* note 6, at 306.
33. LITTLE, *supra* note 15, at 48. Even on this point, we note that mediators are usually directive *as to the mediation process* when structuring the session to discourage participants from interrupting each other, engaging in premature bargaining, or dominating the conversation. There is broad consensus that the mediator should create an open and noncoercive space for the communications to occur. However, we agree that telling parties what to do or which offers they should accept conflicts with the party self-determination upon which mediation is founded.
34. Stark & Frenkel, *supra*, note 6, at 297–304.

Doubt and fear are different shades of the same color. Obligation and guilt are close relatives. Fear and guilt (and—by extension—doubt and a sense of moral obligation) rely on creating an uncomfortable state sufficient to compel the sufferer to escape the problem by fleeing to an immediately available solution.

Resorts to fear and guilt are relatively ineffective and problematic modes of persuasion.[35] With resorts to fear and guilt, "[r]esentment, anger, and a desire to lash out against the message and the messenger are often the result."[36] Reasonable mediators may differ as to whether doubt and moral obligation are fair game in mediation when they allow comparison of an ongoing problem with a less-than-ideal settlement solution. On this point, we urge you to be conscious and conscientious about your core values and ethical boundaries.

3. Narrow the Gap and Move beyond Impasse

Impasse results when the parties have moved toward each other as far as they can but remain some distance apart. By definition, impasse means the parties need you because they have exhausted all attempts to settle. Time to earn your keep. As one sophisticated consumer of mediation services "frankly exclaimed, 'That's what we're paying for. Otherwise we could exchange offers over the phone.'"[37] This sentiment is widely shared by consumers of mediation services. A survey of repeat mediation participants found that "over 98% of the users thought persistence to be an important, very important or essential quality in a mediator, and 93% identified patience in the same way. Users expressed dissatisfaction with mediators who threw in the towel when negotiations became difficult. They *want* mediators who are consistently engaged in the process and willing to work hard to help the parties meet their needs and settle their case."[38]

At impasse, you need a number of tools at your disposal, which might include the following:

- **Engage in a decision tree analysis.** Parties frequently reach impasse by getting stuck on a number to which they attach emotional significance: "My suffering is worth a million dollars!" A telltale sign of this phenomenon is that the parties are stuck on round numbers such as one million, zero, or one hundred thousand. In such an instance, you can help parties to reduce the emotional component of the dollar offer and introduce greater objectivity by engaging them in a decision tree analysis. You can bring copies of the worksheets in Chapter 3 to

---

35. *Id.* at 321–22. *But see* "causing people to forecast how they will feel in the future if their current action or inaction produces harmful effects, or causes them to fall short of their own standards." *Id.* at 324.
36. *Id.* at 323.
37. ABA Mediation Quality, *supra* note 12, at 38.
38. *Id.* at 17 (italics added).

the mediation in preparation. When parties use their own estimates of odds and outcomes, they are frequently surprised at the resulting output and will reconsider their settlement range. If you are working with an overoptimistic party, you can precede the decision tree exercise with the multiple explanations worksheets we provide in Chapter 2.

- **Create movement with hypothetical questions.** If you sense that parties have some distance left toward their best numbers but have lost momentum in exchanging proposals, hypothetical—or "what if"—questions may advance the negotiations. For example, you might ask a party in private caucus: *If the other party were to make an offer of X, would you be willing to make an offer of X+ in return?* After several iterations of this exercise, the parties might close in on a mutually acceptable number and reach agreement without any party having to commit prematurely.

- **Propose brackets.** When parties are far apart in their numbers but making only small movements toward each other, you might advance the negotiations by proposing brackets—that is, a range within which the rest of the negotiations will occur. This allows the parties to get much closer to an agreement without any side's appearing weak or overeager.

- **"Let's split the difference."** When competing offers stall within a relative whisker of each other, the age-old strategy of "split the difference" or "meet in the middle" can be a welcome relief to weary negotiators. It is often easier for the mediator to raise the possibility of splitting the difference than it is for the parties. They may not want to appear overly eager or signal their willingness to compromise further for fear the other side will take advantage.

- **Make a mediator's proposal.** When all else fails, the prospect of a mediator's proposal sometimes comes up. The parties may ask you to make a mediator's proposal. Or you may offer to insert yourself into the negotiation process by suggesting a mediator's proposal.

  A mediator's proposal presents parties with a specific dollar amount (and perhaps other terms necessary to settle the case) that the parties can accept or reject but cannot nibble at with proposed modifications. It is a take-it-or-leave-it proposal that you believe each party might find acceptable (even if only barely so) but that they might not reach on their own. The ground rules for mediator's proposals typically include the following: (1) the parties agree to entertain a mediator's proposal and follow the ground rules; (2) the mediator presents the same proposal to each side in private caucus and allows them a specific amount of time to respond, either during the mediation or after the parties adjourn to deliberate; (3) the parties cannot negotiate the proposal with the mediator or modify it; (4) the parties respond either *Yes* or *No*; (5) if both sides respond affirmatively, the mediator reveals their responses and the case settles, but if one or both sides respond negatively, the mediator lets the parties know they do not have an agreement; and (6) if the process does not result in agreement, the mediator does not reveal the parties' responses to the mediator's proposal.

A mediator's proposal is strong medicine: it is likely to bring quick success or halt the negotiation. Mostly, it results in agreement. It is useful to anticipate the next step should it fail. Here are some ideas we keep in our back pockets for times mediator proposals do not work to settle a case: pick up where you left off, inviting the party who was due to make a counteroffer to do so; invite the parties to restart the negotiation and encourage the party who said *Yes* to reconsider its last offer and propose a number lower (or higher) than the one the other party refused; ask the parties what they would like to do next; or adjourn the mediation with an agreement to check in with counsel the following day.

In addition to the above ideas for overcoming impasse, others have written ably on creative approaches to achieving agreement in the face of obstacles.[39]

4. *Take a Break (Especially for Something to Eat)*

Everything was going beautifully—the parties and attorneys were brainstorming productively and communicating effectively—when something changed. Now everyone's irritable and the clear-eyed analyses have turned into personal attacks. The mediation seems out of control, and you are getting irritable yourself. What should you do? Take a break.

Nothing in your role as a mediator requires you to spend every minute with the participants. However, your role does require you to be helpful and patient with participants when you *are* with them. Late afternoons can be deadly times for patience and the ability to be helpful. Taking a short break to recharge yourself is a relatively easy matter if the parties are already in separate caucuses. Having even 15 minutes to yourself in a quiet room can do wonders. So take a short break!

What should you do during your break? You should eat something. Dana often brings trail mix and fruit for everyone. Having an instant, nonsugary snack can restore your spirits. Being the mediator is a demanding role in which you must continue to demonstrate optimism, patience, concern, and helpfulness. You must also constantly make decisions about how the process is unfolding: Are the participants working well together? Have you completed

---

39. Other teachers and authors offer mediators sound advice about impasse, including BARRY GOLDMAN, THE SCIENCE OF SETTLEMENT: IDEAS FOR NEGOTIATORS (ALI-ABA 2008) (a readable collection of strategies in a slim volume). An excellent, in-depth exploration may be found in ANDREA KUPFER SCHNEIDER & CHRISTOPHER HONEYMAN, EDS., NEGOTIATOR'S FIELDBOOK (2006). Although these works are addressed to negotiators, mediators will nonetheless find much of value in them.

the current phase, or is there more work to do before you can move on? Are the parties emotionally or analytically stuck? By late afternoon, you're suffering from decision fatigue. "No matter how rational and high-minded you try to be, you can't make decision after decision without paying a biological price. It's different from ordinary physical fatigue—you're not consciously aware of being tired—but you're low on mental energy. The more choices you make through-out the day, the harder each one becomes for your brain."[40] Eating something healthy during a break can alleviate decision fatigue.

If you are taking a break and eating something, why not encourage the par-ticipants to do the same? Negotiating is mentally and emotionally exhausting. And "[o]nce you're mentally depleted, you become reluctant to make trade-offs, which involve a particularly advanced and taxing form of decision making."[41] Moreover, when people are hungry, their focus tends to shrink to only their own immediate needs while their sense of entitlement tends to increase.[42] The rem-edy need not be something elaborate since researchers have found that "people snacking on peanuts and soft drinks expressed more agreement with controver-sial issues than those who were not given such refreshments."[43] And after eating something, research participants demonstrate restored decision-making skills and willpower. Tierney notes, "[t]he restored willpower improved people's self-control as well as the quality of their decisions: they resisted irrational bias when making choices, and when asked to make financial decisions, they were more likely to choose the better long-term strategy instead of going for a quick payoff."[44]

After everyone takes a break and has something to eat, you may discover that the mediation process magically resumes a productive tenor and that you feel like you are able to resume your role in helping the parties reach their goals.

5. Keep in Mind What Ultimately Makes a Mediation Successful

Phase 4 demands much of mediators. They must prepare parties to negotiate, facilitate rounds of offers and counteroffers, and maintain optimism and exert effort long after the parties despair of reaching agreement. A good mediator perseveres. A persevering mediator increases the likelihood that the parties will achieve a successful outcome. Parties need and want a successful outcome. But what makes a mediation successful?

---

40. John Tierney, *Do You Suffer from Decision Fatigue?*, N.Y. TIMES MAG. (Aug. 21, 2011), http://www.nytimes.com/2011/08/21/magazine/do-you-suffer-from-decision-fatigue .html.

41. *Id.*

42. Emily M. Zitek & Alexander Jordan, *I Need Food and I Deserve a Raise: People Feel More Entitled When Hungry*, paper presented at the annual meeting of the Academy of Management, Philadelphia, PA (Aug. 2014), http://digitalcommons.ilr.cornell.edu/ conference/34/.

43. Shestowsky, *supra* note 29, at 367.

44. Tierney, *supra* note 39.

Success means achieving the best possible outcome. Some mediators believe the best possible outcome is a settlement agreement—no matter how reluctantly entered into. This is mediating for the sake of the deal, a goal that is undermining of the parties' right to self-determination. A party has a right to refuse an excellent offer and a right to make an offer that is irrationally generous. As mediators, we may provide analytic input where it is welcome and appropriate. But we may not dictate the terms of the parties' settlement.

Usually, a settlement agreement is the best possible outcome of an appellate mediation because a judgment can usually be improved upon for all parties in a settlement agreement. However, the converse is also true. If the mutually acceptable terms are not better for a party than the judgment and the prospects on appeal, a party should rationally reject a proposed agreement. Ultimately, mediators should help the parties to get the result they deem to be the best possible for them, whatever it may be.

C.   Phase 5, Concluding the Mediation

1. *If the Parties Settle at the Mediation, Help Them Conclude with Care*

Encourage parties to complete *all* necessary steps to record their agreement. After a long day of mediation, one party makes yet another counteroffer. Surprise—the other party accepts! It is the magical moment of agreement. Parties are relieved and emotionally, intellectually, and physically exhausted. (You might be, too.) They want to leave, concluding, "We have a deal—that's good enough for now. We can finish up later." But just because the parties have agreed to a dollar amount it does not necessarily follow that they have reached an agreement. If they have not resolved other issues in dispute—such as confidentiality of the settlement, timing of payment(s), tax characterization, and how the terms can be enforced in court—then there is no settlement. Negotiated settlement agreements are interpreted under contract law.[45] And basic contract law requires a meeting of the minds on all essential terms for a valid agreement.

A rush to the door, before the parties expressly agree on and memorialize all terms of the agreement, invites buyer's remorse, second thoughts, additional proposals for new or different terms, and endless procrastination. It is challenging, but rewarding, to help parties overcome the momentum to adjourn. By encouraging them to consider whether they have negotiated all issues and

---

45. Even if the parties mediate as part of federal appellate litigation, "state contract law governs whether they reached an enforceable agreement settling the federal and state law claims alleged" by the plaintiff. Wilcox v. Arpaio, 753 F.3d 872, 876 (9th Cir. 2014). But there remains an unsettled question of whether there is a federal mediation confidentiality privilege on which state law does not bear. *See* Facebook, Inc. v. Pac. Nw. Software, Inc., 640 F.3d 1034, 1041, 1038 (9th Cir. 2011). Nonetheless, parties participating in private mediation of a pending federal civil appeal can contractually agree to mediation confidentiality that federal courts will enforce. *Id.* at 1036.

urging them to memorialize them, you save them much pain (and expense) later.

Ideally, parties record their agreement in writing before the mediation session concludes. Unless the parties agree otherwise *in writing*, the terms of a valid agreement are probably inadmissible and thus unenforceable under mediation confidentiality rules.[46] Moreover, only a written agreement can satisfy the statute of frauds if a negotiated settlement agreement affects ownership of real property.

A written settlement agreement does not need to be fancy, long, or imbued with legalese to resolve a case. There is no need for perfectly formatted, spell-checked, laser-printed agreements. A pen and pad of paper suffice. A handwritten mediated agreement on only 1-and-1/3 sheets of paper was upheld as sufficient to require the transfer of $20 million and more than 120 million Facebook shares to Tyler and Cameron Winklevoss.[47]

Although some mediators are comfortable playing the role of scrivener by writing down the terms of the agreement, you should remember that the parties themselves must agree to all the terms. And while experienced appellate mediators often have an excellent understanding of terms commonly found in agreements to settle appeals, there is a fine line between making parties aware of issues that might be addressed and practicing law by advising them about the inclusion and structuring of particular settlement terms. Ultimate responsibility for crafting a durable and enforceable settlement agreements lies with the parties and their attorneys. Nonetheless, we will briefly review a few considerations unique to settlement agreements reached while cases are on appeal:[48]

- **Someone (probably the appellant) has the duty to request dismissal of the appeal after agreement has been reached.** Usually the appellant has a deadline under the rules of court to inform the appellate court of any settlement agreement.[49] If the appellate record has not

---

46. *E.g.*, Reese v. Tingey Const., 177 P.3d 605, 610 (Utah 2008) (collecting authority for the prevailing view that a mediated settlement agreement must be written to be enforceable by a court). Oregon appears to be the exception to the rule. *See* Kaiser Found. Health Plan of the Nw. v. Doe, 136 Or. App. 566, 903 P.2d 375, 378 (Ct. App. 1995).

47. *Facebook*, 640 F.3d at 1036; Miguel Helft, *Court Upholds Facebook Settlement with Twins*, N.Y. Times, April 11, 2011, http://www.nytimes.com/2011/04/12/technology/12facebook.html?_r=0.

48. Note that we can make only general observations, any of which may be superseded by the law or local rules of the appellate court in which the appeal is pending. And although we do not comprehensively discuss the possible terms that parties may need to explore in reducing their agreement to writing, we provide a sample settlement agreement in the appendix to stimulate thought about what terms might be appropriate or essential for a settlement agreement.

49. *E.g.*, U.S. Ct. App. Fed. Cir. Appellate Mediation Program Guideline 10; Ala. R. App. P. R. 42; Ark. Voluntary App. Mediation Pilot Program R. 7(a). For a cautionary tale, see *Huschke v. Slater*, 168 Cal. App. 4th 1153, 1159–60, 86 Cal. Rptr. 3d 187 (Ct. App.

yet been completed, the appellant may also need to give notice to the court reporter and trial court clerk. Upon being informed of the settlement agreement, the appellate court will *likely* dismiss the appeal.[50] Dismissal of the appeal is *not* the end of the case! Dismissal by the appellate court simply revests jurisdiction in the trial court, which then becomes empowered to hear motions for attorney fees and costs and sometimes to oversee enforcement of the terms of the contract.

- **Enforcement of the settlement agreement is in the *trial court*, not the appellate court.** With fair regularity, parties to an appeal are reluctant to have the appellate court dismiss an appeal before terms of the contract are fulfilled. This reluctance rests on the mistaken assumption that they can enlist the appellate court to help enforce the agreement. Because appellate courts do not make factual findings they do not decide whether parties have fulfilled or breached agreements. Consequently, enforcement actions are properly brought in the trial court (whether by motion or by new lawsuit). And until the appeal is dismissed, the trial court lacks jurisdiction over the case on appeal.[51]

- **There may be special summary enforcement procedures for a mediated settlement agreement.** In contrast to "regular" contracts, numerous jurisdictions provide special summary procedures for quick and efficient enforcement of a mediated settlement agreement. For example, some courts enforce mediated agreements by exercising contempt powers, through entry of judgment on the agreement, or upon motion to compel compliance.[52] However, these special enforcement mechanisms are often highly technical and easily flubbed.[53]

2008) (sanctioning an attorney $6,000 for failure to inform the appellate court of a settlement before the court decided a "pointless appeal").

50. Note that some appellate courts require the appeal to be dismissed *in the trial court. See, e.g.,* CAL. R. 8.244(a)(4). This sort of unusual rule underscores the need to prepare for appellate mediation by reviewing the local rules of court.

51. *See generally* Lyons v. Booker, 370 Utah Adv. Rep. 23, 982 P.2d 1142, 143–44 (Ct. App. 1999) (providing an excellent overview of enforcement of settlements reached on appeal).

52. *E.g.,* Howard v. Louisiana Citizens Property Ins. Corp., 65 So. 3d 697, 700 (La. Ct. App. 2011) (summary proceeding "conducted with rapidity" for mediated agreements).

53. *E.g.,* Wetherby v. Wetherby, 854 N.Y.S.2d 813, 50 A.D.3d 1226 (Ct. App. 2008) (holding a mediated agreement unenforceable for failure to comply with technical requirements of N.Y. DOM. REL. § 236(B)(3)); Haghighi v. Russian-American Broadcasting Co., 945 F. Supp. 1233, 1234–35 (D. Minn. 1996) (mediated settlement held defective for failure to include a statement that the agreement is binding as required by MINN. STAT. § 572.35); Lockwood v. Texas Dept. of Family and Protective Services, 2012 WL 2383781 (Tex. App. Austin 2012) (holding a mediated agreement defective for failure to comply with technical requirements of TEX. FAM. CODE ANN. § 153.0071(d), including the inclusion of particular language in bold type").

- **The appellate court does not want a copy of the settlement agreement.** When moving to dismiss an appeal following settlement, parties sometimes erroneously think they need to include a copy of the settlement agreement with the motion. Because enforcement of the agreement is not made in the first instance in the appellate court, there is no need to attach a copy of the settlement agreement to a motion to dismiss the appeal (unless specifically required by a local rule of court or statute). Thus, a confidential settlement agreement need not be disclosed in a motion to dismiss the appeal.

- **If the parties need to enforce the settlement agreement shortly after executing it, they should include a provision requiring that the motion to dismiss the appeal include a stipulation for immediate remand of the case to the trial court.** Appellate courts have various names—such as "mandate," "remand," or "remittitur"—for the document by which the appellate court transfers jurisdiction over the case back to the trial court.[54] Until the appellate court remands the case to the trial court, the trial court lacks jurisdiction over the case, including, for example, to oversee any terms of the settlement agreement. Stipulation to immediate issuance of the remittitur may allow the trial court to enforce the agreement more quickly. Without such a stipulation, it might take weeks (or even months) for the appellate court to send the case back.

- **A durable settlement agreement should account for the possibility that the appellate court may decide the case and issue an opinion, even if the court was notified of the settlement before it decided the case.** Appellate courts have inherent authority to decide appeals, based on importance to the public and other equitable considerations, even if the parties themselves have resolved the dispute.[55] Especially if settlement occurs late in the appellate process—such as immediately before or after oral argument—the appellate court may decline to dismiss the appeal. Unless the parties have accounted for this possibility, issuance of a written decision may undermine the settlement. Therefore, settlement agreements at the appellate stage need to include language that keeps the agreement intact, even if the appellate court issues a decision in the case.

---

54. *E.g.*, Fed. R. App. P. 41(e) (general rule that issuance of mandate occurs within 30 days after issuance of decision); United States v. Rivera, 844 F.2d 916, 920 (2d Cir. 1988) (explaining that the issuance of mandate is a clerical task); Cal. Code Civ. Proc. § 43 (providing the case "shall be remitted to the court from which the appeal was taken"); Ohio R. App. Pro. R. 12(d) (providing that in the case of error, "the cause shall be remanded to the trial court for further proceedings").

55. Fireman's Fund Ins. Companies v. Quackenbush, 52 Cal. App. 4th 599, 609, 60 Cal. Rptr. 2d 732 (Ct. App. 1997).

- **If a settlement agreement will take time to fulfill, parties may want the trial court to retain jurisdiction for enforcement purposes, even if the agreement will result in the dismissal of the appeal *in the appellate court*.**[56] In some cases, parties agree to conditions that will be fulfilled over time, such as agreements to prepare property for sale or to pay money over time. If these conditions will not be met before the trial court dismisses the case and divests itself of jurisdiction, the parties will not be able to avail themselves of the court's enforcement assistance.[57]

  Although the trial court's dismissal does not affect the settlement agreement's validity, if the trial court has dismissed the case, it becomes more complicated to enforce the agreement should the need to do so arise.[58] If the trial court dismisses the case prior to fulfillment of all settlement terms because the parties failed to request that the court retain jurisdiction to enforce the agreement, the party seeking to enforce the agreement in court must initiate a new lawsuit for breach of contract.[59] However, if the settlement agreement provides that the trial court retain jurisdiction over the original case while its terms are being fulfilled, the trial court will likely retain the ability to enforce the settlement agreement expediently.[60] Thus, when an agreement provides for structured payments, it is prudent for parties to stipulate that the trial court shall retain jurisdiction until after the final payment has been made.[61]

---

56. Mediation participants unfamiliar with the appellate process sometimes do not realize that after the appellant requests dismissal of an appeal in the appellate court, jurisdiction over the case returns to the trial court. In the normal course, the trial court then dismisses the case, divesting itself of jurisdiction over the dispute and ending the legal life of the case conclusively.

57. Fred O. Goldberg, *Enforcement of Settlements: A Jurisdictional Perspective*, 85 FLA. BAR J. 30 (2011).

58. *See, e.g.,* Anago Franchising, Inc. v. Shaz, LLC, 677 F.3d 1272 (11th Cir. 2012); Crawford Logging, Inc. v. Estate of Irving, 41 So. 3d 687 (Miss. 2010); Estate of Barber v. Guilford County Sheriff's Dept., 161 N.C. App. 658, 589 S.E.2d 433 (Ct. App. 2003). Note that in the federal courts a party might be able to reopen the judgment under FED. R. CIV. P. 60. Trade Arbed, Inc. v. African Exp. MV, 941 F. Supp. 68, 70 (E.D. La. 1996) (breach of settlement agreements warranted reopening under FED. R. CIV. P. 60); *but see* Neuberg v. Michael Reese Hosp. and Medical Center, 166 F.R.D. 398 (N.D. Ill. 1996) (declining to reopen).

59. Nicholson v. Barab, 233 Cal. App. 3d 1671, 1681, 285 Cal. Rptr. 441 (Ct. App. 1991).

60. *See* Paulucci v. General Dynamics Corporation, 842 So. 2d 797, 803 (Fla. 2003) (holding that when a trial court "approves a settlement agreement by order and retains jurisdiction to enforce its terms, the court has the jurisdiction to enforce the terms of the settlement agreement *even if the terms are outside the scope of the remedy sought in the original pleadings*") (italics added). In other words, the trial court retains jurisdiction to enforce terms of a settlement agreement reached during an appellate mediation that the appellate court would have been unable to order as part of the disposition on appeal. Encourage parties to be creative in their settlement agreements!

61. In *Interinsurance Exch. v. Faura*, 44 Cal. App. 4th 839, 52 Cal. Rptr. 2d 199 (Ct. App. 1996), the parties agreed that the case would not be dismissed for seven years while payments were being made under a settlement agreement.

- **When parties negotiate for a stipulated reversal of the judgment, they need to understand the procedures for securing them and the potential consequences of conditioning settlement on them.** Some defendants, for personal or business reasons, are troubled by the existence of a judgment against them, even if the judgment is no longer enforceable due to the settlement. In these circumstances, parties can agree to ask the appellate court to vacate the trial court judgment in a procedure known as stipulated reversal. If granted, the judgment "disappears" and the defendant can honestly represent that there are no judgments against him or her.

  Because the appellate court, not the parties, has the power to vacate a judgment, the customary procedure for requesting the court to do so is the filing of a formal request. Thus, negotiations in which parties bargain for this relief will include a term requiring the parties to so stipulate.[62]

  Procedures for vacating judgments vary by jurisdiction. So, too, do the proclivities of courts to grant such requests. Although it is not your job as mediator to advise the parties as to whether the trial court will in fact reverse a particular judgment, parties need to understand that the granting of such a request is by no means a sure thing. You can facilitate this discussion, including whether to condition the settlement on the *submission of a joint request for reversal* or *the granting of the request*. While submission of the request is within the parties' control, the granting of the motion is not, and a settlement conditioned on granting the request will fall apart if the court denies the parties' request. If the parties want their settlement to resolve the dispute once and for all, the only way to achieve that goal is to require the plaintiff to stipulate to reverse the judgment, with the burden to prepare and file the motion resting with the defendant.

  Finally, some jurisdictions and/or appellate courts, or even panels within courts, are loath to permit litigants to buy off a judgment as part of a monetary agreement. California Code of Civil Procedure section 128(a)(8), for example, places the burden on the settling parties to convince the appellate court that a stipulated reversal would not adversely affect nonparties or the public and that the reasons for a stipulated reversal outweigh the potential to erode the public trust if the court vacates the judgment at the parties' request.[63] Because this burden is extremely difficult to meet, the parties need to consider the likely consequence that they will not succeed and the settlement will fall apart if conditioned upon reversal. You can help them consider this possibility and make sure they are prepared to live with this consequence.

---

62. This area of law is arcane and a bit baffling, and reported decisions are rare. Its exotic and abstruse nature therefore makes it a natural magnet for the attention of appellate practitioners. Buy Brendon a beer, and he'll be happy to talk about stipulated reversals of judgments for as long as you like, probably longer.

63. *See, e.g.*, Hardisty v. Hinton & Alfert, 124 Cal. App. 4th 999, 1007, 21 Cal. Rptr. 3d 835 (Ct. App. 2004).

- **If the settlement agreement also resolves collateral litigation, the parties need to take appropriate steps.** Appellate mediations sometimes achieve a global settlement of other cases in addition to the one pending on appeal. If so, the parties must clearly identify the related cases to be settled and ensure that participants in the appellate mediation have sufficient authority to consent to dismissal of the collateral litigation. And they need to follow the appropriate procedures to dismiss any pending collateral litigation.

- **If parties postpone preparation of a final, formal agreement until after the mediation, follow up to check on the status of the agreement and offer your help.** If the mediation session concludes with the parties' signing only a memorandum of understanding or basic term sheet, be sure to follow up to ensure that a formal settlement agreement gets signed by all parties. Although the attorneys for the parties have the duty to complete the agreements, in practice you will find that counsel often benefit from reminders and gentle nudges to finish up a case from which they may have mentally moved on.

- **Court-connected appellate mediations often require the mediator to inform the appellate court when the mediation has concluded and whether the case has settled.** Although mediation confidentiality almost certainly prevents you from disclosing terms of the negotiations or settlement, the local rules of court may require you to inform the appellate court when the mediation has concluded—whether or not the parties have achieved a settlement.[64] This requirement presents a tricky question of timing. When have the parties settled? Is it when they have concluded the mediation session with a term sheet representing agreement in principle that will later be reduced to a typewritten document? Conversely, when has a mediation failed to resolve the case? As we discuss next, many appellate mediations ultimately result in settlement agreements weeks (or sometimes months) after the in-person session has concluded. Mediators should consult the mediation statutes and local rules of court to determine when a mediation is ended.

If the parties agreed to pay for your services, you can follow up on billing for your time. And you may want to elicit feedback and constructive criticism about your role in the mediation session. Satisfied attorneys are likely to be your best source of repeat customers for your appellate mediation services. And dissatisfied attorneys are your best source of information about how you can become a more effective mediator.

---

64. *E.g.*, U.S. Ct. App. Fed. Cir. Appellate Mediation Program Guideline 10; Arkansas Voluntary App. Mediation Pilot Program R. 6(a).

2. *If the Parties Do Not Reach Agreement, Continue to Assist Them after the Mediation Session Ends*

An interesting phenomenon emerges from data of a court-connected mediation program appellate court: a third of appeals settle on the day of the mediation session, a third of mediated appeals just do not settle, and a third settle about four-to-six weeks after the mediation session.[65] Some appellate mediators believe their efforts are limited to the in-person mediation session. Consequently, their settlement rates are much lower than that of their more tenacious colleagues who continue to schedule additional mediation sessions, follow up with repeat telephone calls, and send e-mails that keep the negotiations alive.

Do not give up until the parties tell you to stop! You may be able to double the rate of settlement if you just do not give up after an "unsuccessful session."[66] Equally important, the parties do not want you to give up. In an American Bar Association survey of sophisticated consumers of mediation services, 93 percent "thought that if a mediation session ends without agreement but has some potential to reach one, then the mediator should follow-up with each side."[67] Indeed, "participants criticized mediators who did not do so."[68] Moreover, 82 percent of frequent consumers of mediation services believe "'exerting some pressure' was an important trait, very important or essential for a mediator to be effective."[69] In other words, mediation participants do not just want you to follow up "to see how things are going." They want you to follow up with vigor, to inspire them to keep going, to nudge them toward a solution. They want you to continue to employ the attitude and tools you bring to the process as a mediator—and, of course, the rapport, analytic input, and empathetic listening you brought to the mediation session. So, continue to use them. In addition, consider the following:

- **Conduct a second (or third) mediation session.** Although most cases can resolve through follow-up telephone discussions, occasionally a dispute requires the parties to return to mediation because there is so much distance to travel to reach an agreement, because the parties need time to digest new information gained in mediation, or because in addition to concluding the money negotiation the parties have issues to work out in their relationship. Also, in general, an initial mediation session can be a pressure cooker of emotions, analysis, and negotiations that leave participants well done (if not burned). When participants are done for the day, they are just done. But "[o]nce

---

65. 2013–14 Cal. Ct. App. 3d Dist. (data on file with Brendon).
66. *Id.*
67. ABA MEDIATION QUALITY, *supra* note 12, at 17.
68. *Id.*
69. *Id.*

litigants have expressed their feelings and had time to cool down—which often requires more than a single day—they may be more willing to consider new perspectives."[70] In our experience, when mediators encourage returning for another day of in-person mediation—and the parties agree—the odds of a settlement greatly improve.

- **Facilitate further negotiations by telephone or e-mail.** Some negotiators thrive in the pressure-cooker environment of an in-person mediation session, while others feel defeated. The personalities, emotions, and outbursts can prevent a cool, analytic focus on terms of a settlement that might seal the deal. If so, subsequent negotiations by telephone or e-mail can help analytic negotiators reach agreement. As Professor Donna Shestowsky has noted, "When we communicate via technology, we generally attend less to the other person and more to the message they are disseminating. . . . Thus, communicating via technology can lead negotiators to focus more on the content and quality of your arguments, rather than being distracted and consequently (mis)led into agreement by more peripheral factors like those made more salient in face-to-face interactions."[71]

  Because content-rich, logic-based arguments generally communicate better over the telephone than in person, telephone conference calls or individual calls placed by the mediator may be seen, if not as saving an unsuccessful mediation session, then as the natural progression of a process from one form of communication to another in order to ensure that all of the attorneys and the parties ultimately grasp important information.[72]

- **Follow up at critical points in the appellate process.** Isn't it amazing how many mediation sessions result in a settlement around the magical time of 5 p.m.? Similarly, many appeals seem to settle upon the occurrence of magical moments in the appellate process: the filing of the appellate record, when appellant's counsel begins to write the opening brief, at the completion of appellate briefing, or right before oral argument. Previously stalled negotiations suddenly restart and quickly progress. Mediators who follow up at these crucial points may be startled to find that previously recalcitrant parties suddenly negotiate with fervor. With the advent of electronic dockets, almost all appellate courts make it easy for you to follow the progress of an appeal. Indeed, some courts will even e-mail you notifications when key events occur, such as the filling of a brief or setting of a date for oral argument. Stay abreast of the developments in the appeal and follow up at opportune moments.

---

70. Golann, *supra* note 3, at 25.
71. Shestowsky, *supra* note 29, at 365.
72. *Id.*

But don't beat a dead horse. There is a subtle art in distinguishing between coaxing reluctant parties and beating a dead horse. Again, we remind you that the point of the exercise is not to create a deal for the sake of a deal, to increase your settlement statistics, or to clear the appellate court's docket. Instead, the mediation should empower the parties to settle the case on better terms than they can expect by continuing with an uncertain and expensive appellate process.

Good questions for Phase 5 if a dispute does not fully resolve at the mediation. Once the parties decide to conclude the mediation session short of agreement, it is first important to determine as best you can what the obstacle to settlement is and address it if possible at the mediation, or make plans to do so later. The conversation that happens between when the parties give up and when they actually leave can contribute positively to the potential for settlement following mediation. Here is how you might structure the discussion in a final joint session: *Although you have not reached an agreement today, I hope you leave with the satisfaction of knowing you worked very hard to educate yourselves about the legal arguments and the parties' perspectives on the situation that led to litigation. You also explored the parties' interests and generated a number of ideas about how to resolve the dispute creatively with nonmonetary solutions. You also went as far as you could today in negotiating the financial component of the dispute. Most of the time when cases do not resolve in the mediation, they resolve shortly thereafter, either in a second mediation or as a result of continued negotiations with or without the help of the mediator. Before you leave, I would like us to think together about how to enhance the possibility that this case, like most, will resolve before long. Does that sound like a good idea?*

Once you have agreement to talk about future settlement efforts, we suggest you begin with a broad question to elicit ideas about next steps. Here are some examples: *What are your ideas about how to move the negotiations forward? What do you need to do to be in a position to settle your dispute soon hereafter? What is the next point in time when it makes sense to revisit settlement?*

Assuming the discussion that follows does not lead to a plan, there are a number of directions you could take. You could explore the possibility of another mediation session, by which time you remove the barriers to settlement you encountered in the first session: *Would it make sense to reconvene when the vice-president of operations can join us?* Or you could explore partial settlement: *Is it possible to resolve injunctive relief and damages and design another decision-making process for attorney fees?*

We recommend you clarify your role and your billing practices going forward: *It is my practice to follow up with counsel in cases that do not resolve at the mediation Is that appropriate in this case? Would it be helpful if I call you in the next few days about picking up where we are leaving off? Or I will give the case some thought and get back to you with ideas about how to move the settlement forward? Does that make sense? And would you please call me if you have ideas or would like my help? Our agreement provides that follow up is compensated. Is that still agreeable?*

It is also important to suggest actions the parties and lawyers can take next to move toward settlement. For example, they might reevaluate their negotiation stances based on the information learned during the mediation session, take a closer look at their underlying interests, investigate potential nonmonetary terms, consider other potential participants, and secure additional settlement authority. You might ask the following: *What might your next step be to make further progress toward resolution? Have we missed any opportunities or lacked any resources today? What might they be?*

As we said, most cases that do not settle during the first mediation session do eventually settle. If you take the time at the end of the day to consider the options for postmediation settlement, the case will be more likely to resolve than it will when leaving mediation without any understanding of future efforts. This final reconnoitering also provides a respectful closure to a difficult and, perhaps, discouraging day.

Chapter 16
Grow Your Professional Appellate Mediation Practice

A. Introduction

Appellate mediation is challenging and rewarding. Perhaps more than most types of mediation, appellate mediation demands a high level of legal literacy and analytical ability. Yet even amidst complex legal argument, appellate mediation participants need empathy, help with communicating effectively, and coaching on how to move toward a solution that has eluded them. The ideal appellate mediator represents the best of both worlds: he or she is emotionally intelligent and knowledgeable about appeals. Even if you have taken several mediation training courses, we still highly recommend appellate mediation-specific training. We are also strong believers in continuing educational and learning opportunities for appellate mediators at all levels of experience in order to avoid the ruts and staleness that come from rote repetition. Indeed, a conscious examination of your habits and experiences in your appellate mediations is vital for personal and professional growth. Thus we outline a few thoughts on developing a reflective professional practice. Then we briefly address some of the practical considerations in developing and expanding your professional appellate mediation services in the community.

B. Cultivate Appellate Mediation Skills through Learning Opportunities and Reflective Practice

1. Seek Training and Ongoing Learning Opportunities

Mediation training opportunities abound as the alternative dispute resolution field expands. Many general mediation classes, whether multiday or just a luncheon, address skills that translate well for appellate mediations. Workshops on listening, dealing with strong emotions, strategies for moving beyond impasse, and ethical obligations for mediators are all relevant to appellate mediation.

General mediation courses do not eliminate the need for training specific to appellate mediation, however. As previous chapters demonstrate, many unique aspects of mediating a case that has gone through judgment in the trial court and is currently pending review in a new court call for specialized training in appellate mediation. Because appellate mediation is a somewhat esoteric area of practice, specialized training may be difficult to find. The best source of this training is court-connected appellate mediation programs, which generally

273

provide their panelists with basic training in the fundamentals of appellate mediation and, in some courts, continuing education activities.

You can also create your own appellate mediation training opportunities. Some mediation trainers and experienced appellate mediators allow less experienced mediators to observe their mediations, with the opportunity to interact with the mediator during or after the session to discuss the mediator's approach or to debrief the session. When working with an experienced mediator, we suggest you begin with a clear, express agreement about how you will participate. Some mediators prefer no interaction, and others are open to nearly equal participation. Any approach can be valuable, but to create a positive environment for both mediators and the parties, it is important to be explicit about your expectations and in agreement about the relationship and responsibilities before entering the mediation.

Some mediators are also open to co-mediation, where a less experienced mediator works with a more experienced mediator to plan and facilitate the mediation, particularly if the case comes to the less experienced mediator who seeks to turn it into a learning opportunity rather than mediating the case alone. A co-mediation team consisting of an appellate specialist and an experienced mediator is especially effective. Many mediators would embrace the opportunity to team up with colleagues who compliment their skills. In fact, our association began ten years ago as such a team. Again, prior to the mediation, the mediators should discuss and decide about their respective roles and responsibilities during the mediation as well as how they will allocate any mediator fees.

Peer supervision groups, sometimes known as practice groups or reflective practice groups, are also excellent learning vehicles for appellate mediators. These groups combine beginning and experienced mediators to reflect on their mediations and gain insight from one another. The most effective practice groups have a leader with extensive experience as both a mediator and a mediation trainer. These groups enable the participants to deepen their understanding of the process, of themselves, and of significant appellate mediation issues. They also help mediators develop the habit of continuing education and reflection. And they allow mediators to be part of a learning community.

2. Create a Learning Community

Among the most satisfying and successful trainings Dana conducts are for those court-connected mediation programs in which the panelists coalesce as a learning community—that is, a group of people who engage fully in their own learning and encourage learning in their fellow participants. Creating a learning community for the highly accomplished people who tend to gravitate to appellate mediation requires more than simply putting a bunch of appellate mediators into the same room. Instead, a learning environment must be intentionally and expressly developed.

Professor Chris Argyris, in an article entitled "Teaching Smart People How to Learn,"[1] asserts that the brightest and most successful professionals are often poor learners. He explains that when these professionals, who are used to experiencing success and competence, fail or underperform in trying out a new skill, they often become defensive. They tend to blame someone or something outside themselves for the problem rather than looking inwardly and engaging in critique of their own behavior. They may ascribe to the prevalent belief that motivation is the key to learning, and they confuse learning with problem solving.

Genuine learning, as Professor Argyris points out, requires more than the recognition of a mistake or problem and identification of a remedy. Genuine learning occurs when we examine our *own* contribution to the situation and explore ways to change *ourselves* to address the problem. "Failure" thus constitutes an opportunity to reflect on our assumptions and inferences, thereby enabling us to learn by moving past what we already know. By *intentionally and expressly* making room for mistakes and creating a safe place to explore, a learning community of colleagues and friends focused on appellate mediation makes it possible to engage in genuine learning. Without this intentional structuring, the retired judges, appellate specialists, and experienced mediators who gravitate toward appellate mediation will simply remain within their zones of comfort. This comfort zone feels safe and may be framed by awards, accolades, and admiration, but it tends to be dusty with the old and familiar. Make room for something new and fresh by intentionally creating a space where failure is seen as essential—and an opportunity for reflection and learning.

In such groups, you can also reignite the joy of discovery and creativity described by German professor and neurobiologist Gerald Hüther. Professor Hüther suggests we can realize our highest creative potential by "merging the individual capabilities, insights, talents and ideas that [we] have acquired in [our] own world with those of others."[2] In addition to the commonality of such groups, Professor Hüther also stresses the importance of diversity. He emphasizes that interactions of this quality depend on our ability to strengthen what binds us "beyond . . . different origins, . . . different educations and . . . individual, cultural specific types."[3] And to strengthen these bonds, we must overcome the fear that has kept us apart: "The decisive precondition for the development of our creative potential is overcoming individual fear by strengthening mutual trust."[4] We can strengthen mutual trust by developing learning communities of appellate mediators dedicated to professional development through practice groups and discussion groups (in person and by teleconference) that contain

1. Chris Argyris, *Teaching Smart People How to Learn*, 69 HARVARD BUS. REV. 99 (1991).
2. GERALD HÜTHER, DIE NEUROBIOLOGISCHEN VORAUSSETZUNGEN FÜR DIE ENTFALTUNG VON NEUGIER UND KREATIVITÄT 123 (2008) (includes parallel English translation), *available at* http://www.gerald-huether.de/pdf/neurobiological_preconditions.pdf.
3. *Id.*
4. *Id.*

both the safety and the challenge that we need to harness the creative power of collective endeavor and the opportunities to learn from our mistakes as well as our successes.

The importance of safety in learning groups cannot be overstated. When Dana teaches appellate mediation, she often begins with an exercise in which participants develop guidelines for learning—agreements to create a learning community. Although these principles vary somewhat, they generally include the following guidelines:

- Keep confidences.

- Be present.

- Be curious.

- Be willing to learn something new—to be caught learning, to make mistakes, and to support others to do the same.

These guidelines encourage mutual trust and, in turn, genuine learning.

3. *Engage in Reflective Practice*

Equally important to initial and ongoing training for developing as appellate mediators and being part of a learning community is the *individual* commitment to using mediation experiences as learning opportunities. When you develop a practice of reflecting on your mediations, both the external aspects of what happened and the internal aspects of your own experience, you learn about yourself *and* about appellate mediation. We often encourage the *parties* to "listen to themselves," to become aware of previously hidden assumptions, and to move beyond being stuck in familiar patterns of thinking. If we are to encourage others to become self-reflective, we should first ask the same of *ourselves*.[5]

Reflective practice allows you to be your own teacher. When you develop a student-teacher or mentor-mentee relationship with a great teacher, you experience learning at its most powerful. The teacher recognizes your developmental level and helps you gain knowledge, experience, or insight into your personal qualities and thereby promotes the next level of your learning. Reflective practice gives you the opportunity to develop this intimate student-teacher relationship within yourself.

---

5. For an inspiring and practical guide to developing your ability to explore your inner experience of conflict and reflect on its impact on the mediation process, we recommend GARY J. FRIEDMAN, INSIDE OUT: HOW CONFLICT PROFESSIONALS CAN USE SELF-REFLECTION TO HELP THEIR CLIENTS (ABA Dispute Resolution Program and Harvard Law School Program on Negotiation, 2014).

We have space to touch only briefly on a few approaches to reflective practice. Play around with them. Feel free to adopt them if they work or to customize them—or to disregard them in favor of another approach. The most effective reflective practice is the one you develop for yourself.

Simple journaling reflective practice. At the end of each mediation, or before you go to sleep on the day of mediation, spend 15 minutes writing about your experience. The journaling may be completely unstructured—for example, automatic writing. Or you might develop a brief outline of topics to explore routinely in your journal, such as the following:

- Moments during the mediation when you felt competent

- Moments during the mediation when you felt confused, lost, in doubt, or afraid

- Questions raised by the mediation

- A seminal issue or developmental edge that you are working on in your professional or personal life

A more elaborate reflective practice process. Over years of teaching reflective practice, Dana, with Daniel Bowling, developed a more formalized and elaborate exercise than simple journaling. You can implement this process on your own, but we have found that it works well with a partner or in a group—perhaps a reflective practice group. Because it allows for a more in-depth exploration than journaling, it is especially helpful in the most problematic of our cases—the ones we have difficulty letting go of. This process helps to identify and explore the lessons to be learned—and then to move on.

This process begins with preparation in which you find a space at your office or home where you will be undisturbed for 15 to 30 minutes. Sit quietly alone or with a colleague or group of colleagues. Close your eyes. Breathe naturally. Notice whether you are controlling your breath. Gently release. Relax as completely as possible. Sit quietly, without rushing, until you notice increased focus and an ability to be present. In your own time, do the following:

- **Recall** a mediation session. Focus attention on a recent mediation, recalling it as vividly and in as much detail as you can: the room, setting, time of day, light, participants, what you were wearing, and how you felt emotionally and physically. Allow a story of the mediation to emerge. You may want to visualize it as a film that moves across your mental screen. Notice the story's tone. Is it one of discomfort, feeling incomplete or unfinished, or containing judgments about yourself or another participant? Or do you feel satisfied and successful?

- **Observe** which specific experiences or incidents are most salient, and make a brief written note of them. If none come to mind, ask yourself, "What experiences in the session created opportunities for resolution, and what experiences inhibited it?"

- **Summarize** briefly the background of the mediation and what happened in the session in order to set the context for your learning partners (if you are working with others).

- **Elaborate on the external experience** you want to focus on: the circumstances, the parties' contribution to the difficulty, the lawyers' contribution, and your own.

- **Elaborate on your internal experience.** When were you able to focus your attention, and when did your mind wander? What was the cause of your wandering mind? When did you judge yourself or someone else? When and how did you blame and project your discomfort onto someone else rather than focusing on your internal experience? When something positive happened, what did you notice? When you were challenged, what did you notice? When you were mindful of your own inner experience, what happened?

- **Learn from your reflection.** What conclusions can you draw about the experiences that help you better understand the dynamics of the appellate mediation process? What were the conditions (external to you) that fostered resolution? What were the conditions within you that fostered resolution? Inhibited it? What were the missed opportunities to address these inhibitors prior to the mediation? What were the missed opportunities to address these inhibitors in the collaborative process? What technique or skill did you forget to employ? What knowledge or theory did you forget to apply? How did your internal experience—the quality of your "being"—inhibit or enhance your effectiveness?

- **Record your goals and an action plan** for your professional development. What is the theme of your personal/internal development? What theory do you want to understand better? What skill or technique do you want to develop? What attitudes or awareness do you want to develop? Monitor your progress in subsequent mediations by reflecting on how you have applied the lessons learned.

4. *Realize That Everyone Makes Mistakes*

Mistakes happen all of the time. Indeed, the very idea of an *appellate* court is that smart, hardworking professionals (i.e., judges) make enough mistakes that a whole institution exists to correct them.

Clearly, appellate mediation requires a mediator to embody the qualities of patience, compassion, equanimity, and empathy toward parties and the lawyers who represent them, as in any other mediation. But we often overlook the equally important role that these qualities play in our relationships with ourselves. These qualities not only allow us to hold the awesome responsibility of guiding parties through conflict but also give us the tools to accept the reality that we cannot do it perfectly.

A Personal Reflection by Dana

I still vividly recall mistakes I made in a particular appellate mediation that involved toxic family relationships in a probate matter. I remember how I had difficulty managing my internal conversation about my errors. In my internal evaluation system, I did not live up to my own expectations. I do not like making mistakes. I would like to do this work perfectly, to be at my best always, because it is such important work.

One of my greatest challenges as a mediator—and in life for that matter—is to deal with my "mistakes." With others, I typically have great reserves of compassion, equanimity, empathy, and patience to tap into; but for myself, I have had to work far harder to find such reserves.

Hold on to what is good

even if it is

a handful of earth.

—*Nancy Wood*[6]

Most people—and I include myself in this category—have much more difficulty forgiving themselves than forgiving others. If we have been mediating any significant period of time and have worked to develop ourselves as mediators, showing compassion and loving kindness toward the parties becomes second nature. Showing compassion and forgiveness to ourselves, on the other hand, takes self-awareness and vigilance.

We know from decision-making research that we are hardwired to focus on the negative. Cultural anthropologist and teacher Angeles Arrien described this propensity as "addiction to being fixated on what is not working."[7] Due to the human proclivity toward negativity, it takes more effort to focus on what is working than what is not. However, the payoff for kicking this habit, or overcoming our biological magnetism to the negative, is worth the effort.

6. NANCY WOOD, MANY WINTERS—PROSE AND POETRY OF THE PUEBLOS (Doubleday 1974).
7. ANGELES ARRIEN, THE FOUR-FOLD WAY: WALKING THE PATHS OF THE WARRIOR, TEACHER, HEALER AND VISIONARY 69 (HarperOne and Angeles Arrien 1993).

The research of John Gottman concluded that the most important predictor of a successful marriage is the ratio of positive to negative interactions.[8] To be stable, a marriage needs at least five positive feelings and interactions to each negative one. We propose the same is true in our relationship to ourselves.

Here are a few remedies for those who tend to focus on the negative about themselves:

- Think of each negative thought you have about yourself as creating a debt you must repay by thinking five positive thoughts about yourself. This idea derives from the phenomenon of negativity bias; in other words, "bad is stronger than good."

- For catastrophizers who worry that their mediation practices will dry up as a result of their mistake(s), apply a little cognitive therapy to interrupt the negative thought. It is useful to recall past experiences of thinking such thoughts and remind yourself that your business, contrary to your fears, continued on.

- If the thoughts persist, implement a forgiveness ritual or practice.[9]

As with any change we want to make in ourselves, self-compassion or self-forgiveness begins with the awareness that we lack it, followed closely by the intention to achieve it.

Excellence versus perfection. One obstacle to forgiving ourselves for our imperfections is concern that doing so may lead us to abandon our standards. In reality, when we fail to forgive ourselves or allow room for mistakes, we abandon *ourselves*, not our *standards*. If, instead, we abandon our perfectionism, we remain connected both to our standards and to ourselves.

Angeles Arrien described the difference between perfection and excellence: "Perfection does not tolerate mistakes, whereas excellence incorporates and learns from mistakes. . . . Wherever we are addicted to perfection . . . .[w]e deny our humanness and invest all our energy in maintaining a cultivated image or façade of how we want to be seen rather than exposing who we are."[10] Jungian analyst Marion Woodman has proposed that "[p]erfectionism belongs to the gods; completeness or wholeness is the most a human being can hope for."[11]

---

8. JOHN GOTTMAN, WHY MARRIAGES SUCCEED OR FAIL: AND HOW YOU CAN MAKE YOURS LAST (Simon and Schuster 1995).

9. Jack Kornfield, *The Art of Forgiveness, Lovingkindness and Peace* 48–52 (Bantam Books 2003). For example, Dr. Frederic Luskin, researcher on forgiveness at Stanford Medical School, suggests a nine-step approach to forgiveness in his best-selling book *Forgive for Good: A Proven Prescription for Health and Happiness* 175–76 (HarperCollins 2002).

10. ARRIEN, *supra* note 7, at 55.

11. MARION WOODMAN, ADDICTION TO PERFECTION: THE STILL UNRAVISHED BRIDE: A PSYCHOLOGICAL STUDY 51 (Vol. 12. Inner City Books 1982).

Thus, "[t]o move toward perfection is to move out of life, or what is worse, never to have entered it."[12]

Mistakes as opportunities. We conclude with a thought expressed by James Joyce: "A man [sic.] of genius makes no mistakes. His errors are volitional and are the portals of discovery."[13]

C.   Develop Your Professional Appellate Mediation Practice

We hope to improve the mediator's relationship to business development by demystifying it a bit. You can build an appellate mediation practice by taking a practical, systematic approach to planning and marketing your services.

Lawyers, mediators, and other professionals in private practice already have an infrastructure to support a new niche practice as well as experience with initiating and growing a business that can inform the pursuit of appellate mediation. What works in developing a mediation practice in any sector is applicable to the task of developing an appellate mediation practice. Thus, we suggest the following steps:

- Identify the source of your inspiration to develop your appellate mediation practice, perhaps to help appellants and respondents settle their protracted and painful disputes or to engage in the intellectual challenge of appellate cases.

- Articulate in writing your vision and your mission.

- Develop your appellate mediation skills.

- Create and implement a business plan.

- Increase your personal contacts in the appellate field by joining and being active in appellate law and appellate mediation groups.

- Apply to become a mediator for a court-connected appellate mediation program.

- Volunteer to present programs to educate trial and appellate attorneys about appellate mediation: that it exists, how successful it is, and how to be an effective appellate advocate in mediation.

---

12. *Id.* at 52.
13. James Joyce, Ulysses 125 (Digireads.com Publishing 2004). For further reading, we recommend Michael D. Lang & Alison Taylor, The Making of a Mediator: Developing Artistry in Practice (John Wiley & Sons 2012); Kristin Neff, Self-compassion: Stop Beating Yourself Up and Leave Insecurity Behind (HarperCollins 2011); and Alina Tugend, Better by Mistake: The Unexpected Benefits of Being Wrong (Penguin 2011).

- Create educational content and marketing materials suitable for use on the Internet that make brief explanations of appellate mediation available to the public and to colleagues. These materials can include social media posts, blog posts, articles, brochures, videos, webinars, and teleseminars.

Your **vision statement.** The first, and perhaps the most essential, step in creating a business plan is the formation of an intention for your practice, which in turn forms the basis of your vision. Los Angeles mediator and trainer Forrest (Woody) Mosten advises mediators to begin by articulating their "mediation signature"—the way they are known, or wish to be known, among their peers, referral sources, clients, and the community at large.[14] Your mediation signature encompasses your subject matter focus, the processes you follow, and the way you work with mediation participants. Discerning your mediation signature assures a meaningful beginning to the process of developing your practice because it focuses you on your unique abilities and what matters most to you in your work.

Equally important to examining and describing what is unique about *you* is formulating the vision statement for your appellate mediation *practice*. This clear, concise declaration of what you intend for your business helps you to focus your efforts and informs others about what you stand for and what you offer. It also serves as a guide, at the level of principle, in your future business-related decision making.

The exercise of articulating your vision should involve writing down what you already know and crafting it to be useful to you and your audience. We note that effective vision statements tend to be brief, clear, focused on your purpose and goals, future-oriented, consistent with your criteria for success, and challenging.[15]

Your business plan. With a rough vision statement and a clear idea of what you offer that is unique, you are ready to create a business plan. For Dana, the value of the business plan lies as much in the process as in the end result. The discipline of looking concretely at her mediation practice enabled her to ground her vision in the practical realities of operating a business and to move forward with greater confidence, having, as best she could, anticipated and planned for the challenges and opportunities that lie ahead.

- *Public relations.* Creating a strategy, being alert to and taking advantage of public relations opportunities, and creating public relations

14. FORREST S. MOSTEN, MEDIATION CAREER GUIDE: A STRATEGIC APPROACH TO BUILDING A SUCCESSFUL PRACTICE (Jossey-Bass 2001).
15. Kelly Burke, *Characteristics of a Good Vision Statement: Integrated and paraphrased from various sources including the* Academic Leadership Journal (2011), http://hilo.hawaii .edu/strategicplan/documents/SPC_07_11_vision_characteristics.pdf.

occasions pays off not only for the mediator personally but also for the profession in general. The more people know about appellate mediation, the better off all people will be. Public relations opportunities include the following:

1. Interviews or quotations in articles or books about appellate mediation, particularly in the mainstream media;
2. Publication of articles or books;
3. Social media communications;
4. Awards or recognition; and
5. Programs or trainings you have conducted.

- *Marketing plan.* Approaches to marketing and our comfort level with it vary, so what worked for us may not work for others. However, we offer what has worked for us in the hope it will, at the very least, inspire you to consider the many available options.

  Leverage existing contacts. In Dana's mediation practice, almost all of her business comes by referral from people who have worked with her previously or who know her personally or professionally as a colleague. Mediators can inform existing referral sources about their appellate mediation services. It does not matter if the areas of expertise of those sources seem far afield from appellate mediation; appellate disputes exist across all professions and subject matter areas because any kind of lawsuit can (and, unless settled, or abandoned, eventually will) be appealed! As a first step, make a list of these individuals for inclusion in e-mails. And contact them personally.

  Expand referral sources. Appellate mediation may overlap with your existing or former profession (especially if you are an appellate attorney or retired judge), but that overlap is seldom perfect. Thus, you should look for opportunities to create relationships with other professionals who might see you as a resource rather than as a competitor. An ideal marketing opportunity is one in which you create complementary referral partnerships with professionals whose clients need your services and whose services your clients need.

  Become known as an appellate mediator. The ways people became visible in their existing professional communities are also available to them in the appellate mediation professional context. Here are a few examples. Become active in professional organizations that bring mediators into contact with those who could use their services or refer others to them. Look especially to court-connected appellate mediation programs. Join local bar associations where appellate attorneys congregate. These organizations are another opportunity for reciprocal referrals. Not only will the lawyers be potential referral sources of business but also mediators will cultivate relationships that can also be resources for the parties in their mediations.

Cultivate a positive attitude toward marketing. Marketing can (and should)[16] become an enjoyable part of a professional routine because it primarily involves developing and nurturing relationships. The key to the successful marketing of professional services is identifying strategies and tasks that you are comfortable with and excited to perform.

D. Conclusion

Developing an appellate mediation practice and developing ourselves as appellate mediators are ongoing pursuits, beginning, perhaps, with reading this book and ending . . . well, never. This journey of professional development, as with our life journey, has many ups and downs, twists and turns. It will be at various times exhilarating, anxiety-producing, overwhelming, inspiring, discouraging, heartwarming, humbling, gratifying, and satisfying. If we appreciate at the outset that the journey is long and ends only when we cease to mediate, the process of our development will not seem as daunting or demanding.

If we develop professionally in the company of others who share this journey, we will ensure its richness and enjoyment. And if we also provide ourselves the opportunity for self-reflection as well as a supportive and compassionate inner experience—one in which we not only accept our imperfections but also appreciate them—we will increase the potential for a peaceful journey.

---

16. ROBERT N. KOHN & LAWRENCE KOHN, SELLING IN YOUR COMFORT ZONE: SAFE AND EFFECTIVE STRATEGIES FOR DEVELOPING NEW BUSINESS (ABA 2009).

Section V: Appendix

A. Overview

This section provides sample documents and resources to help attorneys and mediators prepare for appellate mediation. As we discuss throughout this book, effective premediation communications—whether in person, through e-mail, or by mediation statement—enhance the quality and outcome of the mediation process.

Because court rules and governing laws vary widely among the states (and sometimes even within appellate courts in the same state), it is unlikely that all of the information included in the sample documents will apply in your jurisdiction. This is true even of California, the jurisdiction of *Daven v. Douglas*, the hypothetical case we refer to in our sample documents.[1] Likewise, these documents may not contain language for disclosures or contract terms required in your jurisdiction. For these reasons, these sample documents are only *examples*, not products that are ready for use. You will need to adapt them to comply with the rules of your jurisdiction and your particular case.

B. Resources for Appellate Mediators

Although mediators develop their own styles, strengths, and areas of emphasis, all mediators need to address key preliminary issues such as confidentiality, information exchanges between the parties, and additional issues related to preparation of the mediator and parties prior to the mediation session. If you intend to charge for services, you and the parties will also need to agree on the amount, allocation, and manner of payment of fees before the mediation begins. The aids below will help you manage these important premediation tasks.

1. Sample Premediation Telephone Conference

As we discuss in Chapter 4, the premediation call is often your first communication with the lawyers in an appellate mediation. Although parties might also participate because they are self-represented or in some circumstances it has been decided they will join the call with their lawyers, the premediation call is almost always with counsel only. This step in the appellate mediation process is an efficient and effective means by which to gather important information about the dispute and to address logistics. It also gives you a jumpstart on your relationship with the attorneys and allows you to observe and assess

---

1. We introduced the hypothetical medical malpractice action of *Daven v. Douglas* in Chapter 3.

the communication dynamics between them and the quality of their working relationship, important information to help you prepare for mediation. And, as you will see from the example we provide below, the call enables you and the lawyers to collaborate on preparation and the design of the mediation process best suited to the dispute and the people involved.

Every call is unique and raises or emphasizes a unique set of premediation issues. To focus on some of the most problematic and recurrent issues that arise in premediation telephone conference calls, we provide a transcript of a hypothetical call based on the *Daven v. Douglas* case we introduced in Chapter 3. We offer this transcript because many of our mediation students have requested it, but we do so with reservations. By including it, we do not intend to give you a rigid script to follow in conducting your calls. However, we do hope you will find it useful as you develop your own approach for this essential step in preparing for mediation.

> Mediator: *Good morning, my name is Dana Curtis. As you know, the Court of Appeal has appointed me as mediator in the* Daven v. Douglas *appeal. I am grateful for this opportunity to assist you and your clients and look forward to working with you in the coming weeks as we prepare and meet in mediation.*
>
> *I believe we have on the line Takao Normish, who represents Carson Daven, and Christine Kendall, who represents Reshma Douglas. Is that right? And will anyone else be joining us for this call?*
>
> Mr. Normish: *Yes, Takao Normish here on behalf of Mr. Daven.*
>
> Ms. Kendall: *Christine Kendall for Dr. Douglas. I do not expect anyone else.*
>
> Mr. Normish: *Neither do I.*
>
> Mediator: *Have either of you participated in appellate mediation before?*
>
> Ms. Kendall: *No, this is my first time.*
>
> Mr. Normish: *This is my first case, too.*
>
> Mediator: *I take it you have seen the information I sent to you about my background and practice. If you have questions, I would be happy to answer them.*
>
> *To enable the parties to take the fullest advantage of mediation, I requested this call to address issues preliminary to the mediation. In preparation, I sent you a brief agenda. Have you had a chance to look at it? And is there anything you would like to add?*
>
> Ms. Kendall: *Yes, I read it and have no additions.*
>
> Mr. Normish: *I read it, too, and it looks fine to me.*
>
> Mediator: *First, let's address the logistics. Our mediation is currently scheduled for Wednesday, April 20, 2015. We may wish to revisit the question of timing at the end of this call, but for now, does this timing give you adequate opportunity to prepare?*

Ms. Kendall and Mr. Normish: *Yes.*

Mediator: *We are set to meet at the court's Mediation Center located at 1936 Ursula Way, Bridgeport, California. Is that acceptable?*

Ms. Kendall and Mr. Normish: *Yes.*

Mediator: *We are scheduled to begin promptly at 9:00 a.m. I find it is important for the participants to be available as long as they are making progress in the mediation. Is there any reason not to expect this of you and your client representatives?*

Mr. Normish and Ms. Kendall: *No, we will be there as long as necessary.*

Mediator: *If this status changes, please let me know. I am sure you have both had the unfortunate experience that someone unexpectedly announced toward the end of the day that she had to leave. I hope to avoid that circumstance.*

Mediator: *The court's mediation facility is ADA compliant. Even so, I want to ensure that everyone can attend and participate fully. Are there any special needs that we should address in order to ensure the comfort and full participation of those attending?*

Ms. Kendall and Mr. Normish: *No.*

Mediator: *Good. Then let's get started. As I disclosed in my letter scheduling this call, two years ago I mediated another case in which a lawyer from Mr. Normish's firm represented a party. I do not believe this previous association will interfere with my ability to remain impartial but it is essential that the parties have confidence in my ability to conduct a fair process, as well. Does this prior relationship present a problem for either of you or your clients?*

Mr. Normish and Ms. Kendall: *My client has no concerns.*

Mediator: *From the case information form the court sent to me, I gather defendant/appellant Reshma Douglas is appealing a judgment in favor of plaintiff/respondent Carson Daven for $1 million following a jury trial in the malpractice case Mr. Daven brought against Dr. Douglas. Could you please elaborate briefly about the appeal—not to argue the case but to help me understand more about the appeal? Ms. Kendall, I would like to begin with you, since you represent the appellant. Just a brief "Reader's Digest" summary will be sufficient.*

Ms. Kendall: *You are correct. Dr. Douglas believes the runaway jury verdict on malpractice was due to errors on the part of the trial judge. The judge permitted Mr. Daven's so-called medical expert to present extremely inflammatory testimony and show a bloody videotape of Mr. Daven's surgery that had no probative value but greatly prejudiced the jury against Dr. Douglas.*
And the Court of Appeal will strike the jury's award of special damages of $600,000 as a matter of law. The jury based this award on the fact that Mr. Daven did not sign the exact consent form prescribed by the recently enacted

Medical Code section 96734. In fact, Mr. Daven consulted with numerous surgeons who, along with Dr. Douglas, informed him of the risks of his surgery. And he did sign Dr. Douglas's client consent form, which was functionally equivalent to the specified form.

Mediator: *Thank you. So, the two issues Dr. Douglas will raise in her appeal are whether the trial judge erred in admitting testimony and a videotape that you asserted was prejudicial and whether as a matter of law the consent form Mr. Daven signed was sufficient to meet the requirements of section 96734. Is that right?*

Ms. Kendall: *Yes, in a nutshell.*

Mediator: *Briefly, how does Mr. Daven view this case?*

Mr. Normish: *As you can imagine, we strongly believe the judgment will stand. The trial judge had discretion to admit the medical expert's testimony and video and we believe he correctly exercised it. There is no way the Court of Appeal will conclude the judge exceeded the bounds of reason. Likewise, Dr. Douglas will lose her second argument. The statute clearly requires a specific form, not a functional equivalent. Dr. Douglas did not use the prescribed form. End of story. On a practical note, this appeal will cost Dr. Douglas a boatload of money, and even if the court is asleep and Dr. Douglas wins the appeal, all she gets is a second trial, which she will certainly lose, as she did the first.*

Mediator: *So Dr. Douglas will argue that the judge's ruling was well within his discretion. You will also assert that section 96734 required a **particular** form, and Dr. Douglas's form, which you assert was confusing, did not satisfy this requirement. Is that right?*

Mr. Normish: *Yes, essentially. We will put forth many authorities and much more nuanced arguments in our mediation statement, but for now you seem to understand the gist of it.*

Mediator: *I appreciate knowing a bit more about the legal landscape. Thank you. Now, please tell me about your clients' goals for the mediation. I assume, as with most parties, your clients' primary goal is to end the litigation—to find a solution that works better than pursuing the appeal. But are there other objectives your clients would like to achieve?*

Ms. Kendall: *Not that I am aware of.*

Mr. Normish: *My client needs to get on with his life. The surgery devastated his career and made a mess of his life, not to mention his face. He is furious at Dr. Douglas for the damage she caused and equally furious that Dr. Douglas has not taken personal responsibility for the harm she caused. Do you know she has not spoken to my client since before my client sent his first demand letter?*

Mediator: *Mr. Normish, as you speak about the emotional impact of this set of events on Mr. Daven, I wonder whether there is something that could* happen in mediation, in addition to reaching an agreement on a monetary amount, that would increase Mr. Daven's satisfaction with the settlement and perhaps the mediation process.

Mr. Normish: *Nothing comes to mind, except an apology, which I do not think will occur. And if Dr. Douglas were to apologize, it would be too little too late.*

Mediator: *Ms. Kendall, without getting into the issue of apology, is there anything that comes to mind that would increase Dr. Douglas's satisfaction with a settlement?*

Mr. Normish: *No, but I will raise the issue with Dr. Douglas before the mediation.*

Mediator: *Thank you. I suggest both of you speak further with your clients about what they would like to accomplish. As Yogi Bera said, "If you don't know where you are going, you might end up somewhere else."*

Mediator: *I'd like to turn to a new topic: your client's settlement history. Could you please tell me about that?*

Mr. Normish: *There was an early demand of $5 million to which Dr. Douglas did not respond. By the time of mediation, Mr. Daven had lowered his demand to $4 million. The mediation didn't really get off the ground. The parties stalled out at $2.5 million and $250,000. The judicial settlement conference just before trial was likewise unsuccessful. I can't remember the exact numbers. Christine, do you recall?*

Ms. Kendall: *I believe Dr. Douglas offered $300,000 and Mr. Daven proposed $2 million.*

Mediator: *Tell me about the mediation approach.*

Ms. Kendall: *The mediator was a retired judge. The parties were never in the same room. Toward the end of the mediation, the judge brought the lawyers together to see if there was something to be done other than adjourn. I don't know what happened in your room, Takao, but the judge spent most of the time with us talking about why we would lose. I guess she got it wrong!*

Mr. Normish: *I think Christine's description is pretty accurate. We heard a lot about why we were going to lose, too.*

Mediator: *It sounds like the mediation was essentially a settlement conference approach.*

Ms. Kendall and Mr. Normish: *That's right.*

Mediator: *Appellate mediation is an opportunity for a do-over, to try an approach that differs from the one that didn't work so well. Let's keep this in mind later when we discuss the approach to take in this mediation.*

Mr. Normish and Ms. Kendall: *Good.*

Mediator: *It seems unlikely that there are other related lawsuits or collateral actions that could potentially be addressed in the present mediation, but I always ask because, if so, we will need to determine whether other parties or lawyers will be participating and bring them into the premediation planning process. Am I right or are there any other disputes your clients might like to include?*

Ms. Kendall and Mr. Normish: *No, this is it.*

Mediator: *Now, let's talk about who will participate in the mediation. Mr. Normish, I take it you will be there with Mr. Daven?*

Mr. Normish: *Yes, that is right, and he will have full settlement authority.*

Mediator: *Thank you. And is there anyone with whom he will be consulting in making his decision, such as a spouse or partner?*

Ms. Kendall: *No. He will be making all decisions on his own.*

Mediator: *Ms. Kendall, how about Dr. Douglas? I assume she will be present. Is that right?*

Ms. Kendall: *Yes, she will be there.*

Mediator: *And is there insurance coverage in this case?*

Ms. Kendall: *Yes, there is, and we are planning to bring Joan McGrist, the claims adjuster who was assigned to this file at the outset.*

Mediator: *Will Dr. Douglas and Ms. McGrist possess full authority to settle the dispute in an amount up to the judgment, as required by Local Rule 1?*

Ms. Kendall: *I am sorry, it is not possible for Ms. McGrist to come with that amount of authority.*

Mediator: *I see. Then what are your thoughts about how Dr. Douglas's insurance representative can comply with this rule?*

Ms. Kendall: *Our plan is consistent with the insurance carrier's practice in all mediations. Are you saying the rules require otherwise?*

Mediator: *From what you tell me, Ms. McGrist does not satisfy the rule. Local Rule 1(h)(4) requires the in-person attendance of a representative of each insurance carrier whose policy may apply. And it requires that the carrier representative possess full settlement authority. Perhaps there is another representative who would possess the requisite authority or there is a way Ms. McGrist could be vested with such authority prior to the mediation. If neither of these is possible, and there is not another way that the carrier can satisfy the requirement, you can seek an exception by filing a motion with the court.*

Ms. Kendall: *I will check with the carrier and get back to you, if that is okay.*

Mediator: *That is fine. When would you expect to have more information?*

Ms. Kendall: *By Monday noon?*

Mediator: *Good. I will call you Monday at 5:00 pm. If it turns out you need to request an exception, the court will want to know how you propose to deal with the limited authority issue during mediation if the representative believes a settlement above her authority is appropriate. Please discuss that proce-dure with the carrier, as well.*

Mr. Normish, your thoughts?

Mr. Normish: *This is a big case. I can't imagine the carrier will not send someone with the requisite authority. Ms. Kendall, you may file a motion, but please know I will oppose it vehemently! I do not want to waste my time or my client's time in a mediation that results only in a recommendation and not a resolution.*

Mediator: *You want to make sure a settlement can be finalized in the mediation, not through a procedure afterwards. Is that right?*

Mr. Normish: *Yes.*

Mediator: *I will be in touch with you shortly after my call with Ms. Kend-all on Monday. Will you be available?*

Ms. Kendall: *Yes.*

Mediator: *I look forward to talking with you both on Monday. Ms. Kendall, in the meantime if you need my assistance or would like me to speak with the carrier, I would be happy to do so, assuming you do not object, Mr. Normish.*

Mr. Normish: *That's fine with me.*

Mediator: *Let's turn to confidentiality. As you may know, California's medi-ation confidentiality statutes prohibit the introduction of conversations that take place in mediation or documents prepared for mediation in a subsequent civil action, except for very limited exceptions. Your clients cannot introduce this evi-dence, for example, in proceedings to collect on the judgment or in a new trial, should Dr. Douglas prevail. Neither can your clients call me as a witness.*

The mediation and confidentiality agreement I sent to you incorporates the applicable mediation confidentiality rules. Does this agreement meet your clients' needs?

Ms. Kendall and Mr. Normish: *Yes, it is fine as is.*

Mediator: *Now for the mediation statements. I presume you are planning to submit mediation statements and exchange them, as most parties do. Is that right?*

Ms. Kendall: *Yes, appellant is planning to do so.*

Mr. Normish: *I will be sending you a brief, but we haven't decided whether to share it with the other side.*

Mediator: *Please say more about your reservations.*

Mr. Normish: *We find that where our legal analysis of a case differs so drastically from the opposing side, as it does here, that briefs sometimes make it more difficult to settle the case.*

Mediator: *Ms. Kendall, your thoughts about not receiving a statement from Mr. Normish?*

Ms. Kendall: *Well, if Mr. Daven wants the insurer to be able to incorporate the opposing arguments in evaluating the claim, then Mr. Normish needs to let us in on his legal theories. We believe the weight of authority is strongly in our favor. If Mr. Normish has arguments that make sense, then it would be to his client's advantage to make the arguments, nasty as they might be. We can handle it.*

Mediator: *Mr. Normish?*

Mr. Normish: *Mr. Daven is angry and personally offended, as well. Dr. Douglas is not going to like what he has to say.*

Mediator: *One option to address the concern that your zealous advocacy might alienate the opposing party is not to exchange briefs. This option has a significant drawback: you do not have the benefit of understanding each other's legal argument and therefore lack information that is important to evaluating the appeal and advising your clients.*

Other lawyers who share your concerns have resolved the problem by toning down their statements. They approach the statements as an opportunity to **educate** *the other side, not* **debate** *the other side. They sometimes agree to eliminate any commentary that would personally offend the other side and discuss those issues privately with me before the mediation or in a confidential brief for my eyes only. Also, there will undoubtedly be an opportunity to speak with me privately at the mediation. If you feel strongly that this private information needs to be in writing, with your agreement, I am willing to read what you send. What would you like to do?*

Ms. Kendall: *No guarantees, but I am willing to try to tone down my brief and eliminate the personal attacks. I would like to speak with you privately before the mediation, however.*

Mediator: *Mr. Normish, would that be all right with you?*

Mr. Normish: *That is fine.*

Mediator: *I usually receive mediation statements by mail or e-mail a week before the mediation. In some cases, lawyers want to have a staggered schedule for submission, with the appellant submitting two weeks before the mediation and the respondent submitting a week before mediation. This approach works well when the respondent is not entirely clear about the issues for appeal.*

In cases where insurance coverage applies, especially with a large amount of money in controversy, carriers sometimes need briefs earlier than a week before the mediation so they can go through the appropriate channels for analyzing the case. What makes sense here?

Mr. Normish: *I am intrigued by the idea of staggering briefs. Since the mediation is so far away, perhaps Ms. Kendall could send me her brief a week before mine is due. I have a general idea of the issues she intends to raise on appeal, but I could respond much more meaningfully if I had greater detail. Will you do that?*

Ms. Kendall: *Fair enough.*

Mediator: *So, Ms. Kendall will submit Dr. Douglas's statement to Mr. Normish and me two weeks before the mediation on April 6 and Mr. Normish will submit and exchange Mr. Daven's statement one week later on April 13.*

In terms of length, unlike the formal briefs filed with the Court of Appeal, I am perfectly happy with short, informal mediation statements. Important documents such as the judgment, the jury's special verdict form, and post-trial motions are often helpful and I welcome them. Feel free to include any other documents you would like me to review. Any objections?

Ms. Kendall and Mr. Normish: *No.*

Mediator: *Regarding mediation fees, under the court's Mediation Program rules, I have agreed to provide preparation time and the first two hours of mediation session time free of charge. Thereafter, it is my practice to charge my normal hourly fee of $500. Are your clients agreeable with this procedure?*

Mr. Normish: *Yes, that is fine with Mr. Daven.*

Ms. Kendall: *Appellant is agreeable, as well.*

Mediator: *Have the parties agreed how to allocate fees?*

Mr. Normish: *They agreed to allocate fees equally.*

Mediator: *It is my practice to require a deposit of estimated fees within a week of the premediation telephone conference, in this case by March 27. Is that a problem for either of your clients? I will send you a statement of deposit showing the amounts due from your clients following this call.*

Mr. Normish and Ms. Kendall: *I am sure that procedure will be okay with my client.*

Mediator: *Before we end this call, let's take a few minutes to talk about how we will work together at the mediation. Unless there is good reason to proceed otherwise, I would like to begin in joint session to talk about mediation generally and how we will work together throughout the day, and to answer any questions that might arise. I also find it helpful at the outset to hear from the participants about their willingness to work hard toward a settlement or their positive intentions for the day. These declarations, even very modest ones, help to create an atmosphere of collaboration. Would you be willing to make such a declaration?*

Mr. Normish: *Yes, I would do that.*

Ms. Kendall: *Sure.*

Mediator: *And your clients?*

Mr. Normish: *I will check, but it will probably be fine.*

Ms. Kendall: *I am sure Dr. Douglas will agree to do so.*

Mediator: *I also find it most productive in appellate cases, especially appeals in which the parties had a personal relationship, for the parties to remain together for the next phase of mediation in which you educate me and the others about the legal issues. If you are together, there is an opportunity to discuss your theories in addition to just reading about them. Are you willing to do that?*

Ms. Kendall: *I imagine I will understand Mr. Normish's analysis quite well, although I will disagree. I am concerned that we will get off on the wrong foot by arguing with each other. Such a conversation would be counterproductive to our goal of reaching an agreement.*

Mr. Normish: *I agree with Ms. Kendall–for once!*

Mediator: *That is a good start! I hope you will indulge me while I make a case for the extended joint session. I know this will be challenging, as joint sessions seem to be out of fashion these days. I recently had a premediation call in which a lawyer didn't even recognize the term. When he realized I was talking about being in the same room with the other side he exclaimed, "I remember when we used to do that in the old days! Now, we never even see the other side."*

I think this trend is regrettable and has led to the loss of much of the potential of mediation in two ways. First, as lawyers, if you are in separate rooms discussing your case with me, you really do miss a chance to understand the strengths and the weaknesses of your legal case. While I agree that treating the joint session as a forum to deliver your oral arguments is counterproductive, it is very productive to make sure you are not missing something in your or the other lawyer's analysis. After all, the quality of your legal analysis greatly influences your clients' ability to assess whether what is available in settlement is better than going forward with the appeal.

The second potential that is squandered if parties don't meet together is the possibility that they can leave mediation with more than a "deal." If they talk to and listen to each other, they will likely learn something new that can expand their understanding, perhaps cast doubt on negative assumptions they have made about each other, and mend a rift in the relationship. In the course of discussing what matters to them, the parties might also discover solutions that create value or meet the interests of the parties. Finally, these interactions can lead, if not to reconciliation, at least to a sense of closure that goes beyond simply settling a case.

Would there be any value to your clients of such an opportunity?

Mr. Normish: *Well, as I said, my client is upset both about the harm done to him and Dr. Douglas's breach of trust. There is so much water under the bridge in this case that I hadn't considered the possibility of "closure" in this way, but I will discuss it with Mr. Daven.*

Ms. Kendall: *Being sued for malpractice is a very difficult thing for my physician clients, Dr. Douglas included. I will ask her whether she is willing to talk with Mr. Daven and I will discuss with her whether that is a good idea.*

Mediator: *I appreciate your willingness to consider this approach. I suggest I talk with you separately once you have had this conversation with your clients. Could you be prepared to discuss this issue when we talk on Monday? Finally, I share your concern that joint sessions in which you discuss the law be constructive—and I have some ideas about how to ensure that they are, which I will discuss during our call.*

Ms. Kendall: *That should not be a problem.*

Mr. Normish: *That works for me, too.*

Mediator: *Excellent. In the meantime, please assure your clients that I have plenty of experience facilitating difficult conversations such as this. If they agree with this approach, I will want to know of any particular concerns they might have so we can put agreements in place that will allow them to have greater confidence that this exercise will be constructive. I can also talk with you about how you can help your client prepare, if that would be useful. Any questions, comments?*

Ms. Kendall and Mr. Normish: *No. This seems like a good plan.*

Mediator: *I have one final issue to discuss. I find it helpful to have separate calls with counsel after I read your briefs and before the mediation to answer questions and hear any suggestions you have about how to improve the productivity of the mediation. Do either of you object to those calls?*

Mr. Normish and Ms. Kendall: *No.*

Mediator: *Thank you. Is there anything else we need to discuss in order to be prepared for the mediation?*

Ms. Kendall and Mr. Normish: *I think that is it.*

Mediator: *I agree. I appreciate your taking time for this call and considering these important issues with me. In my experience, this forethought pays off in a more effective mediation process. I look forward to talking with you on Monday and the week before mediation and to working with you and your clients on April 20. Goodbye.*

Mr. Normish: *Likewise. Goodbye.*

Ms. Kendall: *Yes, and thank you for volunteering your time to help us.*[2]

---

2. Lawyers take note: in our experience counsel rarely thank volunteer mediators for their pro bono contributions. Appellate mediators perform an important service not only to the court but also to the parties. In addition, they are an asset to lawyers. Remember to show your appreciation and encourage your clients to do so, as well.

2. Sample Confirming E-mail Following the Premediation Conference Call

We suggest you confirm all agreements reached in the premediation conference call with a simple letter or e-mail to counsel, such as the sample we include below, that attaches or encloses a more formal mediation and confidentiality agreement, a sample of which we include after the e-mail, to be signed by the parties and lawyers before or at the outset of the initial mediation session.

3. Sample Confirming E-mail Following the Premediation Telephone Conference

To:	takao@normishlaw.com (Takao Normish); kendall.c@frontstreetlaw.com (Christine Kendall)
Date:	March 20, 2015
Subject:	*Daven v. Douglas* Mediation (Court of Appeal No. 745877)

Dear Counsel,

I appreciated the opportunity to speak with you earlier today. The purpose of this message is to confirm the arrangements for the *Daven v. Douglas* mediation.

Date:	April 20, 2015
Time:	9:00 am
Location:	Mediation Center
	1936 Ursula Way
	Bridgeport, California
Participants:	**Appellant representatives**
	Christine Kendall, counsel
	Reshma Douglas, M.D.
	Joan McGrist, MediPractice, Inc. claims adjuster, or another representative to be determined
	Respondent representatives
	Takao Normish, counsel
	Carson Daven

Mediation Statements

You agreed to the following schedule for submission of mediation statements: Dr. Douglas's mediation statement is due April 6, and Mr. Daven's mediation statement is due April 13.

Below is a suggested format:

- A brief summary of the factual background;

- A brief summary of the procedural background;

- A brief summary of the parties' settlement history;

- For Dr. Douglas, a description of the issues and arguments she intends to raise on appeal, including standards of review and prejudice;

- For Mr. Daven, an analysis of each of the appellant's arguments along with any issues of waiver or forfeiture he expects to assert; and

- For Mr. Daven, an explanation of damages.

Please include in your submission to me copies of the judgment, the jury's special verdict, any post-trial motions, and any other key documents or legal authority you would like me to review. Please provide the other counsel a list of the documents you send to me.

Although you are not required to do so, you may also submit an additional, confidential statement you do not share with the other side. If you submit a confidential statement, you may include any information you believe will be useful, including answers to the following questions:

1. What would you and your clients like to accomplish at this mediation, and what does the mediator need to understand to help you accomplish these goals?
2. What interests of your clients must be addressed in order for a resolution to be reached?
3. What interests of the opposing party must be addressed in order for a resolution to be reached?
4. What do you see as the obstacles to a negotiated resolution, and what ideas do you have to overcome them?
5. What are the consequences for each side if no settlement is reached?
6. What do you estimate it will cost to litigate this case through appeal and a second trial if appellant prevails?

Even if you choose not to submit an additional, confidential statement, I encourage you to review these questions with your clients in advance of the mediation session.

Further Premediation Calls

Mr. Normish, I look forward to talking with you this coming Monday at 5:00 pm to discuss the insurance carrier's authority, your client's goals for the mediation, and the approach we will take in the mediation. Ms. Kendall, I look forward to talking with you shortly thereafter to discuss these same issues.

We have also agreed that I will talk with you separately and confidentially after I read your briefs. I will schedule those calls by separate e-mail.

Mediation and Confidentiality Agreement

Please send me copies of the Mediation and Confidentiality Agreement signed by you and your clients by March 27.

Fees and Deposit of Fees

Consistent with the Court of Appeal's Mediation Program rules, we agree that I will donate preparation time and the first two hours of mediation session time. Also pursuant to this rule, we agree that after two hours of mediation session time, my hourly fee of $500, which shall accrue in one-tenths of an hour, shall apply to all time spent in connection with the mediation, including but not limited to telephone calls; correspondence, including e-mail; in-person meetings; mediation session(s); and follow-up conferences or correspondence. The parties agree to allocate any fees equally.

I look forward to working with you on April 20. In the meantime, please let me know if I can help you in any way to prepare.

With best regards,

Dana L. Curtis

Dana L. Curtis

4. *Sample Mediation and Confidentiality Agreement*

Some court-connected mediation programs provide confidentiality agreements for the participants and mediators to sign at or before the mediation. Others presume the mediators will provide their own. Most private mediators have form agreements that reflect the parties' agreement to mediate, circumscribe the mediator's role, set forth the agreement regarding confidentiality and fees, and address other matters related to mediation. These agreements can either be signed beforehand or at the mediation. Below is an example, tailored to the *Daven v. Douglas* appeal.

Mediation and Confidentiality Agreement
Douglas v. Daven (Court of Appeal No. 745877)

This mediation and confidentiality agreement ("agreement") is made between the undersigned parties or party representatives ("party" or "parties") or other participants in the mediation ("participants") and mediator Dana Curtis ("mediator").

1. Agreement to Mediate

The parties agree to work with the mediator to attempt to resolve their existing controversies with mediator Dana Curtis.

2. Mediator's Role

The mediator will act as a neutral third party. The mediator will not act as an attorney or advocate for any party in this or any future related proceeding and will not provide legal advice.

3. Confidentiality

The parties, participants, and the mediator agree that all statements made in connection with or during the mediation are confidential mediation discussions. All statements shall be inadmissible for any purpose in any civil proceeding. Any information disclosed by or on behalf of a party to the mediator shall be confidential and shall not constitute a waiver of any privilege. The mediator shall not testify and shall not be subpoenaed by a party to testify in any future proceeding relating to this matter. The provisions of California Evidence Code sections 1115 through 1128 shall apply to this mediation. Any files or notes created or maintained by the mediator are solely for the mediator's use and shall be destroyed at the conclusion of the mediation.

This agreement shall not be a confidential mediation communication, but shall constitute a contract that is admissible in a court of competent jurisdiction to prove and enforce its terms.

4. Fees and Deposit

The mediator's fee shall be $500 per hour. This fee shall accrue in one-tenths of an hour and shall apply to all time spent in connection with the mediation after preparation and two hours of mediation session time, including but not limited to telephone calls; correspondence, including e-mail; study time; in-person meetings; mediation session(s); and follow-up conferences or correspondence. The parties agree to allocate fees equally between the appellant and respondent.

In order to reserve the mediation date, the parties shall deposit estimated fees in the amount determined by the mediator by March 27, 2015. The mediator shall refund any unused fees or invoice the parties for fees exceeding the deposit at the conclusion of the mediation. The parties shall pay any additional mediation fees within ten days of receiving a statement showing a balance due. The parties agree that overdue balances are subject to interest at the rate of ten percent (10%) per annum.

5. Cancellation and Rescheduling Policy

If a mediation session is cancelled or rescheduled between 7 and 14 days before the scheduled date, the party responsible for the change shall pay to the mediator a fee in the amount equal to one-half the value of the time reserved. If a mediation is cancelled or rescheduled within 6 days of the scheduled date, the party responsible for the change shall pay to the mediator a fee in the amount equal to the entire value of the time reserved. If the parties disagree as to who is responsible for the change, the parties shall pay their pro rata shares of the forfeited fee without waiving any right to reimbursement at a later time.

By signing below, the following participants indicate their agreement to the above provisions and confirm that they have authority to enter into this agreement:

Date: March 20, 2015   By: Dana Curtis (Mediator)

Dana L. Douglas

Date: March 28, 2015   By: Dr. Reshma Douglas (Appellant)

Dr. Reshma Douglas

Date: March 29, 2015   By: Christine Kendall (Appellant's attorney)

Christine Kendall

Date: March 31, 2015   By: Carson Daven (Respondent)

Carson Daven

Date: March 31, 2015   By: Takao Normish (Respondent's attorney)

Takao Normish

5. *Overview of the Appellate Mediation Process*

Some mediators find it helpful to be able to refer to the appellate mediation process at a glance, especially during their first few cases. Therefore, we include a one-page overview of the process agenda to provide a general roadmap for the mediation. For newer mediators, especially, it can ease some of the "What's next?" anxiety.

Mediation Agenda for *Daven v. Douglas*
(Court of Appeal No. 745877)
April 20, 2015

Phase 1: Introductions and structuring the mediation

- Introduction of the participants
- Mediator comments
- Overview of the appellate process, including confidentiality

Phase 2: Exchanging information and bridging gaps in understanding

- About what happened that led to litigation
- About the legal issues and analysis
- About what matters to the parties; their needs and interests

Phase 3: Identifying issues to be resolved and creating an agenda

- Ensure that the issues comport with the scope of the mediation
- Achieve consensus on the order in which to address the issues

Phase 4: Developing and negotiating solutions

- Reviewing the parties' needs and interests
- Exploring the possibility of creative nonmonetary options to add value and "expand the pie"
- Negotiating monetary issues
- Analyzing risks, opportunities, and costs associated with continued litigation
- Agreeing on terms that are better for the parties than continuing with the appeal

Phase 5: Concluding

If the dispute resolves:

- Refining the agreement for clarity, completeness, and commitment
- Drafting and signing the agreement
- Final comments

If the dispute does not resolve:

- Analyzing why the dispute did not resolve and attempting to address the reasons
- Agreeing on mediator follow-up and next steps

C.   Resources for Appellate Attorneys

In contrast to strictly rule-bound appellate briefs, mediation statements are informal documents that serve the important functions of informing the mediator about the background of the case and educating the mediator and the other party about your client's perspective on the factual background and the legal issues and arguments you will make on appeal if the case does not resolve in mediation. Mediation statements should present your strongest appellate arguments. Thus, they serve to motivate the opposing party to work toward a negotiated settlement that may well offer a better option than proceeding with the appeal.

Mediation statements for both appellants and respondents should include detailed analyses of the standards of review as well as waiver and prejudice. Respondents should also mention the additional cost to appellants of post-judgment interest and the posting of a bond on appeal. They should also emphasize, in the appropriate case, that winning the appeal does not mean the appellate court will reach the result the appellant wanted in the trial court; rather, winning means the appellant has the right to retry the case.

Finally, the length of the brief and any response may be determined during the premediation conference call. Before preparing a brief, be clear about any format or length limitations set by the mediator or the court, in court connected mediations.

1. Sample Mediation Statement for the Appellant, Douglas

**Confidential Mediation Statement
for the Appellant, Dr. Reshma Douglas
Daven v. Douglas, Court of Appeal No. 745877**
April 2, 2015

Sent via express mail and e-mail[3]

Dear Ms. Curtis and Mr. Normish:

On behalf of Dr. Douglas, I hereby submit the following mediation statement. I look forward to working with you and your clients on April 20. If you have questions about the information below or would like additional information, please let me know.

Introduction

This appeal challenges a $1 million verdict in a medical malpractice action filed by Carson Daven against Dr. Reshma Douglas

---

3. **Confidentiality Notice.** The information contained in this transmission constitutes a confidential mediation communication and is intended only for the persons to whom it is addressed. This mediation statement may not be used for any purposes other than the mediation ordered by the Court of Appeal. If you receive this communication in error, please immediately notify the sender. Thank you.

As we will show on appeal, the jury erred in concluding Dr. Douglas was at fault in performing surgery on Mr. Daven's nose. As Mr. Daven's own expert witness acknowledged, Dr. Douglas is one of the premier rhinoplasty surgeons in the country. Having performed thousands of procedures, Dr. Douglas demonstrated expertise in this case by substantially repairing the damage caused by the trauma sustained by Mr. Daven during an auto accident. The finding by the jury that Dr. Douglas's excellent care fell below the standard of care is unsupportable by the record. The only reason the jury found Dr. Douglas liable for $400,000 was due to video footage of a bloody surgery that the court erroneously allowed into evidence. Although gruesome to laypersons since it involved breaking some of the nasal bone, the surgery was exactly what medical professionals acknowledge was the appropriate care. The Court of Appeal will correct the erroneous verdict.

The Court of Appeal will also correct the $600,000 penalty based on Dr. Douglas's alleged failure to use the patient consent form mandated by a new statute: Medical Code section 96734 (hereinafter "section 96734"). Dr. Douglas used a very detailed, clear, and informative patient consent form that was the functional equivalent of (or, we believe, better than) the statutory form. The Court of Appeal will see that Dr. Douglas is being punished by the judgment for using a better and clearer advisement of patient rights and consent than that set forth in section 96734.

The Court of Appeal ordered this case to mediation. Dr. Douglas has been in the business of helping people feel better for more than 25 years and is willing to explore a settlement that helps Mr. Daven. However, any settlement must reflect the strength of Dr. Douglas's arguments on appeal.

Summary of Factual and Procedural History

In short, this is a medical malpractice case involving a former television newscaster, Mr. Daven, and Dr. Douglas, a board-certified and nationally recognized plastic surgeon. After Mr. Daven was rear-ended by a drunk driver, he suffered nasal problems, including a deviated septum. After abatement of the initial physical trauma, Mr. Daven discovered he had a problem when his nose began to whistle when he spoke. He also suffered the inability to swallow properly or sleep comfortably due to his nasal problems. To address these problems, as Mr. Daven testified at trial, he contacted the best plastic surgeons in the country before settling on Dr. Douglas.

Dr. Douglas carefully assessed Mr. Daven's condition, going so far as to order an fMRI to ensure that any surgery would take into account the conditions of the tissue during the movement caused by breathing. Dr. Douglas never guaranteed any particular result. Instead, Dr. Douglas explained how a surgical procedure could possibly reduce the whistling nose sounds and probably improve Mr. Daven's ability to swallow properly as well as relieve some of Mr. Daven's discomfort. Dr. Douglas used a very detailed patient advisement of rights and consent form to go through a checklist of possible problems and complications resulting from the surgical procedure. Item 15 expressly noted that the surgical procedure "may not provide complete restoration of the nasal operation or aesthetics to pretrauma conditions. Such restoration is unlikely to be possible in this case." Mr. Daven acknowledged both that he discussed this point with Dr. Douglas and that he initialed every potential surgical problem listed. This case is not one in which Mr. Daven can claim any lack of information or withholding of any consent.

Dr. Douglas performed the operation in January 2013 and concluded it to be successful. Mr. Daven's pain was almost completely eliminated and his ability to swallow completely restored, as Mr. Daven acknowledged at trial. Scar tissue was removed and the subsequent "look" of the nose was smooth and free of any overt signs of trauma. Mr. Daven's initial complaint was only that the aesthetics had changed. However, as Dr. Douglas explained prior to surgery, the loss of some bone during the auto accident prevented full restoration—at least in *one* surgery.

Mr. Daven subsequently underwent two more surgeries performed by other surgeons—without consulting with Dr. Douglas or considering that Dr. Douglas would be best suited to continue the course of care.

As noted above, Mr. Daven sued Dr. Douglas for malpractice. The jury awarded Mr. Daven a total of $1 million, comprised of $400,000 in compensatory damages and $600,000 in special damages. Compensatory damages were based on the cost of Mr. Daven's subsequent surgeries and his loss of income from "losing" his job as newscaster on *The Daven Report*. Special damages consisted of a special penalty imposed on surgeons who fail to secure a signed advisement of risks on the form specified by a new statute. The jury found the signed patient consent form used by Dr. Douglas was not technically the form specified by section 96734.

Issues and Prospects for Success on Appeal

Dr. Douglas has two strong appellate issues:

1. Mr. Daven's medical expert presented extremely inflammatory evidence, including video footage from Dr. Douglas's surgery on Mr. Daven and some of the bloody dressings worn by Mr. Daven after the surgery. He also testified that Dr. Douglas's surgeries were "medieval barbarism." Although this issue will be reviewed under the abuse of discretion standard of review, it is still a strong argument because the record demonstrates the nature and effect of the error. Proving that the evidence was far more prejudicial than probative was the trial court's repeated admonishment that Mr. Daven's expert witness "tone down" the characterizations of Dr.

Douglas and the surgery. The trial court even noted on the record (after the surgery video was shown) that most jurors were seen cringing during the video.

2. The award of special damages of $600,000 needs to be stricken as a matter of law. The statute authorizing the special damages of 1.5 times compensatory damages for surgeons who fail to use a particular risk advisement form should not apply in this case where Mr. Daven consulted with many surgeons, knew the risks, and actually signed a patient consent form. Although the form was not the statutorily specified form, even the most cursory examination will show the form used by Dr. Douglas to be the functional equivalent of that specified in section 96734.

The Court of Appeal will review this issue de novo without any deference to the trial court, because it is an issue of law. The court will see that *nothing* in section 96734's advisement was omitted here. Indeed, this is such a strong issue that we have already been informed that the Western States Medical Profession (a consortium of more than 5,000 medical professionals west of the Rockies) and Citizens for Smart Reform will be filing amicus briefs in support of Dr. Douglas's position.

If Dr. Douglas succeeds on the evidentiary issue, this case will be reversed and remanded for retrial. If she wins only on the special damages issue, the appellate court will reduce the judgment to $400,000.

Potential Gains and Losses for the Appellant

If Dr. Douglas succeeds on her evidentiary issue, the court will vacate the judgment and order a retrial. If she loses the evidentiary issue but prevails on the statutory penalty issue, the court will reduce the judgment by $600,000. Dr. Douglas did not receive a fair trial the first time and welcomes the opportunity to have a jury properly consider the case without inflammatory evidence. To achieve this remedy, Dr. Douglas is prepared to fund the appeal and retrial. If Dr. Douglas loses on appeal, the judgment remains intact but will never be for an amount that is greater than it is now.

Potential Gains and Losses for the Respondent

We cannot see any gain to Mr. Daven in this appeal because Mr. Daven has not filed a cross-appeal. Thus, the judgment is not going to improve for Mr. Daven—and can only get worse if the Court of Appeal credits either one of our strong arguments. There is no cost-shifting provision at play in this case, which means that Mr. Daven must absorb the cost of litigation regardless of outcome.

A loss by Mr. Daven on the compensatory damages issue would leave him in a worse position on retrial because he would not be able to introduce the same inflammatory evidence, which would weaken his case considerably before the jury. A loss by Mr. Daven on the statutory penalty issue would be conclusive—the Court of Appeal would simply find the consent form in this case to be the legal equivalent of that required in section 96734 with the effect that Mr. Daven would have no opportunity to try to regain this component of damages.

Possible Mutually Acceptable Terms of an Agreement

While Dr. Douglas is confident about the strength of her appeal, she is also willing to explore creative options for a mutually agreeable settlement of this case. The trial court has issued a stay of enforcement as to the $600,000 penalty, and Dr. Douglas has posted an appeal bond for the remainder. Thus, Mr. Daven will not see the proceeds of the judgment before the end of the appeal—and, if he loses, not ever. An appropriate settlement could provide the proceeds to Mr. Daven in a quick manner. Also, a settlement agreement might characterize the entire proceeds as compensation for personal physical injury, meaning that Mr. Daven might receive the entire settlement amount tax free. (To be clear, we are not offering tax advice here, but only exploring possibilities for settlement.)

We have observed that Mr. Daven has been studiously avoiding any reference to his surgeries in his media appearances—even when asked directly about the case *he* brought. Dr. Douglas offers many clients complete confidentiality regarding procedures and can provide the same confidentiality assurances if we settle this case. This confidentiality may also benefit Dr. Douglas who has been wrongly smeared for doing good work.

Conclusion

We are confident that Dr. Douglas has excellent prospects on appeal with two strong issues. Dr. Douglas is willing and able to continue to clear her name. If she must do so by seeking a new trial, so be it. If the parties can agree to do so without further litigation, Dr. Douglas is willing to enter into such an agreement on the appropriate terms.

Respectfully submitted,

Christine Kendall

Counsel for appellant, Dr. Reshma Douglas

2. Sample Mediation Statement for the Respondent, Daven

Confidential Mediation Statement
for the Respondent, Carson Daven
Daven v. Douglas, Court of Appeal No. 745877
April 10, 2015

Dear Ms. Curtis and Ms. Kendall:

This mediation statement is submitted on behalf of the respondent, Carson Daven. This is not a settlement offer but is intended for use only in the mediation of the above-titled appeal. Thus, all mediation confidentiality privileges apply to this statement.

Background

For many years, Carson appeared as the on-air personality for *The Daven Report*. *The Daven Report* was a popular weekly program on Channel 4 that consistently received high viewer ratings. In July 2012, Carson's world changed when he was rear-ended by a drunk driver. Most of his injuries healed relatively quickly—except for the damage to his nose. As a result of the accident, Carson suffered nasal problems, including a deviated septum. Carson privately suffered because he was unable to swallow liquids cleanly or sleep well due to his nasal problems. But what made Carson's heart sink was when he discovered his nose began to whistle as he read the news on his show.

Like any good investigative reporter, Carson did his research and consulted with the top plastic surgeons throughout the northern hemisphere. He settled on Dr. Douglas because she *assured* him that she could *fix* his whistling nose, restore his ability to swallow properly, and relieve some of his discomfort. Although they went over the patient consent forms together, Dr. Douglas's oral statements were not nearly as dour as what was printed on the pages. Indeed, it was her optimism that sold Carson on her.

Dr. Douglas operated and declared the operation a success. However, as the video played to the jury shows, the operation was anything but that. Dr. Douglas used language that would make a sailor blush throughout the operation. After the operation, Carson rightfully became angry because Dr. Douglas changed the look of Carson's nose! In newscasting, one's face is a newscaster's trademark, and Carson felt a loss of identity when the look of his nose totally changed. And although the whistling quieted down considerably, Carson still heard it whenever he talked. As a result, Carson underwent two more surgeries to correct Dr. Douglas's mistakes.

After the subsequent two surgeries, Carson came to accept that his nose "was as good as it's going to get." By that time, the damage was done—he had lost his anchoring role on *The Daven Report* because viewers just don't want to see people with surgery bruises on their faces for months at a time.

The Jury Got It Right

To compensate Carson for loss of income and the cost of subsequent surgeries, the jury awarded him $400,000. This was hardly a runaway jury as Dr. Douglas has complained. (Carson showed that compensatory damages should actually have been $850,000.) The jury also found that Dr. Douglas clearly did not use the form required by state law in order to advise Carson of his rights as a patient and to get a truly informed consent from him. It doesn't take 12 people to find one obvious fact: the papers Dr. Douglas used do not look like the form expressly required by state law. Consequently, the 1.5 times compensatory damages provision set forth by Medical Code section 96734 automatically applies. From judgment entered on this verdict, Dr. Douglas has taken her appeal.

There are no other collateral legal actions addressing the same operative set of facts as presented in this appeal. Resolution of this appeal would entirely resolve the dispute between Carson and Dr. Douglas.

Response to Issues Raised by Dr. Douglas

As the respondent, Carson has the better odds and arguments on appeal:

1. As to the claim regarding erroneous admission of evidence in the form of a videotape of the surgery, the Court of Appeal is almost certain to affirm the trial court's ruling. As Dr. Douglas admits, this issue is subject to the abuse of discretion standard of review, which means that she must show the trial court acted in a manner that was arbitrary, capricious, or beyond the bounds of reason. First, we would like to point out that Dr. Douglas made the videotape in the first place. Second, our medical expert used it to narrate exactly how and when Dr. Douglas committed malpractice. How can it be that the conduct serving as the basis for Carson's legal claim could possibly be erroneously admitted as proof of that claim? Dr. Douglas points out that the trial court informed our witness to tone down the testimony. But Dr. Douglas fails to mention that the trial court admonished the jury to disregard the more colorful descriptions used by our expert— and our case law sets forth the rule that juries are presumed to follow the court's instructions.

2. As to the special damages of $600,000 under section 96734, the amount of the penalty cannot be in dispute: it is set by statute. Thus, this is an all-or-nothing issue for Dr. Douglas. We think Dr. Douglas will get nowhere by trying to persuade the appellate court that what she used even vaguely resembled the form exactly specified by statute. Although de novo review applies, there cannot be any dispute that she didn't comply with the statutory requirements. Moreover, we will show the Court of Appeal that the legislative purpose of section 96734 was to prevent doctors from doing exactly what happened in this case—using their own confusing forms to extract patient consent.

Dr. Douglas Is Unlikely to Succeed in an Appeal That Will Be Costly to Her

We agree that if Dr. Douglas succeeds on her evidentiary issue, the court will order a retrial. And if she loses the evidentiary issue but succeeds on the statutory penalty issue, the court will modify the judgment to be $400,000. This gives Dr. Douglas no more than the opportunity to spend more money to convince another jury that her profanity-laden operating room conduct was somehow excusable. However, Dr. Douglas is paying dearly for the privilege of this appeal, and not just in terms of attorney fees and costs. Postjudgment interest in this state runs at 10 percent (10%) per annum, which means that she is paying $273.97 *per day* to pursue this appeal from a $1 million judgment. Carson may have to wait, but he is getting paid well to wait.

Even If Carson Lost on Appeal, the Case Would Not Be Over for Him

What's Carson's worst case on appeal? Not a total loss, but a remand for a do-over in the trial court. That would be an inconvenient detour, but it would only be a detour toward establishing again that he is entitled to considerable damages. Perhaps on remand, he will find a better jury that will award him full compensatory damages. Carson is willing to take that chance.

We Are Ready to Negotiate in Good Faith

Dr. Douglas says she's in the business of helping people. Let her prove it; we're willing to listen. Carson is willing to mediate in good faith and explore options providing for prompt payment of an amount that properly reflects the strength of his case. Conversely, the poor odds that appellants face, in general, make it worthwhile for Dr. Douglas to explore a settlement as well. We believe that an appeal should be settled if the parties can find an option better than that offered by proceeding with the appeal. If such a solution can be found, you can bet that Carson and I will be in favor of settlement.

We look forward to seeing you at the mediation.

Yours truly,

Takao Normish

Takao Normish

3. Sample Settlement Agreement in *Daven v. Douglas*

We provide a sample settlement agreement to give an idea of the basic contours of such a contract, not as a template or form for ready use. Before drafting settlement agreements in your cases, you should check the requirements in your jurisdiction to ensure that the agreement is admissible in court, enforceable, and avails itself of all the benefits of the laws of your jurisdiction. Consequently, you should engage in your legal research and due diligence before undertaking the delicate task of crafting a valid, comprehensive, enforceable agreement. And we admonish mediators against handing out sample agreements because every case is different, and providing a flawed sample might give rise to legal liability.

Settlement and Release Agreement

This settlement and release agreement ("agreement") is made between Carson Daven ("Daven") and Dr. Reshma Douglas ("Douglas"). Daven and Douglas are individually referred to in this agreement as a "party" and collectively as the "parties." The parties make this agreement in light of the following recited facts ("recitals").

Recitals

A. In July 2012, Daven suffered blunt trauma to his face and nose as a result of an automobile accident caused by a drunk driver. Daven's nose healed only partially, and he suffered the following: a deviated septum, inability to swallow properly, difficulty in sleeping, nasal whistling while speaking, and aesthetic disfigurement.

B. Daven consulted with more than a dozen plastic surgeons throughout the United States and Canada before settling on Douglas to perform reconstructive surgery. Prior to the surgery, Douglas conducted tests to assess the best course of treatment, including a functional MRI of Daven's affected area. Douglas and Daven discussed the findings, proposed treatment plan, and possible adverse consequences. Daven signed patient consent forms provided by Douglas.

C. Douglas performed the nasal surgery on October 3, 2012. The operation was video-recorded by Douglas. Daven thereafter elected to undergo two more operations to his nose, which were performed by two other surgeons and without consultation of Douglas. Between the time of the second and third operations, *The Daven Report* was cancelled by the television network producer.

D. Daven filed an action in Superior Court No. CIV2013-003 against Douglas for medical malpractice, breach of contract, violation of Medical Code section 96734 ("section 96734"), and negligent and intentional infliction of emotional distress. The case was tried to a jury, which awarded to Daven the sum of $1 million, comprising $400,000 in compensatory damages and $600,000 in statutory damages under section 96734. The trial court subsequently awarded to Daven $37,346.91 in court costs. The trial court stayed enforcement of the $600,000 statutory penalty pending appeal. Douglas posted an appeal bond for the remainder, including court costs.

E. Douglas timely filed a notice of appeal in California Court of Appeal case number 745877, which is currently pending.

F. Through this agreement, the parties now wish to resolve their dispute over the pending lawsuit.

In consideration of the above-stated recitals, and the promises set forth below, the parties agree as follows:

Agreement

1. **Payment.** In consideration for the settlement and release of claims in this case, Douglas shall pay to Daven settlement funds of eight hundred thousand dollars ($800,000.00) on or before May 7, 2015. Within seven days of receipt by Christine Kendall ("Kendall"), attorney for Douglas, of an agreement executed by Daven, payment shall be made for the full amount by check made payable to "Takao Normish, Esq." ("Normish") in trust for Daven. Upon receipt of the settlement funds, Normish shall submit to Kendall a request for dismissal of the civil appeal with prejudice as to the entirety of the appeal signed by himself and Daven. Kendall shall promptly acknowledge receipt of the signed request for dismissal, at which point Normish may disburse settlement funds to Daven.

   The parties agree that the payment constitutes compensation solely for tort injuries physically sustained by Daven. Daven acknowledges that neither Douglas nor Kendall has made any representations regarding the federal, state, or local tax consequences of Daven's receipt of the settlement funds. Daven accepts sole responsibility for paying any tax that may be due on any settlement funds he receives. In addition to the other claims released by Daven against Douglas, Daven also releases Douglas and Kendall from any claim arising out of his receipt and their treatment, for purposes of federal, state, or local taxation, of the sums being paid under this agreement.

2. **Dismissal of appeal.** The parties agree to mutually request that the appeal in *Daven v. Douglas* (Court of Appeal No. 745877) be dismissed and further to request that the remittitur issue immediately. The parties agree that this agreement shall remain in effect without any change in terms even if the Court of Appeal denies the request for dismissal and/or issues a decision addressing of the claims on appeal.

3. **Effective date.** This agreement's effective date shall be the date on which the agreement becomes signed by all parties. Each party shall include the date of signing in addition to providing an original signature, and the effective date shall be the latest of these dates. Each party and attorney agrees to personally sign this agreement on or before April 27, 2015.

4. **Representations.** The parties agree they have had adequate opportunity to review and have actually reviewed the terms of this agreement with legal counsel of their own choice and freely and without any coercion or duress accept the terms of this agreement upon the advice of their own counsel and not on the advice or counsel of any other party to this agreement.

5. **Attorney fees and costs.** Each party shall pay its own attorney fees and costs for this appeal as well as proceedings in the trial court in this case.

6. **Notice and delivery.** All notices and delivery of documents under this agreement shall be made in writing and delivered in person or by delivery service in a manner scheduled to require two days or less for transport and with a tracking number to the addresses indicated below:

   If to Douglas: Christine Kendall, Esq., Front Street Law Group, 3 Front Street, Bridgeton, California 99999.

   If to Daven: Takao Normish, Esq., P.O. Box 72453, Bridgeton, California 99999.

7. **Modification.** This agreement may not be altered or modified except by a writing executed by the parties and their attorneys. A party seeking to modify this agreement shall request modification according to the notice provisions in Paragraph 6, above. The other party shall respond to the request within 10 calendar days, and acceptance of the request shall not be unreasonably withheld. The parties agree to execute and deliver any additional papers, documents, and other assurances and take all acts that are reasonably necessary to carry out the intent of this agreement.

8. **Mistakes of law or fact.** The parties recognize that, after the execution of this agreement, they may discover facts or law different from or in addition to those now known or believed to be true regarding claims, causes of action, rights, obligations, liabilities, damages, losses, and expenses arising from the matters stated in the recitals above. The parties agree that even upon new discoveries of fact or law, intervening changes of law, and other changes in understanding, this agreement shall remain in effect.

9. **Release of all known and unknown claims.** Except for the promises and conditions in this agreement, and subject to the limitations set forth below, the parties—as well as their agents, employees, attorneys, and consultants—each release and forever surrender all claims, charges, demands, actions, and causes of action that each has against the other arising out of the facts alleged in the pending action and in the recitals set forth above. This agreement constitutes a full release of claims whether they were actually alleged or could have been alleged by any party in the superior court or in the Court of Appeal. It is the intent of the parties to knowingly and voluntarily waive the application of California Civil Code section 1542, which provides: "A general release does not extend to claims which the creditor does not know or suspect to exist in his or her favor at the time of executing the release, which if known by him or her must have materially affected his or her settlement with the debtor."

10. **Nonliability.** This agreement constitutes a settlement and release of disputed claims and is intended to avoid the burden, inconvenience, and expense of litigating these claims. Thus, this agreement shall not be construed as an admission by any party of liability or wrongdoing to the other party or violation of any law, statute, order, rule, duty, or contract.

11. **No third-party beneficiaries.** Except for the release provisions of this agreement, the parties do not intend by this agreement to create any rights or benefits for any third party.

12. **Severability.** If any part of this agreement is held by a court of competent jurisdiction to be invalid, void, or unenforceable, the remainder of the agreement shall remain in effect and shall be in no way cancelled, impaired, or invalidated.

13. **Press releases.** The parties agree that neither they nor their attorneys will issue a press release regarding this agreement. However, nothing in this agreement shall be interpreted to require the terms of the agreement to be confidential or prohibit any party from discussing the terms of this agreement with any member of the public, including reporters or other members of the media.

14. **Enforcement.**[4] This agreement was reached as the result of mediation held before mediator Dana L. Curtis as part of the

---

4. Note to the reader: In our example, the parties rely on the quick, efficient enforcement mechanism of California Code of Civil Procedure section 664.6. This statute allows

Court of Appeal's Appellate Mediation Program and shall be personally executed by Daven and Douglas. Pursuant to Code of Civil Procedure section 664.6 and Evidence Code section 1123, this agreement is enforceable as a judgment and is admissible in evidence for the purpose of proving and enforcing the terms of the settlement. Moreover, the failure of any party at any time to require performance of any provision of this agreement shall not constitute a waiver of the party's right to enforce the provision or any part of this agreement.

15. **Choice of law.** This agreement shall be governed by the laws of the State of California. The language of all parts of this agreement shall be construed as a whole. This agreement was drafted by all parties and shall not be construed against any party because that party may have initially drafted a particular provision.

16. **Sole agreement.** This agreement is the entire, final, and complete agreement of the parties and represents a present intent to settle the entire case. This agreement cancels and replaces all prior or existing written and oral agreements between the parties, whether made by the parties themselves or made on their behalf by their attorneys. This agreement may be executed in multiple counterparts, all of which shall be deemed originals and with the same effect as if all parties had signed the same document. All counterparts shall be construed together and constitute one agreement, even though it shall only be necessary to produce one counterpart as proof of the agreement.

17. **Authority to enter agreement.** By signing this agreement, each person warrants that he or she is authorized to execute this agreement on his or her own behalf, or on behalf of the represented party.

Date: April 20, 2015   By: *Dr. Reshma Douglas*
Reshma Douglas (Appellant)

Date: April 20, 2015   By: *Christine Kendall*
Christine Kendall (Appellant's attorney)

Date: April 20, 2015   By: *Carson Daven*
Carson Daven (Respondent)

Date: April 20, 2015   By: *Takao Normish*
Takao Normish (Respondent's attorney)

---

enforcement of a judgment upon the filing of a motion without the need for a new or separate lawsuit. This paragraph also reflects the counterintuitive fact that enforcement of a settlement agreement is a matter to be pursued in the *trial* court even if the settlement was reached as part of *appellate* mediation. Why? The question of whether a party has complied with terms of the settlement agreement constitutes a *factual* issue that appellate courts cannot resolve as a matter of *law*. See Chapter 9, part B.2.

D. Our Favorite 12 Books

Other than the book you're holding, there is no other book entirely devoted to appellate mediation. Nonetheless, there are many excellent books that can help you become a more skilled attorney or mediator during appellate mediation. We have narrowed this list to our favorite dozen books. Although the list is subjective, we are confident that these works offer substantial value to any reader. Here they are in alphabetical order by first author:

1. Bowling, Daniel, and David A. Hoffman, *Bringing Peace into the Room: How the Personal Qualities of the Mediator Impact the Process of Conflict Resolution.* Jossey-Bass Inc. Pub, 2003. A valuable collection of essays examining the importance to the mediation process of personal qualities cultivated by the mediator.

2. Cialdini, Robert, *Influence: The Psychology of Persuasion.* Harper Business, 2006 revised edition. This readable book on the psychology of persuasion and cognitive biases is a must-read. For those who find *Influence* as interesting as we do, we offer a bonus recommendation: Kahneman, Daniel, *Thinking, Fast and Slow.* Farrar, Straus and Giroux, 2011. The definitive book on the psychology of judgment by a Nobel Prize winner.

3. Fisher, Roger, William L. Ury, and Bruce Patton, *Getting to Yes: Negotiating Agreement Without Giving In.* Penguin, 2nd ed. 2011. The classic—and very readable—book on interest-based negotiation theory and practice.

4. Friedman, Gary J., *Inside Out: How Conflict Professionals Can Use Self-Reflection to Help Their Clients.* ABA Dispute Resolution Program and Harvard Law School Program on Negotiation, 2014. An entertaining and practical text that makes a strong case that in order to help others resolve their differences, a mediator must be aware of and attend to his or her own internal experience of conflict. This book also provides exercises and insights into how to grow in this way.

5. Friedman, Gary J., and Jack Himmelstein, *Challenging Conflict: Mediation Through Understanding.* ABA Section of Dispute Resolution and Harvard Law School Program on Negotiation, 2008. Provides a thoughtful exploration of client-centered, understanding-based mediation and numerous case studies of mediations conducted entirely in joint sessions. Although not specific to appellate mediation, the philosophy and skills addressed underscore the value of many of the approaches we suggest in this book.

6. Golann, Dwight, *Mediating Legal Disputes: Effective Strategies for Lawyers and Mediators.* ABA 2009. Although not specific to appellate mediation, a comprehensive guidebook for mediators.

7. Little, J. Anderson, *Making Money Talk: How to Mediate Insured Claims and Other Monetary Disputes.* ABA 2007. The only book that focuses entirely on mediating litigated disputes about money, it is a must-read resource full of insight and practical advice for mediators (and

lawyers) to shift the tension-filled and confounding exercise of distributive bargaining in a positive direction.

8.   Menkel-Meadow, Carrie, Lela Porter Love, and Andrea Kupfer Schneider, *Mediation: Practice, Policy and Ethics* 2nd ed., Wolters Kluwer Law & Business, 2013. A comprehensive mediation text that presents case examples in varying gender, race, and cultural contexts and practical advice for lawyers and mediators. Its emphasis on policy and ethics, including critiques of mediation, sets it apart from other mediation books.

9.   Mnookin, Robert H., *Bargaining with the Devil*. Simon and Schuster, 2010. A lively read that addresses important issues in high-conflict, high-stakes cases where trust does not exist and parties demonize each other. It does not address appellate matters specifically, but by the time cases enter the appellate court, parties often believe they are bargaining with the devil, when in fact, as Prof. Mnookin points out, that assessment is unwarranted.

10.   Mnookin, Robert H., Scott R. Peppet, and Andrew S. Tulumello, *Beyond Winning: Negotiating to Create Value in Deals and Disputes*. The Belknap Press of Harvard University Press, 2000. A comprehensive negotiation text focused on a problem-solving approach to bargaining, full of theory and practical advice about creating (and claiming) value in negotiation. It is especially valuable for its consideration of issues related to the role of lawyer as agent negotiation on behalf of a client.

11.   Shell, G. Richard, *Bargaining for Advantage: Negotiation Strategies for Reasonable People*. Penguin Books, 2006. Picks up where *Getting to Yes* leaves off, offering sound advice and tools for becoming a skilled negotiator in both the interest-based and distributive bargaining arenas.

12.   Stone, Douglas, Bruce Patton, and Sheila Heen, *Difficult Conversations: How to Discuss What Matters Most*. Penguin, 2010. An approach to communication that allows parties to conflict to take responsibility for their own part and engage the other in problem-solving conversation. By far the most practical and insightful book we know about communicating in conflict. In cases where parties have an ongoing relationship and agree to talk directly with each other in mediation, Dana often suggests parties read this book in preparation for mediation.

E.   Our Favorite 25 Articles

Articles published in law reviews and scholarly journals provide some of the literature most directly pertinent to appellate mediation. Indeed, the research on reversal rates for civil appeals in state and federal courts is almost exclusively found in law reviews. To help get you started on your research, we present our favorite 25 articles in alphabetical order by first author. Helpful hint: most of these articles are accessible through a search on Google Scholar (http://scholar.google.com).

1.   Clermont, Kevin M., and Theodore Eisenberg. "Plaintiphobia in the Appellate Courts: Civil Rights Really Do Differ from Negotiable Instruments?" *University of Illinois Law Review* 2002 (2002): 947. If you are interested in understanding reversal rates in federal appel-

late courts, this article is required reading because it provides a more insightful analysis than found anywhere else—including in the official published reversal rates (which entirely ignore modifications on appeal!).

2. Cohen, Thomas H., and Donald J. Farole Jr., Bureau of Justice Statistics, U.S. Dept. of Justice, Office of Justice Programs. *Appeals of Civil Trials Concluded in 2005* (2011). A stark reminder of how few appeals make it to decision on merits. This analysis is based on a survey of 26,950 civil trials concluded in 2005 in state courts, resulting in 3,970 appeals, of which 760 appeals were withdrawn by litigants (primarily due to negotiated settlements), 790 summarily dismissed by the appellate courts, 1,580 affirmed, and only 840 reversed or modified. *Id.* at 1, 4. In other words, this study shows that only 3.1 percent of civil judgments were ultimately reversed or modified!

3. Curtis, Dana L. "Reconciliation and the Role of Empathy," chapter in *ADR Personalities and Practice Tips,* American Bar Association Section of Dispute Resolution, 1998: 49–83. An in-depth look at listening, including the various forms of empathy.

4. Curtis, Dana L., and John Toker. "Representing Clients in Appellate Mediation: The Last Frontier," *JAMS Dispute Resolution Alert 1, no. 3* (2000): 1–3. Exploring practical considerations for lawyers preparing their clients for mediation.

5. Eisenberg, Theodore. "Appeal Rates and Outcomes in Tried and Nontried Cases: Further Exploration of Anti-plaintiff Appellate Outcomes," *Journal of Empirical Legal Studies* 1, no. 3 (2004): 659–88. If the federal appellate court reversal rate is an important component of your case evaluation, this follow-up article (to Clermont and Eisenberg, 2002) is also required reading.

6. Eisenberg, Theodore, and Charlotte Lanvers, "What Is the Settlement Rate and Why Should We Care?," *Journal of Empirical Legal Studies* 6, no. 1 (2009): 111–46. Although not directly focused on civil appeals, this study explores the varying settlement rates among various categories of civil cases to show that some categories (tort cases, especially) are more likely to settle than others (such as cases in which constitutional issues predominate). *Id.* at 130. An excellent illustration of the suitability of tort and contract cases to mediation.

7. Eisenberg, Theodore, and Michael Heise, "Plaintiphobia in State Courts? An Empirical Study of State Court Trials on Appeal," *Journal of Legal Studies* 38 (2009). Probably the best examination of reversal rates for various categories of civil appeals in state appellate courts after court or jury trial.

8. Englemann, Kathleen, and Bradford Cornell, "Measuring the Cost of Corporate Litigation: Five Case Studies," *Journal of Legal Studies* 17 (1988): 377. An excellent examination of how the tendency of litigation between companies to eviscerate shareholder value outweighs the potential gain the lawsuit may offer.

9. Hirt, Edward R., and Keith D. Markman, "Multiple Explanation: A Consider-an-Alternative Strategy for Debiasing Judgments," *Journal of*

Personality and Social Psychology 69, no. 6 (1995): 1069. This short but dense article provides what is probably the best single examination of strategies for eliminating overconfidence and other psychological pitfalls in evaluating the odds of an uncertain outcome.

10. Hoffman, David A., "Mediation and the Art of Shuttle Diplomacy," *Negotiation Journal* 27 (2011): 263–309. The most comprehensive look at mediation caucusing, including research studies and ethical and practical considerations that we are aware of.

11. Hoffman, David A., and Richard Wohlman, "The Psychology of Mediation," *Cardozo Journal of Conflict Resolution* 14 (2013): 759–806. A thought-provoking and insightful overview of human behavior and how a wide range of psychological factors apply in mediation, by mediator and lawyer Hoffman and psychologist Wohlman.

12. Kiser, Randall L., Martin A. Asher, and Blakeley B. McShane, "Let's Not Make a Deal: An Empirical Study of Decision Making in Unsuccessful Settlement Negotiations," *Journal of Empirical Legal Studies* 5, no. 3 (2008): 551–91. This fascinating article analyzes 2,054 trial court cases that proceeded to trial after settlement negotiations failed and for which the parties' final settlement positions were verifiable. The authors found that plaintiffs rejected 61.2 percent of offers that turned out to be better than results at trial and defendants rejected 32.0 percent of offers that were better than the trial results. Significantly, the error rates went down to 48.5 percent for plaintiffs and 24.3 percent for defendants when represented by an attorney who also had training and experience as a mediator! *Id.* at 586–87. When plaintiffs rejected offers and did better at trial, they gained only an average of $43,100 over the last offer. However, when defendants rejected a demand and went to trial and fared worse, they fared much worse: an average of $1,140,000 worse! *Id.* at 566.

13. Nolan-Haley, Jacqueline, "Mediation: The 'New Arbitration,'" *Harvard Negotiation Law Review* 17 (2012): 61–118. Winner of the International Institute for Conflict Prevention & Resolution's[5] Outstanding Original Professional Article award of the year in 2012, this article laments the trend toward evaluative mediation as "in effect, a watered down version of adjudication," which lawyers prepare for accordingly. This thought-provoking critique warns that the drift toward a focus almost entirely on lawyers and the law marginalizes fundamental principles of mediation, such as party self-determination and interest-based bargaining, and stifles the important values of dignity and participation. It is a must-read for those who never knew or have forgotten their mediation roots.

14. Peters, Amanda J., "The Meaning, Measure, and Misuse of Standards of Review," *Lewis & Clark Law Review* 13 (2008): 233. The best single article describing the various standards of review employed by the

---

5. Based in New York City and often referred to as CPR.

appellate courts. If you are new to the appellate arena, begin with this article.

15. Philbin, Jr., Donald R., "The One Minute Manager Prepares for Mediation: A Multidisciplinary Approach to Negotiation Preparation," *Harvard Negotiation Law Review* 13 (2008): 249. Although primarily directed at trial court mediations, this is an outstanding overview and primer for attorneys preparing for appellate mediations. The author shows how multidisciplinary understanding of risk, psychology, opportunity costs, and negotiating skills helps tackle complex litigation.

16. Rack, Jr., Robert W., "Thoughts of a Chief Circuit Mediator on Federal Court-Annexed Mediation," *Ohio State Journal of Dispute Resolution* 17 (2001): 609. A worthwhile look into the development of a mediation program in the federal appellate courts.

17. Riskin, Leonard L., "Decisionmaking in Mediation: The New Old Grid and the New Grid System," *Notre Dame Law Review* 79 (2003–2004): 30–53. An insightful reflection on—and update to—Professor Riskin's seminal article "Understanding Mediators' Orientations, Strategies, and Techniques: A Grid for the Perplexed," cited next.

18. Riskin, Leonard L., "Understanding Mediators Orientations, Strategies, and Techniques: A Grid for the Perplexed," *Harvard Negotiation Law Review* 1 (1997): 7. A classic article that proposed a paradigm of four mediator styles based on evaluative-facilitative and narrow-broad focus dichotomies. Useful in understanding the differences among multiple mediation styles and their underlying assumptions. Readers do well to remember that most mediators use varying styles and approaches over the course of a single mediation session.

19. Robbenolt, Jennifer K., "Apologies and Settlement Levers," *Journal of Empirical Legal Studies*, vol. 3 (2006): 333–76. For those who want to learn about the effect of apology in negotiation and settlement, this article is an interesting analysis of the research findings.

20. Stark, James H., and Douglas N. Frenkel, "Changing Minds: The Work of Mediators and Empirical Studies of Persuasion," *Ohio State Journal on Dispute Resolution* 28, no. 2 (2013): 263. A fascinating, enlightening compilation of social science and other research about persuasion— what works (and doesn't work), how it works, and why.

21. Storm, Timothy J., "Standard of Review Does Matter: Evidence of Judicial Self-Restraint in the Illinois Appellate Court," *Southern Illinois University Law Journal* 34 (2009): 73. A useful article showing how the standards of review yield different reversal rates according to how deferential the appellate court is under the particular standard. For example, how reversal rates for de novo review greatly exceed those for abuse of discretion.

22. Sussman, Edna, "A Brief Survey of U.S. Case Law on Enforcing Mediation Settlement Agreements over Objections to the Existence or Validity of Such Agreements and Implications for Mediation Confidentiality and Mediator Testimony," *Mediation Committee Newsletter* (April 2006): 32. A good start for any research into crafting enforceable mediated settlement agreements.

23. Table B-5, Statistical Tables—*U.S. Courts of Appeals*. Available at http://www. uscourts.gov/statistics/table/b-5/statistical-tables-federal-judiciary/2014/12/31. This table is cited with such frequency for reversal rates in the federal Courts of Appeals that we include it here to caution that it does *not* provide a reliable picture into odds for litigants. Although it claims a 10.5-percent reversal rate in civil appeals, the data does not reflect modification of judgments or include any appeals in which the appellant secures any kind of relief from the appellate court. Also, cases arguably civil in nature are included even though they fall into categories of disputes unlikely to be disputed or successfully appealed. For a much better survey of federal appellate court reversal rates, the law review articles authored by Theodore Eisenberg are recommended.

24. Taft, Lee, "Apology Subverted: The Commodification of Apology," *Yale Law Journal* 109 (2000): 1135–60. A fascinating and incisive critique of the use of apology in mediation, including the ethical and moral implications, written by trial lawyer *cum* Harvard Divinity School student Lee Taft.

25. Wissler, Roselle L., and Robert W. Rack, Jr., "Assessing Mediator Performance: The Usefulness of Participant Questionnaires," *Journal of Dispute Resolution* (2004): 229. An excellent reminder, based on a study of federal appellate court mediators, that the most important attributes of an appellate mediator are having sufficient knowledge of appeals and the substantive law to help evaluate the merits of the appeal. The other three most important appellate mediator abilities, according to this article, are eliminating issues unnecessary for a settlement, helping clarify the issues, and dealing with procedural problems. *Id.* at 250. In short, mediators need skills both in facilitating the process and in understanding the substantive law bearing on the appeal being mediated.

F. Our Favorite Internet Resources

1. American Bar Association, Section of Dispute Resolution, http://www .americanbar.org/groups/dispute_resolution.html. This section of the ABA has just under 13,000 Members, 25 committees, and several ongoing task forces. It has published the Model Standards of Conduct for Mediators in cooperation with the American Arbitration Association and the Society of Professionals in Dispute Resolution. The Section of Dispute Resolution operates an excellent and in-depth website that provides extensive online resources for all participants in the mediation process. In addition, the Section also publishes periodicals and books for alternative dispute resolution (ADR) professionals and participants.

2. Mediate.com, http://www.mediate.com. Dedicated to "mediators and everything mediation." For professionals seeking to develop an appellate mediation practice, this site provides timely information and advice. For consumers of the ADR process, it includes a search function for local mediators. For both, each week it publishes a wide array of mediation-related articles, many of which are archived and available on the website.

3. Appellate court websites. For almost all court-connected mediation programs, mediators, and attorneys will find information about local rules, mandatory forms, and staff contact information on the appellate court's website. Many provide information about appellate mediation and how to prepare for and participate in it.

Index

A

Abandonment of appeal, 46–48
Abuse of discretion, 6, 12–14, 16
Acceptance, 223
Accuracy, of odds on appeal
    estimations, 37–43
Action, 223
Administrative remedy, 47
Advertising, 144
Advocacy, counter-attitudinal, 232
Affirmation, defined, 20
Agenda
    creation of, 137, 237
    for mediation session, 124
Agreement. *See also* Settlement
    assisting parties without, 268–271
    attorney fees and, 153
    clarity of, 157–158
    completeness of, 157–158
    compliance checkpoints in,
        153–154
    confidentiality in, 155
    enforceable language in, 153
    follow up to achieve, 161
    handwritten, 193–194
    implementation of, 158
    insurer consent and, 154
    reasons for not reaching, 159–160
    release of liability and, 152–153
    signing, 155–157, 194
    tax characterization and, 154–155
    understood by client, 193
    when mediation ends with,
        152–159

when mediation ends without,
    159–161
in writing, before conclusion of
    mediation, 193–195
Allen v. Zurich Ins. Co., 20n41
Alyeska Pipeline Service Co. v.
    Wilderness Society, 28n7
Amenability, to mediation,
    115–117
"American rule," 28–29
Analysis, 223
Angelou, Maya, 217
Anger, 131–132, 189–190
Animosity, 189
Anxiety, 222, 224
Apology, 142, 248–249
Appellant. *See also* Parties
    decision tree analysis for, as
        defendant, 83–91
    decision tree analysis for, as
        plaintiff, 62–73
    meaning of winning for, 26–27,
        28–29
    mediation statement from,
        302–306
    odds considered by, in case
        evaluation, 34–36
    special concerns to discuss with,
        181
Appellate brief, mediation statement
    vs., 174
Appellate court
    preventing decision by, 170
    trial court vs., 1, 2–3
Appellate issues, discussion of, 167

E

Easement, 166
Eating, 186, 259–260
Economic value, negative, of appeal, 47
Effectiveness, in working with lawyers, 224–226
Egocentrism, 246
E-mail, confirming, 296–298
Emotional climate, 208–209
Emotional cost, 29, 106–107, 107–108
Emotional discussions, 226–227
Emotions, in mediation, 131–132, 189, 218, 257–258
Empathy, 217–224
Employment contract cases, 36
Energy, low, 222, 224
Enforceability provisions, 236
Enforceable language, 153
Environment, emotional, 208–209
Error(s)
    clear, in standards of review, 8–11
    determination of, standard of review and, 5–6
    invited, 20
    multiple, 17
    no reversal in absence of, 16–18
    qualifying as prejudicial, 16
    single source of, as most common, 45n52
    in view of appellate law, 5
Estimation, gut feelings and, 54
Evidence
    additional, 9
    ambiguous, 10
    for cause of action, 11
    credibility of, 9
    emotional impact of, 10
    gaps in, 10
    inadmissible, 14
    insufficient, 10–11

new, 9
relevance of, 12
reweighing, 10
silence on, 21
substantial, as standard of review, 6, 8–11, 16
in trial vs. appeal, 2–3
vague, 10
Evidentiary protection, 122
Evidentiary standards, standards of review vs., 7–8
Excellence, perfection vs., 280–281
Exchange, information, 112, 125–133
    confidentiality and, 129
    current circumstances in, 128–130
    facilitation of, 215–235
    in joint session, 128, 130–131, 187, 227–229
    legal merits in, 126–128
    listening in, 132
    mediator in, 130
    negotiation vs., 131
    private caucuses in, 132–133
    separation of topics in, 125–130
    shift from debate to dialogue in, 215–217
    tips, 186–189
    underlying problem in, 128–130
Expectations, client vs. attorney, 54–55
Experts, help from, in case evaluation, 44
Exploring interests, 244–245

F

Facebook, Inc. v. Pacific Northwest Software, Inc., 176n5, 261n45, 262n47
Fairness, prejudice and, 18

Trial counsel, 167
Trial court
   appellate court vs., 1, 2–3
   issue not raised in, 18–20
   return to, 22
"True" costs, 108–109
Trust, 117, 209–210

U

Understanding, 217–224
Uniform Mediation Act, 129n2

V

Value
   decision-tree analysis and, 53,
      56–61, 106–109
   negative economic, 47
   real numbers in, 54–55
Venue, change of, 12
Verdict, in decision tree analysis, 59
Verdict forms, 166

Vision statement, 282
Visitation orders, 12
Voluntary mediation, 169–170

W

"Walk-away number," 24
Wants, needs vs., in case evaluation,
   23
Weakness analysis, 167–168
Wetherby v. Wetherby, 263n53
Wilcox v. Arpaio, 261n45
Willingness, to mediate, 116–117
Winklevoss, Cameron, 262
Winklevoss, Tyler, 262
"Winner," in trial vs. appeal, 2, 3
Winning, meaning of
   for appellant, 26–27, 28–29
   for respondent, 27, 28–29
Witness, single, 10
Woodman, Marion, 280
Worry, 222, 224